Vestiges

Spirit-History of Man

S. F. Dunlap

Alpha Editions

This edition published in 2019

ISBN : 9789353959623

Design and Setting By
Alpha Editions
email - alphaedis@gmail.com

VESTIGES

OF THE

SPIRIT-HISTORY OF MAN.

BY

S. F. DUNLAP,

MEMBER OF THE AMERICAN ORIENTAL SOCIETY, NEW HAVEN.

"I caused blind HOPES to dwell within them."
ÆSCHYLUS, *Prometheus Bound.*

NEW YORK:

D. APPLETON AND COMPANY,

346 & 348 BROADWAY.

1858.

PREFACE.

THE basis of the world is power. It lives in us and in every thing. From the beginning it came forth from God, and was uttered in the philosophies of great teachers and prophets of the ancient world. God has not placed it here to remain inactive: it strives, creates, institutes. So long as the world is filled with it so long will its efforts continue, for power expresses the will of God. This work proceeds upon the conviction that there has been a gradual rise of systems, one cultus growing out of another. Thought grows like a plant. New fruits become the bases of further developments. The present perpetually evolves new power.

The first three chapters of this book are a kind of general introduction to the main body of the work. The third chapter has been extended by additional matter, in order to afford a broader basis for the subsequent chapters to rest upon. The authorities are given at the bottom of the page, and notes are added: particular notes to certain pages will be found in the Appendix of Notes and some remarks (p. 387) in reference to reading Hebrew without the vowel-points. These are not to be used in reading Hebrew proper names in this work. Corrections and additions will be found in the Errata.

The author most prominently referred to in this treatise is Movers, Phönizier, Vol. I. Movers is authority among scholars: his work bears the highest reputation. Reference has also been made to Roth, Lassen, Weber, and other prominent Sanskrit scholars; Rawlinson, Spiegel, Haug, students of the Old-Persian; Seyffarth, Lepsius, and Uhlemann, on Egyptian antiquities; Pauthier on the Chinese; Duncker on the Persians, Hindus, &c.; Adolf Wuttke on the Chinese and Hindus: on the American races, to J. G. Müller, Von Tschudi, Schoolcraft, Squier, Stevens, Gallatin, Prescott, Larenaudiere, Lord Kingsborough, La Croix, Adair, the Dacotah Grammar, "Mounds of the Mississippi Valley," &c.: on the Polynesians, to Hale, Ellis, and, on linguistik, to a number of recent and earlier European publications, besides the works of Grimm, Bunsen, Lepsius, Bopp, and many other Sanskrit, Old-Persian and other Oriental authorities. The author has used Tischendorff's as well as Lachmann's edition of the New Testament in Greek, a translation of Griesbach, Sebastian Schmid's Hebrew and Latin Bible, Leipsic, 1740, also Cahen's Hebrew Bible, De Wette's Version and the Septuagint, ed. Tischendorff.

In compiling the brief account of Buddhist doctrines in the last two chapters, the following works have been used: Duncker's Geschichte des Alterthums; Wuttke, Geschichte des Heidenthums, Vol. 2; Burnouf, Intr. to Bouddhisme; Neve, sur le Bouddhisme; Weber, Akad. Vorlesungen; Weber, Ind. Skizzen; Prof. Salisbury's article in the Journ. of the Am. Oriental Soc. Vol. I.; Spence Hardy's Eastern Monachism, also his Manual of Buddhism, and other authorities: the reader can also examine the

Lotus de la bonne loi, by Burnouf, and Koeppen's Religion des Buddha.

The language of an author has generally been closely followed without putting the extract in quotation marks : these however are frequently employed. As this work is a collection of studies (Studien), frequent use has been made of parentheses to insert explanations, collateral ideas, or suggestions of any kind, and words in the *original* or in the German translation. J. G. Müller is quoted as J. Müller, D. M. G. is an abbreviation for Deutschen Morgenländischen Gesellschaft and R. A. S. for Royal-Asiatic Society. Seyffarth's *Berichtigungen* &c. is quoted as *Computationssystem.* The word Dios, Dius, Deus, has been used both in the genitive and nominative cases for "God." In Greek it is the genitive case of Zeus. As Oriental names are sometimes spelled differently in different authors, no attempt has been made to establish a uniformity in this respect, but the words have frequently been taken as the author found them, even where a more elegant usage has since sprung up.

Use is made of names, which, having been handed down from remote ages, stand in the place of inscriptions and records ; for if there was a name, there must have been a thing named. They are evidences of ideas, persons or things that once existed; and where they happen to be compound words, several ideas are often recorded in a single name. The *terminations* as, es, is, os, us, i, ya, &c., usually form no part of the proper word or *root*, but are merely case-endings, &c. In this volume the proper names are divided by hyphens in many cases, to show that they are composed of shorter words. The *termination* syllable is occasionally separated by a hyphen from the *root* of a word. Sometimes the letters forming the *original root* have been printed in small capitals, and those letters that have been added by a later usage left in ordinary type. Occasionally the article (*H*=Ha) prefixed to a Hebrew word is printed with a capital letter italicised, to divide the article from the word proper. The references to Sanchoniathon are taken from Eusebius, Praeparationis Evangelicae, Liber I., cap. Phoenicum, Paris, MDCXXVIII.

The aim of the author has been to state verified facts with as few of his own inferences as possible. The order of arrangement follows the march of thought from the first conceptions and untaught speculations of the religious sentiment, passing rapidly through the classic period of ancient philosophy and religion to the field of modern controversy.

TABLE OF CONTENTS.

SPIRIT-HISTORY OF MAN.

CHAPTER 1.

FROM the earliest times, among all nations, man has sought to recognize his God; to define that inscrutable Providence which rules the world. Like the successive changes of the forests, the infinite variety of the harvests, the differing notes of the birds, the opposite languages of men, the varied fragrance of the flowers, such is the contrast of religious belief which man's spirit brings, as its first fruits, to its Creator.

From Constantinople to the shores of India, China, and Japan, four great world-religions meet in conflict. Each asserts its claims to be regarded as the civilized and saving religion of mankind. Brahmanism has an antiquity of more than three thousand years, Buddhism of twenty-three hundred, the Christian religion of eighteen centuries, the Mahometan of twelve. The number of Christians is perhaps two hundred and fifty millions; that of the Mahometans, Brahmans, and Buddhists united, may be set down as not far from eight hundred millions. This enormous mass of human beings, whom we call pagans, are adherents of systems which are founded on the religious convictions of many

1

centuries, and are improvements upon former modes of worship that have long since passed away. The Christian religion holds possession of Europe and America; the Mahometan, of North Africa, Turkey, Lesser Asia, Palestine, Arabia, Mesopotamia, Persia, and even Northern India; the Brahman holds Hindustan, and some isles; Buddhism predominates in Ceylon, Thibet, the countries north-east of the Ganges, the Birman Empire, Siam, China, Japan, and the Indian Archipelago; also in Russian and Chinese Tartary.

Man has his worth—his mission. To properly estimate our own, we must consider it in its relation to that of all other men; not only those who at this day cover the surface of the globe, but those who have preceded us and contributed in action, thought and sentiment, to form the present.

Nature, to man in the most primitive state, is all alive; she is a congregation of distinct existences, each moved by the soul or spirit that dwells in it.[1] There is no harmony, no unity. All is separate, independent life. Hence, almost every object is a subject of suspicion to the savage. He is environed by agencies visible and invisible. Legions of spirits are seen in the woods, the flowers, the fruits, the grass, the mountains, the seas, the lakes, the rivers, the brooks, the fountains, the waterfalls, the birds, and the stars. Trees have their protecting spirits; the animals have their spirits, and are themselves divine spirits.[2] Songs were sung and fasts celebrated in honor of the guardian deities of the bears in Canada.[3] Every appearance is the work of a spirit. If thunder is heard, the mighty god of the thunder is adored. The snow, the frost, the hail, and the storm-winds, have each their especial divinities, which lie con-

---

[1] "And to every beast of the earth, and to every fowl of the air, and to every thing that creepeth upon the earth wherein is a living soul."—1 Gen. 30.

"Like man, all nature separates into body and spirit."—2 Duncker, 66; Castren, Vorl. über Finnische Mythologie, 59, 163.

[2] J. Müller, 61, 74, 75, 107, 114, 120.

[3] J. Müller, Am. Urreligionen, 75, 91.

cealed in the material substances to which they belong, like the soul in the human body. Spiritual existences inhabit almost every thing, and consequently almost every thing is an object of worship. Gods are seen " in the mist of the mountain, the rocky defile, the foaming cataract, the lonely dell, the shooting star, the tempest's blast, the evening breeze." [1] The Dacotah has " his god of the north, his god of the south, his god of the woods, and god of the prairies; his god of the air and god of the waters." [2] The savage has his war-god, his fire-god, and his sun-god. The child of Nature reveres the lovely morning-red and the zephyrs that attend the path of the sun; [3] he adores the " great star" Venus [4] and other planets, the clouds, or the shining nymphs of the waters above, [5] and locates souls of the distinguished dead, as deified spirits, in the regions of the air, or among the countless host in the starry heavens. The Milky Way is the " path of souls leading to the spiritland," or the stars are their lights seen in heaven. [6] The soul, an airy form, is borne on the wings of the wind, following the sun in its course to the heaven in the west. [7] The Northern Lights are the dances of dead warriors and seers in the realms above. [8] The Iroquois and Algonquin tribes call the souls " shades" (otahchuk), like the Greeks and Romans. [9] The sunbeams are themselves the pious souls in the old Vedic ideas. [10]

[1] Ellis. Polynesian Res., vol. i. 331.   [2] Introd. to the Dacotah Grammar.
[3] Rinck, i. 50.   [4] J. Müller, 53, 220; Squier, Serpent Symbol, 123.
[5] Weber Vorlesungen über Ind. Literaturgesch. 31 ; Ind. Studien, ii. 301 ; Wuttke Gesch. des Heidenthums, ii. 248.
[6] J. Müller, 54; quotes Wied, ii. 152; Lafiteau, i. 406 ; Squier, Serp. Symb. 70, quotes Wied, 360; Weber, Zeitschrift der Deutschen Morgenländ. Gesell. vol. ix. 238 ; quotes Rigveda, vi. 5, 4, 8.
[7] Weber, Vorles. über Ind. Literaturgesch. 31; Weber, A Legend of the Çatapatha Brâhmana, Zeitschrift der Deutschen Morgenländ. Gesell. vol. ix., 238, note.
[8] J. Müller, 54. The Dacotahs call the Aurora Borealis "Old Woman." She is the goddess of war.—Schoolcraft, part iii. 487.
[9] J. Müller, Amerikanische Urreligionen, 67.
[10] Rigv. i. 9, 3, 10, in Zeitsch. d. D. M. G. ix. 248, note.

> " And now Cyllenian Hermes summoned forth
>   The spirits of the suitors ;
>   The sun's gate, also, and the land of dreams
>   They passed, whence next into the meads they came
>   Of Asphodel, by shadowy forms possessed,
>   Simulars of the dead."—COWPER'S ILIAD, *Book* 24.

The American aborigines believed falling stars to be
divine beings.[1] The Greeks worshipped the stars in common with the most ancient nations.[2] The Zendavesta says,
" I invoke and praise the stars, heavenly people of excel-
lency."[3] The stars in Charles's Wain were believed by
some of the New England Indians to be men hunting a
bear. The Seven Stars were seven dancing Indians.[4] Stars,
in the Arya-Hindu belief, were considered abodes of the
gods, or visible forms of pious persons after death.[5] The
Californians believe the sun, moon, morning and evening
stars, to be men and women, who every evening leap into
the sea, and reappear in the morning on the other side of
the earth.[6] Agni, in India, is thought to rise in the morning in the shape of the sun out of the ocean.[7] The
Mexicans adored Tlavizpantecutli, the god of the dawn and
of the twilight. It was the first light which appeared in
the world. The Peruvians worshipped Venus by the name
of Chasca, "the youth with the long and curling locks," the
page of the sun whom he attends so closely in his rising and
his setting. The Romans adored Aurora ; the Greeks, Eos ;
the Dorians, Auos ; the Old Prussians, Aussra ; the Persians,
Ushasina ; and the Vedic Hindus, Aushasa (Ushas), impersonations of the rosy-fingered morn. Among our Indians, the
Rainbow is a spirit, who accompanies the sun. He is worshipped by the Peruvians as a direct emanation from the
sun. Among the Greeks, she is Iris the Messenger. The

---

[1] J. Müller, 54.
[2] Eschenburg, Manual 465 ; Rinck, Religion der Hellenen, i. 38.
[3] Kleuker's Zendav. 83.   [4] Squier, Serp. Symbol, 71.
[5] Wilson's Rigv. Veda, i. 132.   [6] J. Müller, 53.   [7] Wilson, Rigv. i. 248.

Camanches worship the moon as god of the night. The moon was also a male deity among the Cherokees, as well as among the ancient Germans and Egyptians. The elements are deified. Air, fire, and water, have each their divinities.

The Mandans think the stars are the spirits of the dead.[1] The Egyptians accorded divine honors to the dead. The Madagassians consider the dead evil spirits. The Hebrews held notions like those of the Egyptians and other neighboring nations. They had a dim conception of existence after death. They had their "Sheol," which is the same as Hades, Orcus. There the shades assemble, who no more have either blood or flesh. Moses could not deprive them of these ideas, for he had nothing to replace them with.[2] "They joined themselves unto Baal Peor, and ate the sacrifices of the dead."[3] The Jews regarded the souls of the dead as demons. So did the Greeks. "Their term demon, in its ancient acceptation, meant a divinity."[4] In like manner the Chinese erected temples to their ancestors. The Hindus and Greeks, before Homer, honored them by invocations and libations. At the time of the new moon, the Hindus made offerings (pitri-yagna) to the spirits of "the fathers;" also on the birthdays of the dead; and water was sprinkled every day in their honor, besides certain days of the month specified in the laws of Manu. They were said to have adorned the heaven with stars. The Romans believed in lares of all sorts, spirits of the departed, protecting spirits, lares of gentes, lares publici, and lares that stand where cross-roads meet.[5] They held an annual festival (Feralia) in honor of the dead. It began the 18th of February, and lasted to the end of the month. The manes were both good and hostile powers. They were subordi-

---

[1] Squier, Serp. Symbol, 70. [2] Friedlander, i. 92.
[3] Psalm cvi. 28. [4] Compare Euripides, Phœnissæ, 1607, 1608.
[5] Zeitschrift der Deutschen Morgenl. Gesellsch., vol. ix. p. lx.; Duncker Geschichte des Alterthums, vol. ii. 171; Wuttke Gesch. des Heidenthums, vol. ii. 251, 393.
[6] Creuzer, Symbolik, 586.

nate to the authority of Pluton. Ataensie, a death-goddess in America, dwells in the moon, like the Greek Persephone, and stands at the head of all the bad spirits ; and in
the belief of the Apalachis, Cupai, the adversary, rules over
the underworld.[1] The Indians believe in the transmigration of souls, not only into the bodies of animals, but into
the stars.[2] The soul is considered immortal among the
Algonquins, passing from one object to another.[3] The
Caribs believed that the insignificant and inferior souls
were changed into animals.[4]

The Phœnician deities were personified *powers of
Nature*, which gradually came to be regarded as beings
"considered human," until at last Euhemerism made mere
men of them. The Phœnician religion was Nature-worship, in which the sidereal element was prominent; and
the gods, which elsewhere appeared visibly in the ver-
dure of the trees, in the beauty and grace of plants, in the
manifold stirrings of the animal kingdom, in consuming
fire, in the murmuring of streams and fountains, in the
mountains, in the glowing poisonous simoom, in short,
every where in Nature, where life and death reveal themselves, had especially their "idols" (symbols and carriers of
the deity), in the lights of heaven.[5] The Khonds, in India,
had a sun-god, an Earth-goddess, a moon-god, a war-god, a
god of hunting, a god of births, a god of the small-pox, a
god of grain, and many other gods.[6] The religion of the
first inhabitants of India consisted in the worship of local
deities, some supposed to be benevolent, some malevolent.
They were originally supposed to be spirits of deceased
persons, who still retaining the feelings they had when
alive, haunted the places of their former residence. They

---

[1] J. Müller, 140, 150.   [2] J. Müller, 209, 67

[3] Schoolcraft, Indian Tribes, i. 33; J. Müller, Geschichte der Amerikan.
Urreligionen, 66, et passim.

[4] J. Muller, 209.   [5] Movers Phönizier, i. 157.

[6] Allen's India, 425.

were thought to have the power of assisting their friends and injuring their enemies. Thus able to interfere at pleasure in human affairs, they became objects of great anxiety.[1] The Father-Genii possess wonderful powers; they bless and protect the pious, bestow possessions and wealth; they resemble the heavenly bands who help the gods in their works like the Feruers of the Zend legends.[2] The Persian liturgy says: "I invoke the fearful and mighty Fravashis of the saints, of the pure men, of the men of the Old Law and the New Law, the Fravashis of my ancestors, and the Fravashi of my soul."[3] The Persians venerated rivers, trees, mountains, herds of the resurrection, stars, spirits, feruers. Feruers were in all places; in the streets, cities, and provinces, heaven, water, wind, earth, animals, etc.; in Ormuzd, the Amshaspands and all the deities. Spirits of the departed were feruers. Connected with the worship of the stars is the worship of the Fravashis, or Feruers. The Fravashis are souls, and are stars also. "All the other numberless stars which are visible, are called the Fravashis of mortals: for the whole creation which the Creator Ormuzd has made, for the born and the unborn, for every *body*, a Fravashi, with like essence, is manifest,"[4] (mit gleicher Essenz ist offenbar.) All the stars are considered metamorphosed Indians, by the inhabitants of the Caribbean Islands and the Patagonians.[5]

The Hindus believed the stars to be spirits called Gandharvas and considered to be heavenly choristers.[6] At the close of the year, during the last five days, the Persians celebrated the "Festival of All Souls." On these five in-

[1] Allen's India, 361.

[2] Begleitende Helfer der Götter bei ihren Werken wie die Feruer der Zend sage. Roth. 4 D. M. G. 428.

[3] 2 Duncker, 375. So, in the New Testament, we find, "I will say to my soul: Soul, thou hast many good things," etc.—Luke xii. 19.

[4] Spiegel Die Lehre von der unendlichen Zeit. Zeitschrift der D. M. G. 1851. Minokhired S. 343. Paris MS.

[5] J. Müller, 256, 220.

[6] 1 Weber, Ind. Stud. 196, 224. Milman's Nala, p. 122.

tercalary days the souls of the dead come again on earth
and visit their friends. At this festival every one must
pray twelve hundred times a day, "Purity and glory is for
the just, who is pure ; " and the prayer, "That is the will of
Ahuramazda," with other prayers. Noxious animals must
be killed, entertainment and dresses prepared for the pure
spirits, and they must be invoked with prayers,—customs
which have evidently the same origin as the banquets of
the dead among the Hindus.[1] Festivals in honor of the
dead were celebrated by the American tribes every eight
or ten years, and even by the Aztecs and Tlascalans in
Mexico.[2]

The ancient Chinese religion was that of all the earliest
forms of society,—the worship of the visible powers of Nature or of the stars. The Chinese sacrificed to the Shin,
that is, to the superior spirits of every rank, and to their
virtuous deceased ancestors, and addressed the wind, rain,
thunder, diseases, etc., as divinities. Confucius says,
"Shun then offered the sacrifice called lui to Shangti, he
presented a pure offering to the six venerable ones, he
looked with devotion towards the hills and rivers, and
glanced around at the host of Shin."[3] The Micronesian
islanders, in the Pacific Ocean, worship the spirits of their
ancestors. Their word "anti" means deified spirit. They
believe that as soon as a person dies, his spirit or shade
ascends into the air, and is carried about for a time by the
winds. At last it is supposed to arrive at the Kainakaki, a
sort of elysium.[4] In Ellis's Polynesian Researches, the
name of a spirit is "varua," which means a "god" likewise. "Varua ino" are the bad spirits. Oramatuas tiis,
"spirits of the dead," were greatly feared by the islanders.[5]
Among the Old Persians the bad spirits were, in part, spirits
of the dead.[6] Some of the Indians of our Southern States
believed the higher regions above inhabited by good spirits,

[1] 2 Duncker, 377, 378.   [2] J. Müller, 86, 647.

[3] Canon of Shun. Shu King, book ii., Chinese Repository.

[4] Hale, 99.   [5] Ellis, vol. i. 334, 335.   [6] J. Müller, 209.

called "Nana ishtohoollo." The evil spirits, "Nana ook-proose," were supposed to possess the dark regions of the west.[1] The conception of souls of the dead as changed into airy shapes, which the wind attends to their resting-place, is the old belief of the Indogerman races extending from Britain to the Ganges.[2] In Tahiti, the dead are elevated to the rank of gods, and the "First man" (the Creator) had the same name, Tii or Tiki.[3]

Every Indian, in youth, seeks a protecting spirit for himself. There are also bad spirits; but all spirits are to be feared: for the protecting spirit of one is to be feared by others.[4] Throughout the spirit-realm the same spirits are both good and hostile, or they are divided into those which are favorable and those which are unfavorable.[5] According to Philo, the Alexandrian Jew, the air is filled with invisible inhabitants, spirits free from evil, and immortal. The best of them are the angels. God uses them as inferior powers and ministers to benefit mankind.[6] The angels were the souls of the stars.[7]

> "When the morning stars sang together,
> And all the sons of Elohim (God) shouted for joy."

The Septuagint gives this verse differently:

> "When the stars were brought forth they approved me,
> All my angels with a loud voice."[8]

In Homer, the same gods are favorable or hostile to different persons; but there is no formal division into good and evil deities among the gods; bad spirits, spectres, etc., were generally, among the Greeks, believed to exist. Bad angels are not known to the Hebrews before the exile; although the angels work evil.[9]

[1] Adair, 43, 57, 80, 81.
[2] Weber, Ind. Studien, 31.
[3] J. Müller, 135.
[4] J. Müller, 72.
[5] J. Müller, 151.
[6] De Wette, Bibl. Dogm. i. 146.
[7] De Wette, Bibl. Dogm. 82.
[8] Job xxxviii. 7.
[9] De Wette, Bibl. Dogm. i. 82.

The ancient Irish worshipped the sun, moon, stars, and the winds;[1] the Gauls, natural phenomena, the elements and heavenly luminaries, stones, trees, winds, rivers, thunder, the sun, etc. The ancient German and the Scandinavian religions were based on nature-worship. They adored spirits of every kind, in the sun, moon, and stars, air-gods, water-gods, etc. The Esquimaux, the Greenlanders, the people of Siberia, and the Polynesians, worship spirits. The Baktrian Hindus worshipped spirits of the sun and moon, the air, the heaven, the water, the rivers, the winds, celestial singers, nymphs and demons, patron deities of the villages, and the souls of their ancestors. The American Indians worship the fire, the sun, the elements, and innumerable other spirits.[2] The Peruvians, Mexicans, Romans, Greeks, Assyrians, Arabs, Hindus, Babylonians, Tartars, Persians, Massagetæ, Egyptians, and Hebrews, adored the sun. The primitive Magian religion was the worship of the heavenly bodies.[3] The old Canaanites adored the sun, moon, and stars. Some of the Mexican races considered the stars sisters of the sun. In Peru they were the moon's maids. Among the Hebrews they were the sons of El (the Sun). "They fought from heaven. The stars in their courses fought against Sisera."[4] "And suddenly there was with the angel a multitude of the heavenly host praising God."[5] "Take heed that ye despise not these little ones; for I say unto you, that in heaven their angels do always behold the face of my Father which is in heaven."[6] "Notwithstanding, in this rejoice not that the spirits are subject unto you."[7] The demons enter the herd of swine. Jesus walking on the water is thought to be a spirit. "What shall a man give in exchange for his soul?" "Je-

---

[1] Vallancey, Essay on the Celtic Language, 51, 65.
[2] Schoolcraft, i. 38, et passim.　　[3] Heeren's Asia, vol. ii. 190.
[4] Judges, v. 20.　　[5] Luke ii. 13.　　[6] Matthew xviii. 10.
[7] Luke x. 20.

sus perceived *in his spirit* that they so reasoned within themselves." [1]

"For so *the Spirit* of the Theban seer
Informed me." [2]

"For when they rise from the dead, they neither marry nor are given in marriage, but are as the angels which are in heaven." [3] "The chariots of God are twenty thousand; thousands of angels." [4] "And it shall come to pass in that day, that the Lord shall punish the host of the High Ones that are on high, and the kings of the earth upon the earth.[5] "The stars are not pure in His sight." [6] "His angels he charged with folly." [7] "Who maketh His angels spirits." (Winds.) "Then a spirit passed before my face." [8]

Ovid says in his Metamorphoses, " that no region might be destitute of its *peculiar* animated beings, the stars and forms of the gods possess the tract of heaven." [9] Human figures were sculptured by the Assyrians, having stars upon their heads.[10] The same are found in Egypt, representing the twenty-four hours of the day.[11] Others have a huge star in the middle of the figure.[12] The Persians, Chaldeans, Carthaginians, Assyrians, Egyptians, Old Canaanites, including the Phœnicians, worshipped the spirits of the stars. In the language of Mr. Prescott, " As the eye of the simple child of nature watches through the long nights the stately march of the heavenly bodies, and sees the bright host coming up one after another, and changing with the changing seasons of the year, he naturally associates them with those seasons as the periods over which they hold a mysterious influence." [13] "And they had no sure *sign* either of winter, or of flowery spring, or of fruitful summer; but they used to do every thing without judgment, until I showed to

---

[1] Mark ii. 8.   [2] Odyssey, xxiii. 251.   [3] Mark xii. 25.
[4] Ps. lxviii. 17.   [5] Isaiah xxiv. 21.   [6] Job xxv. 5.   [7] Job iv. 18.
[8] Job iv. 15.   [9] 1 Metam. p. 7. Riley.   [10] Layard's Nineveh vol. i.
[11] Champollion Egypte, p. 131.   [12] Gesenius, Jesaia, vol. ii. 529.
[13] Prescott's Mexico, i. 121.

them the risings *of the stars* and *their settings,* hard to be discerned.'" So, in the opening of the tragedy of Agamemnon by Æschylus, the watchman says:

> "I have beheld the gathering of the nightly stars,
> Both those that bring winter and summer to mortals,
> Brilliant Lords, Stars conspicuous in the Æther."

And Job:

> Canst thou fasten the bands of the Pleiades,
> Or loosen the chains of Orion?
> Canst thou lead forth the Signs in their season,
> Or guide Arcturus with his sons?
> Knowest thou the ordinances of the heavens?[2]

Let them be for signs, and for seasons, and for days, and years.[3] The Mexicans regulated their festivals by the Pleiades.[4] The Polynesians determined their two seasons by this constellation. "Matarii i nia," "Pleiades above," "Matarii i raro," Pleiades below" (the horizon).[5] The Cherokees venerated "the Seven Stars;" and they were called "the dancers" by some of the Northern tribes of Indians. The Peruvians consecrated a pavilion of the great temple at Cuzco to the stars, and especially to Venus and the Pleiades.[7]

In India, the Maruts, the Rudras, the Ribhus, and the Pitris, were protecting spirits, originally men.[8] The Maruts are the wind and storm gods; a spirit-band formed by the souls of the dead. Hence the oft-repeated expression "they were once mortals," and hence probably their name; Maruts, "morts," mors.[9] In the Vedas, the Manes are called "the fathers" (pitris), and Yama, an old

[1] Æschylus, Prometheus bound, 454—457

[2] Noyes, Job, p. 198. Job xxxviii. 31. 32. 33. Munk, 424.

[3] 1 Genesis, 14.   [4] Prescott 146. Mexique 29.

[5] Ellis, Polynes. Res. i. 87.

[6] J. Müller, p. 54. Squier, Serp. Symb. 69.

[7] Lacroix, Univers pitt., Perou, p. 370.

[8] Wuttke, Gesch. des Heid., p. 568.

[9] 4 Kuhn's Zeitsch. für Vergleichende Sprachforschung, p. 116.

sungod or firegod, is their king. Yama was the "first man," like Manu.[1]

> "Agni zertrümmere nicht die heilige Schale,
> Die lieb den Göttern und den hehren Vätern;"

> "Geh' hin, geh' hin, auf jenen alten Pfaden,
> Auf denen unsre Väter heimgegangen;
> Gott Varuna und Yama sollst Du schauen,
> Die beiden Könige, die Spendentrinker.
> Geh' zu den Vätern, weile dort bei Yama."[2]

The Hindus poured out libations to the dead like the Greeks. The Peruvians made libations to the Sun; they searched the entrails of victims, and believed in auguries like the Romans, Babylonians and Greeks, and their idols were thought to speak after the manner of the ancient Greek pythonesses.[3] The flight of birds, especially vultures, was ominous among the American savages, as amongst the ancient Italians.[4] "So sang the birds in the branches to Sigurd, after he had destroyed Fafni, what yet remained for him to do.[5]"

> "Fataque vocales præmonuisse boves."[6]

In Italy genies were supposed to reside in the mid air, where the tempests have their origin.[7] All the Sabellians, but especially the Marsians, practised divination: principally from the flight of birds.[8] "The seer, the feeder of birds, revolving in ear and thoughts, without the use of fire, the oracular birds with unerring art."[9]

---

[1] Müller, Todtenbestattung, D. M. G., vol. ix., page xxi.—4 Kuhn 101.

[2] Müller Todtenbestattung, D. M. G. vol. 9. ix. xiv.

[3] Univers pitt. 371, 372, 376; Prescott, Peru, i., 106; Ezekiel xxi. 21; D'Orbigny, l'homme Americain, i. 303.

[4] J. Müller, p. 84. 278.; D'Orbigny, L'homme Americain, i. p. 303.

[5] Jacob Grimm, Ursprung der Sprache, p. 14.

[6] Tibull. ii. 5. 78.   [7] Italie ancienne, p. 386.

[8] Niebuhr's Rome. Am. ed. i. 71.

[9] Æschylus, Septem contra Thebas, line 24—26.

" Nor does bird send forth the notes of propitious omen." [1]

The "fifty races of birds, sharp-darting, divine," are mentioned in the old Persian sacred books.[2] Gods were among our Indians thought to reside in the upper currents of the atmosphere.[3]

" And the pure Æther, highway of the feathered race." [4]

Birds which dart lightning from their eyes are the children of Thunder.[5] The bird belongs to " the Heavenly " as one of them ; he raises himself by superhuman power above the earth, and is lost in the realm of the invisible.[6] Hence the Indian conception of the Deity manifesting himself in the form of a bird.[7] " Either this bird is the god himself, or the Great Spirit reveals himself as a bird, or he dwells in him." On great occasions, Kitchi Manitu shows himself in the clouds, borne by his favorite bird Wakon.[8] This is no other than the Great Spirit himself. " The bird of the Great Spirit is throned above, while the noise of his wings is the thunder ; he looks spying around, so arises the lightning; also he causes rain." [9] Other Indians ascribe the thunder to a great white cock in heaven.[10] The Dogribs tribe supposed that the earth was originally covered with water. No living being existed but a great Almighty Bird, whose eyes were fire, his looks lightnings, and the flap of his wings the thunder. He leaped down into the water, then the earth rose, and, at the Bird's command, animals came forth out of the earth. When his work was ended, the Bird withdrew, and was seen no more.[11] According to the Minitarree

---

[1] Antigone, line 1020.

[2] Yaçna. Kleuker, vol. i, p. 129, Note, *et passim*.

[3] Schoolcraft, part i. p. 33.   [4] Æschylus, Prometheus, 280.

[5] J. Müller, p. 91.   Schoolcraft, Algic Res. ii. 114.

[6] J. Müller, p. 120.   [7] J. Müller, 61, 63, 64, 111, 120, 121.

[8] J. Müller, 120 ; Chateaubriand, i. 192.

[9] J. Müller, 120.   [10] Ibid. 121; Heckewelder, 627.

[11] J. Müller, 121, quotes Klemm, ii. 155, 160; Schoolcraft, Wigwam, 202, etc., etc.

version of this myth, *the Bird had a red eye*, which refers to *the Sun ;* he dived under, and himself brought the earth up.[1]

Baal (the Sun) was represented with the wings and tail of a dove, to show the association with Mylitta.[2] Compare the Orphic idea of Zeus as Eros or Cupid; also Noah's dove with the doves of Mylitta (Venus), the Sun's dove, as the Spirit of God, that moved on the face of the waters. "The Spirit descending from heaven like a dove."[3] Among the Egyptians and Assyrians, hawk-headed divinities were those of the first order. " God is he that hath the head of a hawk."[4] The winged Sphynx resembles the Greek Gryphon, which is evidently an Eastern symbol, connected with Apollo (the Sun).[5] The eagle is the bird of Jove. In Persia the bird Asho-Zusta contends against the fiends. Other birds fight the devils, especially the bird Sinamru (Simurg). The Parsees asserted that Sinamru was the eagle.[6] "Serosch is holy, one of the four Heaven-birds : Corosh, radiant with light, far-seeing, intelligent, pure, excellent, speaking Heaven's language."[7] " I invoke the five races of the birds, ... the numerous birds of rapid wing."[8] In the comedy of Aristophanes, the chorus of birds is made to say :

> "The black-winged Night first lays a windy egg,
> Whence in the circling hours, sprang wished-for Love,
> He begot our race, and brought us forth to light.
> The immortal kind, ere Love (Eros) confounded all things,
> Had no existence yet ; but soon as they
> Were mingled, Heaven with Ocean rose, and Earth
> And all the gods' imperishable race.
> Thus are we far more ancient than the Blest."[9]

[1] J. Müller, p. 121
[2] Layard's Nineveh, 449.   [3] John i. 32.
[4] Layard's Nineveh, p. 458 ; Movers Phönizier, vol. i. p. 68, 59.
[5] Layard, p. 459.   [6] Dunker, vol. ii. p. 385.
[7] Serosh-Yesht. Kleuker i. 145.
Serosh, "the god of obedience, shows the law to the 7 Keshvars of the earth." Corosh—the Raven; the Carrion Crow.
[8] Kleuker, 129.   [9] Aves, 768—772.

J. Müller says of our Indians that in all things they recognized a *divine* Spirit, except in living men.[1] To the worship of Spirits is to be added that of the souls of the dead, which not unfrequently is one and the same thing. The souls of the dead, like other spirits, exert on the destiny of the living a *divine* influence; they manifest themselves, and are worshipped like gods. Festivals in their honor were celebrated every year; or every eight or ten years. They erected not merely monuments, but temples to them. Many Indians believe that before their birth they were animals. The Iroquois believe that at their decease men may become animals, or their souls transmigrate into stars. The southern heaven is chiefly the abode of the departed, and the stars of the Milky Way are the road to it. Among the Apalaches and Natchez, the sun is the abode only of the souls of the brave.[2] The Comanches believe the Indian paradise is situated beyond the sun.[3] The Mexicans prayed to their chief god, "We beseech thee that those whom thou lettest die in this war, may be received with love and honor *in the dwelling of the Sun*; that they may be gathered to the heroes (mentioned by name) who have fallen in former wars."[4] The souls of warriors escorted the Sun in his progress through the heavens, and, after four years of this life of happiness, were transformed into clouds, birds of brilliant plumage, lions, or jaguars.[5] "It is manifest that between the periods of Homer and Pindar a great change of opinions took place, which could not have been effected at once, but must have been produced by the efforts of many sages and poets." Whilst in Homer (about B. C. 884) only a few favorites of the gods reach the Elysian fields on the border of the Ocean; Pindar, not far from B. C. 550, makes the "Islands of the Blessed" a reward for the highest virtue. In Hesiod's "Works and Days" all the *heroes* are described as collected by Zeus in the "Islands

[1] J. Müller, 78.   [2] J. Müller, 72, 63.   [3] Schoolcraft, ii. 225.
[4] J. Müller, 620.   [5] Univers pitt. Mexique, 25.

of the Blessed."[1] The Hindus believed that those who fell
in battle went to Indra's heaven, where was light a
thousand times more brilliant than the sun. Those who
died in bed, the women and servants went to Jama in the
shades below.[2] The nations of Northern Europe believed that the beautiful maids of Odin conducted the
souls of fallen heroes to Valhalla. Those who died of
old age or sickness went to Hela, the goddess of the under-
world. The souls of the common people enter the bodies
of animals, in the conception of the Natchez tribe ; those of
the distinguished migrate into the stars.[3]

Our Indians believe that spirits or gods abide in
animals. The more primitive the Nature-worship, the more
frequent is the worship of animals.[4] Animal worship prevailed over Persia, India, Greece, Asia Minor, and Egypt.
The adoration of the bull, the goat, and the serpent, is too
well known to need remark. The Egyptians held most
animals sacred. So, in America, the Great Spirit appears as
a beaver. The beaver was sacred to the Great Spirit. The
same is true of the snake and the opossum among the Natchez Indians.[5] The transmigration of deities and the spirits
of the dead into animals was a prevalent notion. In Peru,
one of the deities is represented in the shape of a bird, just
as in the Polynesian islands, gods take the shapes of birds
or sharks.[6] Separate distinct spirits were regarded as
causes of the individual phenomena of Nature. Nowhere,
in the primitive condition of mankind, ruled the conception
of order, or subordination, or unity ; but all things had separate spirits assigned to them as their causes. Every object wears the aspect of a separate living being—and when
the mute and dead nature of some is too apparent for the

---

[1] See K. O. Müller, Lit. Anc. Greece, 230, 232.
[2] Duncker, ii. 68, 69. Inde, 196.   [3] J. Müller, 67, 66.
[4] J. Müller, 120, 59 ff.   [5] J. Müller, 123.
[6] Ellis, Polynesian Res., vol. i. 225, 329 ; Univers pitt. Mexique, Guatemala
et Perou, 371, 377.

exercise of this belief, it exerts itself in the idea that the inanimate object has a soul, a *life* about it somewhere; or a
genius loci, a nymph, or protecting spirit. Thus, to the
savage, the larger part of Nature becomes a legion of
animated powers, independent in existence and character.

Life and power are associated together in his mind, and
the most important distinction of the nature of gender,
which he thinks fit to make in his language, is the division
of objects into those which have life, and those without it.
With him, the Sun, Moon, Stars, Thunder and Lightning are
of the animate, or *living* gender.[1] The Mexican gender
distinguishes rational beings from irrational animals and
inanimate objects. "In the nouns of inanimate things the
plural is the same as the singular, such excepted as are
personified and *considered animate*, as the stars, sky, etc."[2]
Dr. von Tschudi, in his grammar of the Kechua (Peruvian),
remarks, "substantives in gender are divided into animate
and inanimate. To the first belong men, beasts, plants,
especially trees, the sea, rivers, the sky, the stars. To the
inanimate belong stones, all inanimate masses, works of
man's artificial production, little plants, small animals,
etc., etc."

The most primitive condition of mankind was that of
separate tribes, families or gentes, speaking different
tongues; and these tribes often assimilated in language to
their neighbors, producing resemblances of some sort, we
can scarcely say dialects; for all the dialects we know of in
Europe and Asia, and possibly in America, date some
thousands of years after the earliest period. The totally
different character of the languages of the American tribes
favors this view. It has been said that the grammar of
these tribes and nations is very much the same, from the
Esquimaux to the Patagonians; but that such a resem
blance is not to be found in the word-material. It is confined to the grammar, which would naturally be crude,

[1] Schoolcraft, ii. 366.   [2] American Ethnol. Soc. i. 216.

because the American tribes were not, generally speaking, civilized. Ranke, at the commencement of his History of the Popes, says: "If we take a general survey of the world in the earliest times, we find it filled with a multitude of independent tribes. We see them settled round the Mediterranean, from the coasts as far inland as the country had yet been explored, variously parted from each other, all originally confined within narrow limits, and living under purely independent and peculiarly constituted forms of government." The historian Niebuhr remarks: "The farther we look back into antiquity, the richer, the more distinct and the more broadly marked do we find the dialects of great languages. They subsist one beside the other, with the same character of originality, and just as if they were different tongues.'" The variety of the Grecian tribes, and Homer's enumeration of the various races that assembled at the siege of Troy, are well known. Additional evidence of this early multiplicity of distinct tribes is perhaps to be found in the oriental system of government. A great king had many tributary kings under him. Each of these petty kingdoms preserved in the main its ancient customs and form of government, paying an annual tribute to the power whose superiority it acknowledged. The Old Testament bears constant testimony to the variety and number of distinct nationalities. In Persia and India, the same thing appears, and even in China. The tribes of Tartary and the remains of countless races that even now appear between the Caspian and Black seas, the tribes of Germany, Gaul and Britain, and the ancient and even modern condition of Africa, all point to the same primitive tribal organization. In North America, we have the almost infinite variety of distinct tribes, speaking different languages. Mexico was filled with distinct nations having different dialects. The Aztec armies were incessantly occupied in attacking "a multitude of petty States," some unconquered, and others

[1] Niebuhr's Rome, Am. ed., vol. i. p. 49.

endeavoring to shake off the yoke.[1] The Mexican grea chiefs or nobles exercised complete territorial jurisdictioi each in his own district; they raised taxes, and followed th standard of the monarch in war with forces proportionat to the extent of their domain, and many paid tribute to th king as their legitimate sovereign. All this resembles th ancient state of things among the tributary peoples of Asia In Guatemala, according to Juarros, the number of natior alities and languages was greater than in any other part c the New World. The number of different peoples exceed that of the languages.[2] In South America, in the kingdon of Quito, in its narrowest acceptation, two hundred and fifty-two nations existed, with as many dialects, which hav been divided into forty-three distinct separate languages The nations, dialects and languages to the south, toward Cuzco, were hardly less numerous.[3]

"The Indian languages *generally have few words or ever roots in common*, except when they belong to some grea family. The Apaches may be taken as an example. They extend from Texas to the Colorado of California, swallow ing up many tribes with which they were not supposed to have any relationship, until affinities were discovered ii their languages. Professor W. W. Turner, to whom I sen a few words of the Apache language, ... discovered striking affinities between it and the language of the Atho pascans who occupy a far northern region near the Esqui maux. I have been able to trace analogies in the lan guages of several Indian tribes in New Mexico and Cal ifornia, quite remote from each other. *Unless there is such a relationship, no innate radical resemblance can be traced in the word-stock of the Indian languages. This charac teristic, I can safely say, applies to the group of languages on the Pacific as well as on the Atlantic side of North*

---

[1] Univers pitt. Mexique, p. 21.   [2] Buschmann, pp. 130, 131.
[3] Von Tschudi, Grammar of the Kechua language.

America." [1] Mr. Gallatin says : " Taking into view the words or vocabularies alone, although seventy-three tribes (east of the Rocky Mountains, within the United States and the British possessions) were found speaking dialects *so far differing that they cannot be understood without an interpreter by the Indians of other tribes*, yet the affinities between the words of many of them were such as to show clearly that they belonged to the same stock. Sixty-one dialects, spoken by as many tribes, were thus found to constitute only (?) eight languages, or rather families of languages, *so dissimilar that the few coincidences* which might occur in their words appeared to be accidental. [2] The investigation of the languages of the Indians east of the Rocky Mountains, and north of the States as far as the Polar Sea, has satisfactorily shown, that however *dissimilar their words*, their structure and grammatical forms are substantially the same. [3] " Mr. Gallatin has found in North America alone thirty-seven families of tongues, comprising more than one hundred dialects." [4] It is well known that tribes emigrate and change their language entirely ; and that two tribes will coalesce, forming a new language, in which it is almost impossible to recognize either of the original tongues. Von Tschudi says, " The number of American languages and dialects is extraordinarily great, and scarcely the twentieth part of them has been even superficially known. Also these languages have undergone great alterations. Many have become extinct. It is a well-known fact, that individual tribes or bands (Rotten) of Indians separate from the main stock, remove into remote regions, and there form, in a manner, a new language, that contains an altogether new word-material, and is not understood by the original race. Other races mix, and form a new

---

[1] John R. Bartlett, Nov. 25th, 1854.
[2] Jour. Am. Ethnol. Soc., vol. i. p. 2.
[3] Notes, etc., p. 10 ; Squier's Serp. Symb., p. 26.
[4] Indigenous Races of the Earth, p. 82.

language, which only a close and thorough examination can trace back to its source.[1]

It is important, while showing that the primitive organ ization of mankind was that of tribes, speaking differen tongues, to notice in this connection certain characteristic common to all primitive languages, which are evidences o the simple and unphilosophical mode of thought of the early peoples. "Crude and primitive languages are redundant in grammatical forms."[2] "In general it may be observed that in the lapse of ages, from the time that the progress of language can be observed, grammatical forms, such as the signs o cases, moods and tenses, have never been increased in number, but have been constantly diminishing." "The luxuriance of the grammatical forms which we perceive in the Greek, cannot have been of late introduction, but must be referred to the earliest period of the language."[3] Jacob Grimm says, "the state of language in the first period can not be called one of perfection, for it lives nearly a life of plants, in which high gifts of the soul still slumber, or are but half wakened. The word-material pushes forth rapidly and close together like blades of grass."[4] Not only are many moods and tenses formed, but many cases of nouns, numerous inclusive and exclusive forms of verbs, and a great variety of particle usages, that later lingual develop ments have caused to entirely disappear. Thus the Sanskrit has eight cases of nouns—the Peruvian nine, the Greek five, and the Latin six. The Peruvian (Quiqua) is a more primitive language than the Sanskrit, and possesses a greater abundance of grammatical forms.[5] "The genius of the American languages, like that of the Sanskrit, Greek and the Germanic tongues, permits a great number of ideas in a single word."[6]

[1] Von Tschudi, Grammar of the Kechua Sprache.
[2] Schoolcraft, vol. ii., 342.   [3] K. O. Müller, Hist. Greek Literature, 5.
[4] Ursprung der Sprache, 46, 47.
[5] See Von Tschudi, Grammar, passim.
[6] Larenaudière, Univers pitt. Mexique, 49, b.

The Indian's crude conception of Nature pervades his language. It is description with an attempt to paint in words a scene just as it occurred, taking in all its details and particulars *in one long word.* It is a constant effort to speak of objects *in groups,*[1] or rather to find a single word to express two or three ideas, where we should use one word for each. These well-known *agglutinated forms of words* among our Indians are mentioned by Von Tschudi (p. 11) as a characteristic of the Quiqua (the Peruvian); but the Mexican had dropped this mode of expression probably, as it is said not to exist in this language.[2] The Indian, instead of using one verb "to wash," no matter what undergoes the process of washing, employs a verb signifying in itself "to wash the hands," another meaning "to wash the face," and so on. Without perceiving that the idea of washing is common to each, he gives a new word for each variation of idea, which includes every thing—one main idea with all its adjuncts. It is language prior to generalization and philosophic analysis.

[1] Schoolcraft, ii., 342.   [2] 1 Am. Ethnol. Soc., 242.

CHAPTER II

The great number of the Nature-gods is gradually increased by abstractions which are borrowed from ethical and social relations, and to which divine powers, a personal existence and agency are attributed.[1]

From the spirits of Natural objects and phenomena, it is an easy step to spirits which preside over substances, as the deities of corn, gold, salt, wine; over diseases; over abstract ideas; the first moral conceptions and mental qualities; as wisdom, beauty, truth, justice, sin; over blindness, sleep and death. In Homer, sleep and death are personified. The Algonquin god of sleep is Weeng, whose ministers beat with little clubs on the foreheads of men, producing slumber. Their Pauguk is a god of death. He has a bow, arrows and clubs.[2] Spirits preside also over days, months, and periods of time generally, as in Yucatan, Mexico, Egypt, Persia, and other countries. There is a god of carpenters, of thieves, of persons who thatch houses, of ghosts, surgery, husbandry and physic, among the Polynesians.[3] The Chinese had a god presiding over agriculture, an ancient patron of the silk manufacture, a god of the passing year, an ancient patron of the healing art, a god of the road where

---

[1] Weber, Akadem. Vorles., 4.   [2] J. Müller, 98.
[3] Ellis, Polynes. Res., 333.

an army passes, a god of cannon, and gods of the gate, besides ghosts of faithful statesmen, scholars, etc.[1] The Mexican had his gods of gold, sin, blindness, wine, pleasures, frost, salt, and butterflies, his goddesses of the chase, the flowers, and medicine. The Greek had his Wisdom, Justice, Sleep, Death, Fortuna, as divinities.

When the savage perceives the operations of Nature that we call *laws*, he conceives a Being working and revealing himself in them.[2] Spirits govern the elements and the seasons. The people of Western Europe considered Kronos to be Winter, Aphrodite Summer, and Persephone Spring.[3] The American Indians worshipped the Earth as the mother of all things.[4] " Rhodos (Rhodes), the daughter of Aphrodite, bride of the Sun,"[5] Erde, the Earth, Gothic Airthô, Aritimis,[6] the Scandinavian Earth-goddess Jörd, the Old-Persian deity Armaiti, the Earth, the Sanskrit Aramati, Acal, Ocol, Col (Cœlus), " Acalus and Calus names of the Cretan Talus "[7] (the Sun), Kleio (Klea), Ascl, Sol, the Etruscan Usil, the Sabine Ansel, Sauil, Sahil, Sigel, Heli(os), Eelios, Aelios, Azel and Azael (a god adored in Damascus),[8] Ab,[9] the old god Av, the Oscan god Iiv, Iove, Ievo, (Ιευω),[10] Evi-us (Bacchus), Aphaia, (Artemis,[11] the E-arth) Apia (the Earth), Kronos "the beaming Sun" (Krona, a sunbeam in Phœnician, Karan, in Hebrew " to shine," Karnon, in Arabic " a sunbeam,"[12]) Zeus (Seus ?) god of Æther and the storms, the old god Asius in Asia Minor, " the Spartan Sios" (Zeus), the Old Testament Aishi (Baal =Jehova),[13] the Assyrian "As," father of the gods,[14] " Iasius

[1] Martin's China.
[2] J. Müller, 57, 254, 361.   [3] Plutarch, de Is. et Os., lxix.
[4] J. Müller, 56 ; Tanner, 203, in Müller.   [5] Pindar, Olymp. vii. 25.
[6] Donaldson's Varronianus, 37.
[7] American Encycl. Art. Talus. Movers, i. 381.
[8] Movers, i. 368. Jacob Grimm, Trans. Berlin Akad. 1845, 197.
[9] J. Brandis, 40, 100.   [10] Movers, i. 128.
[11] Donaldson's Pindar, 351.   [12] Rinck, i. 40.
[13] Hosca, ii. 16. (18.)
[14] Rawlinson, Journal Royal Asiatic Soc., vol. xii. 426.

(Bacchus), the husband of Ceres,"[1] Smun (Esmun), Apollo, "Summanus (Pluto), god of the nightly lightnings," Amanus or Omanus, the Sun in Pontus and Cappadocia, Amon, god of light and fire, Iapetos, the Titan, Phut or Ptah (Vulcan), Oannes, 'Ωην, Ani, Ina (the Sun in Sanskrit), Anu,[2] Æolus, Boreas, and Rudra, "the rushing storm-blast," Adan, Odin, Adonis, Inachus, the Phrygian Annakos, Enoch, Asar, Asarac, Ahura, Dagon, Dakan, Agni "the four-eyed Hindu fire-god" (Ignis), Am, Ami, Aum, Om, Aoum,[3] Aoymis, Iama, Ioma, Iom (day), Yima, Jamadagni, Saad, the Arab god, Seth, the god of the "Sethites," Seth-Typhon (Moloch, Pluto), Sol-Typhon[4] = "Apop, the brother of Sol,"[5] Abobas (Adonis), Phoibos, Papaius (Zeus), "Apellōn, the fighter,"[6] Abel,[7] Abelios, the Sun in Crete,[8]Babelios, the Sun in Pamphylia,[9] Apollo, are all spirits. It is enough to say, generally, that for nearly every idea which the human mind could conceive, a god or presiding spirit would seem to have been somewhere created.

Hence Fetichism is explained. It is as easy for the mind of the savage to locate a spirit in a stick of wood, a square stone, or a rude idol, as for the Mexican to conceive a god of gold, of butterflies, or of frost. If spirits transmigrate into stars from the forms of the animals or human bodies, if they reside in trees, why may they not enter an artificially prepared substance? The African con-

---

[1] Hesiod. Theog. 970. Compare the Hebrew names Iesaias, Iesaiah, Ishiah, Ishiaho, 1 Chron.xii. 6. Iesus, Asiah (in the Cabbala), and Iasiaho (Ioshua). Jeremiah xxxvii..

[2] Bopp, Berlin. Akad. 1838, 194; Brandis, 80. See also Zeitschrift d. D. M. G. viii. 596.

[3] Aμοῦς. Plut. de Is. cap. 9. Herodot. ii. 42.   [4] Movers, i. 300.

[5] Kenrick, ii. 354; Movers, i. 399.

[6] Müller's Dorians, Book ii., ch. 6. §. 6; Donaldson's Varron. 37 ; Rinck, i. 175.

[7] The Phœnicians and Syrians call Saturn (Kronos) El and Bél and Bōlatēn. Movers, i. ch. 8. 256. Damascius in Photius, 343.

[8] Jacob Grimm, Trans. Berlin Akad. 1845, 197   [9] Ibid.

siders the material substance which he adores endowed with intelligence like himself, only superior in degree. He has housed a spirit within it.

The Dacotah Indian worships a painted stone.[1] In Peru, a stone was observed to be a tutelary deity.[2] The Arabs adored a great black stone. The worship of idols in the human form is a more cultivated, but a similar conception. The Teraphim in Genesis are a kind of portable household gods or penates, such as the Greeks and Romans possessed.[3] The Manitus of the visible objects of Nature, or of natural phenomena, are considered so united with the material appearance, as to form one being, like soul and body.[4] "If the spirits are sometimes looked upon as without a visible form, yet their appearance and revelation are connected with these objects and signs."[5]

"Then Samuel took a stone and set it between Mizpeh and Shem, and called the name of it Eben-Ezer."[6] This means Dionysus (Bacchus = the Sun); for, as the Maltese stone-inscription translates Ebed-Esar by the Greek Dionysus, we feel no hesitation in translating Eben-Ezer (Aban-Azar) the same. Bacchus-Ebon was represented in Campania as an ox with a human head, and Oben-Ra is said to be Ammon-Ra.[7] Rawlinson reads Aben; Aban is Pan.[7] Jacob sets up a stone on end, and pours oil on the top of it, and says; "This stone which I have placed as a statue, shall be God's house."[8] "And Jacob set up a statue (statuam) in the place where he talked with him, a statue (statuam) of stone; and he poured a drink-offering (libation) thereon, and he poured oil thereon."[9] "No man is with us; see, Elohim is witness. Behold this heap, and behold the

---

[1] Intr. to Dacotah Gram. [2] Univers pitt. Perou, 77.

[3] Parts 4, 5, vol. v., Bunsen, Ægypt's Stelle, 326. [4] J. Müller, 92.

[5] J. Müller, 95. [6] 1 Sam. vii. 11, 12.

[7] Movers, i. 373, 326; Munter Babylonier, p. 27; Bononi, p. 78; Journal Royal Asiatic Soc. 15, Part 1, p. xvii.; Christian Examiner, July, 1856, p. 95.

[8] "Quem posui statuam," Version of Sebastian Schmid.

[9] Gen. xxxv. 13, 14, Version Schmid.

statue (statuam)." [1] The adoption of the human form
in images is a more advanced conception. The human
form symbolizes the superiority of man's nature over the
rest of creation, and is so much the better fitted for the representation of the forms of the gods. In Asia, the representation of the Divine in human shape was forbidden in
the earliest period, and the Persians, at first, were greatly
displeased on seeing such images. [2] The Persians, the
people of Central America, the Egyptians, the Hebrews,
and other nations, used animal forms as the symbols of
divine qualities. The highest employment of these symbols is seen in the Sphinx, the Cherubs, the Serpent, the
Winged Bulls with human faces at the doors of the Assyrian palaces. The highest conception of God clothed him
with the human form. "The Greek anthropomorphism is
a higher stage than the Pelasgic Nature-worship." [3] God
is represented in the legends of Genesis with the human
shape. The Egyptian and Hindu sacred writings often ex-
hibit the same conception of the deities.

The fetichism of the savage confines its regards to the
individual phenomena and objects of Nature. To him the
idea of unity (Einheit), of " a whole," of " a creation," must
necessarily be strange. He thinks not of " a whole," of " a
world; " and does not ask himself, " Who has made that ? " [4]

From among the multiplicity of powers whose existence
was obvious to the perception of the child of Nature, he
selected some that were more prominent as the chief objects
of his regard—the sun and moon, some of the stars, the
earth, air, fire, water, and gods of matters connected with his
daily wants. Every kind of spirits (and there are many) has
its own leader or chief. This idea forms an intermediate
step from the infinitude of individual spirits to the conception of a Great Spirit, who stands at the head of all spirits. [5]

[1] Gen. xxxii. 50, 51, Schmid's Version.
[2] Mover's Phönizier, i. 181, et passim.
[3] J. Müller, 96.   [4] J. Müller, 75.   [5] J. Müller, 104, 75, 91.

The Great Spirit is a spirit like any other; he wears all the peculiarities of the other spirits of Nature-worship, and his idea or the conception of him fastens itself to any visible object, which exercises a striking influence upon the whole of Nature, like the Sun, the Heaven; or to one which reveals to us a power of Nature (Naturkraft) as an animal, or, finally, which expresses the personality as the human figure.[1] The Greenlanders worshipped the Great Spirit, but did not associate the idea of a Creator with him.[2] Northern races, like the Esquimaux and Greenlanders, know nothing of a Creator, but recognize a Great Spirit.[3] The Great Spirit dwells in waterfalls, in birds and animals, such as the hare, beaver, wolf, bear, buffalo, and serpent.[4] He is a Nature-god, like the other gods: a part of the many gods, primus inter pares.[5]

In the progress of conception, the primitive spirit-worship is in some sort systematized. The number of distinct existences is divided into classes. Spirits preside over these divisions. A god of all the rivers, winds, fishes, classes of animals, etc., is conceived. Æolus presides over the winds, Oceanus over the waters, Unktahe is the god of waters of the Dacotahs. In Mexico, Nahuihehecatl is ruler of the four winds. Tlaloc is the chief of the water-gods. A rise takes place to the conception of "Great Gods," who preside over the elements, the winds, and the most prominent circumstances of life. These chief gods are generally of a certain number, which is fixed; although the deities are not always the same. In Egypt the number remains the' same, but the deities differ in different districts.[6] The number is taken from some calculations respecting time, or has an astronomical origin, like the numbers thirteen, twelve, and seven.

Thirteen was the sacred number of the Mexicans and

---

[1] J. Müller, 99.   [2] J. Müller, 104.   [3] Ibid. 115. 116, 149.
[4] Ibid. 122, 123, 125.   [5] Ibid. 102.
[6] Lepsius über den ersten ägyptischen Götterkreis, Trans. Berlin Ak. 1851.

the people of Yucatan; "twelve" of our Indians, and almost all the nations of antiquity; "seven" was taken from the Babylonian idea of the Sun, Moon, and five great Planets, as prominent rulers over the destiny of mortals. The number twelve is the twelve moons or lunar months. "The names of these twelve gods often show that they were only the old deities, presiding over the elements and most important circumstances of every-day life. The Mexican and Maya sacred number was thirteen. The method of computation among the priests was by weeks of thirteen days. The thirteen names of days are those of the "Great Gods."[1] The origin of the period of thirteen days to a week was this. The year contained twenty-eight weeks of thirteen days each, and one day over—just as our year contains fifty-two weeks of seven days, and one day over. Thirteen years would make an indiction or week of years, in which the one day over, each year, would be absorbed in an additional week of thirteen days. Four times thirteen or fifty-two years made their Cycle. The period of thirteen days resulting from their first chronological combinations, afterwards became their sacred number."[2] Lepsius says, the Great Gods of Egypt had not an astronomical origin, but were very likely distributed on an astronomical principle, when it was advisable to form and arrange the nome deities into one system on the consolidation of the kingdom.[3]

The number of stones of which Druidical structures consist is always a mysterious and sacred number, never fewer than twelve, and sometimes nineteen, thirty, sixty. These numbers coincide with those of the gods. In the centre of a circle, sometimes external to it, is reared a larger stone, which may have been intended to represent the Supreme God.[4]

[1] Gama, Astronomy, Chronol. and Mythol. of the ancient Mexicans, 51, 97, 98, 99, ff. Compare the thirteen snake-gods of Yucatan. Müller, 487.

[2] Stephens, Yucatan i. 434; Appendix, 94. Müller, 94.   [3] Berl. Ak. 1851.

[4] Pictet, 134; Michelet, Hist. France, vol. ii. 382, quoted in Squier, Serp. Symb. 48.

Janus is the Sun-god, or god of the year, among the Romans. He is represented with twelve altars beneath his feet, referring to the twelve months of the year. (He is called Ani by the Assyrians, Ion, Jan and Dionysus by the Greeks, Eanus in Italy, and On by other Eastern nations.) The first day of the first month of the year was sacred to him.[1] Two ancient names of the sun were On and Ad; or, doubled, Adad, Atad, Tat, Thoth, &c. The composition of Tat and An is *Titan*, which name for the Sun is used by Ovid and Seneca.[2] The twelve Titans, of whom Saturn is the chief, are the earlier deities of the primitive Grecian tribes, corresponding to the twelve months of the solar year. Later, the Olympian twelve (of whom Jupiter is chief) take their place, and the early Titans are transformed into the conception of Primæval Powers, or Elements.[3]

After the twelve moons (or months), the American Indians made a classification of their more prominent gods. The Lenni Lennape have twelve highest Manitus, to whom a higher importance is attributed than to the other spirits. Twelve staves or posts are set up in a circle in the midst of the council-house, each of a different wood, and connected together above. Into this circle twelve burning-hot stones are rolled, sacred to twelve Manitus. The greatest stone to the Great Spirit of Heaven, Walsit Manitu, the others to the Manitus of the sun (or day), moon, earth, fire, water, of the house, of maize, and the four quarters of the heavens.[4]

The twelve months are, in the Zendavesta of the Persians and Baktrians, named after the Fravashis,[5] Ahura-Mazda, " the six holy immortals " (the Amesha-Çpenta), the Sun-god Mithra, the star Tistar, the Water and the Fire.[6] Like the months, the days also were assigned to particular

[1] Eschenburg, Manual, 409.   [2] Metam. i. 5; Medea, 5; comp. " Tithonus."

[3] 1. Rinck, Religion der Hellenen, 41; Hesiod. Theog. 424.

[4] 3 Loskiel, 565, ff.; Bromme, R. A. 231; quoted in J. Müller, 92.

[5] The first month is named after the Fravashis.

[6] Duncker, vol. ii. 376, 363, *note;* Gerhard, Griech. Myth., i. 314; Movers, Phönizier, vol. i. 86, 27, 255, 256, et passim.

gods and spirits. The first seven days of each month were
named after Ahura-Mazda and the six Amesha-Çpenta—
just as the seventh day of the week was sacred to El,
among the Hebrews and Arabs, and to Saturn among the
Eastern nations generally. The Sun-god Apollo has the
epithet ʽΕβδομαῖος, and the number seven is sacred to
Mithra, the Sun-god of the Persians.

The number twelve is very common, as a sacred number, among the American tribes. Twelve Indians dance the
bull dance.[1] In Florida, twelve wooden statues, of superhuman dimensions, and wild and threatening aspect, each
with a different weapon, stood before the temple at Talo-
meko.[2] In Central America, at Momotombita, Squier found
a group of twelve statues of the gods together.[3] The Peruvians divided the year into twelve lunar months, each of
which had its own name and its appropriate festival.[4]
Such groups of twelve gods were found in Thessaly, Olympia, Achaia, Asia Minor and Crete. Also in Italy among
the Etruscans, Sabines, Mamertines, Romans. The division
of the year at Rome came under the head of religious affairs, and was in the charge of the priests.[5] The Babylonians worshipped the sun, moon (Baal and Astarte), and five
planets, also the twelve leaders of the gods, corresponding
to the twelve months, or signs of the Zodiac.[6] The
Hebrews, like the Chinese and Saracens prior to Mahomet,
had their division into twelve tribes, in reference probably
to the sacredness of this number.[7] The twelve gods are
found among the Egyptians,[8] Phœnicians, the inhabitants
of Cyprus, Bithynians, Syrians, Persians, Greeks, Chaldeans,
Hindus, Japanese and Lithuanians. Among the Scandina-
vians Odin had his twelve chief names.[9] The younger

---

[1] Catlin, 121; J. Müller, 92.   [2] J. Müller, 98, 92.
[3] J. Müller, 92.   [4] Prescott, Peru, i. 126.   [5] Eschenburg, 570.
[6] Munter, Babylonier, 13.   [7] J. Müller, 93.
[8] Herodot. ii. 4; Lepsius, über den ersten ägyptischen Götterkreis, Berlin.
Ak. 1851.
[9] J. Müller, 93.

Odin is chief of the Aser, the later gods, who are descended from him.

The Hebrews worshipped the twelve gods of the Zodiac.[1] The twelve labors of Hercules are the twelve signs of the Zodiac. Hercules is here the Phœnician Hercules (the Sun). Solomon's "molten sea," ten cubits from the one brim to the other, stood upon twelve oxen, three looking toward the north, and three looking toward the west, and three looking toward the south, and three looking toward the east. "And on the borders between the ledges were lions, oxen and cherubims."[2] The Irish god Cromeruah, whose image was of gold, was surrounded by twelve brazen statues of the gods.[3]

Among the Persians, the first seven days of each month were sacred to Ahura-Mazda and the six Amesha-Çpenta; they call the eighth day "that which *precedes* the Fire;" the ninth day is named after the Fire, the tenth after the Water, the eleventh after the Sun, the twelfth after the Moon, the thirteenth after the star Tistar, the fourteenth after the Holy Bull. The fifteenth belongs to Mithra, the seventeenth to Çraosha, the nineteenth to the Fravashis (souls), the twentieth to Verethragna, the rest of the days of the month to subordinate spirits; the last but one, however, to Manthra-Çpenta, the "Holy Word." Thus every day has its protecting deity, as among the Egyptians, Babylonians, Mexicans, and other nations.[4] Of the Jewish months, Nisan or Abib, Thammuz (Adonis), Ab, Elul, Ethanim, Bul and Adar are names of sun-gods or prominent deities. Some Old as well as New Persian names of months are also names of deities: Ab, Aban, &c. The same is true of the Roman, Greek, and Egyptian months.[5]

The division of the great gods into seven, which is very ancient in Egypt and Palestine, probably sprung from the

[1] 2 Kings, xxiii. 5; Munk, Palestine, 424; Job, xxxviii. 32; Movers, i. 80, 287, 164.

[2] 1 Kings, vii. 23, 25, 29.   [3] J. Müller, 93.

[4] Duncker, vol. ii. 366.

[5] With the deity-name "Bar," often found in Nineveh, the god Bar can

3

division into four quarters of the moon, just as the number
"twelve" had its origin in the division of the year into
moons. The "seven" is the seven days of the week, named
after the Pagan gods and Planets. The first day of the
week was Saturday, which was sacred to Saturn, or, as the
Saxons called him, Seatur. His name in Palestine was El.
Sunday (Sontag) was Dies Solis, and sacred to the Sun
and Hercules (or Sandak).[1] Monday, the Moon's day,
Dies Lunæ. Tuesday was sacred to Tuisco, or Mars. Wed-
nesday to Odin or Woden. Among the Romans it was the
day of Mercury. Thursday was the day of Thor, Odur,
Adar, Adar-melech, Dorus, Jupiter, Donar—Donnerstag,
the day of the god of thunder. Friday was sacred to Freia,
Aphrodite, Venus. The Egyptians assigned a day of the
week to the sun, moon, and five planets, and the number
seven was held there in great reverence.[2]

"And Balak took Balaam and brought him up into the
high places (mounds) of Baal, that thence he might see
the uttermost of the people. And Balaam said unto Balak,
Build me here seven altars, and prepare me here seven
oxen, and seven rams. And Balak did as Balaam had
spoken, and Balak and Balaam offered on every altar a
bullock and a ram."[3] It is obvious that Balak and Balaam
were priest-kings like Melchizedec, who was both priest and
king in Salem. This combination of offices was found
among the Natchez, whose caziques, called "Suns," were
both chiefs and priests.[4] The caziques of the Guaramis
were called "Suns," and claimed the Sun as their father.[5]
As the mounds of the American aborigines who inhabited

alone be compared, who is occasionally named on the Egyptian monuments.
In like manner we may compare with "Ab," the same name (Ab) of the As-
syrian-Babylonian month, and Diodor's relation that the Babylonians appointed
a month to each of their twelve gods. What is meant, is obvious from the
names of the tenth and sixth month, Tamus and Adar, both *deity-names*, one
of Adonis, the other of Mars.—Brandis, Assyr. Inschriften, 40.

[1] Movers. 240, 459.   [2] Kenrick, Egypt, i. 283.
[3] Numbers, xxiii. 1, 2.   [4] Serp. Symb. 129.   [5] Ibid. 129.

the Valley of the Mississippi, originally contained but two bodies, one a male, the other that of a female, it is not unlikely that the chief of the tribe, like the Natchez chieftains, united the priestly functions on the mound with the office of cacique or king.[1]

Noah took of every clean beast *seven* pairs into the ark. The ark rested on Ararat in the *seventh* month; and Noah rested *seven* days longer, and *seven* more besides, before he went from the ark. We also find the *seven* lean kine in Pharaoh's dream, the seven archangels, the seven Amshaspands of the Persians, the seven "great gods" of the Egyptians, Greeks and Romans, the seven Cabiri of Phœnicia, "the seven eyes of Jehovah," "a stone with seven eyes," "a candlestick with seven lamps," seven heavens, and finally, in Japan, the *seven* Sintoo (Hindu) gods. Jehova-Elohim created the world in seven days.

It is stated in "Cory's Ancient Fragments," on the authority of Berosus, that according to the Babylonian cosmogony, "Bel, who is Jupiter, divided the darkness, separated the heavens from the earth, and reduced the universe to order—he created the stars, the sun, moon, and five planets." [2] The number seven was a sacred number in the "light religions." *Οἱ δὲ σύμμαχοι Ἴτου τοῦ Κρόνου Ἐλοεὶμ ἐπεκλήϑησαν, ὡς ἂν Κρόνιοι· οὗτοι ἦσαν οἱ λεγόμενοι ἀπὸ Κρόνου.*[3] El is the leader of the other Elohim, or Elim who go by his name. "Who is like thee among the Elim?" (plural of El, God.) [4]

In Italy, the seventh day was sacred to Saturn, "die Saturno," Seaturday, Saturday. In Judea, the seventh day was sacred to "the Lord," as the Sabbath. The symbol of an oath was seven sheep—it was a bargain.[5] Abraham gave Abimelech seven ewe lambs as a witness that he dug

---

[1] See Squier and Davis, Mounds of the Mississippi Valley.

[2] Cory, p. 75.

[3] Sanchoniathon, A. vi. Eusebius, p. 37.   Movers, i. 256. Ἴλον τὸν καὶ Κρόνον. Sanchon. vii.

[4] Exodus, xv. 11.   [5] Hengstenberg, i. 277.

a well.[1] The number seven was sacred to El (Saturn) throughout the East.[2] "The planet Saturn, at any rate, very early became the chief deity of Semitic religion, at least before the Sabbath was established, long before Moses consecrated the number *seven* to him, perhaps earlier than Saturn was father of Jupiter and the other gods in Greece and Italy."[3]

The city of Ecbatana, which was erected on or near the site of Hamadan in Al Jebel, had strong walls built in circles, one within another, rising each above each by the height of their respective battlements. The city being thus formed of *seven* circles, the king's palace and the royal treasury stood within the last.[4] A hymn was sung to Python (the Sun-Serpent) at Delphi every seventh day.[5] On the first and *seventh* of every month, the Lacedæmonians give to each of the kings a perfect animal, which is sacrificed in the temple of Apollo.[6] On the way from Sparta to Arcadia, stood seven planetary columns, at which horses were offered to Helios (the Sun), as in Persia.[7]

[1] Gen. xxi. 30.
[2] Movers, i. 315; Lepsius, Berlin, Akad.; Kenwick, i. 283.
[3] Movers' Phönizier, i. 313.
[4] Beloe's Herodot. Clio, i. 149, 150.   [5] Deane, Serpent-Worship, 89.
[6] Heredotus, Erato, lvii. 274.   [7] Movers, i. 51, 52.

CHAPTER III.

In Egypt, Atmu (Atumu, Athom, Tom) is the night-Sun; Mentu, the day-Sun. The god Mu is "light," "brilliance." Seb is "father of the gods,"[1] "Sun-worship was the earliest germ and the most general principle of the Egyptian mythology."[2] "It was the primitive national religion of the Egyptians."[3] Ra was the Sun.[4] "Not Ammon, but Ra is the real ' king of the gods.' "[5]

Baal-Adon(is) was the morning-Sun.[6] Sandan is Baal (the Sun) and Hercules.[7] Shun is the Sun in Mandshu-Tartar.[8] A god San is read on the Assyrian monuments.[9] Asana is the name of the Spartan Minerva, the wife of Apollo, the Sun.[10] Azania is Arcadia.[11] Zano is Juno.[12] Sunna is Gothic for Sun;[13] the German Sonne, the feminine Sun. Asan must have been the original word, a compound of " As" (the Sun) and An (On, Ion, Ani, Eanus,

[1] Lepsius,Berlin Akad. 1851, 187; Kenrick, i. 330; Lepsius,Berlin Akad. 1856, 191.

[2] Ibid. 1851, 193.　　　　[3] Ibid. 195.　　　　[4] Kenrick, i. 328.

[5] Lepsius, ibid. 193.　　　　[6] Movers, i. 227.

[7] Movers, i. 458–480; Johannes Brandis,Historische Gewinn, etc. 40.

[8] Bunsen, Philosophy of Univers. Hist., i. 356.

[9] J. Brandis, 104. Sani-el, an angel.–Gallaeus, 274.

[10] Liddell and Scott's Lexicon; Rinck, i. 296, *note*, quotes Aristoph. Lysistr. 170, 989, 1251, 1256; see also 913, 1209. Assan-ias, Assana, 1 Esdras vii, 54, v.

[11] Beloe's Herodot., iv. 201, *note*.　　　　[12] Greek Lexicon.

[13] Grimm, Berlin Akad. 1845, p. 197. Shanah, a solar " year " in Hebrew.

Ianus, Janus). We have in the Bible the names AzanIah,[1] אֲזַנְיָה, IaazanIaho, וְיַאֲזַנְיָהוּ, written iazaniaho in Hebrew.[2] We have Zion, Ezion-geber, Aison the father of Iason (Jason), the Sun. His "Medeia" is named among the goddesses by Hesiod.[3] Iason is probably Dionysus, who was called Amadios and Omadios.[4] We find Zan (Ζην), Jupiter; Zanoah[5] (Noah), a Hebrew proper name, and Chorazin, a compound of Kur, the Sun (Kurios, "Lord;" the river Kur, Curus=Cyrus), and Azin (Asan) the Sun. Dorsanes is a compound of Adar (Thor), the fire and thunder god, the Assyrian Mars, and San, the Sun-god's name. Zan and Asana would then be the Sun and his goddess (Danae), Apollo and Minerva. Asanai, the Laconian name of Athenai (Athens), is the city of the Sun (San, Atten, Adonis) and his goddess of light.

In Florida, the first-born male infant was offered up to the Sun, in honor of him or of the rulers of the people as "sons of the Sun."[6] Human offerings were made to the Sun even in this century.[7] The Natchez Indians and their affiliated tribes worshipped the Sun, to whom they erected temples and performed sacrifices. They maintained a perpetual fire,[8] and the chiefs claimed the Sun as their father. The Hurons also derive the descent of their chiefs from the Sun.[9] The great chief of the Natchez bears the name of the Sun. Every morning, after the Sun appears, the great chief goes to the door of his hut, turns towards the east, and chants thrice, prostrating himself to the

[1] Nehemiah, x. 10.   [2] Ezekiel, viii. 11.
[3] Theog. 992; Anthon, Art. Jason.   [4] Movers, 232, 234,347, 372, 381.
[5] Joshua, xv. 34.
[6] J. Müller, 58, quotes Hazard, 418; Picard, 129; Benj. Constant de la Religion, i. 348; Arnold, 949, after Ross Reisen xvi. 503; Mayer, 1811, 94. ["The account rests on the testimony of an eye-witness."]
[7] J. Müller, 85. Fried. Schmidt, i. 346. See Schoolcraft, Algic Res. i. 203.
[8] J. Müller, 69, 70.
[9] Charlevoix, Nouvelle France, vi. 177 ff.
"Sun" was also a title in Egypt, Greece, Persia, Palestine, Mesopotamia, India, etc. The titles Ra (Coptic Erra), Bel, Melek, Sar, Adonai, Nasi, Suten,

earth.¹ The Peruvians offered to the Sun the blood and heart of animals ; the rest they burned in the sacred fire.² In Mexico, Yucatan, and Nicaragua, human victims were slaughtered, and the heart held up to the Sun by the officiating priest. They offered only the blood and the heart to the Sun.³

The Peruvians sacrificed coyes and zaco to Ataguju (whom they considered the creator of all things) at the period *when the maize is in flower.* He is the creative power in the sun.⁴

" And Moses took the blood, and put it upon the horns of the altar round about with his finger, and purified the altar, and poured the blood at the bottom of the altar, and sanctified it to make reconciliation upon it. And Moses sprinkled the blood upon the altar round about.

" And Moses took of the blood of it (the ram), and put it upon the tip of Aaron's right ear, and upon the thumb of his right hand, and upon the great toe of his right foot.

" And he brought Aaron's sons, and Moses put of the blood upon the tip of their right ear, and upon the thumbs of their right hands, and upon the great toes of their right feet, and Moses sprinkled the blood upon the altar round about." ⁵

" Moreover ye shall eat no manner of blood, whether of fowl or of beast.

" Whatsoever soul eateth any manner of blood, even that soul shall be cut off from his people." ⁶

Saran, Nebo, and others, mean " prince," " lord," " god," " sun," " ruler," etc. It was etiquette to call the king " god " or " sun."

It is not unlikely that Nissi in the inscription Jehova-Nissi (Exod. xvii. 15), written without vowel-points, יהוה נסי, Ihoh N si, is merely a different pro-nunciation of Nasi, " prince," or a change of the word on purpose. See Ahohi (Ahoh), 2 Sam. xxiii. 9.

¹ Charlevoix, Nouvelle France, vi. 177, 178.

² Univers pitt. Perou, 372a.

³ Journal American Ethn. Soc., i. 126, 141. J. Müller, 476, 478. Squier's Nicaragua ; Stephens Yucatan.

⁴ Perou, 368, 369, 376.   ⁵ Leviticus, viii. 15, 19, 23, 24.   ⁶ Ibid. vii. 26, 27.

"It shall be a perpetual statute throughout all your dwellings that ye eat neither fat nor blood. All fat is the Lord's." [1]

"For the *life of the flesh is in the blood;* and I have given it to you upon the altar, to make an atonement for your souls: for it is the blood that maketh an atonement for the soul."

"*For it is the life of all flesh,* the blood of it is for the life thereof." [2]

"If ye walk in my statutes, and keep my commandments, and do them;"

"Then will I give you *rain* in due season, and the land shall yield her increase, and the trees of the field shall yield their fruit." [3]

All persons afflicted with leprosy were considered displeasing in the sight of the Sun-god by the Egyptians. Lysimachus says, "That in the reign of Bocchoris, king of Egypt, the Jewish people being infected with leprosy, scurvy and sundry other diseases, took shelter in the temples, where they begged for food; and that in consequence of the vast number of the persons who were seized with the complaint, there became a scarcity in Egypt. Upon this Bocchoris sent persons to inquire of the oracle of Ammon respecting the sterility; and the god directed him to cleanse the temples of all polluted and impious men, and cast them out into the desert, but to drown those that were afflicted with the leprosy and scurvy, inasmuch as their existence was displeasing to the Sun: then to purify the temples; upon which the land would recover its fertility." That these notions of the Egyptians were shared by the Hebrews is evident; for in the 21st and 22d chapters of Leviticus, it is said:

"For whatsoever man he be that hath a blemish, he shall not approach; a blind man, or a lame, or he that hath

---

[1] Leviticus iii. 16, 17.   [2] Ibid. xvii. 11, 14.

[3] Ibid. xxvi. 3, 4.

a flat nose, or any thing superstitious, or a man which is broken-footed or broken-handed."

" No man that hath a blemish of the seed of Aaron the priest, shall come nigh to offer the offerings of the Lord, made by fire."

" Or whosoever toucheth any thing that is unclean by the dead, &c."

" The soul which hath touched any such shall be unclean until even, and shall not eat of the holy things unless he wash his flesh with water."

" And *when the sun is down*, he shall be clean, and shall afterwards eat of the holy things, because it is his food."

" When the plague of leprosy is in a man, the priest shall shut him up *seven days :* if the plague spread not in the skin, the priest shall shut him up seven days more."

" He is a leprous man, he is unclean." [1]

A leprous *Persian* must neither enter the city, nor have communication with any of his countrymen ; this disease they always think occasioned by some offence committed against the Sun. When Æschines touched at Delos on his way to Rhodes, the inhabitants of that island were greatly incommoded by a species of leprosy, called the white leprosy. They imputed it to the anger of Apollo (the Sun), because, in contradiction to the custom of the place, they had interred there the body of a man of rank.[2]

Among the American aborigines the Moon was generally the wife of the Sun. Sun-worship and fire-worship are found every where, as well as traditions of an *ancient* worship of the Sun in the United States,[3] Peru, and other parts of this continent. Mounds were erected for sun-worship as "high places;" and the mound-builders seem in religion, culture, and social condition to have very much resembled the Floridian tribes. The "Suns" of the Natchez, and the priest-caciques of Florida would seem to have had their types in the rulers of the races that built the mounds, having

[1] Leviticus xiii.   [3] Beloe's Herodotus ; Clio, 187.   [2] Müller, 56.

like the Southern tribes, but one ruler, who dwelt upon the mound, as both priest and chief, and, at his decease, was interred within it.[1]

Compare the mounds of Assyria and ·Palestine, and the " great High-place" or mound of Gibeon.

"The people sacrificed in High-places, because there was no house built unto the name of the Lord (Iahoh) until those days."   .

"And the king went to Gibeon to sacrifice there; for that was the great High-place."[2]

"And as they (Saul and his servants) went up the hill to the city, they said, 'Is the Seer here?' And they answered: ' He is; for there is a sacrifice of the people to-day in the High-place.'

"And Samuel said, 'I am the Seer, go up before me unto the High-place. There shall meet thee three men, going up to God to Beth-El."[3]

"Samuel called unto the Lord, and the Lord sent voices (thunder) and rain that day; and all the people greatly feared the Lord and Samuel."[4]

Joshua was buried in mount Ephraim.[5]

" And the Lord spake unto Moses that self-same day, saying :

" Get thee up into this mountain Abarim, mount Nebo, which (*is*) the land of Moab, that (is) over against Jericho ;

" And *die in the mount* whither thou goest up, and be gathered unto thy people ; as Aaron thy brother died in mount Hor (Ahura, Horus), and was gathered unto his people."[6]

" Adoniaho sacrificed sheep, oxen and fatted cattle, at the stone Hazoheleth, which is by the fountain of Rogel.[7]

---

[1] Müller, 69.   See also Squier and Davis, Mounds of the Mississippi valley, passim.

[2] 1 Kings, iii. 2, 4.   [3] 1 Sam., ix. 11, 12, 19; x. 3.
[4] Ibid. xii. 18.   [5] Judg. ii. 9.
[6] Deut. xxxii. 49, 50.   [7] 1 Kings, i. 9.

"Even unto great Abel, whereon they set down the ark of Iahoh (the Lord.)[1]

"Then Joshua (Iahosha) built an altar unto Iahoh Elohi of Israel in Mount Aibal." (עיבל.)[2]

It is probable that the name of the God of Israel, at that time, was the name of the mountain; because, in Hosea ii. 16, the Hebrew God is represented as saying: "Thou shalt call me Aishi and no more *Baali.*" We find also Mount Baalah (compare Allah, Elah, Elohi, Elohim, Alahoh, Eloah, names of "God."[3]) The valley of Elah (Alah).[4] "And the children of Israel made Baal-Berith their god."[5]

The Camanches worship the Great Spirit, the Sun, the Earth, and the Moon as gods.[6] In Greece, the Pelasgi worshipped the Heaven and Earth, Sun, Moon, and Stars.[7] The Cherokees sometimes worshipped the Sun as male, and the Moon as female, sometimes *vice versâ.*[8] Mr. Squier says, "Bartram observes of the Creeks that they pay a kind of homage to the Sun, Moon, and Planets, as the mediators or ministers of the Great Spirit in dispensing his attributes. They seem to particularly revere the Sun as the *symbol* of the power and beneficence of the Great Spirit and as his minister. They also venerate the Fire." The Cherokees worshipped Fire, paid a kind of veneration to the Morning Star, and also to the Seven Stars.[9] The Virginians worshipped the Great Spirit as well as the Sun, Moon, and Stars.[10]

The Camanches believe that the Indian Paradise is beyond the Sun where the Great Spirit sits and rules.[11] The Mexicans[12] and Natchez[13] believed that the chief place of

---

[1] 1 Sam. vi. 18.　　[2] Joshua, viii. 30.　　[3] Ibid. xv. 11.

[4] 1 Sam. xvii. 2.　　[5] Judges, viii. 33.

[6] Schoolcraft, Ind. Tribes, ii. 129.　　[7] Rinck, i. 38.

[8] Serp. Symb., 68.　　[9] Ibid. 69.

[10] Hackluyt, iii. 276 in Squier's Serp. Symbol. 70.　　[11] Schoolcraft, ii, 129.

[12] Gomera in Purchas iii. 1137, quoted in Serp. Symb., 128.

[13] J. Müller, 67.

glory was near the Sun. Pindar says, "Their souls she (Persephone) sends in the ninth year to the Sun of heaven."[1]

The Mandans on the Missouri were not less devoted Sun-worshippers than the Cherokees. All their principal sacrifices were made to the Sun, or to the "Master of Life" (Omahank Namakshi), who was supposed to inhabit that luminary. They consider the thunder the Lord of Life, when he speaks in his anger.[2] The Minitarees adored the Sun, and regarded the Moon as the Sun of the night. The morning-star Venus they esteemed the child of the Moon. The Chippeways regarded the Sun as the symbol of Divine Intelligence, and its figure, as drawn in their system of picture-writing, denoted the Great Spirit.[3] The symbol of Osiris was an eye. The Sun is the eye of Jove.[4]

The ancient Mexicans had apparently reached the same stage of progress at which we first observe the more advanced nations of the ancient world,—the period ante-Homeric and Old Etruscan. They worshipped one God invisible, the Supreme Being, Creator and Lord of the universe, omnipresent, that knoweth all thoughts and giveth all gifts.[5] Tlavizcalpantecutli, the god of the dawn; Huitzilopoctli their Mars (once a sun-god according to Müller); Teoyomiqui, his goddess, who leads the souls of warriors to paradise; Tlaloc, the Rain-god, and Chalchiucueje, his goddess; the Fire-god Xiuhtenctli, "Master of the Year," the Lord of Vegetation, and his goddess, Xochitli, goddess of Earth and Corn; Mictlanteuctli and Mictlancihuatl, the god and goddess of the dead; Centeotl,[6] goddess of agriculture; Tazi, Mother Earth; Quetzalcoatl, Air-god and god of civilization (Culturgott), and two hundred and sixty, or

---

[1] Thren. fr. 4, ed. Bœckh, in K. O. Müller, Hist. Greek Lit. 230.
[2] Serp. Symbol, 70.   [3] Ibid. 71.
[4] Macrob. Sat. ed. Bipons, 314;. Martianus Capella, book ii. 54; Nonnus ed. Marcellus Notes, 170.
[5] Prescott's Mexico, i. 57 ff.
[6] "Mother of Men."

probably many more inferior deities.[1] Every month was consecrated to some protecting deity, as among the Persians, Babylonians, Egyptians, etc. The Mexicans and Etruscans agree in the computation of the solar year.[2] The Maya and Toltecan faith inclined to Sabaism, the Old Assyrian religion. Astral worship existed among the Toltecs and Tezcucans.[3] The Toltecs were great idolators, and worshipped the Sun and the Moon. The Pyramids of Teotihuacan, already *old* when the Aztecs arrived in Mexico, were consecrated to the Sun and Moon. The pyramid of Cholula was consecrated to the same worship.[4]

The Peruvians also worshipped the Sun and Moon. The Sun-god is Creator. Pachacamac, the Great Spirit of the Peruvians, produced the world out of nothing. " When King Atahualpa was told that our Lord Jesus Christ had created the world, the Inca responded that he did not believe any being but the Sun could create any thing; that he held him for God, and the Earth for mother—that, for the rest, Pachacamac (Sun-god) had drawn the great world from nothing.[5] In spite of the belief in Pachacamac, the Sun, as the sole visible Creator of material Nature, was the principal object of Peruvian worship.[6] The ancient Peruvians worshipped the Sun as the visible image of the god Pachacamac.[7] Manco Capac taught that the Sun was the greatest Spirit.[8] Among the North American Indians the Sun-god is generally the *Great* Spirit; or the Great Spirit resides in the sun.[9] The Delawares and the people of Persia considered the God of Heaven the chief god; the Sun-god is the second in rank. So the Greek Helios is second to Jupiter, and sometimes even to Hyperion. The Creeks worshipped the Sun as " Great Spirit." The Apalachis regarded the Sun as Creator and cause of life.

[1] J. Müller, 494, 503, 506 ; Serp. Symbol, 160, 162.
[2] Niebuhr, i. 85.   [3] Prescott, i. 194.
[4] Univers pitt Mexique, 200.   [5] Perou, 368.   [6] P. 369.
[7] P. 380.   [8] J. Müller, 321
[9] Ibid. passim, 116, 117 ; quotes Schoolcraft, Wigwam, 303.

The Sun gives life to all things, to all beings. Ani is the Sun,[1] Ani-ma is the life, the soul, A ni-mare means to animate. Our very language to-day recognizes the Sun as the source of animation or existence. Sel or Asel (the Sun) is the source of the spirit, "Seele." "Soul" comes from "Sol."

Among the nations of Mesopotamia, Syria, Palestine, and even India,[2] the word "As" meant "*life*," and the Sun was called "As." The softened pronunciation of this word was "Ah;" for the s continually softens to h from Greece to Calcutta, from the Caucasus to Egypt. Ah is Iah, Ao and Iao. God tells Moses that his name is "I am" (Ahiah), a reduplication of Ah, or Iah. The word As, Ah, or Iah means "life," existence. The Assyrians and Persians called their chief God Asura, Ahura (Hor), "As" and Assarac.[3] The Greek Ουραν-ος, God of Heaven, Saturn, is a compound of Ar, the Sun (Ares), Ur, Aur, Our (Uro, to burn), and On, Ani, the Sun. Almost the same word among the Hindus for Saturn is Varuna; compounded of the shining "Bar" of the Assyrians, or Var of the Sclavonians, Persians and Baktrians (the god Abar), and Ani or On, the Sun.

"The Lord of Life," "the Master of Breath," "the old man of the sun," "the Old one who never dies" (like El Saturnus, the Old Bel of the Babylonians), is either the Sun, as among the Mandans, Minitarrees, and Blackfeet, or, what is the same thing, the Lord of Life, has his seat in the sun.[4] According to Herodotus, the Massagetæ sacrificed horses to the Sun.[5] This custom prevailed among their neighbors, the Persians, and is found in ancient India. Osiris was the Sun, and, like Saturn and Varuna, judge of the dead also. Soranus (=As-Uran-us) was god of the

---

[1] Christian Examiner for July 1846, 83; Journal of the Royal Asiatic Soc., vol. xii. 427, 432.

[2] Journal of the Am. Oriental Society, vol. iii. 324.

[3] Rawlinson, Journal Royal Asiatic Soc., vol. xii. xiv.

[4] J. Müller, 117; Squier, Serp. Symbol, 71; quotes Hopkins, Housatonic Ind., 11.

[5] Kuhn's Zeitschrift für 1853, 183.

dead ; in very name, akin to Saturn (Sat, or Seth-Uranus). The Great Spirit, worshipped by the American tribes, is Creator, as sun-god and as god of heaven. So, among the Siberians, the chief god and creator is sun-god and god of heaven.[1] The *Great* Spirit is frequently considered separately as god of heaven, like Zeus and Jupiter.[2] The Mexican Tezcatlipoca is sun-god, and Jupiter also.[3] The Great Spirit thunders in the heavens.[4] The Germans called him Donar. The sun-god is the cause of rain, Jupiter Pluvius, Indra, Agni, Noah. He is the author of light and heat. In these three qualities, without mentioning any thing further, is enough to account for his pre-eminence above all other spirits or Nature-gods as *Great* Spirit *par excellence*, and creator.

" I extol the greatness of that showerer of rain, whom men celebrate as the slayer of Writra : the Agni Waiswanara slew the stealer of the waters, and sent them down upon earth, and clove the obstructing cloud.[5] "

" The seven pure rivers that flow from heaven, are directed Agni by thee.[6] "

The Sun, Sun-god, or God of Heaven, seems thus to be god of the waters, of fire, and light. So in Florida Aguar was worshipped as " the Creator of all things who dwells in heaven, whence the water and all good things come.[7] " The water was considered as an original, creative principle, and appears in innumerable myths of the Indians as the fruitful principle.[8] Thales considered water the first principle in the formation of the world. It is so regarded in the Babylonian, Phœnician, and Egyptian cosmogonies, and in the first chapter of the Old Testament. All was a damp moist mass, into which the Sun-god, the Great Spirit, El or Bel, introduced light, the creative principle and the principle of

---

[1] J. Müller, 114, 116.   [2] Ibid. 116, 117, 118.

[3] Ibid. 420 ; Torquemada quoted in Serp. Symb., 174.

[4] J. Müller, 133.   [5] Wilson, Rigveda, i. 158.

[6] Ibid. 192.   [7] J. Müller, 119.   [8] Ibid. 316.

order and harmony—the first cause of all animal and vegetable life.   The Peruvian Viracocha or Pachacamac, under the name of Con, is originally a Water-god, and cause of all things, just as Agni of the Hindus is god of the waters as well as Fire-god and Sun-god.[1] The Mexican Sun-god, Tezcatlipoca, is Sun and Fire-god.   At his feet are represented a serpent (the emblem of the Sun), and a heap of fire.[2]   In his temple there is a shrine for Huitzlipoctli and for Tlaloc who is god of the rain.   As, in this triad, there is an identity of nature between Tezcatlipoca and Huitzlipoctli, it is not improbable that the Fire, Sun and Water are, as in Peru, here ascribed to the chief god or Sun-god.[3]   Mr. Squier says that from the foot of Tezcatlipoca proceed the signs of fire and water.[4]

Sisuthrus, the Babylonian Noah, is the Sun in the sign of the Waterman in the Zodiac.[5]   The name is a composition of Asis in Edessa, the Sun (Asas and Azaz),[6] and the god Adar (of the Assyrians and Dorians), the Thor of the Germanic races, like Sisi-Mithres (Mithra), the Sun, Sosares (Ares, the Sol-Mars), and Sisera of the Old Testament. Ar means the Sun and the Fire, אור. The Deluge is called by Isaiah "the waters of Noah"[7] מֵי נֹחַ.

"Noah is the Aiōn of Nonnus."[8] *AION* is the Sun with four wings, referring to the four seasons,[9] the "First-born," (Ulom), the Πρωτόγονος of Sanchoniathon; he is Osiris and Adonis (two names of the Sun).   He is Iao and Iahve.[10] 'Noah was Neptune, the ancient Proteus of Orpheus, who bore the keys of the Ocean.   He is the ancient Nereus of Apollonius Rhodius, and the Osiris whom Plutarch calls

---

[1] J. Müller, 316.   [2] Codex Vat. Lord Kingsborongh, vol. vi. 172.

[3] J. Müller, 616 ; Squier, Serpent Symbol, 176.

[4] Ibid. ; Cod. Vat. p. 172.   [5] Movers, 165, 589, 634 ; see 384.

[6] Zeus, Sios, Ushas, Sais (Minerva); Movers, 644, 645, 69 ; Christian Examiner, 1856, July, 79, 95, 96.

[7] "Aquae Noachi : " liv. 9. Version of Sebastian Schmid.

[8] Williams, Primitive Hist., 273.

[9] Movers, i. 9, 283, 288, 391.   [10] See Movers, 9, 59, 544, ff.

Oceanus."[1] He is the water side of Ianus, the god Eanus[2] in Italy, the gods Anos and Oannes in Babylon, the sun-god as Fish or Man-fish, the rivers Oanis,[3] and Noas in Thrace.[4]

" *Αἰὼν Κρόνου παῖς*,"[5]

" Aion, son of Saturn."

Aion, of varied form, holding the key of generation. . . . .
O Father, born of thyself, director of the eternal years.[6]

"Annos is Belus" (Bel). In Italy "Annus, more anciently Anus," was god of the sun; Anna was the Moon.[7] Ion was the Sun in Greece. In Babylon, his name (Anos) is found mentioned with those of Aos (As) and Illinos (Elon) among the twelve cosmogonial Powers (Titans) which precede Creation.[8]

At the time of the new moon of the month Phamenoth, the Egyptians kept the festival of the "ingress of Osiris into the moon."[9] Osiris was supposed to enter the moon to fertilize the earth. The moon-bark is inscribed "Ship of the Creator on which the Good Deity rides."[10] The Sun's bark is called "Boat of the Sun, the Lord of the two regions who fares in his boat to weave seasons for the house of the world."[11] The sculptures of the temple of Apollinopolis represent the progress of the Sun, called Phre-Hor-Hat, Lord of Heaven, in his bark or bari through the hours.[12]

It was a most natural idea to the mind of a Hebrew or Egyptian writer of "sacred tales," that the sun-deity Noh should enter his ark. He did the same thing every time that his priests took his image in the bari (sacred boat) in solemn procession upon the Nile.[13] Ammon had his

[1] Williams, 273, 292. Plut. de Is. xxxiv. [2] Creuzer, Symb. iii. 595.
[3] Pindar, Olymp. Ode v. [4] Herod. iv. 9.
[5] Euripides, Heracl. 900; Rinck, i. 40. [6] Nonnus, vii. 22, 73.
[7] Movers, 94. Donaldson's Varron, 163. [8] Movers, 276.
[9] Plut. de Iside, xliii. [10] Seyffarth, Theolog. Schrift. 36. Kenrick, i. 303.
[11] Seyffarth, ibid. [12] Kenrick, i. 329.
[13] Kenrick, i. 177, 318, 385, 386; Movers, 355, 356. Wilkinson, second series, i. 254, 255, ii. 275, 296, 297.

bari.[1] The boat of Ptah-Sokari-Osiris was borne in solemn
procession.[2] The "ship of Osiris" is mentioned by Plutarch.[3] He calls the Argo "the image of the ship of Osiris
become a constellation." Osiris is both the Sun and the
Inundation; and therefore, in this respect, is the same as
Noh, the god of the annual overflow of the Nile.[4] Plutarch calls the Nile "Osiris," and the "outflowing of Osiris."[5] The sacred bark of the Sun was carried in procession by twelve priests.[6]

Jupiter is the sun-god, become chief of the gods. He is
not merely a Nature-god, but also ruler of all human destinies and interests. He is a war god besides.[7] His name
is derived from the old sun-name Op or Ap, and Adar or
Atar, Thor, the Thunderer, the name of the Assyrian Mars.
The wife of Op is the Earth Ops (Opis). The Scythian form
of Ap is Apap, doubled, as in Papaios. The Egyptian is
also the doubled form Epaph-us, the Bull-god. "O Sun...
called *Apis* on the Nile, Kronos in Arabia, Belus on the
Euphrates, Ammon in Lybia."[8] Iabe was the Samaritan
god, and Ab the name of a Jewish and Syrian-Babylonian month.[9] In Homer we have Apia γαια, "the land of
Ap." Iap-ygia was the name of Magna Græcia in Italy.
"The Scythian name for the goddess of the Earth is Apia,
and the root Ap, or Op, was of frequent occurrence both in
Greece and Italy."[10] In Media Appi meant "god."[11] Sa-
turnus-Ops was Saturn.[12] Epaphus was the Ox-god of
Memphis.[13] The Hebrew month Abib, Phoibus (Apollo),

[1] Kenrick, i. 385.
[2] Wilkinson, second series, i. 254; Champollion Egypte, 131.
[3] De Iside xxii.
[4] Kenrick, i. 339; Osburn, Monumental Hist. 240, 280.
[5] De Is. xxxii. xxxvi.   [6] Kenrick, i. 21.
[7] Gerhard, über die Gotth. der Etrusker, Berlin Akad.
[9] Nonnus, Dionys. xl. 392, 393.   [8] Brandis Hist. Gewinn, 40.
[10] Buttmann, Lexil. i. 68, note; Donaldson, Varr. 49.
[11] Norris, Journ. Royal Asiatic Soc. xv. 175.
[12] Donaldson, Varr. 36.   [13] Movers, 46. Herodot. ii. 38 chapter.

Abob-(as), a name of Adonis,[1] Baba (Bηba) a name of the god Amon in Egypt;[2] Boubou "fulgentis," shining,[3] Bebon (a name of Seth-Typhon) in Egypt,[4] Apophis, and Aphōph the Giant, and Apop (the Serpent-Devil), are also the doubled form of Ab (Ap).[5] Ap (Op) is Ap-is (the Sun's sacred Bull), who is the Egyptian Jupiter-Taurus, Iapet, Phut (Ptah), the Egyptian chief god, and Iapetos the Titan. Apis has his counterpart in the Persian Bull, Abudad, who takes the place of Saturn in the Greek Mythology.[6]

Jupiter is the Bull of Europa (the Earth) like the Persian Sun-Bull Abudad, "in whom Ormuzd has laid the seed of all life,"[7] or the Persian "Ox-Man" Kaiomors, the "First Man," the Great Spirit.[8] The Manobozho of the Chippewas was at the same time the Creator and Ancestor of men after the flood. The same is said of Messou of the Canadians.[9] The "First Man," according to Hennepin, was stated, in an Indian myth, to have raised himself into heaven, "*and thunders there.*" In Germany, Mannus (the Sun, Amanus), in Hindustan, Manu, are the "First Man."[11]

[1] Movers, 199.   [2] Seyffarth Grammar, App. 7.   [3] Ibid. 88.
[4] Plut. de Is. lxii.
[5] Andr. Müller in Movers, 199, 202; Kenrick, Egypt, i. 353.
Apis (Hapi)=a symbol of the Nile and of the Moon.—Lepsius.
Osiris entering the Moon fertilizes the world.—Kenrick, i. 347.
The Scythians make Pap-aeus and Apia (husband and wife) to be Jupiter and the Earth.—Herod. Melpomene, lix.
The Abii were a Scythian nation. The Ep-ians are mentioned by Homer. —Il. ii. 619.
Ab-ia was a city on the Messenian gulf. Epeius was the son of Endymion (the Sun). Babel is called Bapilu (Journ. R. A. Soc. vol. xv. 104), as Abelios becomes Apellōn.—Müller, Dorians, ii. 6, § 6.
Ab-ib-al was a Phœnician king, Aphobis, an Egyptian king; Hobab, Iobab and Bebai, Hebrew proper names.
[6] Rinck, i. 72. The name Ab-udad is compounded of Ab and Adad (the Syrian Hadad), two names of the sun-god.
[7] Ibid.
[8] Kleuker, Zendav. 112; see J. Müller, 133. 135.
[9] Ibid. 133.
[10] J. Müller, 133, quotes Hennepin, ii. 91.
[11] Kuhn, Zeitschrift, iv. 102, 91.

" As thou, O Indra, with Manu the Vivasvat (the Sun) drinkest the Soma, as thou with Trita enjoyest the song, so thou delightest thyself also with Aju.[1]

Compare with Manu, the Hindu lawgiver, Minos, the Cretan lawgiver, and his Bull (Minotaur),=the Bull of Manu, whose lowing annihilated the Asura.[2] "Astronomically, Mithra is the *producing Sun* borne by the Equinoctial-Bull, the Seed-preserver. The Sun enters into the Sign of the Bull."[3] Kaiomorts, "the Man-steer," was of both sexes—originally Bull, then Ox-man, later "First and Ideal Man."[4] Kaiomorts issues from the right side of the Bull.[5] The bull was in India the symbol of the sun's generative force.[6]

The Crows, Mandans, and Minitarrees call the "First Man" "Numank Machana," the only one saved from the great flood; the Lord of Life gave him great power, and therefore they bring offerings to him.[7] Sometimes the Lord of Life, sometimes the "First Man" is invoked, as having power over the spirits. The "First Man" is thought by the Dogribs Indians to have created men, the sun and the moon.[8] The Caribs believed that Loguo, the "First Man," created the earth, and then returned to heaven. In Tahiti, the "First Man" had the same name (Tii or Tiki) as the souls of the dead who had been raised to the rank of gods.[9] The Chinese have Puan-ku, their "First Man," as the Persians their Kaiomorts or Meschia.[10] Adam Kadmon, the "First Man," was considered by the philosophers of the Jewish Cabbala to unite in himself the powers emanating from God.[11] The Phœnician god K-*adm*-iel was Hermes-Kadmus the minister Mercury (der dienende Mercur) and aid of the Creator in the Phœnician myth.[12] The later Jews

[1] Roth, Djemshid-Sage; Rigv.
[2] Vedic Legend in Weber's Ind. Stud. i. 195.
[3] Creuzer, Symbolik, i. 249.   [4] J. Müller, 136.
[5] Rinck, i. 72; Kleuker, Anh. zum Zendav. i. 275.
[6] Movers, 374; Duncker, ii. 21; Benfey Samaveda, p. 268.
[7] J. Müller, 133.   [8] Ibid.   [9] Ibid. 134, 135, 136.   [10] Ibid. 135.
[11] J. Müller, 135; Munk, Palestine, 523.   [12] Movers, 21, 142, 513.

considered the wisdom of the "First Man," Adam, greater than that of the angels.[1]

In ancient philosophy, the Bull was an emblem of the creative or fertilizing Sun. The union of Heaven and Earth in the fertilizing rains which alternate with the rays of the sun in penetrating the soil and imbuing it with productive power, was treated of as a holy marriage of Saturn with Mother Earth. Anthropomorphism early proceeded, in America and on the other continents, to invest the gods with human forms. The gods of the Indians, Mexicans, Peruvians, Greeks, Assyrians, Hindus and Egyptians, are represented in the human shape. Saturn, Jupiter and Tezcatlipoca are human forms; Saturn is an old man bent with age. When the doctrine was promulgated by the ancients that the gods were originally men whose virtues had raised them to the skies, old Bel-Saturn, the oldest and chief god, the Great Spirit of all antiquity, would naturally be the "First Man," Adam. Adam is the sun-god Saturn, "Zeus-Demarus,"[2] whose wife was the Earth, just as Jupiter united with Europa, Ouranos (Heaven) with Ge (Earth). As the Great Spirit of the skies appears as "First Man," so Adam, by the doctrine of Euhemerus, was like Saturn, but a mortal raised to the rank of god. As first god he is euhemerized into "First Man." In this way antiquity disposes of its sun-gods. The Hebrews turned them into Patriarchs. Adam, Abraham, Israel, were names of Saturn.[3] Edom is Adam; and the ancient usage was to name the nation, the land or city after the chief god. The Greeks made these deities founders of tribes. Annos and Belus are mentioned by the emperor Julian together as the oldest sages of the Babylonians.[4]

The serpent was the Sun's symbol.[5] Great honors were said to have been paid by the Natchez to the wooden figure

---

[1] J. Müller, 135.   [2] Sanchoniathan, vii.   [3] Movers, 86, 130.
[4] Ibid. 92.   [5] Squier, Serpent Symbol passim. J. Müller, 62.

of a rattle-snake.[1] The Maya god Votan was a serpent-deity, as were the Mexican Quetzalcoatl, the Athenian Apollo, and the Bel-serpent of the Babylonians.[2] Torquemada states that the images of Huitzlipoctli, Quetzalcoatl and Tlaloc were each represented with a golden serpent, bearing different symbolical allusions.[3] At the festival of Huitzlipoctli, a great serpent was borne in procession.[4] He is in some points hardly to be distinguished from Tezcatlipoca, and their festivals were similar.[5] For him the hearts of prisoners, taken in war, were reserved. This identifies him with the Sun, to whom the heart was held up at the sacrifice.[6] Huitzlipoctli, like the Roman Mars, and the Phœnician Adonis, was probably the spring-sun.[7] In Mexico, Tezcatlipoca was the Great Serpent.[8] At his feet a serpent was represented in the paintings,[9] and at his festival a wooden collar in the form of a coiled serpent was placed around the neck of the victim.[10] The wood which held fast the head of the blood-offering sacrificed to Huitzlipoctli, had the form of a coiled serpent.[11]

The wife of Tezcatlipoca (Saturnus-Jupiter) was Cihuacohuatl, "the Woman-serpent," like Minerva at Athens.[12] Athena (Minerva) is goddess of wisdom, because she is serpent-goddess and the Sun is "all-knowing." She is the feminine part of Bel (Bolaten), who, as "Man-woman," se-

---

[1] Charlevoix, Nouvelle France, vi. 175.
[2] J. Müller, 487 ; Movers passim.
[3] Book ii. ch. 8. ; quoted in Serp. Symb. 193.
[4] Mexique, 25, par Larenaudiére ; Serp. Symb. 56.
[5] J. Müller, 605, 478, 505, 610, 614, 616, 620, 623, 624, et passim.
[6] Prescott, Mexico, i. 76.
[7] J. Müller, 588, 592, 597, 602, 604, 607, 609, 610, 615, 660 ; Movers, 21, 28, 30, et passim.
[8] Serp. Symbol. 181, 199, 161, 163, 164.
[9] Cod. Vat. Lord Kingsborough, vi. 172, 178.
[10] Mexique, 29.
[11] J. Müller, 485.
[12] J. Müller, 484, 494, 612 ; Bulwer, Athens, iii. ch. 7, p. 94.

parates into Bol and Atena, Apollo and Athena.[1] In Nicaragua a representation of a coiled serpent was called the Sun (Sol).[2] Saturn was the "dragon of life."[3] This is the Great Spirit, as cause of life. Hercules (Chronos) was represented as a serpent with the face of a god, but the head of a lion and an ox.[4] Jupiter in the form of a dragon begets Dionysus Zagreus.[5] The Great Spirit was worshipped by the American Indians in the form of a serpent.[6]

The Egyptians and Phœnicians had their serpent-deities. The Gnostics taught that the ruler of the world was a great serpent.[7] Apollo (Abal, Epul) was called Python. The Phœnicians represented the god Noum by a serpent.[8] The serpent was the emblem of the Sun and its fruitful influence. It was the symbol of life, immortality, "the spiritual," and wisdom. In the Mysteries, it was the emblem of Jupiter.[9] Apis-Osiris is generally represented with the globe of the Sun, and the asp.[10] Ptah is represented with the asp, and Horus the same; because they were sun-gods.[11] The symbol of Kneph (Chon-uphis) was a hawk-headed serpent.[12] Ammon was called "the renowned Serpent."[13] The Orphic god Phanes (Sun) has a serpent on his head.[14]

The decrees of Destiny (for the world) which the divining hand of the First-born Phanes has written.[15]

The following names of the Sun and his serpent-emblem appear to be the same:—Ak the Sun (Ag, Ukko in Scan-

---

[1] Demarez (Jupiter Demarous) separates into Adam and Araz (Aras), the Sun and the Earth, Araz, Eraz, "the Earth" ארץ, Eraze, in Homer, in Chaldee, Aroah, in Samaritan Arah.

[2] Squier's Nicaragua, i. 406.   [3] Rinck, i. 67.

[4] Ibid. 65; Movers, 446.

[5] K. O. Müller, Hist. Greek. Lit. 237.

[6] J Müller, 123, 366; see Stephens' Yucatan, passim.

[7] Deane, 107; quotes Epiphanius, 91.   [8] Kenrick, i. 314.

[9] J. Müller, 611.   [10] Wilkinson, Second Series, ii. 350.

[11] Ibid. i. 256; Champollion, Egypte; Univers pitt. 131a.

[12] Beloe's Herod. i. 369, note; Movers, 506.   [13] Kenrick, i. 315.

[14] Rinck, i. 96.   [15] Nonnus, Dionys. xii. 34.

dinavia, Gau-as a name of Adonis,[1] Agu-ieus a name of
Apollo, Iauk in Arabia), Echis, " serpent;"[2] Ako, " vi-
per," in Egyptian;[4] " Og, the serpent-god;"[4] Ap the Sun
(Op), Ab the Sun, Af the Sun, in Persian;[5] Ophis (ὄφις),
"serpent," in Greek; Hob, Hp and Hof, " serpent," in
Egyptian;[6] Ob, "serpent;"[7] Achad the Sun, Echidna,
"serpent;" Cal-us, Col, Acal (a name of Talus, the Sun, in
Crete); Achel (Αχελι, Χελι, Mod. Greek), " serpent;"[8] Aban
Phanes, Pan (sun-gods, originally), Obion = " Serpent;"
Ophion=" Serpent;" Iah (Ah), the Sun; Iao (As, Asu,
Ahû), Iahi and Ahi, serpent-demons in Persia; Dag
(Tag, Dagon, Dakan, Dagur, god of day), the Sun; Dahak,
the Serpent, or cloud-demon, in Persia; Pharo (Φαρο=
Mithra), the Sun; Varuna, Var; Varitra (compare Vere-
tra-Agna), the cloud-demon; Puthon, Apollo, Pytho the
Sun-serpent, pethĕn a snake (Hebrew); Abāb (Abobas,
the Sun, Adonis), Apop, the serpent, the devil;[10] Sat, Set,
the Sun (Seth, Asad), Set, a serpent (Egyptian); Adad,[11]
the Sun, " Adodus,"[12] Dood (in Arabic), a snake;[13] Asam,
Shem the Sun, Semo, Smu (Typhon), "Zom (Hercules) the
powerful,"[14] Asamın (in Arabic), a serpent, adder;[15] Ani
the Sun, Ayn " serpent,"[16] the Zyrianian Yen;[17] Akar, Kur
"the Sun," Akore " a viper," in Egyptian;[18] Af, the Sun,
afₑa, afäₑi, " serpent;"[19] Ilahat=sun, Ilahat " a serpent;[20]
Adar (Adar-Melech), Ajdar dragon;[21] Nahash king of the
Amorites,[22] " Nahash, " a serpent " in Hebrew; Sarp-edon,

[1] Movers, 199.　　　　　[2] Kuhn Zeitschrift, for 1833, p. 46.
[3] Seyffarth Grammar, App.　　[4] Deane, Serpent-Worship, 93.
[6] F. Johnson, Persian and Arabic Dict.　[6] Seyffarth Grammar, 3.
[7] Deane, 80, 84, 128.　　　　[8] Kuhn iii. 46.
[9] Deane, 165.　　　　　　　[10] Kenrick, i. 353.
[11] Seyffarth Gram. 73 ; Uhlemann, Ægypt. Alterthumskunde, 172.
[12] Sanchon. ed. Orelli, 34.
[13] F. Johnson, Persian, Arabic and English Dict.
[14] Uhlemann, Thoth. 35.　　　[15] F. Johnson, Dict.　　　[16] Ibid.
[17] Journal of the Royal Asiatic Soc. xv. 127, 94.
[18] Seyffarth, Grammar, App.　　[19] F. Johnson, Dict.　　　[20] Ibid.
[21] Ibid.　　　[22] Kings bore sun-names.

a god of the Lycians and Cretans;[1] Seraf, an Assyrian god or angel (Seraphim) ; Serap-is, a sun-god of the Egyptians ;[2] Sarpa, "a serpent" in Sanskrit and in Welsh,[3] "In Serpente Deus;"[4] Apollo Sarpedonius in Cilicia.[5]

Some of the New-England tribes believed the Sun to be God, or at least the body or residence of the Deity.[6] "Among the North American tribes, the graphic Ke-Ke-win, which depicts the Sun, stands on their pictorial rolls as the symbol of the Great Spirit."[7] The Great Spirit is Creator, as sun-god. Nature and its laws are regarded as one great whole, which, every year, assumes new life through the power of the sun, and all the life-giving influences of Nature, and is preserved and continued by the same agencies by which it was created. Therefore the sun-god was regarded as the Creator by the Muyscas, and so many other nations of America and the other continents of the globe.[8]

The Great Spirit is a Nature-god, identical with Nature, and subjected to it. He is a personification of the highest powers of Nature ; not a being "supreme above Nature." Therefore he is controlled by inevitable fate or destiny. The decrees of destiny cannot be changed. Müller says that this destiny is personified under "the name of the old one (Woman) who never dies," whose son is the Sun, in whom the Lord of Life dwells. This is the conception of the Mandans, Minitarrees, and Hurons, who regarded Destiny as a hostile old woman, a kind of Proserpine or Persephone, a queen of the dead.[9] In Homer we find Destiny playing the greatest part in the control of human affairs.

[1] Movers, 16.
[2] Williams, 276.   [3] Ibid. 27.
[4] Ovid. Met. xv. 670. Movers, 533.   [5] Movers, 16.
[6] Hopkins, Hist. Housatonic Indians, p. 11 ; in Squier, Serp. Symbol, p. 71.
[7] Schoolcraft's Address before the N. Y. Hist. Soc. 1846, p. 29, quoted in Serp. Symbol, 130.
[8] J. Müller, 116, 117.
[9] J. Müller, 148, 149, 150.

3*

The Great Spirit is the "Giver and Taker of breath." He is the Lord of Life, the Master of Breath, the all-pervading spirit, the old one (Man) who never dies.[1] The Great Spirit is death-god as well as Lord of Life. The Great Spirit rules in Paradise, as the Comanches believe.[2] The Great Spirit receives the dead in the happy hunting-grounds, the beautiful prairies of the other world, ideas which correspond to the Grecian conception of the Elysian fields, or the Isles of Cronos, the "Islands of the Blessed" in the Western ocean. Or the Great Spirit dwells on an island of the sea above, and wanders about in the light of the moon. To him resort the warriors who have fallen in fight, and enjoy the pleasures of hunting.[3] The Great Spirit of the Indians is as great a friend of warriors as the Scandinavian Odin or Huitzlipoctli, the Mexican war-god. Tezcatlipoca is called "God of Battles." Lord Kingsborough translates one of his appellatives " the Chastiser of Evil," and another "He who requires an account of our thoughts." [4]

Mantus was the death-god, Pluto, in Italy.[5] Amenthe was the name of hell in Egypt. The Egyptian god Mentu (Mandoo, Month[6]) is, in name, the same as the Italian Mantus, and therefore, probably, the night-sun. Compare the god Rhad-*amanth*-us, the Judge of the dead. Huram is a deity-name (Ophion).[7] The name of the death-god Hermes (Hermaos, 'Ερμαων) in Greece, and Hermode (compare the name Har-m-odi-us), the Scandinavian Mercury, are compounds of the names of the Sun, Har (Ar), Am and Ad (Adi, Deus). Hermode is also a compound of Har and Amad[8] (Muth) who is Pluto and Dionysus. Mercury is a form of Zeus (Jupiter) and Pluto. He is the Arcadian

[1] J. Müller, 117, Serp. Symb. 115. 152.

[2] Schoolcraft, Indian Tribes, Part. ii. 129.   [3] J. Müller, 139.

[4] Serp. Symbol, 176, 177.   [5] Creuzer, iii. 624.

[6] Kenrick, i. 331.   [7] Movers, 506, 668; ii. Chron. ii. 2, 12; iv. 16.

[8] Amad, a city of the tribe of Asher, Josh. xix.26; and the sun-city Hamat, or Hamath is Emath. Seldeni opera, iii. 387.

sun-god who steals the herd of Apollo.[1] He is rain and fire-god, and, like Vulcan, husband of Aphrodite and the Earth.[2]

Bring wealth, thunderers, and give it to us; protect us, Indra and Agni, by your deeds; may those *rays of the Sun*, by which our forefathers have attained together a heavenly region, shine also upon us.[3]

The natives of Honduras worshipped the rising Sun, and had two idols, one in the shape of a man, the other in the shape of a woman, which were called the Great Father and Great Mother.[4] The Sclavonians adored Bog, the rising Sun, the Old Persians Baga, the Romans Bacchus, the Hindus Bhaga, the Aditya or sun-deity.[5] Bog-es was a governor of the city Aïon;[6] Bal-Pegor was a Babylonian god,[7] Bag and Bagir Arab deities.[8] Bak meant "sunbeam" in Egyptian, and Bok "prince."[9] The Phœnicians and Syrians worshipped Adad[10] or Hadad, the Sun, (Adodus, Taut, Tot, Thoth, "the all-knowing," the Divine Wisdom). They also adored Azael,[11] who is Asal and Sol. The priests of Jupiter were called Selli and Helloi, the priests of Hercules and Mars "Salii," "Janes" or "Eani," from Ani (An) the sun-god.[12] "I swear by the Sun, the great God of the Massagetæ."[13] "By that Jove that dwells amid the constellations."[14] In Mexico the form of an oath was "I swear by the life of the Sun."[15]

The Homeric hymn represents the Sun as seeing and

---

[1] Movers, 159, 655; Beloe's Herodot. vol. i. 337, 338, 341, 342.

[2] Gerhard, Griech. Mythol. p. 260, 265, 266, 273; Preller, 240—245; Creuzer, Symb. iii. 417, 420, 504, 634; iv. 124, 310.

[3] Wilson, Rigv. i. 282, 283.

[4] Squier, Serp. Symb. 56, quotes Herrara, Hist. Am. iv. 155, 138.

[5] Weber, Ind. Stud. ii. 306, et passim; Wilson, Rigv. passim.

[6] Herodot. vii. 107.   [7] Munter, Bab. 19.

[8] Osiander, Zeitschr. der D. M. G. vii. 499; Universal Hist. vol. xviii. p. 387.

[9] Seyffarth, Grammar, 30, 13.   [10] Munter, 20.

[11] Movers, 368.   [12] Creuzer, Symb. iii. 595, 692; Movers, 188.

[13] Herodot. Cleio, ccxii.   [14] Euripides, Phœnissæ, 1005.

[15] Serp. Symb. 55.

knowing all things that happen, and giving information to the other gods.[1] Ani under the name of Oannes is represented in Babylon with the appendage of a fish's tail, like Odakon, the Man-fish of the Chaldean legends. Oannes appeared as the civilizer of the primitive people, instructing them in the arts. In Etruria, Tages (Tag, the Sun, the day), in Peru, Manco Capac, an ancient sun-god anthropomorphized, were the authors of the national civilization. In Mexico it was Quetzalcoatl, the serpent-deity.

His coursers bear on high the divine all-knowing Sun, that he may be seen by all.

(At the approach) of the all-illuminating Sun, the constellations depart with the night like thieves.

His illuminating rays behold men in succession like blazing fires.

Thou, Surya, outstrippest all in speed; thou art visible to all; thou art the source of light; thou shinest throughout the entire firmament.

Thou risest in the presence of the Maruts, thou risest in the presence of mankind, and so as to be seen in the presence of the whole of heaven.

With that light with which thou, the purifier and defender from evil, lookest upon this creature-bearing world,

Thou traversest the vast ethereal space, measuring days and nights, and contemplating all that have birth.

Divine and light-diffusing Surya, thy seven coursers bear thee, bright-haired, in thy car.

The Sun has yoked the seven mares that safely draw his chariot, and comes with them self-harnessed.

Beholding the up-springing light above the darkness, we approach the divine Sun among the gods, the *excellent Light.*

Radiant with benevolent light, rising to-day, and mounting into the highest heaven, do thou, O Sun, remove the sickness of my heart, and the yellowness of my body.

Let us transfer the yellowness to the parrots, to the starlings, or to the Haritala.

This Aditya (sun-god) has risen with all might, destroying my adversary, for I am unable to resist my enemy.[2]

Among the sun-deities mentioned in the Hindu Vedas are Savitar, the Creator-sun with golden hands (rays), Mithra, the day-Sun, Varuna (the Saturn of the Vedic period), Bhaga, the Sclavonic and Old Persian sun-god, Ar-

---

[1] Hymn to Ceres.　　　　[2] Wilson, Rigv. i. 134, 135.

iaman, Pushan (Apason), Agni who is Sun, fire-god, the lightning, &c., Surya (Asur). Vishnu is also mentioned. Manu, the ancestor of men, the Hinduh Noah, is the sun-god as "First Man," the German hero and ancestor Mannus, the Cretan king Minos, the Egyptian god Amon, the Babylonian god Haman, the god Amanus, Manes, Omancs or Omanus of Pontus, Cappadocia and Persia.[1] Amon was a Hebrew king, Manes a king of Egypt. The Al-*emanni* and Marc-*omanni* in Germany have the name Aman or Omanus compounded with El and Makar (Baal), or Mirrich (Moloch, Mercury). The Semitic and Indo-Germanic deity-names are *ancient* in Italy and Germany, Greece, Asia Minor, &c. Bharata is an Aditya, a name of the Sun.[2]

Another Indo-Germanic and Semitic sun-god is Nar, a name of Adonis in Cyprus,[3] Ner=the light;[4] the god Anar, the "forming Principle" in the Scandinavian religion, Nereus, the old (sun and) water-god; the German Onar, the Egyptian god "Onur-is" (in name), Nero, "the shining,"[5] Nerio, the Sabine Mars, and Neriene, his wife;[6] the Hindu deity Narayana (Vishnu, the Sun), "the water-movement" (the movement of the waters from the sun, their source); Aner-ges, the Babylonian sun-god,[7] the god Nirrig, the god Noragal,[8] or Nergal, who is Merodach (Baal, the Sun). Compare the Babylonian proper name Nerigl-issar, the Hebrew name Igal, and Gallos, the Sun. Nergal was the Chaldee fire-god Mars.[9]

Akal was the Sun, "Gallus." Gallos was a name of the god Attes or Atys, who was an incarnation of the Sun,

---

[1] Movers, 348; Duncker, ii. 487, et passim; Kuhn's Zeitschr. iv. 121, 94, 95.

[2] Wilson, Rigv. ii. 73, note. The god Berith, Baal-Berith? Judges ix. 46.

[3] Movers, Phönizier, 217.   [4] Munter, Babylonier, 25.

[5] Rawlinson, Journal of the Royal Asiat. Soc., xii. 486, ff.

[6] Creuzer, iii. 543; Gerhard, ii. 281.

[7] Munter, Bab. 24.

[8] Seldeni Opera, iii. 382.   [9] Movers, 384.

and is first of the Galli (Selli). The worship of the god
Agal is also mentioned, and *Agl*-ibal.[1]

Agni, the Hindu Fire-god, is the Latin Ignis (Fire). He
is the god Chon of the Egyptian and Palestine races, called
Kan (Achan), Chion, Chaon, Iachin, Kin, Cain, Agni
(Agoni). His name is found compounded with Apollo (Apel)
Epul, in the names of the Pelignians in Italy, the Pela-
gonians in Greece. The New Fire for the hearths was taken
from Apollo's altar at the "renewal of the fire" at Lemnos.[2]
The word Akan (Akani=Ak+Ani) becomes Agoni, Agni,
Igni northwest and east of Babylon; but, dropping the "A,"
Chon, "Baal-Chon," Vulcan, Kan, Chion, Chiun, etc., in
Palestine, Egypt, or Arabia. His feminine is the Earth-
goddess Aigina, the island. Aigaion was the hundred-
armed centaur; Chuns-Aah was the Egyptian Hercules.[3]
Agenor (Agen-or), the ancestor of the Phœnicians, was
father of Phœnix, Cadmus and Europa (deities).[4] Agni or
Kan is the god Ogēn ('Ωγῆν-ος),[5] a name of Okeanus (Ωκε-
ανός), the Sun, as god of the World-Ocean (Akan, Okean).[6]

The path of the revolving (Sun) has been lighted up by rays: the eyes of
men (have been lighted) by the rays of Bhaga: the brilliant mansion of Mitra,
of Aryaman, of Varuna (has been lighted up by his rays).

Mitra is the animator of mankind, and so is Varuna; Aryaman is the
animator of mankind.

I proclaim veneration to the mighty Sun, to Heaven and Earth, to Mitra,
to the benevolent Varuna, to the conferrer of happiness, the showerer of
benefits. Praise Indra, Agni, the brilliant Aryaman, and Bhaga, so that,
enjoying long life, we may be blessed with progeny.

Mitra and Varuna bestow abundantly that unenduring water which you
obtain from the Sun through your own energy;

[1] Ibid. 379, 687, 99, 401: Anthon. Dict. "Atys." Muys, Griechenland
und der Orient, 30. Aglaos ἀγλ-αος means "brilliant."

[2] J. Müller, 520.

Apollo is Mars. Movers, 188.—Adonis was Mars in Bithynia. Movers, 21.
—Mars is Baal fervoris and Hercules (Ibid. 188,) "the wild, destroying fire."

[3] Bunsen, Egypt's Place, i. 504, 507.

[4] Movers, Phön. Alt. i. 129. Ibid. Phönizier, 20, 45.

[5] Anthon's Classical Dictionary.

[6] Wilson, Rigv. i. 178, 250; Weber, Akad. Vorl. 31.

May he who is one with light, who has fleet horses, the invoker (of the gods), full of joy and borne in a golden chariot, listen to us: may that irresistible yet placable Agni conduct us by the most efficacious (means) to that desirable and accessible (heaven). Both his associated mothers blackened (by combustion) are in movement, and give birth to an infant whose tongue in the east dissipates darkness.

The drops of rain enveloped (by the solar rays) are renewed in the dwelling of the divine (Sun) their birth-place.

His radiance is undecaying: the rays of him who is of pleasing aspect, are everywhere visible and bright: the intensely shining, all-pervading, unceasing, undecaying (rays) of Agni desist not.

Glorify the three-headed, seven-rayed Agni.

How have thy shining and evaporating (rays), Agni, supported life and supplied food; so that, enjoying both, the devout, possessing sons and grandsons, may repeat the hymns of the sacrifice.

The tresses of Agni minister, Mitra and Varuna, to your sacrifice, when you honor the sacrificial chamber: send down of your own accord (the rain) and prosper our offerings, for you have command over the praises of the pious men.

You bring the cattle to their acceptable pasture upon earth, whence the milk-yielding cows, protected by your power, return unharmed to their stalls; they cry to the Sun above, both at evening and at dawn, as one (cries) who beholds a thief.

The vigorous Bull (the Heaven) daily milks the pellucid milk (of the sky).

We behold the lover of maiden (Dawns) ever in movement, never resting for an instant, wearing inseparable and diffusive (radiance) the beloved abode of Mitra and Varuna.

Without steeds, without stay, borne swift-moving and loud-sounding, he travels, ascending higher and higher, connecting the inconceivable mystery with the radiance in Mitra and Varuna (which men) eulogizing glorify.

Agni is awakened upon earth; the Sun rises; the spreading Dawn exhilarating (all) by her radiance, has dispersed (the darkness); harness Aswins your chariot, to come, that the divine Savitri may animate all beings to their several (duties).

Earnestly I glorify the exploits of Vishnu, who made the three worlds; who sustained the lofty site (of the spheres), thrice traversing (the whole); who is praised by the exalted.

May I attain his favorite path, in which God-seeking men delight; (the path) of that wide-stepping Vishnu, in whose exalted station there is a perpetual flow of felicity.

Man, glorifying, tracks two steps of that heaven-beholding (deity); but he apprehends not the third; nor can the soaring-winged birds (pursue it).

We pray that you may both go to those regions where the many-pointed and wide-spreading (rays expand); for here the supreme station of the many-hymned, the showerer, shines great.

Waters are the most excellent, said one: Agni is the most excellent, said another; the third declared to many the Earth (to be the most excellent), and thus speaking true things the Ribhus divided the ladle.

Ribhus, reposing in the solar orb, you inquire, "Who awakens us, unapprehensible (Sun) to the office (of sending rain)?" The Sun replies, "The awakener is the Wind; and, the year (being ended), you again to-day light up (this world)."

Sons of strength, the Maruts, desirous of your coming, advance from the sky: Agni comes from the earth, the Wind traverses the firmament; and Varuna comes with undulating waters.

, Let neither Mitra nor Varuna, Aryaman, Ayu, Indra, Ribukshin, nor the Maruts censure us; when we proclaim in the sacrifice the virtues of the swift horse sprung from the gods.[1]

When first thou neighest at thy rising mounting out of the Sea of Air or from the waters, with the wings of the falcon, with the limbs of the deer, then great glory arose for thee, O Horse.

Yama gave him (created him), Trita harnessed him, Indra first mounted him, Gandharba seized his reins: Vasus, out of the sun you have made a horse.

Thou, Horse, art Yama: thou art Aditya, thou art Trita with the mysterious sway: Thou art fraternized with Soma; threefold affinity, they say, hast thou in heaven.[2]

They have said that three are thy bindings in heaven; three upon earth; and three in the firmament. Thou declarest to me, Horse, who art Varuna, that which they have called thy most excellent birth.

I recognize in my mind thy form afar off, going from the earth below, by way of heaven, to the Sun. I behold thy head soaring aloft, and mounting quickly by unobstructed paths, unsullied by dust.

I behold thy most excellent form coming eagerly to thy food in thy (holy) place of earth: when thy attendant brings thee nigh to the enjoyment (of the provender), therefore greedy, thou devourest the fodder.

The car follows thee, O Horse: men attend thee: cattle follow thee; the loveliness of maidens waits upon thee; troops of demigods following thee have sought thy friendship; the gods themselves have been admirers of thy vigor.

His mane is of gold; his feet are of iron; and fleet as thought, Indra is his inferior. The gods have come to partake of his (being offered as) oblations: the first who mounted the horse was Indra.

The full-haunched, slender-waisted, high-spirited, and celestial coursers (of the Sun) gallop along like swans in rows, when the horses spread along the heavenly path.

Thy body, Horse, is made for motion: thy mind is rapid as the wind: 'the hairs (of thy mane) are tossed in manifold directions; and spread beautiful in the forests.

---

[1] Wilson Rigv. ii. 52–112.   [2] Zeitschr. der. D. M. G. ii. 223.

The swift horse approaches the place of immolation, meditating with mind intent upon the gods: the goat bound to him is led before him; after him follow the priests and the singers.

The horse proceeds to that assembly which is most excellent: to the presence of his father and his mother (Heaven and Earth). Go (Horse), to-day, rejoicing to the gods, that the sacrifice may yield blessings to the donor.[1]

Yama is the Sun, the source of the souls and of all life; later, he becomes, like Osiris, king of the dead. The Earth-goddess Nirriti is his wife.[2]

Agni as Yama, is all that is born: as Yama, all that will be born.[3]

Garuda the messenger of Varuna, Bird that producest in the womb of Yama the All-controlling (Agni).[4] . . .

Those who from their hearts desire union with the Divine Being, in the heavens in the bosom of Yama, look with steady vision to thee.[5]

"Yama of Sunlike glory." [6]

In India Vivasvat is one of the forms of the Sun, and is father of Yama. So in Ancient Persia, Vivanghvat is father of Yima.[7] This Yima is Yama.[8]

Ahura-mazda (Ouranos-Varuna) is asked by Zarathustra (Zoroaster) in the Persian Liturgy : " With whom as the First of Mankind hast thou conversed beside me ? " Ahura answers: "With Yima, the beautiful . . . . with him as the First of the men I have conversed, I who am Ahura-mazda." Ahura says to Yima, " Spread out my worlds, make my worlds fruitful, then obey me, Protector, Nourisher and Overseer of the worlds." Yima answers : " I will spread out thy worlds, I will make thy worlds fruitful, I will obey thee (I who am) Protector, Nourisher, and Overseer of the worlds . . ."[9]

Then Yima went forth up to the stars, about mid-day, to the way of the Sun. He divided this earth with his golden lance.[10]

Yima is the Jemshid of the Persian legends, and the

---

[1] Wilson Rigv. ii. 125.   [2] Weber, Ind. Stud. i. 290.

[3] Wilson, i. 179.   [4] Stevenson, Samaveda, p. 278.   [5] Ibid. 60.

[6] Wuttke, ii. 250.   [7] Burnouf, Journal Asiatique, 1844, 475.

[8] Spiegel, Vend. 7, 70.

[9] Ibid. Vend. 70, 71.   [10] Ibid. 72.

5

Hindu Jama.[1] He has the Chaldean name of the Day (Sun) Ioma, the Hebrew Iom (yom) and the First-born in the Chaldean philosophy, called Aoum, or doubled, Moum, the Hindu "Word" of Creation, the Word of Light; " Om," " Aum," the Sclavonic " Um," " Oum," meaning "spirit," "soul;"[2] Ium, in the Scandinavian Thunder-god's name Ium-ala, Iumjo (Iumio), the Thunder-goddess; Ami, Ammi, and Ammi-Shaddai, Hebrew proper names, Oma " the holy fire" in German;[3] Om in Omanus (Ammon) the Persian firegod's name; Aom in the Hebrew proper names Immer and Aomar,[4] and the Dorian Amar, meaning " day" (Mar, the Phœnician Sun); Bal-*aam*, Ah-*iam*, a Hebrew name; Iam (Day) in Egyptian;[5] Iem-uel, a Hebrew name (Iam or Am and El); compare M-iel, the name of an angel, and Kadmiel=Ak-Ad-*am*-El. This old Indo-germanic and Semitic sun-god Am, Yama in India, Yima in Persia, Euimos (Dionysus),[6] Am-ous in Egypt,[7] Iam-us in Greece, is mentioned in a myth, related by Pindar.[8]

Meantime Evadne, laying aside her girdle, woven with purple woof, and silver ewer, under dark bushes brought forth a boy *instinct with divinity*. To her the deity of the golden locks (Apollo) sent, to assist her, gentle Ilythia,[9] and the Fates; and from her womb, and from the yearning pang of childbirth came forth Iamus to light at once.

In Asia Minor, his goddess bore his name, in the feminine Amma (Ama), Ma, the Moon; Ammia, Amaia, and Maia, the Earth,[10] Ma the Egyptian goddess of truth.

I have beheld the unwearied protector of the universe, the Sun, travelling

[1] Duncker ii. 300; Roth in der Zeitsch. der D. M. G. iv. 426; Kleuker, Zendav. ii. 305.

[2] Grimm, in the Trans. of the Berlin Akad. A. D. 1854. 309.

[3] Movers, 348; Grimm, Deutsche Mythol. 674.

[4] Gen. 36, 11.   [5] Seyffarth, Theol. Schriften, 23.

[6] Movers, 546. Scholia ad Aristoph. Aves, 583.

[7] Rinck, i. 223; Williams, 316; " Amos," 319.

[8] Olympiad, vi.   [9] Ilita, a name of Agni in India (Alat, Lot). Alitta, and Ilythia, would be his goddess.

[10] Duncker, ii. 499; Gerhard, Griech. Mythol. i. 451; Movers, 586.

upwards and downwards by various paths: invested with aggregative and diffusive radiance, he revolves in the midst of the regions.[1]

The wonderful host of rays has risen; the Eye of Mitra, Varuna and Agni, the Sun, the Soul of all that moves, or is immovable, has filled (with his glory) the heaven, the earth, and the firmament.

The Sun who traverses alone the path of heaven with the speed of thought, is at once Lord of all treasures: the two kings, Mitra and Varuna, with bounteous hands, are guardians of the precious ambrosia of our cattle.[2]

Yama is evidently related in nature to Agni and to Aryaman.[3] Agni is thought to rise in the morning in the shape of the Sun, from out of the ocean.[4]

He verily upholds the heaven: he, the brilliant, the leader of the herd (rays, or waters which are called "cows"), pours forth the flowing (water) for the sake of food: the mighty Indra manifests himself after his own daughter (the Dawn).

May he, illuminating the purple (dawn), listen to the invocation of old, daily bestowing wealth upon the race of Angirasas.[5]

Curtius speaks of the chariot of Zeus drawn by white horses in the host of the last Darius, behind which a horse remarkable in size, the Horse of the Sun, was led.[6] The Old Persians anciently adored the Sun, Mithra, who rose in the East over the mount Berezaiti. So, in India, Mithra was originally adored, then Mithra and Varuna (Saturn), just as Mithra and Ahuramazda in Persia. Later it becomes necessary, in the course of arrangement of the religious system, that Mithra should be subordinate to Ahuramazda, the Supreme God.[7] Mithra and Ahura are (originally) both names of the sun-god. Every lie and all deceit are in the Zendavesta an uncleanness, and at the same time an offence towards the all-seeing and *all-knowing* sun-god, Mithra.[8]

When I made the wide-ruling Mithra, I created him just like myself in godliness and dignity, I Ahuramasda.·

Go up, shining Sun, with thy swift horses, rise above Mount Berezaiti,

---

[1] Wilson, ii. 137.	[2] Ibid. i. 189, 304.	[3] Wuttke, ii. 250.
[4] Wilson, i. 248.	[5] Ibid. i. 325, 326.	[6] Duncker, ii. 363.
[7] Ibid. 323—325.	[8] Ibid. 351.	

and shine to the creatures on the way which Ahuramasda has made in the air, which the gods have created. Praise to the Sun who drives on with four horses, and works purity.[1]

The names of the Sun are those of the Day.

Ahan, " Day " (in Sanskrit).	Ahan is *therefore* the Sun.
Amar " the Day " (in Pindar).	Mar, a god of Gaza.
Meri "the Light," the Sun (in Egyptian.)[2]	*Mar*-na, *Mer*·odach=Baal, the Sun.
Iom, " the Day " (in Hebrew), Ioma (in Chaldee), Iam (in Egyptian),[3]	Am, " Ami," Iama, the Sun in India; Mei, Mu, Egyptian gods.
Mu (in Egyptian) "Radiance."	In Egypt " ham " meant " created." [4] The same root must have been used for " Creator."
	Ham " the Sun," the oldest Cronus (Saturn) of Eupolemus.[5]
Dag, " the Day," Tag (in German).	Dagur, the Sun (in Scandinavia), Tages in Italy, Dach-os in Babylon, Dag-on in Phœnicia.
Dies, " a day."	Dius, Deus, the Sun-god, later Saturn, Attis in Asia Minor, Ata, Ta, Tai, in Arabia.
Coptic, Hou, Hu, " day." In Sanskrit Ahû "Light," "the Word of Light." Iaho.	In Egypt, Ehou, the god of Day, the Sun, Chons-Aah (Hercules). Iah in Israel and Phœnicia, Aoos-Memnon, the morning-Sun.
In Greek Abōs (Aβωs), Φῶs (Phōs), Phaos "light."	Busi, the Sun in Assyria, Abas, Iebus.

In the Assyrian period the Hebrews worshipped the Sun, Moon, Planets, and all the host of heaven.[7] The Hebrew names Shemuel, Samael, Samuel, are composed of Sem or Shem, the Sun, and El, the Sun. Isaiah puts in the mouth of the Babylonian king " gainst Heaven I mount forth, over the stars of El I set my throne, make myself like the El-ion " (Ion).[8] El is the name " God " (Sun) in many parts of the Bible. It is the Homeric Eel and the

---

[1] Duncker, ii. 361.
[2] Seyffarth, Theol. Schr. 99.   [3] Ibid. 28.   [4] Ibid. 99.
[5] Williams, 223.   [6] Exod. xl. 38.
[7] 2 Kings, xxiii. 5; Movers, 164.   [8] xiv. 13, Movers, 256.

Doric Ael, the Sun. It is used four times in Numbers xxiii., and four times in chapter xxiv. The terms Elion and El Sadi (Shaddai) are also used in chapter xxiv. El is used for "God" in Job xii.—6, xv.—4, and elsewhere. Eli occurs in the New Testament. It is the Hebrew name Heli[1] and the Greek Helios. The name of the Hebrews was taken from Eber (anciently Abar or Obar), and would seem to be the name of the god Bar, the sun-deity Abar of the Assyrians and Iberians, the Egyptian god Bar, Baru or Bore, the Persian god Pars, Perseus and Pharo (Φαρο); the name of the Sun's rivers Iberus in Asia, Ebro in Spain, and the Latin iubar, jubar, "sunbeam."[2]

And he (Iasiaho) took away the horses that the kings of Judah had given to the Sun at the entrance of the house of Iahoh, and burned the chariots of the Sun with fire.[3] Here we find the Hebrews as sun-worshippers. The Amorites were probably sun-worshippers, because the nations bore the name of the national or tribal god. Amori אמרי is Amar, the Doric name of the Day.[4] The Sun and Day are the same in name, and the Phœnicians worshipped a god Mar (Amar), and Marna, god of Gaza.[5] Amar gives his name to Amor or H-imer-os, Sol-Cupid, just as Ar (Ares, אור ,אר Mars), the Sun ("Hor," Horus, "Har") gives his to Er-os. He is the sun-god Erra (Ra, Re) of Memphis. The Danai (Greeks) worshipped the Assyrian god Adan (Adonis). The Danes worshipped the Carthaginian god Don.[6] The Hebrew tribe of Adan or Dan worshipped Adoni, אדני. The Amalekites were sun-worshippers, because the name of Amalak (Baal-Malach or Moloch, the Sun) was borne by this race.[7] Baal-Gad was the Sun.[8]

---

[1] Luke 3.

[2] Lepsius, Berlin Akad. 1851, p. 206, 163; Benfey, in der Zeitschr. der D. M. G. viii. 466.

[3] 2 Kings xxiii. 11.   [4] Donaldson's Pindar, Pyth. iv. 256.

[5] Movers, 28, 30, 16.   [6] Ibid. 479.

[7] Ibid. 400; Grotefend, Erläut. einer Inschr. des letzten Assyrisch-Babyl. Königs, 28   [8] Movers, 197, 174, 175, 291.

The tribe of Gad were probably sun-worshippers, Achad meaning the Sun, and the Persian Khoda (Choda) " God" being the royal title of the ancient kings of Bokhara and Gnzagan.[1] The name Baal-gad is found in the Bible,[2] and the word is also in composition with Omanus or Amanus, names of the sun-god, in the name *Cod*omanus (Darius). It is "Achates," and, in the feminine Hecate (Gad), is the Moon.

As kings were called by sun-names, Gauda, the king, son of Mastanabal, has probably the name Achad or Agad, Mastanabal is a compound of the god-names Am, Asad. Anabal (Abal, Bel, Baal). Asatan, or Satan, the name of an Egyptian king Staan (Set or Sat-An), is the sun-god Siton [3] (Dagon), and is also the Persian Iasdan, a name of the good god Ormuzd, the Agathodemon. It is also the name of the bad god Shitan of the Persians, the Hebrew Satan and the Egyptian Seth (the Devil, Typhon); also Set the Assyrian god. Asad, Sad, or Saad, the Arab god, and Shaddai of the Hebrews (the Almighty), the Arab Shadad and Shadid (Hadad) the Almighty Sun. Plutarch says that the name of the Egyptian Seth signifies "that which overpowers or forces," like the Arabic " Shadid," which means " a strong man."[4] Sadid was a Phœnician god:[5] Κρόνος υἱόν ἔχων Σάδιδον.[6] " Seth " (Aseth), was the name of a deity.[7] Compare also the Assyrian god Sut (in Egypt Hut,[8] the Celestial Sun), the royal title " Suten," and the proper names Pal-estina, (the names Bel (Pal) as, atina), Schetina),[9] Sadi, the poet (Sadai), Sidon, the Sun's city, and Sthen-elus (Satan-El), the strong man El, Hercules, the strong Phœnician Sun, who had "his good and his bad

---

[1] Rawlinson, Journ. R. A. Soc. xi. 124.

[2] Josh. xi. 17. xii. 76.   [3] Sitô is Demeter, the Earth.

[4] De Iside, xli.   [5] Movers, 657.   [6] Ibid. 144, Sanchon, 30

[7] Movers, 107, and the authorities there quoted.

[8] Bunsen, Egypt's Place, i. 45.

[9] Brandis, p. 36.

side."[1]   Satan is the Phœnician Hercules, who torments
with his fire and his heat the hot countries of the Levant.[2]

In Egypt the Sun was "father of the gods."[3]   Ammon
was father of the gods.[4]   Osiris was "king of the gods."[5]
In Assyria, Assur, Ahura (the Sun), As or Assarac, was
"father of the gods."[6]   Jupiter is "king and father of the
gods." The Phœnician Elon or Elion was the "highest
god," whom Abraham invoked, calling him "El, Elion."[7]
The Babylonian chief deity, Baal (the Sun), was "king of
the gods," as was also the Syrian Adad, the Sun.[8]   "The
old Dorians called Adon-is Ao."[9]   Iao is the sun-god
Adonis.[10]   Iao (Dionysus) is the highest of all the gods.

$$\text{Φράζεο τὸν πάντων ὕπατον Θεὸν ἔμμεν᾽ Ἰαώ.}\text{[11]}$$

The Orientals generally adored Shem (Asam) as the
Sun; the Italians worshipped Semo (Hercules);[12] the Egyptians Som. Shemes and Sur are well-known names of the
Sun.[13]   Assur for Assyria is written with the phonetic
letters, As, and Sur, disunited.[14]

"Ani, at Khorsabad, is usually joined with Ashtera
(Astarte)."

"In the north-west palace of Nimroud there is an inscription of Sar-dan-apal-us repeated more than a hundred
times: 'This is the palace of Sardanapalus, the humble worshipper of Assarac and Beltis, of the shining Bar, of Ani,

---

[1] Movers, passim.
[2] Mattan-bukus is Satan, Berial=Belial.
   Mattan is Mithra, the Sun.   Rawlinson, R. A. S. xi. p. 10, part 1st.
   Mattan is priest of Baal, the Sun.
   Mattan-iah is a proper name.   2 Chron. xx. 14, xxiii. 17.
[3] Uhlemann, Thoth. 27.   [4] Egypte, 253.
[5] Wilkinson, Second Series, ii. 344.
[6] Rawlinson Journ. etc., xii. 414, 432, 486 ; xiv. 14.
[7] Sanchoniathon, Eusebius, Pr. Ev. 36 ; Gen. xiv. 19, 20, 22.
[8] Munter Babylonier, 20.
[9] Rinck, i. 171, quotes Etymolog. M v. 'Aώ.   [10] Movers, 554, 544, 545.
[11] Oracle of Apollo Clarius Vindicated, Movers, 539.
[12] Creuzer, iii. 672, ii. (iv.) 86.
[13] Rawlinson Journal R. A. S. xii. 461.   [14] Ibid. vol. xiv. p. xviii.

and of Dagon, who are the principal of the gods.' An obelisk inscription also runs as follows: 'Asarac, the great lord, king of all the great gods; Ani, the king; Nit, the powerful, and Artenk, the supreme god of the provinces, Beltis, the protector, mother of the gods.' . . . Shemir who presides over the heavens and the earth. . . . Bar. . . . Artenk, Lama, Horus. . . . Tal and Set, the attendants of Beltis, mother of the gods.'

The God Assar, the great Lord, and the gods inhabiting Assyria, to them I made adoration.[2]

" As " is Assur; Bushi (Abōs, Abas, the Dawn, Iebus= Ierusalem) is the sun-god ; Bushi-cham (Apollo Chomaeus) is the glowing sun.[3] Jerusalem (Iebus) bore his name.

There was rest on account of the fear at the bidding of the seer Sarak, in accordance with the direction of Assur, Bushi-Cham and Seraf, etc.[4]

" As" is the sun-god. Ar is the sun-god (Ares). As-ar (Assar) is the sun-god of Assyria and Syria. Prof. Whitney says, "As" means "life." Benfey says, "Asu" is " spirit," and Asura, "the living." Asurya is an appellative of the Sun, and Surya, in Sanskrit, is the Sun.[6] It is a universally recognized rule that *s* softens to *h*.[6] It is admitted by all the Sanskrit scholars, and instances are familiar to every student. The Spartan Asana, the Assyrian San, the German Sonne, are softened in Sanskrit into Ahan.[7]

Ahana (Ushas, the Dawn), charged with downward bending light . . . comes perpetually diffusing light.[8]

In like manner " As," the Spartan Sios (Zeus), the Asius of the nations of Asia Minor, and Assyria, softens to Ah,

---

[1] Journal of the Royal Asiatic Society, vol. xii. pp. 427, 432.

[2] Rawlinson, Journal of the R. A. S. xii. 14.

[3] Grotefend in der Zeitchr. der D. M. G. vii. 81 ; Bunsen Hist. Phil. 1. 79.

[4] Grotefend, ibid. vii. 86.

[5] Benfey, Samaveda, Gloss.

[6] Ibid. ; Bunsen, I. p. 111. Haug. Zeitschr. der D.M.G. vii. 321 ; Pictet in Kuhn's Zeitschr. for 1856, 349, 350.

[7] Bopp, Gloss. Sanscritum.   [8] Wilson Translat. Rigv. ii. 7.

Iah, and Asas to Ahiah, in Palestine. The Asura of the Assyrians softens to the Zend Ahura.

In Arabia, the Hamyarites chiefly worshipped the Sun, Misam, Al Debaran, Lakhm and Iodam (Adam?) Al Moshtari (Jupiter); Tay, Sohail or Canopus; Kais, Sirius and *Asad*, Otared or Mercury. The Arabs adored U*rotal* (Ar and Tal, the Sun), and Allah Taâla, the Most High God.[1] As they were Sun-worshippers, they must have worshipped Ashem and El (Ishmael) for these were the deities of the whole Semitic race. They had the idols of Asaph (Sabus) and the goddess Nailah.[2] Their tribes had deity names, as Ad, Thamud (a people called Thamudeni), Amalek, Hashem, Abil and Bar.[3] They worshipped, among others, three angels called the goddesses Allat (Alitta, Alilat, Venus), Al-uzza (Venus), and Manah (a large stone), "the daughters of God."[4] They had the idols Saad an oblong stone (Seth), Jagut, Yaghuth, (Achad), in the shape of the lion (Sun), Iaak (Ak, Ag, Aguieus), Hheber (Abar, Eber) a most ancient idol, Al Auf (Ap. Aph), Hobal, Sair,[5] Madan,[6] Halal, Yalil (Ialil, Eliel), Awal ("Wale the god of the bow in Scandinavia, Epul, Phul, Evil=Bel=Apollo), Bag (the Persian sun-god Baga, the Sclavonian Bog, the rising Sun) or Bagh, the god Nash or Nosh (Anos, Enosh) in Arabia, Baiar, Dar (Adar) Al Sharek (El Assarak), Asaf (Asaph), and Saiva, goddess; Sams or Sums (Shems), Huza'ah, Anazah, 'Uzza Salama, Aud, H-umâm, Rudâ (Arad and Erde), Amr, Durrigl (Adaracol), Fuls or Fils (φελλης, Apel, Epul), Addar*iban*, Ukaisir, Kuzah the cloud-god, Wadd.[7] The Musnad inscription reads: "In the name of God: this edifice Samir Jar'as has erected to the Lord, the Sun."

---

[1] Universal Hist. xviii. 378, 379.

[2] Zeitsch der D. M. G. vii. 493; Universal Hist. xviii. 361

[3] Ibid. 370.   [4] p. 380.   [5] p. 387.

[6] A king of Madon. Josh. xii. 19.

[7] Oslander, Zeitsch. D. M. G. vii.

[8] Zeitschr. der Deutschen Morgeul. Gesellsch. vii. 468: Domino Soli or Dominæ Soli (the Sun's Goddess). Ibid. note.

Countries and cities were named after the gods worshipped there.[1] The Carians said that Lud, Car and Mus (the gods or ancestors of the Lydians, Carians and Mysians) were brothers.[2] Alad, Lud, or Lot was probably a Hebrew-Phœnician god. Car is Kur the Sun; Kurios "Lord." Mus is found in the names of the gods Amous, Ch-*emosh*,[3] the Arabian god K-*amus*, *M-az*-eus, a Phrygian name of Zeus,[4] and Mis-or a Phœnician god (Misraim in Egypt), Amasia, a city of Asia Minor, Art-*emisia*, a queen.

Gallia (Gaul) is the feminine of Akal (Gallos), and Sikelia (Sicily) the feminine of Sigel the Sun.[5] The name Agal is found compounded in Hebrew and Assyrian proper names, as Iecol-iah, Nab-*ocol*-assar, Bar-*achel* and Ar-*chal* the Phœnician Her-*akles*. In Greek, *agl*-aos means "shining."

Let Asher be blessed with children.[6]

Assur (As, Asarak, etc.) was the god of the Assyrians, and (Sur) of the Syrians. Assyria was called Athuria on the coins, from Athur (Adar, Atar), another Assyrian sun-god.[7]

Moses was king in Ishoron . . . "There is none like El, O Ishoron, riding upon the heaven in thy aid, and in his magnificence the clouds."[8] This Isoron (Sharon) is the name of the Italian death-god Soranus, a name of Apollo.[9] It is the city or district named after the sun-god as death-god.[10] The Surani (Soranus) dwelt north of the Caucasus. The five Seran(im) (compare Surena="regent," "serene highness,") were rulers (sons of the Sun) in the five cities of the Philistines.[11]

---

[1] Rawlinson, Journal of the Royal Asiatic Soc. xii. 426.
[2] Movers, 17.   [3] Judges, xi. 24.
[4] Hesychius in Williams' Prim. Hist. 270.
[5] Jacob Grimm. Berlin Akad. 1845, p. 197.
[6] Deut. xxxiii. 24.
[7] Zeitschr. der D. M. G. viii. 57.   Journal of the Royal Asiatic Soc. xi. 10.
[8] Deut. xxxiii. 26, 5.   [9] Donaldson, Varron. 148.
[10] Gerhard Griech. Mythol. ii. 277. Creuzer, Symb. iii. 673.
[11] Judges xvi. 23; iii. 3.

Adar (Dorus, Thor) was god of the Dorians. The city Tur (Tyre) and the Arab tribe Dor were named after him. The Chaldee Targums give Athor for the Hebrew Asur.[1] He is Odur, the husband of Freia (Venus), in Scandinavia, the Syrian god Adar-melech and Adramelech, the Egyptian god Thore, Hator, Atur, Addir (God).[2]

The Horites in mount Seir (Sair, an Arab god) wor-shipped the Assyrian god Hor-us, the Persian Ahura, (?) the Egyptian god Hor, called also Iar, Har, Or, Ar, Aroer. Ar was a god in Asia Minor,[3] and the cities "Ar of Moab" and "Ur of the Chaldees," bore his name. Mount Ama-nus[4] is the mount of the god Amanus or Ammon.

The Hittites worshipped Atat, Tat, Adad, Hadad, the Sol-Mercury Taut; the Kenites worshipped Kan, Chon, Cain; the Kadmonites Adam-Kadmon, the god Cadmus, Kadmiel;[5] the Kenizites the god Akanaz, Kenaz (Ak-Anos, or Ash-kenaz); the Perizzites Paras, Rimmon-Parez,[6] Pars or Perseus, the Sun; the Zuzims worshipped Aziz (Azaz) the Dev, Asis the Sun; the Reph-aims Orpheus, the Emims (Aim-im) Am the Sun, the Canaanites the god Canaan mentioned in Eusebius among Phœnician divini-ties, the Edomites Adam; the Hivites and the Avvim wor-shipped the god Av, Af (Aph, Ab), Evi, the Oscan god Iiv, Jove or Bacchus (Evius), the Sinites the god San (Asan).[7] The Elumaeans (Elamites) were named after Elam (Ulom), the Sun. The Solumi, a people of Lycia in Asia Minor, were the children of the god Shalom ("As" and Ulom, Elam).[8] The Pelasgi were the Bel or Apel-Sacae (Bel and Asac, the god).

[1] Rawlinson, Journ. etc. xi. p. 10.   [2] Uhlemann, Thoth, 37.
[3] Movers. 441.   [4] Grote, xii. 118.   [5] Movers, 520, 521.
[6] Numb. xxxiii. 19. Baal-Perazim, 1 Chron. xiv. 11.
[7] Compare the Hebrew names Asana, Iashen, Shen, Shuni, Numb. 26-15. Azzan, Numb. xxxiv. 26. Nibshan, Josh. xv.; also Zeno, the Sen-on-es, a people of Upper Italy and Gaul.
[8] Jehova-Shalom (Ihoh-Sh lom), the name of an altar, Judges vi. 24; She-lumiel.

Duma[1] was the tribe of the god Adam (Adom) Atho
and Athumu the Sun in Egypt, Adamas, the god Tammı
of Ezechiel (viii. 14, a name of Adonis), Athamas a Gree
Ancestor or god ; compare the names Thomas called I
idum-us (Ad-*adam*), Duma a town in Achaia (Adom).[2]

The Aram-eans were the children of the god Ara
(Hermes). The Ammonites were the children of Ammo
(the Sun), the Israelites of their god Azar-iah or Azar-
(EzrAel, Azrael, Israel). The Paion-ians in Thrace were tl
children of Paian, a name of Zeus ; the Sap-aioi we:
perhaps the children of the god Asap, Asaph, or Sev. Tl
Paiti, a people of Thrace, may have worshipped the g(
Abad, Aput, or Iapet.[3] The city Aphutios was probab
named after this god Phut, Ptah, or Apet.[4] The city Eïc
was perhaps named after the god Aion ;[5] and Bog-es, tl
governor of the city, has the name of the Sclavonia
"Bog," the Sun, like the eunuch Bago-as.

Beth-Chanan[6] was the abode of the Phœnician g(
Canaan,[7] the Kanoon, after whom the Syrian month w
named. Cana of Galilee had the name of the god Aca
" Chon," " Kan." Beth Abara,[8] the house of Abar (the g(
Bar), is translated "house of passage." Beth Achara
house of the god Achar (Kur=the Sun),[10] is translate
"house of the vineyard." Beth Agla, house of Agal,[11] tl
god Agal (Gallos, the Sun), translated "house of festivity
Beth-Anath,[12] house of Nit (Anad) the Assyrian. god, A
ata, Anaitis or Neith, goddesses both of Egypt and countri
near the Black Sea. Beth Arabah, "house of Arabah."[13]
"The name of Hebron before was Kiriath-Arba, who (Arb
Araba) was the great Adam among the Anak people."[14]

[1] Movers, 338, 353.   [2] Crucius Hom. Lex. p. 140.
[3] Herodot. vii. 110, 113.   [4] Ibid. vii. 123.   [5] Ibid. 113.
    1 Kings, iv. 9.   [7] Sanchon. see Cory Anc. Frag. Preface
[6] John i. 28.   [9] Jer. vi. 1.   [10] Movers, 198.
[11] Josh. xv. 6.; xviii. 19, 21; Movers, 379.
[12] Josh. xix. 38; Judges i. 33.   [13] Joshua xviii. 22
[14] Ibid. xiv. 15; Movers; Arab, Iarob.—Baal; Horeb.

In the most ancient times there was a continual change of the myths. Gods become men or angels, and human adventures are ascribed to them. This is seen in Persia, India, Arabia, Palestine, Asia Minor, Greece, Italy, Phœnicia and Egypt. Thus Aigaion (Agan, Agni) is the hundred-armed centaur; Jubal (Iubal, or Bel, Baal, Apollo) becomes the inventor of musical instruments, instead of Apollo, Epul, playing on his lyre. 'Uagnis (Agni) is the inventor of the melody of the double flute.[1] Bel becomes a giant.[2] He is also Hercules,[3] and an ancient king, the ancestor of all the Semitic royal families.[4] Tat, the Sun (Adad) becomes Tituos, the giant. The Titans, whom Hesiod expressly calls the earlier gods,[5] are sun-gods and "giants." The Carian god Osogo (Asak, Asag) becomes (in Nonnus) Aisak, the chief of the horned centaurs.[6] Chom (Bel and Apollo[7]) becomes an ancestor of the Æthiopians, as Adam and Israel are ancestors of the Hebrews.[8] Vulcan, god of fire, is become Tobalcain, the smith. Sam, the Persian god (Shem?) mentioned in the Yasna, becomes an ancient hero in Firdusi's Shah Nameh. The god Amar or Mar (Jupiter-Sol) becomes, apparently, the World-giant Ymer in Scandinavia. "At last they brought the gods on earth, where they underwent human experiences and died, and the partisans of Euhemerism showed everywhere their monuments or the spot where they had been buried as evidences of the fact."[9]

The names of the angels Raph-ael, Sam-ael, Asas-iel,

---

[1] Nonnus, xli. 374. [2] Movers, Phön. Alt. i. 52.

[3] Movers, Phönizier, 14, 178, ff. [4] Ibid. 17.

[5] Hesiod, Theog. 424. [6] Dionysiac xiv. 190.

The Sacæ in Germany, the Iazug-ians in Sarmatia, Tac. xli—§ xxx. Ar-sac-es, Isaac, Asa-Ak, Ukko the German god, Ugo (Hugo), Æes-c-ulap-ius (in Hebrew Aloph is the title "Prince," "Duke," and therefore it was previously a name of the sun-god. Compare Eliph-al, Eliph-alaho, Hebrews. Aleph, ox.

[7] Movers, 189, et passim. Ibid. 347, 130, 189.

[9] Ibid. 152, 153.

Sat-ael, Rachiel (compare Archal = Herakles) Am-abiel,
Sachi-El, Seraph-ael, " Och (the spirit of the Sun)," Asmo-
deus, Amon, Berith, Oriph-iel,[1] give the gods Arab or
Orph-eus, El, Set, Shem (Semo), Sach (Asak, Isak), Och
(Ak), Asas, Arachal (Hercol in Etruria=Hercules), Serapis, &c. When the Arabs wished to rid themselves of their
numerous gods, they called them ancestors, patriarchs,
heroes, great and good men. Thus " Iauk " (Iacch-os) was
said to have been a man of great piety, and his death much
regretted : whereupon the devil appeared to his friends in
a human form, and, undertaking to represent him to the
life, persuaded them, by way of comfort, to place his ef-
figies in their temples that they might have it in view,
when at their devotions. This was done; and seven others
of extraordinary merits had the same honors shown them,
till, at length, their posterity made idols of them in earnest."
By such means were their old sun-gods withdrawn from the
Arab devotees; for it is evident that Iauk was the Sun, as
he was worshipped in the form of a horse, the universal
emblem of the Sun.[2]

The Arab Iaghuth (Achad, the Sun, Choda) was an idol
in the shape of a lion.[3] Lions were the solar emblems of
Horus and El. Live lions were kept in the temples. The
idol of Hobal (Saturn) is supposed to have been the same
with the image of Abraham, found and destroyed by Mo-
hammed in the Caaba, when he took Mecca. That image
was surrounded with a great number of angels and prophets as inferior deities, among whom, as some say, was
Ishmael with *divining arrows* in his hand.[4]

Beth Aven (Βαιτάβεν) is a place. Avan or Havan was
a Persian deity, after whom the Jesht-Aven was named.
Beth Azamoth (Asmaveth) is the place of Asamad (Sem-o-

---

[1] Agrippa, 3, 24 ; quoted in Williams' Prim. Hist. 326. Elih-oreph, 1 Kings,
iv. 3.

[2] Universal Hist. xviii. 384, Pococke not. ad spec. hist. Arab. 94.

[3] Ibid. xviii. 384.   [4] Universal Hist. 386.

Deus, Asmodius). Beth Horon is the house of Uranos, Sor-anus or Huranos. Beth-Baal-Maeon, a place, is the abode (or city) of the god "Baal-Maeon." Beth Maon is the house of Maon (Amon). Beth Shan, "the house of the tooth," was probably the "house of Asan, Zan, or San," the Assyrian god. Beth Shemesh[1] the house of Shemes the Sun; Beth Basi, the house of Abas (the god Busi); Bethel, the house of El; Beth Car, the house of Acar or Kur; the Sun, Beth Anoth[2] is the residence of the god Anad or Anat, the god of the Eneti, a people of Italy, the Assyrian god Nit (Nid). Anath-oth,[3] a place, is a compound of the names of the gods An and Athoth, the god Tot, Taut, Thoth (Mer-cury); Beth-Barah[4] is the house of the god Abar, Pharah. (Ab and Arah=Aras). Bethany was the abode of Ani, the Sun. We find Beth-Ezel, "the house of Asel" (Sol), Beth-Lomon, "the house of the god Lomon" (lumen=light), El-Amon the luminous (or Ulom the Sun and On the Sun); Beth-saida, the house of Asad, or Seth, Set; Gur-baal, a place,[5] bearing the names of the sun-gods Achar, Agar and Baal; Beth-Aura, "the house of אור Aur," the Sun; Succoth, a place,[6] and Succoth-benoth, a deity; Adami; a place,[7] and Adam, a god; Beth Dagon, the house of Dagon (the sun-god); Beth-Aran, the house of Aran (Uranos). Beth Haram, the house of Harameias (Hermes); Beth Om, the house of the Sun (Am, Iom=Day); Beth Peor, the house of Beor (the god Bar or Abar in Assyria), "the stone Ezel,"[8] (Asal the Sun), the city Adam,[9] Beth Marc-aboth, the house of the Arab god Mirrich;[10] Abad, Obodas (Mercury-Dio-nysus). Rimmon-Parez, a place, was probably the seat of the worship of the gods Hermon (Ariman), Rimmon, and Paras (Paraz, Perseus), as the same divinity. Beth

---

[1] 1 Kings iv. 9.   [2] Josh. xv. 59.   [3] Jer. xxxii. 9.
[4] Judg. vii. 24.   [5] 1 Chron. 26—7.
[6] Gen. xxxiii. 17.   [7] Josh. xix. 33.
[8] 1 Sam. xx. 19.   Compare Azel, Asael, Iasael, Ioseel, Azael, Sela, Salo, Hebrew names.
[9] Josh. iii. 16.   [10] Movers, 365.

Ieshimoth [1] was probably the city of Ashim (Shem th
Sun), At (Atys, the god). We find Aroer, ערוער [2] a city, an
Aroer the name of the god H-or-us or Har in Egypt. Th
four cities " Ain, Remon and Athar (Ether) and Ashan,
are names of the gods An(i), Ariman(ios), Atar and Asha
or " San." [3] Eder, a city, is the name of Adar, the go(
Eden or Adan, a town of Mount Libanus, not far from th
river Adonis,[4] is named from the god Adan. Beth-Lehen
was the house of Eloham (Elohim) and Beth-Pazzez,[5] th
house of AP-Asas (Ap and " Asis," being names of the Su
(compare Asas-el, Azazel). Gath-Rimmon [7] was the plac
of Achad and Rimmon, the two deities (compare Hadac
rimon, a god).[8] The names of the places Ashthaol, Ai
Shamesh, Shalabbin, Ailon, Eilon, Akron עקרון, cor
tain the deity-names As, Tal, Ar, Shemes, Sal (Sol), Abai
Elon (Alon) and Kronos (Ak-Uranus).[9] The place Alan
melech [10] was named after the god Alamelech or Elimelect
Compare Melech, Adarmelech and Anamelech, gods o
Syria and Sepharvaim. The places Mar-alah and Iphtah(
(Iephthah-El, Phth-ah-El or Phut-Ahelios) were obviousl
named after the gods Amar, Alah (Eloah),[11] Ptah and E
Arad, a city, Arada, Arath (in Arabia Petræa),[12] an
Arad-us, a seaport, were named after the god Arad
Ruda, an Arab god, Rta, an Egyptian god,[13] the god Baa
Melk-*arth* of Tyre, Melic-*ertes* of the Greek legends (Ama
lak-Arath).[14]

On, or Heliopolis (Aon, אין Numb. XVI. 1.), was th
city of An, the Sun, in Egypt, and in Syria (Baalbec). A(
was a frequent name of cities in Asia Minor and neighboi
ing countries.[15] En-rogel [16] was the well of Archal i

---

[1] Josh. xiii. 20.   [2] Ibid. 16.
[3] Ibid. xix. 7.   [4] Calmet, Dict.   [5] Josh. xix. 15.
[6] Ibid. 21.   [7] Ibid. 45.   [8] Movers, 197, 206.
[9] Josh. xix. 41, 43.   [10] Ibid. 26.
[11] Ibid. 14, 11. Polyglott Bible, Stier & Theile.
[12] Calmet.   [13] Bunsen, Egypt's Pl. i. 410.   [14] Movers, 14, 153, 43(
[15] Christian Examiner for July, 1856, p. 86.   [16] Josh. xv. 7.

Phœnicia (Arcules), Hercol in Etruria a name of Hercules, called Herakles.[1]

Asdod was the city of Sadad (As Adad) or Sadid, the Arab and Phœnician god.[2] Iptah, Iphthah,[3] was the city of Ptha, Aphthas,[4] Apet, Phut, Iapet. Abot was the word for the solar "year."[5] Abod was the Sun. The city Abydos (Abidos) was named after the god Abad, "Ebed," Apet, "Iapet," "Phut," "Ptah" or "Aphthas." The name Beth (in Hebrew "house") was probably in the proper-names above quoted, originally the deity-name Abed or Abot (the Sun). S-*ebad*-ios a name of Bacchus (Dionysus), Zebedee and S-*ebaoth* contain the deity-names As and Abad (Ebed). Compare Bethobalus, Obadilus.

Amad, Amathus, Emath, id est, Hamath,[6] was the city of Amadios (Dionysos).[7] " And the men of Babylon made Succoth-benoth, and the men of Cuth (Achad) made Nergal, and the men of Hamath made Ashima, and the Avites made Nibhaz and Tartak."[8]

Lukia, the country Lycia, is named from Alak, Lauk, Luke, λύκη, "light," the sun-god. Laconia and Elicon are the names of the gods Elac and An, On, the sun. The cities Alalah and Nebo were the places of the gods Alah and Nebo.[9] Askelon was the city of the god Asak-Elon, the Phœnician Elon, the Hebrew deity Elion. Amam[10] was the city of Amam (Moumis) the sun-god of the Babylonian philosophy,[11] the Arab god (H)umam; Yamama, a part of Arabia is the name of Amam or Yom-Am, the Sun. Adad-ah, a city, is evidently the name of Adad, Ah, the Sun.[12] Compare the name Adah in Genesis. Apharath*ah* Gen. xxxv. 19, is the city of the god Abaratha. Temani

---

[1] Movers, 336. [2] Ibid. 144, 657. Sanchon.

[3] Josh. xv. 43. [4] Suidæ Lex. [5] Seyffarth, Gram. Preface, xxvii.

[6] Seldeni Opera, iii. 387. [7] Movers, 232, 372, 381.

[8] 2 Kings, xvii 30, 31. [9] Numb. xxxii. 3.

[10] Josh. xv. 26. [11] Movers, 266, 276. Damascius l. c. p. 258.

[12] Munter, Babylonier 20; Josh. xv. 22. Iedidah, 2 Kings xxii.

is the land of Temen (Atman, Atumnios), Athom — Ami.[1]
Abel and Abila were cities of Abel or Bel, Shushan in
Persia the city of Asas-An (Asan), the Sun; Aloth or
Alath was the city of Alad or Lot, the Sun, and his goddess
Alitta (Venus). Arad, a city, Aradus, Rhodos (Erde) were
named after Arad, the Sun. Shamir was the city of
Shamir, the Sun.[2] Melita (Malta) was the isle of Venus
(Mylitta), Samaria was the land of Shemar or Shemir.
Berytus was named after Berouth or Barad, the Sun, "the
god Berith."[3] Bublos (G-ebal) was the city of Abab-El,
Babel, the Sun in Pamphylia and Babulonia. The city
Beroe was named after Bar (Abar): she was the bride of
the Sea-god.[4] Ekron was the abode of Kronos (Saturn,
Baal-*zebub*).[5]

The Phœnician-Hebrew month-god Abib (Ab, Abab),
the name of Adonis (Abobas), Phoib-os (Apollo), gave his
name to Boiba, in Homer, a Thessalian town.[6] Compare
πέπων, " cooked by the sun," " ripe." Here we have reached
the ante-Homeric period of Palestine, Phœnicia, Asia Minor
and Greece. Ahaz-iah sent messengers, saying, " go con-

---

[1] Gen. xxxvi. 24.   [2] Josh. 15. 48.

[3] Judges, ix. 46. Compare the Vedic deity Bharata.

[4] Movers, Phön. Alt. I. 111.

The Phœnician Kron-os appears as sea-god (Movers, Phön. Alt. i. 112).
Pindar, Ol. xiii. 98, calls the Water-god (Poseidon, the Sun) " Father *Dam-
aios*." Kuhn's Zeitschr. i. 468. Damia is Demeter, the Earth-goddess. Ibid.
Chom was Apollo (Movers, 189); the Arab word Kamus is a deity-name, and
means " Water" (Anthon, Class. Dict. quotes Ritter, Erdkunde, 2nd ed. i. p.
570), like the gods Agni, Ogen, and Ocean-us, the Assyrian god Adar ('Udor,
water), Bal-ak, Peleg and Pelagos " the sea," Poseidon, water-god and Lybian
sun-god, Mar, the Phœnician god, and Mare " sea," Banoth, a god, Pontus,
" the sea," Pontus a country of Asia Minor, and the Helles-pont.

[5] 2. Kings, i. 2.

[6] Il. ii. 712.

Vib-ulen-us (Abib-Elon), Tác. Book 6, xl.

Vib-ill-ius, ibid. xii. 29.

Vip-sanius, ibid. ii. xxiii.

Vip-sania, a Roman lady.

sult Baal-zebob (Bel-"As "-*Abob*) God of Akron, whether I shall recover from this sickness."[1] He must have sent them to the oracle of *Abib or Phoibos-Apollo*, the oracular god.

In Homer Azeus ($A\zeta\epsilon\upsilon\varsigma$[2]) son of Clumen-os (the gods Col, Agal, and Omanus), brother of Ærg-īnus (Erech and Ina, the Sun), is the name of the Greek-Asiatic god Zeus, who is the Spartan god Sios (Zeus), the god Asi-os in Asia Minor, Jupiter Asius in Crete,[3] the god "Husi " (Ashi?) north of the Euphrates, the god " Aishi" in Palestine a name of Jehovah,[4] I-asius (a name of Bacchus),[5] "As " the name of Asar and Asarac in Assyria[6]; (H)uas and Euas, names of Bacchus.[7] Compare the names of Asa, a Hebrew king, Aso, queen of Ethiopia, Is-ias, a Corinthian general, As-Iah in the Cabbala, and As-Ah-Iah.[8]

Mercury, in Hesychius, is called *Such*-os.[9] Chr-usaor, and *Osog*-o (Asac) were Carian gods.[10] Chr-*usor*, M-*isor* (Taut), S-uduk and *Ousō-us* were Phœnician deities.[11] The Greeks, Assyrians and Persians adored Per-seus (Bar-Asius; compare the Perazim and Parsees). The Germans worshipped Hesus ('Esus), Zeus was called C-*asius* (Ac-Asius, like Ac-Mon, Ak-Amon) on the river Orontes,[12] M-*azeus* in Phrygia ;[13] D-*asius* is a Chaldean month-name (a god), evidently the name of "Thasos," the "Tasian Hercules."[14] Seb-*azius* is Bacchus (Seb=Saturn),[15] Sabus was a name of Bacchus,[16] Seb is Saturn. Sebub is probably the same god. Zebul was the title of a ruler of a city. Kings bore sunnames.

---

[1] 2 Kings, i. 2.   [2] Crusius, Iliad. p. 82.   [3] Anthon, Art " Asi."
[4] Hosea, ii. 16, (18).   [5] Hesiod. Theog. 970.
[8] Rawlinson, R. A. S. xii. 426.   [7] Eckermann, i. 199 ; Movers, 546.
[8] 2 Kings, 22, 14; Ishiah, 1 Chron. xxiv. 25 ; Ah-iah, Exod. iii. 14; Ahah, "Ahob," 1 Chron. ch. 27, 4 ; 2 Sam. 23, 28.
[9] Eckermann, i. 141.   [10] Movers, 19; Strabo, xiv. 2, p. 204.
[11] Sanchon. 16, 18 ; Movers, 653 ; Eusebius, Pr. Ev. 35, 36.
[12] Movers, 668 ; Eckermann, i. 119.   [13] Hesych. in Williams, 270.
[14] Herodot, ii. 44 ; Movers, 21.   [15] Ibid. 547.   [16] Ibid. 23.

In connection with the god Adad the Sun, Hadad, Athoth, Tat, Taut in Phœnicia, Thoth in Egypt, Teut in Germany, compare the Irish words *Tiota*, Titin, Tetin, meaning "sun," the Welsh Tydain "sun " (Titan, Teutonic), Titha, a Sanskrit word, meaning " fire," Titho-es, an Egyptian word, meaning "light," Adittha, a city of Arabia (Audattha).[1]

With Acar or Kur, the Sun's name in Crete, Palestine &c., compare the Irish c rios "sun"[2] (Kurios "lord"), Car-ni a people of Italy, *Kr*-onos, a name of Saturn, *Acar*-nania, part of Greece.

With Sol, Sul, in Irish "the sun," compare in Italy Sol, Ausel, *Usil* (Asel), names of the Sun, Sulla, a Roman, Usal (Genesis x. 27), Azael, a god in Damascus, [3] the Gothic Sauil, the Lithuanian Saulé, the French Soleil, the Greek Helios (Asel, Ahel), the Welsh haul "sun," [4] heol in Armorica.[5]

With Abel, Bel, Babel, the Sun in Babylon, Pamphylia and elsewhere, also Evil, Phul, compare Abelios in Crete, the Irish beal, beol, bel, the Sun, the Sanskrit Bhala, the Sclavonian Bjelbog (Belbog), the god of day (Bog, Baga);[6] Awal, the Arab god, and Wale (Apollo), " the god of the bow" in Scandinavia.

Oseiris the name of the sun-god is Asar in Assyria, Seirios " the sun " in Greece,[7] Sair is an Arabian god,[8] the names Ashur and Mount Seir are found in the Old Testament, Asura and Surya " the Sun " in Hindustan, Sour the name of the city Sarra (Tyre).

The god Asan or San (the Sun) is Ahan " day " in Sanskrit, in Welsh Huan.[9] We have Asam, Shem (Shemes,

---

[1] Universal Hist. vol. 18, 348. Bopp, die Celtischen Sprachen, Berlin Ak.; Seyffarth, Theolog. Schriften der alten Agypt. p. 4 ; Munter, Bab. 20 ; Pictet in Kuhn's Zeitschr. vol. 4, p. 358.

[2] Pictet in Kuhn's Zeitschr. iv. 359.   [3] Movers, 368.

[4] Pictet in Kuhn, iv. 349.   [5] Ibid.   [6] Ibid. 361. 362.

[7] Kuhn, iv. 351.   [8] Movers, 263, 317, 414.

[9] Pictet in Kuhn's Zeitschr. iv. 353 ; Bopp, Gloss. Sanskr.

Shemir, Shems), Ṣmu the Egyptian Typhon,[1] Zom, the Egyptian Hercules,[2] Sams or Sums an Arabian god, Samh and Somh the sun in Irish,[3] Semo in Italy a name of Hercules 'the Sun.'[4] With the Babylonian Alorus אל-אור, the god of light,[5] compare the Scandinavian god Uller, the son of Thor, the Thunderer. With Asarak the Assyrian chief god compare Serach, a name of the Egyptian god Memnon, the Sun,[6] the Arab god Al Sharek, and the Siraci, between the Black and Caspian seas.

The Sun Arak ('Erc-ean Jove), Arg-us, "all eyes," whom M-erc-ury slays), is the Irish Earc, Erc (the Sun), the Sanskrit Arka (sun).[7] From this name of the Sun comes Erech, a kingdom,[8] Arg-os, a kingdom of Greece, Iericho, a city, and the wanderer Ark-as, the inventor of the measure of the twelve months and the journey of the Sun.[9] Arch-al was the name of Heracles in Phœnicia, Herc-ol in Etruria.[10]. Luc-urg-us was a Thracian and Arab god.[11] Compare the names Arg-aios, Archel-ous (Archal), Mam-erk-us (the god Moum or Moumis, the First-born), Anakas-arch-us (Anaxarchus, Annakos, Erech). The Homeric Orchomenos [12] was the city of the sun-god Arka or Erech-Omanus the Hindu, Persian, Asia Minor and Egyptian deity.

The Arabs adored a god Ta תא.[13] Attis אתא is the beloved of Cybele, just as Adonis is of Venus. "Hail Attis, the Assyrians call thee thrice desired Adonis (the Sun); Egypt, the holy celestial horn of the Moon; the Greeks Ophias, the Samothracians (in their mysteries) Adam the holy (σεβάσμιον), the Mæonians Korubas, and the Phrygians sometimes Pappas"[14] (Pappæus=Zeus.

---

[1] Plut. de Iside, lxii.　　[2] Uhlemann, Thoth, p. 47.

[3] Pictet in Kuhn, iv. 352,　　[4] Donaldson's Varr. p. 37.

[5] Munter, Bab. 31.　　[6] Movers, 229.　　[7] Pictet in Kuhn, iv. 355.

[8] Gen. x. 10.　　[9] Nonnus, xli. 376, 377.　　[10] Movers, 55, 432, etc.

[11] Ibid. 22.　　[12] Il. ii. 511. The Egyptian Harka the Sun, Kenrick I 323.

[13] Tuch in the Zeitschr. der D. M. G. iii. 153.

[14] Schneidewin, Philologus, 3, 261, quoted in Gerhard Griech. Mythol. i.

The old German Tis or Dis was Mars (the Sun).[1] This
god At (Ad) is the Sun Ad-ad. He is the Arabian deity
Aud (Saturn),[2] and, as names of the deities were given to
the tribes that adored them, he was probably the god of the
Aedues (Ædui). Ad is the name of an Arab tribe, of the
mountain Athos (At or Adas), the river Adda or Addua,
and is compounded with El, Eli (the Sun) in the Hebrew
proper-name Eli-ada. It is the name of the altar called Ed
עד (Ad, Adi, Deus, Dius, Tius, Thios in Crete, Theos) by
the sons of Re-oben and Gad.[3] "I swore by the blood-be-
sprinkled *Aud* and by the pillars of Sair."[4] These are the
Arabian chief gods Obod-as (Abad, Ebed) and Dusares.[5]

Iacch-os is the Sun, Bacchus. Iauk was an Arab sun-
god. The Ach-æans were the children of Ak, Ag-uieus
was Apollo, Gau-as was Adonis.[6] We find Ukko, a German and Scandinavian chief god, Agis, a Spartan king, Og
king of Bashan, Ag*esila*-us, a Spartan, Ac-*usil*-aus, Heg-
esil-aus (Grote, II.) As kings bore the sun-names, Ag-*ag*
king of the Amalekites, has the name Ag doubled, as in
Og-ug-es, the sun-deity of the flood-legend, Gog and Guges.
The Ciconians and C-auc-oni-ans have the sun-names Ak-
ak, Ani. Og-ug-ia was an island bearing the Sun's name,
as usual. Og was a serpent-god.[7] Eac-us, a god, was one
of the judges in hell. The Armenians had their Haik (Ak),
the Egyptians their god Kai (Ka, Ki), Ki-os meant "Lord".[8]

115, 116. "The hawk was the sacred bird of Adam or Re-Athom." Osburn's
Monum. Hist. of Egypt i. 340. "God is he that hath the head of a hawk."
Layard, Nin. 'The Creator is represented by a hawk. Seyffarth, Theolog.
Schriften der alten Aegypter, p. 35. The sun-god Phre is a hawk-headed di-
vinity. Movers, 68. Cherub (Korub-as) a Hebrew. Ezra, ii. 59.

[1] Uhlemann, Thoth, 22.

[2] Movers, 263; Universal Hist. xviii. 370, 387; Zeitschr. der D. M. G.
vii. 499.

[3] Josh. xxii.   [4] Kamus, in Movers, 263.   [5] Ibid.

[6] Movers, 199, 545.

[7] Lampridius, Jablonski, quoted in Deane, Serp. Worship, 93.

[8] Lepsius, Berlin Akad. 1851, p. 170 : Seyffarth, Grammar, 3.

in Egyptian, and the Greeks had their *Aig*aios Pelagos, the Sea of *Aig*. *Ac*-mon (Ak and Amon or Monimus) was a fire-god, *Coi*-os a Titan, and Ki-os a god in Bithynia.[1]

Esmun (Saman, Baal) is Kronos (Saturn), and corresponds to Pan.[2] Zeus was named Paian in Crete. Phaon was a name of the sun-god Memnon.[3] Phanes was the Phœnician sun-god. Pan was sun-god and fire-god. He had an altar at Olympia, on which the fire burned day and night. He is represented on a monument " blowing upon a shepherd's pipe before an altar on which the fire burns. Above the altar is a star. A goat leans his forefeet on the altar. The whole is surrounded by the twelve signs of the Zodiac." [4]

Lam(us) was a god, Elum-as, a Lybian prince.[5] And the sons of Shem were *Ailam*, אילם, Ashur, Ar-phach-sad and Aram.[6] *Lam*-ech is Elam and Ach. In Homer Laomedon is a compound of Elam and Adan (Adonis), the Assyrian god. The Hebrew name Elm-Odam [7] or Almodam is a compound of Alam and Adam. Elm-odad is a Hebrew name—Elam and Adad, the Sun. The god Oulom or Ulom (the male and female Baal) " the Sun as Soul of the world," is the union of El and Am, two names of the Sun. We find the name Lama (Ulom) in the list of Assyrian gods, given by Rawlinson. The Latin Illuminare and lumen, and the name of the god Lomon are allied to it. The goddess Lamia, the daughter of Poseidon (Neptune) would seem to have been the feminine of Lama, the sungod. It is the name of Lamos, a river of Helicon,[8] and Lamos, the son of Poseidon, king of the Læstrigonians.[9]

The goddesses are chiefly regarded as *wives of the Sun under various names*. Next, they have their appropriate characters, as goddess of wisdom, the Earth, the fruits, etc.;

---

[1] Eckermann, i. 204.   [2] Movers, 332.   [3] Ibid. 26, 227.
[4] Creuzer, Symb. iv. 69, 70, note, 212; Gerhard, i. 532, 533.
[5] Movers, 476, 477; Grote, xii. 412.   [6] Gen. x. 22.
[7] Luke, iii. 28.   [8] Nonnus, Dionys. Notes, ix. p. 34.
[9] Odyssey x. 81. *Abish-alom*, 1 Kings, xv. 10.

but they all have something in common. Rhea, Cybele, Demeter, Pallas and Cotys are very much the same.[1] Venus is Onka, Isis is Neith, Hathor, Bubastis.[2] Isis is made to say, "Me the first-born Phrygians name Pessinuntia, the mother of the gods : hence the indigenous Attici (call me) Cecropia Minerva, thence fluctuating Cyprii (call me) Paphia Venus, the arrow-bearing Cretes, Dictynna Diana, the three-tongued Siculi, Stygia Proserpina, the Eleusinians, old goddess Ceres, Juno some, others Bellona, these Hecate, those Rhamnusia, and those who are illuminated by the commencing rays of the Sun at his birth, the Aethiops and Arii and Egyptians, strong in ancient learning, . . . call (me) by (my) true name, queen Isis." [3]

Aurora is sometimes the wife, sometimes the sister of the Sun, and is called by his name. In India we find Aushasa, the Dawn, the feminine of Asas (Ushas) the Sun. The Vedic name of this goddess, Ahana,[4] is the feminine of the Assyrian sun-name San (Asan, Azan,[5] Azanes, Zan), Ahan, Ohan (Iohan), the name of the Huns. The Assyrian sun-god Abas, Busi, Bushi-Chom " the burning sun," gives his name to Abōs (Αβως, the Dawn) in Lakonia.[6] Asas, Asis, the Edessa sun-god, lends his name to the Persian and Sanskrit Ushas and Azesia (Cora).[7] The Babylonian sun-god Aos (the Sun, Titan), finds his name borne by Aos (Eos) the Dawn, who leaves the rosy bed of Tithonus (the Sun). Ar-oer (Horus) from " Aur" the name of the Sun (Ar) has Aurora to bear his name.

It was a principle of ancient mythology that the female forms an essential part of the conception of the deities. They are found in pairs. The Greeks, Romans, and other nations did not hesitate to pair those of different names together. Venus is the wife of Vulcan, but she bears the

---

[1] Gerhard i. 115. [2] Movers, 150.. [3] Apuleius in Gerhard, i. 115.

[4] Wilson, Rigv. Sanhita, ii. 7 ; Bunsen, Hist. Phil. I. 111 ; Ausonia, the name of Southern Italy. [5] Gerhard, Griech. Mythol. ii. 144.

[6] Bunsen, Hist. Phil. i. 79. [7] Gerhard. i. 451 ; Williams, 296.

name of Pan (Aban), Phanes, Avan or Havan. Juno is the spouse of Jup-iter, yet she has the name of the Etruscan deity Jonn. If they were paired according to their names we should have—

Ab, Ap the Sun, Ob, Op, the Samaritan god Iabe, the Arab god Auf (Af).
Av, "the Oscan god Iiv."
"Iuve," Iove (Jove), "Evi," Evi-us (Bacchus.)

Apia the Earth-goddess (Greece), Aphaia (Artemis, the Earth).
Ava, Eva the Earth.
Heva, Eve.
Euboia (Euboea), an island, Ops, the Earth, "Opis," Upis." [2]

The Assyrian god As, Aishi, a name of Jehovah and Baal, Asius the god of Asia Minor and Crete, the Spartan god Sios, the Homeric Zeus, Iasius (a name of Bacchus the husband of Ceres).[6]

Asia, 'Uzzâ in Arabia, a name of Venus, Ias (Greece),[3] Esi,[4] Hes (Isis), Sai,[5] Aisa the goddess of Fate in Homer; Iaso.

Aos in Babylon, Ashi, Asha in Persia, Iao in Phœnicia, Aoos-Memnon (Adonis).[7]

Aia, the Earth, Aue, a meadow in German.

Ehou in Egypt the god of day, Hou, Hu, the day, in Coptic; Ahû in India, Iah, Iaho in Palestine, Ao (Adonis), Aah (Hercules).[9]

Ioh the Moon in Egypt,[8] Io the Moon.

El (Al), Il, Heli-os, Ael, Eel, the Sun in Homer.

Elle (Isis),[10] Lua, wife of Saturn (in Italy), Ila the Earth (Sanskrit).

Am, the Sun, Iamus in Pindar, Iama in India, Ioma in Chaldee, Iom in Hebrew, Am-ous in Egypt, Euimos (Bacchus), Yima in Persia.

Ma the Moon in Asia Minor,[11] Ma the goddess of truth in Egypt, Amaia,[12] Maia the Earth, Ammia, Amma.[13]

[1] Donaldson's Pindar, 351.
[3] Strabo in Williams, 341.
[5] Seyffarth, Theol. Schriften, 99.
[7] Movers, 285, 555, 225.
[8] Lepsius, in the Berlin Akad. 1851.
[9] Bunsen, Egypt's Place, etc., i. 504, 507.
[10] Williams, 296, quotes Hesychius.
[12] Gerhard Griech. Mythol. i. 451.

[2] Williams, 296.
[4] Kenrick, i. 353.
[6] Hesiod, Theog. 970.

[11] Duncker, ii. 488.
[13] Movers, 586.

Ad (Adi), Dius, Deus. The gods Aud, Ieud, Aides and At.

Ada (Juno in Babylon),[1] Dia "the beloved of Jupiter;" Aida, Ida (Sanskrit) the Earth-goddess, Adah.[5] Dηŏ (Ceres).

An, "Ani," "Anus," Jonn, "Ianus," Ion, Ina (Sanskrit), the Sun.

Anna the Moon,[4] Ino "the white goddess," Enuo the Moon, Iuno, Anna, the Carthaginian Venus;[5] the goddess Anaia,[9] Aonia, Ionia.

Ar, Aur, the Sun, אר, אור.[7]

Rhea, the Earth.

Ar-es (Mars), Erra, Ra, Re, Iar, the Sun in Egypt, Hari the Sun in the Vedas,[9] Ari-el in Judæa, Er an Armenian god, Ar a god in Asia Minor.[10]

Aria a country, Hera (Juno), Aeria (Venus).[8]

Ak the Sun, Och the Spirit of the sun, the god Aug "the brilliant Auges."[11] Agu-ieus (Apollo).
Iauk (Yauk the Arab god), Iacch(os) a name of Bacchus, Eac-us the hell-god. Ukko in Germany.

Achaia (Greece), Gaia the Earth, Acca Larentia.

Aras the Sun, הֶרֶס 'Aras, the Sun, PHC (Resh) in Egyptian,[12] the Sun, Arah.

In Hebrew, Eraz, אֶרֶץ the earth.
Eraze in Homer.
Arah, in Samaritan, the earth.
Aroah, in Chaldee, the earth.
Irah, the Moon, ירח.

Alas, Alah, Eloah.
Elas? Ilus, Elias? Helios the Sun.

Aluzza the Arab Venus, Elousia (Diana),[13] Elissa the goddess Dido, Elis, Hellas (Greece).

Abram (Saturn), Bromius (Bacchus) the Sun. Abarim.

Obrimo,[14] Brimo a name of Hecate.

---

[1] Movers, 340.   [2] Weber Ind. Stud, i. 170.   [3] Gen. iv. 20.
[4] Donaldson's Varronianus, 163.   [5] Movers, 600, 615.   [6] Ibid. 627.
[7] Movers, 334, 335, 473; Job xxii. 28, xxxi. 26.
[8] Movers, 231.   [9] Wilson Rig Veda Sanhita, i. 247.
[10] Movers, 336, 431, 432, 434.   [11] Nonnus, xiv. 44.
[12] Seyffarth Grammar App. 80. Aruas, a son of Moses, Kurtz ii. 178. Arusei-us, a Roman; Tacitus, book vi. § xl. Ars-al-us, a Phœnician god; Movers, 19. Arah, 1 Chron. vii. Iaras-Iah; ibid. viii.
[13] Movers, 616.   [14] Rinck, i. p. xx.

Asan (Azan) Zan (Jupiter) Ζῆν, San, the Assyrian god, Ahan (Day in Sanskrit), the Gothic Sunna (Sun).

Zano (Juno), Asana the Spartan Minerva, Ahana (Aurora) in the Vedas, Sonne the German female Sun.

The Egyptian god Thore, a name of Ptah, the German god Thor (Thorr), Adar (Atar) the Assyrian Mars, Htore (Hator?) meaning "God" in Egyptian, Adar-melech the fire-god, Baal-Thureus.[1]

Hathor (Venus in Egypt), Terra the Earth-goddess, *Atar*gatis, *Tar*kat and Derketo, names of Venus.

Athro, an Assyrian-Persian goddess ; Thuro, a Phœnician name of Harmonia.

Asad, the god Seth, Sadi, Set, deity-names, "Sate god of light."[2]

Satis (Hera, Juno), Istia, 'Istia, Hestia, Eseet, Sit, Sito.

Amar, the Sun, "Day," Meri the sun, Mar (Dominus imbrium),[3] a Phœnician god. Mor-Iah.

Mer, an Egyptian goddess.[4]

Asak, the Sun, Osogo the Carian god,[5] "Suchos," a name of Mercury, the god *Sich*-ae-us.[6]

Zugia (Juno),[7] Siga (Athena,) a Phœnician goddess.[8]

Alor-us, the Babylonian god of light, Uller the son of Thor the Thunderer (a Scandinavian god).

Illuria (Illyria).
'Ilaira.

Hermaõn (Mercury),[9] Ahariman, Ahriman (Sol-Mars-Devil-Ophion), the god Rimmon.

Harmonia, the goddess.

Anan the Sun, Ninus the king or god, Noun (Water).

Nana (Venus), Nanaia.[10]

Assur the Sun, Surya,

Assyria the Earth.

Arad, the Sun, Iared, *Urot*-al (a name of Dionysus), Melk-*arth* (Moloch).

Erde the Earth, the Gothic Airthô the Earth-goddess, the Scandinavian Jörd the Earth-goddess, "*Arit*-imis," Artemis, names of Diana ; the German Earth-goddess Hertha.

---

[1] Movers, 25. [2] Seyffarth Gram. 40, App. 6. [3] Movers, 663.
[4] Bunsen, Egypt's Place, i. 410.
[6] Movers, 232, 616. [6] Ibid.
[7] Nonnus Dionys. xxxii 57. [8] Movers, 642.
[9] Nonnus, Dionys. x. 303 ; Josh. xii. 5. [10] Movers, 627.

Adam (Adar, Thor), Zeus-Dem-arus (Demarez), Athamas a god,[3] the sun-god Atumu, Atmu, Tom, Tumi, Re-Athom in Egypt, Thamus a name of Amon,[5] Thammuz (Adonis), Baal Tamar, Thamyras.[6]

Damia (Isis).[1] Demeter,[2] the Earth. Damia (Ceres) the Earth.[4]

Ad-Adam.

Diedumos, a Phrygian goddess.[7]

Adan, Adonis, Ethan a name of Baal.

Athena (Minerva) Tanais, Danae the Earth; [8] Diana, Earth-goddess; the goddess Than-ake (Tanais).[9]

Avan the Sun, Ven the Sun (in Sanskrit), the god Phanes in Phœnicia, the god Phaon, Evan a name of Bacchus,[10] Havan in Persia, Aban in Egypt, Oben-ra in Egypt, Pan the Sun. Bhanu, Sun in Sanskrit.

Vena the Moon (in Sanskrit), Avani, the Earth-goddess in Sanskrit,[11] Venus, the Earth-goddess.

Benoth (Abanad) a god.

Bendis (Artemis),[12] Pontus, a country.

Uran-us, Saturn.

Uran-ia, the celestial Venus.

Asar (Ahura) [13] Hor, Horus, the Sun, the God of light, In Coptic, hor="day."

Hera (Juno, queen of heaven), Sara the Moon in Syria and in Calmuck-Tartar.[13]

Azar, Saturn,

Azara.

Asher (Baal, the sun).

Ashera, Baal's goddess in Israel.[14]

Asis [15] (sun) Mars, Asas.

Saosis, Sais, goddesses, Ushas the Dawn; Sosa, a nymph united to Mercury.[16] Asis (Asia).

Adad (sun), Tat, Taut, Thoth.

Tit-aea, the Earth, Tethys, Thetis.

Silen-us

Selen-e, the moon.

Hephaestus (fire-god of Greece), Aphaistos in Pindar.

Vesta, Roman fire-goddess.

---

[1] Williams, Prim. Hist. 296; Gerhard i. 451.   [2] Kuhn Zeitschr. i. 468.
[3] Nonnus, v. 557, x. 78.   [4] Creuzer, iv. 380. 321.
[5] Rinck, Relig. der Hellenen. 164.   [6] Movers, 661.   [7] Movers, 570.
[8] Creuzer, iv. 242.   [9] Movers, 14.
[10] Eschenburg Manual, 436.   [11] Spiegel, Vend. 155.
[12] Rinck, i. 99.   [13] Bunsen, Hist. Phil. i. 356.
[14] Movers, 79; 2 Kings xxiii.   [15] Movers, 368.
[16] Nonnus, ed Marcellus, p. 126.

Apollo (sun),	Pallas.
Acar, Kur (the sun),	Cora, the Earth.
	Cer-es, goddess of corn, etc.
	Charis, wife of Vulcan.
Wodan,	Evadne.
Anakos, the sun,	The Egyptian Anuke, the Earth.
Inachus, "	
Samael (Moloch),	Semele, mother of Bacchus ; Earth.[1]
Nit (the Assyrian god),	Nut, " she who bears," Neith, Anata, Anta,[2] Egyptian war-goddess, Anaitis,
Dionysus *Amad*-ios,[3]	Amadia, Media, Mōt, chaotic matter,
Muth (Pluto),	Mouth (Isis).
Mirrich (Moloch),	Amorka,· Omorka, and Omoroka,
Mercur, Makar,	names of the Babylonian goddess Chaos.
Alad,[4] Ialda-Baoth,	Allât, Allitta, the Arabian Venus.
Lud, Lot, Ilita, (Agni),	Ilythia, the Greek goddess of birth.
Ebed, Abod, Japhet, Beth,	Buto,Baauthe,Baoth, Boeth (Venus),
Apat, Phut, Ptah, Aphthas, Iapetos.	Apt, an Egyptian goddess.[5]
Agni, Akan, Kan, Chōn, Kin.	Gnạ, Scandinavian goddess who floats about with the sun's rays.—Χνᾶ, Οχνᾶ ἡ Φοινίκη. Ken, Aigina.
Sabos, Seb (Saturn), Asaf, Sev, Ahab, Sabi,	Hebe. Saiva, an Arab goddess.
Elon (Sun, "the king"), Elioun, Elion (The Most High).	Luna, the Moon.
" Apellōn, the fighter."[6]	Bellona, goddess of war, the Armed Minerva of Homer.
Adak, Dachos, Tag, Dag, the Sun.	Dakia, the Earth, Dacia; Dauka, a
Adag-ous, a god of the Phrygians.[7]	Babylonian goddess.
	Attica, the Earth.

---

[1] Creuzer iv. 242.   [2] Bunsen, Egypt's Place, i. 410.

[3] Amada, Amittai, Hebrew priests, Amida a city in Eastern Asia Minor, the Maedi a Thracian tribe, Grote xii. 4 ; the Medes, Madai, Mata ("a Mede.")

[4] *Elat*-us, king of the Lapithae, father of Caiu-eus, grandfather of the Argonaut Coronos (Kronos = Saturn, Baal-z-ebub, god of Ekron); Eloth, a city, 1 Kings, ix. 26. Aluatt-es, *king* of Ludia. ALɒos (Zeus).

[5] Bunsen, ibid.   [6] Müller Dorians, ii. 6, § 6.   [7] Hesychius, in Movers. 668.

Asel (Sol), Usil, Helios

Hela, Scandinavian Hell goddess.

Huram,[1] Suram,[2] Hermes death-god, Surm-ubel, the god.

Sarama, Hindu death-goddess.

Asadan, Satan, the sun-god,[3] Iasdan (Ormuzd),

Stheno, a Gorgon.

Orpheus (Pharo, the Sun),

Eüruphaessa, wife of Hyperion ;

Iarbas (Apollo), Baal-Iarob,[4] Arab the god, Arba (Adam).

Europa the Earth-goddess. Eëriboia, wife of Aloeus.

Sarpedonius (Apollo),

Sarpedonia (Diana).[5]

Atal, Talus, the Sun in Crete, Tal the Assyrian god, Talaios in Crete, Atlas, Talos.[7]

Tholath (Isis,[6] Omorka), Tellus the Earth, Dalos the Isle De-los,[8] Italia, Aitolia (Aetolia).

Atab, Tobi the Sun (Ad-Ab) or Saturnus-Sol ; Davus, Divus, Dev, " the land of Tob,"[9] Tab Rimmon, Tob-Adon-Iaho, Tobi, an Egyptian month-god. Tuphöi.

Tupe (Typhe or Type), the Heaven, a goddess in Egypt; Neith-Pe, (Neith Urania).[10]

Papaios (Zeus in Scythia), Abib, Phoib-os (Phoebus), Ahobas (Abob) a name of Adonis) Apop and Apophis (names of Typhon) the Devil, Bab-el, the Sun, Babys-Typhon (compare Sut-Baba). •

Paphia (Venus), Aphaia (Diana), Apia (the Earth) in Scythia.

Am the Sun, Ham, Sam, Semo, Anam, Noum, a Phœnician god.

Humus the earth. Naama (Venus).[11]

Abar, Epure (a name of Apollo), Bar the Assyrian god, Bore in Egypt.

Pyrrha, Deucalion's wife.

Narayana (Vishnu the Sun), Nerio.

Neriene, wife of Mars.[12]

Achad the Sun ; Gad.

Hecate the Moon, the goddess Gad,[13] the goddess Cotys.[14]

Moloch   "

Melechet his goddess.

Isaac, Asac (the god of the Sacae, Scythians).

Succoth (Venus).[15]

Amanus the Sun,

Mana the Oscan goddess of birth.

---

[1] Movers, 506.   [2] Ibid. 505.
[3] Satnios, a warrior in Homer. Il. 14, 443.
[4] Movers, 398.   [5] Ibid. 17.   [6] Munter, 22, 40.
[7] Movers, 381.   [8] Pindar, Nem. i. 4.   [9] Judges, xi. 3.
[10] Uhlemann, Thoth. 37.
[11] Movers, 371, 205, 585, 576.
[13] Isaiah, lxv. 11.   [14] Gerhard, i. 112.   [12] Creuzer Symb. iii. 543.
                                                    [15] Movers, 484, 483.

Omanus, Amon,	Mena the Moon.[1]
Manes, Minos, Manu, Menes,	Meni the Babylonian Venus,[2]
Abōbas (Adonis),	Bub-astis (Bobasatis?) Isis, Satis the goddess.
Barad, Bharata the Aditya, Baal-Berith (Eljon), Berodach, "the god Berith,"[3] "Barat-os" in Sanchon.	Berouth (goddess of Elion), the Earth.[4]
Salam the Sun; Iahoh-Shalom,	Salama an Arab goddess, Salamis the Island, Salambo (Venus), Salem (Ierusalem).

The reader will find in the first part of the preceding table eight monosyllables, each a name of the Sun. As scholars have reduced ancient words used in ordinary conversation to one-syllable roots, it is reasonable to suppose that the same principle holds true as respects *proper names* generally.*

The following Hebrew (and other) names are supposed to contain deity-names. Shem, the sun-god, Shim-eah, Sem-ach-Iah, Shemuel (Shem and El, a name of Saturn and Sol), Samu-el, Sam-ael,[5] Semo an Italian god, Sem-Heracles[6] (Hercules the Sun),[7] Asom, a Hebrew name, ("Zom the powerful," the Egyptian god Hercules,[8] Smu a name of the god Typhon in Egypt.[9] Hercules is in the Sun and goes round with it.[10] Hercules was called Desan(us) in Phœnicia.[11] Odison, Idisan, and Disan are Hebrew proper names.[12] Beth-Shean (house of the god Shean or San), and מאן (San, Shan), are found,[13] Nib-shan (Nebo and San or Asan)[14] Azzan[15] Asana, a Hebrew name, Hassau a Turkish name, Bil-shan (the gods Bel and San), Sh-eshan (As-Asan), Sbuni[16] Ashan,[17] Nah-shon (Anos, or Anas, Nah, and Asan, Son, Shon, names of the Sun).[18] Shinar is As, An, Ar; or, the gods Asan and Anar=Onuris, Anerges, etc. Ieshim-on, Sim-on, Sim-eon, the Asm-on-ean dynasty, compare the Assemani, the people of Asaman or Saman (Baal), Esm-un (Apollo), (Sm-un=Osiris, Ammon, Ptah),[19] Aishbosheth (Asab-Aseth, the god),[20] M-ephibos-eth (Abib, Phœbus, Seth), בתואל Bethuel, the Syrian[21] El-beth-el, Shimi, Bal-Aam, Bal-Ak, Ibleam, Pel-Eg, Bash-an (the god Busi and An

---

* See my article on Ancient Names in the Christian Examiner for July, 1856, page 78, ff., also the Appendix of this volume.

[1] Pindar, Ol. 3.　　[2] Munter, 14; Isaiah lxv. 11.　　[3] Judges, ix. 46.

[4] Munk, Palestine, 89, 92; Movers, 575, 584.

[5] Movers, 397.　　[6] Creuzer, iv. 86.　　[7] Donaldson's Varronianus, 37.

[8] Uhlemann, Thoth 35; Zames the brother of the goddess Rhea.—Williams 248 quotes Cedrenus.　　[9] Plutarch, de Is. lxii.

[10] Plut. ibid. xli; Movers, 444.　　[11] Movers, 460.

[12] Geu. xxxvi. 21, 26.　　[13] Josh. xvii. 16.　　[14] Josh. xv. 62.

[15] Numb. xxxiv. 26.　　[16] Gen. xlvi. 16.　　[17] Josh. xv.

[18] Numb. vii.　　[19] Movers, 150.　　[20] 2 Sam. ii. 10.

[21] Gen. xxviii. 5.

the Sun),[1] Elon the Phœnician god, Elion the "Most High God," by whom
Abraham swears, Eln-*athan* (Bal-*adan*, Bel-*itan*=Baal), Ion-*athan*, N-*athan*,
N-*athane*-el, N-ethan-iah (compare Baal-*Ethan*),[2] Bil-*dad* (Bel-*Adad*), El*idad*,
El*dad*, Eth-Baal, Tub-Al, Teb-Al-iah, Eli-jah or El-iaho, Eli-El, Eleazar, Iedid-
Iah (Adad and Iah), Tob-iah, Ah-itob (Tobi, a month-god in Egypt), Tab-Rim-
mon,[3] a Damascene king, Tob-Adon-Iaho, Tubal-cain (Baal-chon, Vulcan,
Phulchan), Ierub-Abel (Baal-Iarob or Orpheus), Rub-ellius, a Roman, Amr-
aphel (Amar-Apel), Ash-Bel,[4] Baal-ah [5] (Allah), B-eal-Iah,[6] Bealoth, Baalath,[7]
Aliah, Azar-iah, Abi-Ezer, Ah-i-Melech, Ah-isham, Ah-imoth, Ah-iman (Amon)
Pela-iah, Bela, Amal-ak (the god Ag, Ach), Im-uel or Iem*uel*,[8] Ammiel, Miel,
the name of an angel,[9] the god Milcom (Mal-cham, a fire-god), Lem-uel, El-
am-uel, An-i-am[10] (the gods An or Ani, and "Iom=Day"), El-iam, Ah-iam;[11] Ah-
noam a Hebrew name, Noum (a Phœnician god), Naomi, the king Ab-iam,
Ab-Iah, Ada-Iah, Mor-Iah, Amar-Iaho,[12] Hav-il-ah, Obad-Iah, Shephat-Iaho,[*]
Shemar-iaho,[13] Nahum, Nehem-Iah, M-enah-em, Ier-iah, Ier-emi, Ier-em-iah,
Iar-m-uth,[14] Ramoth [15] (Ar or Ra, the Sun, and Amuth, Muth=Pluto) a city,
Shemir-amoth,[16] Aram, a Hebrew name ('Aram-es, Hermes?) Ram, a Hebrew
proper name, Hermei-as, a leader or king, Herm-*ot*-us, a city of Asia Minor,[17]
Herom-en-es,[18] the city Harm-ozica (Huram or Herm-es Asac), 'Ραμας, Ramas
a name of the Highest God in Phœnicia,[19] Ram-ah, Ram-iah,[20] Baal-Ram,[21] mount
Baal-Hermon, the mount of Hermaōn who is Hermes,[22] the Hermundorians,[23]
the god Hermon (a name of Mercury) and Adar (Thor); *Rem*-us a Roman god,
T-*urmieus* a name of Hermes; [24] Arm-amithres (Mithra the Sun),[25] *Rom*-ulus a
Roman god, Roma the city of Aram the god, Huram, a deity-name (Ophion),[26]
the Rhemi in Germany the children of Remus, the Aequi worshippers of Ako
(Ukko), the Decii in Rome having the name of Dak, Dag, Tag the Sun, the
Babylonian god Dach-os; Beth-H-aram,[27] Ram-athl-ehi, P-adan-Aram,[28] the
Arimoi, people of Aram [29] (Hermes), Rem-phan, a god,[30] (Phanes, Aban), Bas-
emath,[31] Pos-eidon, Bil-hah (Bel-ahah),[32] Al-ameth,[33] Ber-iah[34] (Bar and Iah),

---

[*] Iah-osha-phat, king of Judah. Hushai the Arch-ite, 2 Sam. xvii.

[1] Josh. xvii. compare *Ebus*-itan-us, Abas, Busi the god, Boaz, the Abas-
ians, Abassides, etc.

[2] Movers, 150.   [3] Ibid. 197.   [4] Numb. xxvi. 38.

[5] Josh. xv. 29.   [6] 1 Chron. xii. 5.   [7] Josh. xix.

[8] Gen. xlvi. 10.   [9] Williams, 326.   [10] 1 Chron. vii. 19.

[11] 2 Sam. xxiii.   [13] 2 Chron. xix. 11.   [12] 1 Chron. xii. 5.

[14] Josh. xii. 11.   [16] 1 Chron. vi.   [16] 1 Chron. xv. 18.

[17] Grote, xii.   [16] Ibid. ii. 517.   [19] Movers, 173.

[20] Ezra, x. 25.   RemAllaho, 2 Kings xv. 27.   [21] Movers, 173.

[22] Joshua, xii. 5; Nonnus, x. 303.   [23] Tac. xii. 29.

[24] Varronianus, 150.   [25] Movers, 337.   [26] Ibid. 506, 668.

[27] Josh. xiii. 27.   [28] Gen. xxv. 20.

[29] Crusius, Homeric Lex. 81.   [30] Acts vii. 43.   [31] 1 Kings, iv. 15.

[32] Gen. 29. 29.   [33] 1 Chron. viii. 36.   [34] 1 Chron. vii. 23.

Bena-iah, Iaaz-iah, Uzz-iah, Sadok, Zedek, the Most High God of Phœnicia, Zedek-iah, Zebad-iah (compare Dionysus-Sabadios), Azal-iah, Athal-iah, Onan, Ananias, Ch-enan-ah (the Phœnician god Canaan), Ch-enan-Iah, the god Chon, Cainan, the patriarch, Avan and Havan a Persian god, Aven, a Hebrew deity (Beth-aven), Iavan a Hebrew Patriarch, Evan (Bacchus),[1] Esh-ban, Hesh-bon, Ish-pan, Hebrew names, the Sabines in Italy, the As-ibun-oi[2] in Phœnicia, Art-apan-us,[3] the Assyrian proper name Neb-ushas-ban, Nebo, Ushas, the Sun, and Aban the Sun, Eben-ezer (a compound of Ahan ; the god Aban=Amon in Egypt),[4] the Sanskrit Bhanu the Sun, the Egyptian Oben-Ra[5] (said to be Am-mon-Ra), the sun-god Pan, the Mysian god Phanak (Phanax), the Phœnician god Phan-es, the Hebrew priest H-ophni,[6] the Campanian god Ebon (Bacchus-Ebon),[7] the god Phaon,[8] Phaon Nero's freedman, Aponius, a Roman, Art-aban-us, king of Parthia, the father of Orod-es; Herodes, Al-ban-ia, a river and town on the Caspian, a city of Media ; M-evan-ia, a city of ancient Italy, Evan, a name of Bacchus, Homer's Dam-ophoon, the Sanskrit Ven (the Sun), the Ahani an African people,[9] the Hebrew proper names Abin-adab, 1. Sam. xvi. 8, Shal-abin or Shal-abbin, Josh. xix., Re-uben, Ben-hadad, the son of the Sun (Aban-Hadad), Phan-ocl-es (Calus,Ucal, Iecol-iah), Hachilah, Keilah,[10] Asaf an Arabian god, Asaph a Hebrew name (Sabus, Sabi=Dionysus) Sh-aph-an, Sh-eban-iah ; the deity-name Baal-Zephon,[11] Zaphon, a city (Josh.xiii. 27), Zephan, El-zeph-an, Elizaphan, El-i-asaph, Ioseph, Ios-ibi-ah, Ios-iph-iah, Z-eph-an-iah, Van-iah, Vanas-pati (Agni). Iahin a king of Canaan, "Aban, named Gabriel," Anael, Raph-ael, Obnos an Egyptian king.[12] "And Jacob sent messengers be-fore him unto Esau his brother, unto the land of Sair, the country of Adom."[13] Countries were named after the gods there worshipped; Adam is the name Athamas, husband of the goddess Ino, Thomas, Didum-us (Adad and Am, or Ad-Adam.) Baal-Thamar, Tham-ur-us, the god Tham-us (Amon),[14] Thamus a Macedonian god,[15] the Hebrew god Thamm-uz (Adonis), Atm-an, the Hindu Soul of the World, the Sun ; Daimon="God" in Greek, Domin-(us) "Lord," Temen (Ataman), an Assyrian deity-name, and Temen-bar[16] L-aodam-as (El-Adamas) translated "subduer of the people," the L-aodok-os (El-Adachos the Babylonian deity Dachos), Dam-ocl-es, Iph-icl-es, the Odom-antians (Adam and Anat, Nid, Nit.) "The wise En-dum-ion (Ani the Sun, Adam and Ion) spouse

---

[1] Eschenburg, 426.

[2] Sanchoniathon, Wagenf. Γ. xvi.   [3] Movers, 125.

[4] Seyffarth, Grammar App. 60.

[5] Bunsen, Egypt's Place, i. 371 , Bononi, 78.

[6] 1 Sam. iv. 4.   [7] Movers, 373.   [8] Ibid. 227. Phan-odem-us.

[9] Lacroix, Hist. Numidie et Maur. 88.   [10] 1 Sam. xxiii. 12, 19.

[11] Movers, 175 ; Numb. 33—7.

[12] Seyffarth, Grammar, Pref. xxxiv.

[13] Gen. xxxii. 4.   [14] Rinck, i. 164, 224.   [15] Williams, 275.

[16] Rawlinson, in the Journ. of the Royal Asiat. Soc. xii. 427, 432.

7

of the Moon," [1] C-*adm*-us, a Phœnician god,[2] Athamas, king of Thebes, Adamas, son of the Trojan Asius,[3] Dumas, father of the Phrygian Asios,[4] *Autom*-edon, (Adam, Athom in Egypt; Adonis), Eur-*udam*-as (Aur, the fire, the Sun, and Adam), the Greeks twisted it into "the wide subduing; " Ph-Aidimos, king of the Sidonians, Iph-*idam*os in Homer, G-*atham*; "the city of Adam," [5] K-*edem*-oth (Ak, Adam, At, or Achad, and Muth), [6] R-emeth,[7] Amad,[8] Hamath, Amadios (Dionysus). Pindar [9] calls the Water-god Poseidon (the Sun) Dam-aios.[10] Damia is Demeter the Earth-goddess.[11] In Ezechiel (viii. 14) women bewail Tammuz (the Thammuz of the Septuagint), Thammuz is a name both of Adonis and a Syrian month.[12] We find Daim-ōn="God" in the Greek dramatists, and the proper names *Dem*-ad-es, Dem-ar-atus, *Dem*-oced-es (Adam, Achad), Iotham, king of Judah, Ram-*athaim*-zoph-im,[13] Chon-*odom*-ar-us, king of the Alamanni,[14] Rh-*adam*-anth-us, a god in Hades, *Autom*-edon (in Homer), Athamas, Eidam (Talaos),[15] S-*odom*, the Spartan king Arch-*idam*-us, Pol-*udam*-as, *Dam*-as, a rich Syracusan, *Dam*-on, *Tim*-on, Char-*idem*-us, *Dem*-ochar-es, Athenians, Di-*otim*-us, *Dem*-osthen-es (Adam, Asatan), D-*eidam*-eia, a princess of Epirus. Iesus, Ioses, Susi, Sosi-osh, Aseas, Oseas, Iosias, Az-iaho, Asas-el.

T-ub-al, T-eb-al-iah, Tubal-cain, Chon, Baal-chon, Vul-can, Tab-Erah,[16] Tobi an Egyptian month-god, Adoni-jah or (in Hebrew) Adoniaho, Tob-adoni-jah, Hebrew names, Beal-Iah, Id-al-iah, Ig-dal-iah, Tal the Sun in Crete, the Assyrian god Tal, Dal-os (Del-os) the island,[17] the Dol-ians, Aetol-ians and Ital-ia, Ash-tal,[18] Ash-taol,[19] Ham-utal, Athal-iah, Tal-mon, Zalmon the Ahohite, Amon, Hebrews, Tel-amon in Homer, Tola a Hebrew, Tellus the Athenian, Attalus king of Pergamus, Tullius, Thales, Atlas the god, Amalak, Moloch, Milichus, Adar-melech, An-amelech, fire-gods, the Amalek-ites, Az-emilchus, (Grote, xii.) Ar-*sam*es, Azaz, Azaz-Iah, Azaz-El, Ieho-ahaz, M-eshez-abel, Asahel, Sahil Sun, "the stone Ezel" Sol (1 Sam. xx.), Beth-Ezel, Azael a god.

The god Mars called M-amers, the Hebrew name Lah-mam, Maresh-ah, Mam-*erc*-us, a Roman, Amam, a Hebrew name. The Osi a German people.[20] Aor-si and Ador-si [21] the ancient *Dor*-ians (the Ador-ians), the Mar-si in Italy, the Mars-aci in Germany, Mar-abod-ius a king, (Mar and Obodas an Arab god), and the Mars-igni-ans in Germany, the Bur-ians, and Ans-*ibar*-ians,[22] Aper, the name of a Roman of rank, Bari a city of Apulia (anciently Bar-ium), Pharas-manes a German king, the Car-*aman*-ians a German tribe, the gods Bar and Adan in Assyria, the Danes, *Bar*itania (Britain), *Bar-dan*-es an Orien-

---

[1] Nonnus, xli. 379, xlviii. 668. [2] Movers, 513, ff. [3] Iliad. xii. 140.
[4] Iliad xvi. 718. [5] Joshua, iii. 16. [6] Josh. xiii. 18.
[7] Ibid. xix. [8] Ibid. [9] Pindar. Ol. xiii. 98.
[10] Kuhn, Zeitschr. i. 468. [11] Ibid.
[12] Movers, 195. [13] 1 Sam. i. 1. [14] Murphy, Tac. v. 336.
[15] Gerhard, Mythol. ii. 155. [16] Numb. xi. 3.
[17] Pindar, Isth. i. 4. [18] Judges, xviii. 2.
[19] Josh. xix. 41. [20] Tac. xliii. [21] Ibid. Book xii. §. xvi.
[22] Tac. xiii. §. lv.

tal, T-*uber*-o, a Roman, Epir-us in Greece, Purrh-us (Pyrrhus) a king. Ari-*obar*-zan-es, a noble Persian, Mithr-*obar*-zan-es, satrap of Kappadokia, (Mithra is the Sun), Rh-*omithr*-es, Sat-*ibar*-zanes, satrap of Aria, N-*abar*-zan-es, Bars-*aen*-t-es, a satrap, Phar-n*ab*-*az*-us, Art-*abaz*-us, satrap of Baktria, *Per*-seus the god, Par-menio (Abar-Aman), Per-*icl*-es (the gods Bar and Calus, or the god Agal), Per-*dikk*-as (the gods Bar and Dag), Bari (Bar-ium), a city of Italy, Pari-um, a city of Asia Minor, the kings Datt-*amithra*, *Mithr*-idat-es, and the proper name Sp-ithridates. Hazez-ont-amar, Nar-asan-sa, Idum-aea.

Adan, Adonis, the Edon-ians, K-udon-ians, the river Udon, M-adon,[1] the M-ak-edon-ians, Maked-ah,[2] L-usitan-ia, Shitan, Asarelah, Ieshar-elah,[3] Ar-tem-is, Ar-tem-idor-us, Ar-tem-bar-is, Abar-is, a Greek priest, Par-is, Iedid-iah, Adad, Hadad, Adadrimmon, Hadad-rimmon, Adad-ezer, Hadad-ezer, Hen-adad, Senn-acher-ib, Achor, Ereb-us, Ch-erob a Hebrew, Elib-oreph, Orpheus, Baal-Iarob, Reba, king of Midian,[4] Ierubb-ab-el, Abel, Azar-Iah, Hazar-Addar, Ami, Ammi, Ammi-Shaddai, Zur-ishaddai, El-shaddai, Asad an Arab god, Sodi a Hebrew proper name. (H)asad-iah,[5] the god Aseth or Seth, the Arab idol Sad,[6] Asad="lion" and the sign Leo. Zatha==Creator,[7] Zaota,[8] Zethos, son of Jupiter, Izad (God), Yezad==Hormuzd.[9] Abidan a Hebrew, Bedan,[10] Abyden-us, Ohed, Obed-iah, Obed-Adom(Abed-Adam),[11] Batt-us,[12] Potifar or Πετεφρὴς,[13] a compound of the gods Apat and Abar, or Afar, Far=="light," Pire, Phrē the Sun in Egypt, Ophir, Iephthah (Jephthah),[14] Aphthas or Phthah the Egyp-tian god Ptah, Petbab-Iah.[15] Phæth-ων, "shining," "bright," Φειδων a Greek name, the name of a town Alona ('Ηλωνη), Elon and Elion, the Highest god of Phœnicia and Israel, Alani, the Alans, Am-elon, "Ap-ellon (Apollo) the fighter," Ak-Elion==Geleōn, a name of Zeus, Ch-ilion,[16] Ilion (Troy), Dag the Sun, "Dagur whose horse illumines with his mane the Air and the Earth," Dakan (Dagōn the Sun), Dauc-alion (Deucalion), the Eteoc-retans, the Cretans, Iaanai a Hebrew,[17] Ani the Sun; Hushai,[18] Husi is Shemir the Sun: "In the first year of my reign I crossed the Upper Euphrates and ascended to the tribes who worshipped the god Husi" ("As," or Asas, Ahas);[19] Ishoi,[20] L-us-i-tania.

Iahaz-akal, Ses-ach, an Arab and Babylonian deity, Ez-ekiel. Evil-Merodach, king of Babylon, Beradach Bal adan[21] (compounded of the gods Bar, Amar, the Day-Sun, Adag, Dag or Tag the Day-Sun, Bal the Sun, and Adan, Adonis, the Sun); Nabuchadonosor (composed of the names of the gods An, Abach, or Baga, Adan, Assar), Nehuchadr-ezzar (Nebo, Achad, Adar,

---

[1] Josh. xii. 19.   [2] Ibid. x.   [3] I Chron. xxv.   [4] Numb. 31, 8.
[5] 1 Chron. iii. 20.   [6] Osiander in Zeitschr. der D. M. G. vii. 498.
[7] Haug in D. M. G. vii. 511.   [8] Spiegel, Vend. 127.
[9] Universal Hist. v. 158.   [10] 1 Sam. xii.   [11] 2 Sam. vi. 11.
[12] Beloe, Herod. iii. 42.   [13] Septuagint Version.   [14] Judg. xi. 34.
[15] 1 Chron. xxiv.   [16] Ruth i.   [17] 1 Chron. v. 12.
[18] I Kings iv. 16.   [19] Rawlinson, Journ. R. A. Soc. xii. 432.
[20] Gen. xlvi. 17.   [21] 2 Kings xx. 12. בראדך

Azar, or Asar), Nab-onad-ius, (the goddess Anata, the Eneti, the children of
the god Anad or "Nit,") Apar-anadisus (the gods Abar, Anad, As), Erigebalus,
(Erech and Abal), Rigebalus, Nirigasolasarus (the gods Nirrig, Asal, or Sol,
Assar), Niricasolassarus, Illoarudamus (the gods Alor-us and Adam), Saosdu-
chimus (the gods Asas, Adag, Am), or (As, Asad, and Chom, Acham), Meses-
imordacus (Am, Asis, Amar, Dag),[1] Sisimerdak, Amarames (Am, Armes—
Hermes, or Amar the Sun and Am the Sun),[2] Miriam (Amar, Mar, and Iam or
Iom the Day), Tig lath pil esar (Dach(os, Lot, Apol (Bil) Asar), Nergalsarezer
(Anar, Gall(us), Asar, Azar). Milcom (Amal-Chom=Apollo), Malcander
(Amel, Chon, Adar), Scamander (Asac, Aman, Adar), Sochi a city, Dam-asc-
us a city, the river Oski-us, Harm-ozica a city on the river Kur, Aesch-ines,
Isok-rat-es, orators, Rh-æssak-es,[3] the Assak-eni, a tribe on the Southern slope
of the Hindu Kush,[4] Akragines,[5] Solsicottos, Andra, Andracottos, Sandra-
cottos, Sosicottus,[6] Nic-odem-us, Anak-os, ἄναξ, Chush-an-r-ish-athaim a king,[7]
Com-bab (Adonis),[8] Babys-Typhon,[9] Abibal,[10] Cobab (Saturn),[11] Iobab.[12]

Pharao gives Joseph (the god Asaph or Asap) the illustrious name Zaph-
nath-paan-eah (Asaph, Anat, Pan, Iah) ; Osarsiph, an Egyptian name of Moses,
is Asar-Asaph. Compare the Usip-ii, a German people.[13] Resh-eph, Ram-ath
m-izp-eh (Aram, Baal-Ram, Atham or Adam, Azap or Asof, Ah or Iah),[14] Ked-
eshn-apht-ali, (Achad, Asan, Apat or Phut, Eli or Ali),[15] Ram-athaimzophim,[16]
Ichos-aphat (Iahoh-Phut or Aphthas), Kir-haraseth (Kur, Ahara or Ahura, Seth
or Aseth the deity),[17] Baal-Shal-isha,[18] Nit the Assyrian god, Nabo (Mercury).
Nabo-nid, an Assyrian name, the god Anebo,[19] Anab, a Hebrew name of a
place, Anebus, a Babylonian king,[20] Anubis the Egyptian deity, Anabesin-eus,
a proper name in Homer[21] (Anab-Asan), the Assyrian names Nab-urian, Nab-
uzar-adan, Nabon-assar, (Nab-on-assar), Nabo-nabo, Nab-ocol-assar, Shal-man-
esar, Sal-em, Ier-usal-em, Shelemiah, Meshelemiah, Jehoh-shalom (Ash-Alom)
"Jehovah-Peace"(?), Ulom, Lama, S-al-omo, Sal-omi, Shel-umi-el, Sal-mon,
Sal-m-unna, Ab-sal-om, Abishalom, Am-on, Ab-el, B-el, B-al, Evil, Phul, Awal,
B-aal-an, "Apellon," Anibal, N-abal a Hebrew, Hann-ibal, Baal-Chon, Vul-can,
Och-us and Bel-Ochus, Archal (Hercules), Ar-chil-ochus, Or-sil-ochus, An-til-
ochus, Asad (Mercury), Ş-et, S-eth, S-ut-pal-adan, Sardan-apal, Seb-pal-utak-ra
Sut-Baba, Iobab,[22] Sut-bel-herat, Babi-us a Babylonian king, Cinn-ereth, Ar-
odi, Arad[23] a Canaanite king, Addi, Baga-Sut, Sut-m-esitek, Sut-athr-asar-am,
Kat-ibar, Ari-el, Ari-obar-zan-es, the Hebrew names Shut-Elah (Numb. 26),

[1] Cory, Ancient Fragments, 79—83.		[2] Lepsius, Einleit. 368.
[3] Grote, Greece, xii.	[4] Ibid. xii. 225.	[5] Movers, 463.
[6] Ibid. 488, 489.	[7] Judges, iii. 10.	[9] Movers, 154.
[9] Ibid. 233.	[10] Ibid. 129.	[11] Ibid. 306.
[13] Gen. x. 29.	[13] Tac. Mores Germ. xxxii.	
[14] Josh. xiii.	[15] Judg. iv. 6.	[19] 1 Sam. I. 1.
[17] 2 Kings, iii. 25.	[18] 2 Kings iv. 42.	[19] Movers, 43.
[20] Williams, 249.	[21] Od. viii. 113.	[22] Gen. x. 29.
[23] Numb. xxxiii. 40.		

Abar-ban-el, Abr-avan-el, בּרע Bara,[1] בּרשׁא Bir-sha (Bar-Asha),[2] Adm-ah a district,[3] שׁמאבּר Shem-abar,[4] Bar-adod-os, Adod-os,[5] Nitit-paal, Nadit-abira, the Babylonian name Nidit-baal,[6] אזנותתבּור Az(a)noth(a)t-abor (Azan, Atat—Thoth, and Abar),[7] the Abors on the southern exposure of the Himmalaya,[8] the Avars in Russia, Pharo the Sun (Mithra), Far="light," "splendor," "lustre," "brilliancy." [9] Af(a)rica, "Var "=a heavenly sea in Persian, Var-kash, Aphar-eus (in Homer), Pur (πῦρ), "fire," in Greek, Afer the Roman (Terentius Afer), the river Var, Varus, Verres, Varro, Roman names, Avar-masta in Persia a name of Aura-masta,[10] the Ebur-on-es in Gaul, Bar-iana, north of the Euphrates, the god Bar (Abar), the names north of the Euphrates, Assar-ani-met, Sar-doch-æus, Bel-et-sira, the Babylonian Baal-at, and the As-syrian Assar, Assar-ac, Sar-gon, Chon, Achan,[11] Chion, Chaon, Chiun, Akan, Agni, Ignis, Kau, Dakan, Dagōn, Odacon, Attag-inus, Tal (the Sun), Tel-egon-us, in Homer, the Pel-agoni-ans (in Greece), the Pel-igni-ans (in Italy), the Eugan-eans (in Italy near Lake Garda),[12] Aigina (Aegina), the M-agn-esi-ans, Achan, Iecon-iah, Con-iah, Iconi-um, Philo's god Genos (Γένος), Chuns-Aah (Hercules in Egypt), Canaan the Phœnician god, the god Kan, "Chen-aan-ah," "Chenan-iah," Can-opus and Kn-eph, Egyptian gods, Ham, Ami, mount Hæ-mus, Am-am,[13] Aim(im),[14] Ahol-ibam-ah, Apom-uos (Zeus), Apamea a city, Hal-ubin-er-us north of the Euphrates, Aban, Pan, Iabin, the Ven-eti, Phanes, Iphinoos in Homer, Anata,[15] Anaitis, Neith, Nut, Ianthe, goddesses from As-syria and Asia Minor to Egypt; the Eneti, a people, Andi a district north of the Euphrates, Teut-at-es, a German deity, Teut-oBachus, king of the Cimbri,[16] Bacchus, a Roman deity, Hobal (Saturn), Shobal, a Hebrew, the Sabell-ians in Italy, Ash-bel, a Hebrew,[17] Soth-elah, Bag-ilah, an Arab tribe, the god Iar, Iour (in Sanchouiathon), Iair, Iairus, Iarah.

In Homer we have the names Ne-opt-olem-us (Ani, Apet or Phut, Elam), Ialmen-os, a proper name, "lumen," "light," Eumai-us (Iom, Am the Day, the Sun), Telamon in Homer, Talmon a Hebrew, Pelamon (Amon a Hebrew king), Iamenos a Trojan, (Iamin, a Hebrew), Eurum-edon, Eur-upul-os (Ar-bela), Memnōn the Sun (in Egypt), Ag-Amemnon, the god Atlas, Talus the Sun in Crete, Tal in Assyria, Talaos, king of Argos, father of Adrastus. Asmodius (Semo-deus, Shem-dius, As-Amadios), Shem-ida,[18] the Abyssinian king-names

---

[1] Gen. xiv. 2. [2] Ibid. [3] Ibid.
[4] Ibid. [5] Sanchoniathon, Δ. ii.
[6] Norris in the Journ. Royal Asiatic Soc. xv. 196.
[7] Josh. xix. 34. [8] Bunsen, Hist. Phil. i. 376.
[9] F. Johnson, Persian and Arabic Dict. Compare Pharah, Pharaoh.
[10] Journ. Royal Asiatic Soc. xv. 198.
[11] Josh. vii. 19. [12] Bunsen, Hist. Phil. i. 89.
[13] Josh. xv. 26. Iemima. [14] Gen. xiv. 5.
[15] Layard, Nineveh, ii. 211. [13] Tacitus, v. 388.
[17] Numb. xxvi. 38.
[18] Josh. xvii. ; Numb. xxvi. 32.

Al-Ameda, Ela-Amida, Del-naod, Anbasa-Udem, Udedem (Adad and Adam the Sun), Elaljon, Ela-Samara (Shemir the Sun), Ela-Auda (El and Aud, Ad).[1]

The translation of proper names by the common colloquial language of the country where the name is found is later than the period of the composition of the word. Thus Grotefend remarks " Although many Pelasgic deity-names have a Phœnician origin, yet they are generally so transformed to suit the pronunciation of the Greek language that they may also be translated by it, but in a different sense from the original." [2]

The usual translations given to the Hebrew and other oriental names are not to be taken as their *primitive* meaning, but as a *later* interpretation of them.

The sun-gods Ab, Ak, Am, Ar, As, Ad, El, An (On), Adag, Abel, Abak, Bacch or Baga, Amar, Asad, Sadi, Seth, Elon, Adan (Adonis), Abos, Ani, Amon, Nebo (Anab), Atal or Tal (Talus), Aban, Asar (Azar), Asam, Sam, Shem, Zom, Asab, Sabos, Sabi, Asaf, Asaph, Iah (As, Ias, Ah, Iah), Adad, Atat, Tat, Taut, Thoth, Asas, Abab (Abob, Obab), Apap, Epaph, Abel, Apel, Adam, Edom, Abam, Abar, Akar (Kur the Sun), Acal, Col, Cal (Calus), Asal, Ausel, Usil, Sal, Sol, Sel, Ahel, Helios, Elam, Ulom, Anam, Alad, Alar, Alor, Uller, Asan, San, Adar, Atar, Thor, etc., are the basis of the Old Testament nomenclature, and of that of the other nations extending from the Mediterranean sea to Bactria and India, Germany, Britain, Italy, Carthage, and Spain.

LANGUAGE IN ITS EARLIEST PERIOD.

" The *first appearance of language* is simple, artless, full of life, as the blood in the young body has rapid course. *All words are short, monosyllabic,* formed almost entirely with short vowels and simple consonants: the word material crowds itself quick and thick like blades of grass. . . . With every step, the loquacious language unfolds fulness and capability, but it works in the whole without measure and harmony. Its thoughts have nothing lasting, nothing steady ; therefore, this *earliest* language founds no monuments of the Spirit, and dies away like the happy lives of those oldest men without a trace in history. Numberless seeds are fallen into the soil, which make preparations in advance for *another* state of things."—Jacob Grimm, Ursprung der Sprache, p. 47.

The Chinese, the Mon, and other Oriental languages are monosyllabic ; so is the Ottomi in America.[3] In Hale's Dictionary of the Polynesian, the words

---

[1] Dillmann, in der Zeitschr. der D. M. G. vii. 341.
[2] Grotefend, in der Zeitschr. der D. M. G. viii. 811.
[3] Gallatin, in the Journ. of the Am. Ethnol. Soc. vol. i.

are with very few exceptions one and two syllables. Mr. Schoolcraft has observed, that, in the Chippewa, almost all the roots are of one or two syllables. It is not unlikely that this original tendency of language to express itself in short words, was at first assisted by the earliest alphabets, which were "syllabic,"[1] and this probably led the earliest grammarians to reduce words as much as they could, to one-syllable roots, as in the Sanskrit. According to Von Tschudi, agglutination is very marked in the Kechua (in Peru). Schoolcraft says of the principle of the American languages, "It is a fixed theory of language built on radices which retain the meaning of the *original* incremental *syllables.*"

[1] Lepsius, Zwei Sprachvergl. Abh. 23, 24, 25, 37, 67, 77. Norris, in the Journ. of the R. A. S. xv. 5, 47, 48, 49. Compare Bopp's Sanskrit Grammar, p. 3. Seyffarth, Grammar Aegypt. pref. p. vii., 11, etc. Uhlemann, Handbuch, 51, 70, 71, 120, 123, 124, ff. 131, 205. Sequoia Guess's Cherokee Syllabarium, Schoolcraft, part ii. 228.

CHAPTER IV.

FIRE-WORSHIP.

———— Τὴν γοῦν πάντα βόσκουσαν φλόγα
αἰδεῖσθ' ἄνακτος Ἡλίου.

SOPHOCLES, ŒD. TYRR. 1425.

Reverence the *flame* of the king Sun
That feedeth all things.

———————— The life-bearing fire descends
As far as the material channels.

CHALDEAN ORACLES. CORY, 258.

The fire-heated idea has the first rank,
For the mortal who approaches the Fire shall have light from God.

PROC. IN TIM. 65 ; CORY, 271.

SUN-WORSHIP and fire-worship were closely connected with the worship of the Great Spirit, from the Gulf of Mexico to Canada.[1] The fire-worship belongs to all the American tribes. The lighting the New Fire at the feast of "first fruits" was in honor of the Sun. It was observed by the Southern tribes at the beginning of the first new moon after the corn became full-eared. The old hearth or altar was dug up and removed from the sacred square. A new one was formed by order of the chief priest. For two days an unbroken fast was maintained. On the evening of the third day, as the sun began to decline, the fires were extinguished in every hut. The chief priest then kindled a fire by friction and placed it on the altar in the great circular

---

[1] J. Müller, 125.

temple amidst acclamations. This festival was celebrated annually in July or August. The Cherokees said the Master of Breath gave the festival to the Indians as necessary to their happiness.[1]

The Creeks also worshipped the fire.[2] The Delawares were given to fire-worship. The Iroquois yearly celebrated the *renewal of the fire*.[3] The Natchez worshipped fire in connection with the Sun-worship. In their Temple of the Sun the sacred fire burned continually.[4] In New Mexico the same custom obtained.[5] The Creeks, Cherokees, Choctaws and the tribes related to them worshipped Loakishtohoollo-aba the Great Holy Fire of the heavens. He is the author of warmth, light and all animal and vegetable life.[6] The Muyscas and Mexicans kept the festival of the New Fire in honor of the Sun.[7] The fires were extinguished in the temple and all the private dwellings of the Mexicans at the festival of Xiuteuctli, the god of fire. It was held in August.[8] Xiuteuctli, "Master of the year," "Lord of vegetation," is the Sun as father of the gods.[9] Pacha-camac, the Supreme Deity of the Peruvians, has his "fire-nature;" he is the life-inspiring Fire.[10] At the feet of the Mexican Tezcatlipoca are represented " a serpent and a heap of fire.[11] "

When the Mexicans built a new house they called in their friends and neighbors to witness the ceremony of lighting the New Fire.[12] At the close of their great cycle, the Mexicans lighted the New Fire at night by the friction of sticks when the constellation of the Pleiades reached the zenith. On the top of their Teocallis were two lofty altars on which fires were kept as inextinguishable as those of Vesta. There were said to be six hundred of these altars on smaller buildings within the great temple of Mexico, which, with those

[1] Squier, Serp. Symbol, 115.
[2] Serp. Symb. 68.
[3] Schoolcraft, Iroquois, 37, in J. Müller, 70.
[4] Charlevoix, Nouvelle France, vi. 173.
[5] J. Müller, 54, 55.
[6] Adair, 80, 19. Squier, Serp. Symb. 112.
[7] J. Müller, 54.
[8] Squier, ibid. 113.
[9] Ibid. 162.
[10] J. Müller, 320, 368.
[11] Codex Vatican, Lord Kingsborough, vi. 178.
[12] Serp. Symb. 118.

on the sacred edifices in other parts of the city, shed a brilliant illumination over its streets through the darkest night.[1]

And the altars of all our city-guarding gods, of those above and those below, gods of heaven and gods of the forum, are blazing with offerings: and in different directions different flames are streaming upward, high as heaven, drugged with the mild unadulterated cordials of pure unguent, with the royal cake brought from the inmost cells.[2]

It was their custom to pass new-born infants through the fire. At the festival of the god of fire, a human victim was first plunged in the flame and instantly withdrawn, to be sacrificed alive in the usual way by the knife.[3]

At the great Raimic festival which the Peruvians celebrated at the summer solstice, at the same time as the Cherokees, the fire used in the solemnities was given to the Inca priests by the hand of the Sun. The rays were concentrated in a focus, and cotton set on fire. When it was bad weather, they were obliged to obtain it by the friction of sticks. For three days previous there was a general fast, and no fire was lighted in the dwellings.[4] The sacred flame was intrusted to the care of the Virgins of the Sun; and if by any neglect it went out, the event was regarded as a calamity that boded disaster to the monarchy.

The Indian tribes burn tobacco instead of incense as a propitiation to the Sun. The fire in the temple of Vesta was renewed every year by fire produced from the rays of the sun.[5] The Romans had their Vestal Virgins who kept up the sacred flame, and there were virgin priestesses of the Assyrian Artemis.[7] Among the Greeks, human victims were offered to Dionysus (the Sun) as they were to the Hebrew Moloch.

---

[1] Prescott, Mexico, 72, 73.   [2] Æschylus, Agamemnon, 88–98.

[3] Mexique, 28.

The Peruvians sacrificed human beings, a child or beautiful maiden, on great occasions.—J. Müller, 103 ; Prescott, 105. A tribe of the Pawnees offered up human beings to the Great Star Venus.—J. Müller, 53.

[4] Perou, 372 ; Prescott, 104.   [5] Prescott, 107.

[6] Eschenburg, Manual, 429.   [7] Movers, 404.

Thou four-eyed Agni *blazest* as the protector of the worshipper.[1]

The fires being kindled, the two (priests stand by) sprinkling the clarified butter from the ladles, which they raise, and spreading the sacred grass (upon the altar).[2]

Agni, thine offering and thy glory and thy flames beam high.[3]

Blessed are ye holy men—in your sacred fires.[4]

The Vedas allegorically figure the Deity with a head of fire, and the sun and moon are his eyes.[5]

Homer, the Vedas, the laws of Manu and the Old Testament make frequent mention of fire-worship. The Sepharvites burned their children in fire to Adrammelech and Anammelech, the gods of Sepharvaim.[6]

Will Iahoh be pleased with thousands of rams, with ten thousand rivers of oil? *Shall I give my firstborn for my transgression,* the fruit of my body for the sin of my soul?[7]

And they have built the "High Places" of Tophet, which is in the valley of the son of Hinnom, *to burn their sons and their daughters in the fire;* which I commanded not, neither came it into my heart (saith the Lord).[8]

Manasseh "built again the high places which his father had broken down." And he caused his children to pass through the fire in the valley of the son of Hinnom. And he set a carved image, the idol which he had made, in the house of God ('Elohim).[9]

Manasseh set up an image of Jupiter with four faces in the temple at Jerusalem.[10] Movers, in speaking of the influence of the Phœnician religion on the Hebrews from the earliest times, says, " Jehova, here earlier adored as Moloch-Apis, was now Baal besides." [11] In Egypt the ox is sacred to Ptah, the god of fire, the Moloch or Great Spirit of the Egyptians.[12] A holy bull, called Apis, was kept in his temple and venerated.

Among the Old Israelites the image of Moloch was a

---

[1] Wilson, Rig. Veda, i. 82. [2] Wilson, ii. 278.

[3] Benfey, Samaveda, 294. [4] Nalas and Damayanti.

[5] Stevenson, Samaveda. [6] 2 Kings, xvii. 31.

[7] Micah, vi. 7. [8] Jeremiah, vii. 31, 32.

[9] 2 Chron. xxxiii. 3, 6, 7 ; Levit. ix. 24.

[10] Suidas (Manassēs), quoted by Movers, p. 542. B. C. 698–643.

[11] Movers, Phönizier, p. 9. [12] Duncker, i. 50.

statue with the head of an ox, in whose outstretched hands
children were laid and roasted by a fire heated in the idol.[1]
In Crete, Jupiter was represented in the form of a bull
(Minotaur), the same as in Persian and Egyptian symbolism.
The oxen of the sacred vessels of the Hebrew ceremonial
will not be forgotten. They constituted an important part
of the Hebrew symbolik. The idol of the Cretan sun-god
or Zeus Talaios (Talos was the name of the Sun) is compared by Böttiger to the image of Saturn in Carthage and
among the Old Israelites, in whose burning arms children
were laid, and to whom in Crete children were sacrificed.[2]
The Carthaginians anciently sacrificed to Saturn the children
of the first families of Carthage. While Agathocles besieged
the city they immolated two hundred children chosen from
the most illustrious families.[3] The story of Saturn devouring his own children is thought to refer to the practice of
offering children in the fire to this Saturn-Moloch.

Πῦρ δέσποτα ἔσθιε.

"Fire Lord, eat." [4]

"For Iahoh your God is a consuming fire."—Deut. iv. 24.

The Phœnicians in great misfortunes, in war, drought
or pestilence, offered up the best-loved child to Saturn.
The king of Moab was besieged in his city by the allied
armies of the kings of Samaria, Jerusalem and Adom, and
reduced to the last extremity. In vain he had attempted
a sally with seven hundred men for his preservation.
"Then he took his first-born son who would be king after
him and offered him up as a *burnt-offering upon the wall*"
(in sight of the besiegers). "And there was great wrath of
God against Israel; they marched off and returned to their
own land." [5]

---

[1] Beyr, Annot. ad Selden Syntagm. 256, Munter, Rel. der Karthager, 9, in
Movers, 379.

[2] Movers, 31.   [3] Carthage, p. 23, Univers pitt. Afrique.

[4] Maximus Tyrius, in Movers, 328.   Ezek. xvi. 20; xxiii. 37.

[5] 2 Kings, iii. 27.   Movers, 303.

The Phœnicians held that Cronos (Saturn) offered up his Only-Begotten son to his father Ouranos.[1] Abraham (a name of Saturn), in the Old Testament, prepares to offer up his only son as a burnt sacrifice to the Hebrew God.

I will destroy him out of the midst of his people, for of his seed has he given *to Moloch to defile my sanctuary.*[2]

We find El-imelech and Ah-imelech, names of Hebrews. The first is El (God) and Moloch; the second is Iah and Moloch. Elijah said, "Call ye on the name of your gods and I will call on the name of Iahoh: and the god that answereth by *fire* let him be God."[3] The Oriental God whom the Greeks name Dionysus, and who was first known to them through the Phœnicians (according to Herodotus), was originally Moloch, since the Arabian Dionysus-Urotal, with his fire-pillars, his sacrifices of men and children (the Libyan Dionysus Milichus with the ox-head), is no other than the fire-god. In Greece, the oldest Dionysus appeared as this fire and pillar god Moloch, to whom men and children were offered.[4] Offerings were made to Moloch as to a modification of the Tyrian sun-god on Baal's altars, where was earlier El, then Jehova the consuming Fire. The worship of Malach, or Moloch (compare Malach-Bel, Malachi, Malchi-El and Malchi-Jah) had in the most ancient period united itself with that of El-Saturnus.[5] Melech is Camus and Ariel; and is worshipped in conjunction with Bel-Saturn, the national god of the Semitic races.[6] Later, the Israelites swore by Jehovah and by Malcham (Moloch).[7]

The mountains quake at him and the hills melt and the earth is burned at his presence.[8]

The fire-god Ariel, worshipped by the Ammonites and Moabites, gave his name to Jerusalem, the Ariel! Ariel! of the prophet.[9] El eats up children, the Babylonian Bel-

---

[1] Sanchoniathon, Λ, vii.; Cory, 14.   [2] Levit. xx. 3.
[3] 1 Kings, xviii. 24.   [4] Movers, 372.   [5] Movers, 317, 324.
[6] Movers, 358.   [7] Zephaniah, i. 5.
[8] Nahum, i. 5.   [9] Movers, 323, 324, 337.

Mithra changes to Moloch, Sol to Typhon the consuming heat.[1] The Egyptians worshipped Typhon with the usages of the Moloch worship. The Greek Dionysus was originally the fire-god Moloch.[2] To the Tyrian Baal children were offered in the character of Moloch the devouring Fire. The same is true of the Tyrian Uso(v) (Mars), called by the Egyptians Chom and Moloch.[3] The old Phœnician and general Semitic chief deity, Bel-Saturn, assumes the character of Moloch; his worship is connected with fire-worship. The old Canaanite deity Moloch was worshipped in remotest antiquity by the Canaanite races settled in Egypt, and in conjunction with the national deity of the whole Semitic race, Bel-Saturn.[4] Baal and Moloch are the two sides of the same deity. The Carthaginian, Libyan and Greek Dionysus is this same fire-god Saturn-Moloch.

In Babylon the sun-god Bel was worshipped as the fire-god Moloch.[5] Moloch was the Sun.[6] Dionysus was both sun-god and fire-god. Baal-Ethan, Baal-Chon (Vulkān), is the Preserving, Baal-Adonis the Creative, and Baal-Moloch or Baal-Makar the Destroying Principle, according to Movers. These are Saturn, Sol, and Mars, Winter, Spring and Summer Sun; and are parts of the conception of Baal. Rinck says, " Hephaestus (Vulcan) seems to mean the Divine Breath which inspired the earth-clod with the fire of life, like that Dragon of Life, Chronos, who produced the egg of the world."[7]

The Virginians kept up a perpetual fire in their temples.[8]

I straightway essayed the divination by fire on the blazing altars.[9]

"The seer . . . revolving in ear and thoughts *without the use of fire.*"[10]

And the gods no longer accept from us the sacrificial prayer, nor the *flame* of the thighs.[11]

---

[1] Movers, 300, 301.   [2] Ibid. 372 ff.

[3] Movers, Cap. ix.   [4] Ibid.   [5] Movers, 299.

[6] Grotefend, Inscription of the last Assyrian Babylonian King, p. 28.

[7] Rinck, i. 67; Movers, 150.   [8] Serp. Symb. 128, 129.

[9] Antigone, 1010.   [10] Æschylus, Septem contra Thebas.

[11] Euripides, Ant. 1020.

And do the creatures of a day possess *bright fire?* [1]

There too is the fire-wielding DIVINITY the Titan (Sun) Prometheus.[2]

Saith the Lord ("Iahoh") whose *fire* is in Zion, and whose furnace in Jerusalem.[3]

These words (the ten commandments) the Lord spake unto all your assembly in the Mount, *out of the midst of the fire*, of the cloud and of the thick darkness, with a great voice. . . . And it came to pass, when ye heard the voice out of the midst of the darkness (for the mountain did burn with fire), that ye came near to me, all the heads of your tribes and your elders: And ye said, Behold, the Lord our God hath showed us his glory and his greatness, and we have heard his voice *out of the midst of the fire;* we have seen this day that God doth talk with man, and he liveth. Now, therefore, why should we die? For *this great Fire* will consume us: if we hear the voice of the Lord our God any more, then we shall die. For who is there of all flesh that hath heard the voice of the *living God* speaking out of the midst of the *fire*, as we have, and lived? [4]

And the sight of the glory of the Lord was like devouring *Fire*.[5]

Here is fire-worship (Moloch, the Destroying Fire) plainly enough. It is both fire-philosophy and fire-theology. It is the worship of the Divine Fire which is seen in Mexico, and among the Creeks and Cherokees in the United States; it is the Persian and Hindu fire-worship. It is the Divine Fire of Pythagoras and the Chaldean Oracles. Jah, the God to whom the blood was an offering (Leviticus), as it was in Egypt and Central America, is the El-Moloch, the Saturn-Malach of the ancients in his character of " God of Life,"—Adoni, Adōnis, Adoni*jah*, Malchi*El* and Malchijah. In his character of *Cause of life*, the bull (Apis), the twelve oxen of the "sacred sea," the cherubs are his symbolik; and the first-born "that openeth the womb" holy to him as his *sacrifice*. Moses sees God in the burning bush. The lower orders adhered to the Apis-worship while Moses was engaged in the fire-worship on the mount. "Jehova spoke to you in Horeb out of the midst of the fire." [6] "Did ever people hear the voice of God speaking out of the midst of

---

[1] Æschylus, Prom. Bound, 253.

[2] Sophocles, Œdip. Col. 55.

[3] Isa. xxxi. 9.

[4] Deut. v.; vi. 22–26.

[5] Ex. xxiv. 17.

[6] Deut. iv. 15.

the fire, as thou hast heard, and live." [1] "The Lord talked
with you face to face, in the Mount, out of the midst of the
fire." [2] "And the Lord said unto Moses, Take all the heads
of the people and hang them up before the Lord *against the
Sun*, that the fierce anger of the Lord may be turned away
from Israel." [3]

The Sun had his chariot in Cyprus, in Hierapolis, and in
the temple at Jerusalem; and the Rhodian Colossus corresponds on the one hand to the brazen statue of Sol-Talaios
in Crete to which human sacrifices were made, on the
other, to the idol of Moloch among the Carthaginians and to
the gigantic statue of Baal-Thureus in Babylon, mentioned
by Daniel, before which the sacred fire flamed and human
victims were offered amid the strains of a wild music. In
later times, in Rhodes as well as in Phœnicia, Egypt, and
other parts of Africa, on account of the summer heat, a man
was annually offered up to Saturn. [4] In Deuteronomy, the
Israelites were forbidden to let their children pass through
the fire to Moloch; but the fire ceremonial was continued
as carefully as in India, Persia, Assyria, or Babylon.
"Nadab and Abihu offered strange fire before the Lord,
which he commanded them not. And there went out fire
from Iahoh and devoured them." "And the fire upon the
altar shall be burning in it; it shall not be put out; and
the priest shall burn wood on it every morning, and lay the
burnt-offering in order upon it; and he shall burn thereon
the fat of the peace-offerings." "The fire shall ever be
burning upon the altar; it shall never go out." [5]

The Tyrian Baal or Hercules was worshipped as the
fire-god Moloch. On his altars the eternal fire was kept
up: irrestincta focis servant altaria flammæ, sed nulla ef-
figies, simulacrave nota Deorum. [6] "They keep altars of
flame with unextinguished fires, but no effigy or known
images of the gods." This is the "Sacra Herculis" carried

---

[1] Deut. iv. 33.   [2] Deut. v. 4.   [3] Numb. xxv. 4.
[4] Movers, 25.   [5] Levit. vi. 12, 13.   [6] Silius, iii. 30; in Movers 401.

from the Ariel of the temple at Tyre to the Tyrian colonies. "It is evident that in Tyre, in the temple of Heracles-Baalsamim, a perpetual fire was preserved, from the account of Herodotus that the emerald-pillars lighted the sanctuary at night, which is only supposable if the fire flamed upon the altar, and its glare was reflected by the pillar. The worship here was without an image." [1] The fire-worship in the Hercules temple at Gades was, according to the Phœnician custom, imageless.[2] Nothing but the pure fire as a symbol of the Divinity was used by the Assyrians at one period. So, in India, the fire on the altar is the symbol of Agni, the Fire-essence of the Hindu Soul of the World.

For ye saw *no manner of similitude* in the day when the Lord spake unto you in Horeb out of the midst of the fire.[3]

And the Lord spake unto you out of the midst of the fire: ye heard the voice of the words, *but saw no similitude*, only a voice.

These words the Lord spake unto all the assembly, in the mount, out of the midst of the fire.

The Lord talked with you face to face in the mount, out of the midst of the fire.

For who is there of all flesh that hath heard the voice of the living God speaking out of the midst of the fire as we have, and lived?

For it came to pass, when the flame went up towards heaven from off the altar, that the Angel of the Lord ascended in the flame of the altar . . . .

And Manoah said unto his wife, We shall surely die, because we have seen God.

Astrochitón Heracles, King of fire, Chorus-leader of the world, Sun, Shepherd of mortal life, who castest long shadows, riding spirally the whole heaven with burning disk, rolling the twelve-monthed year the son of Time, thou performest orbit after orbit. Nonnus, xl. 369.

The Assyrian armies were always accompanied by the Magi carrying the Fire, the visible presence of the Deity, in which the idols of the conquered nations were consumed. Smoke or fire pillars preceded the Assyrian armies;[4] and in the exodus from Egypt the Lord went before the Israelites "a cloud by day and a pillar of fire by night." "In the

---

[1] Movers, 401.   [2] Movers, 76.   [3] Deut. iv. 15.
[4] Movers, 70, 339, 340; Isaiah, xiv. 13, 31; Jer. i. 13, 14, 15.

daytime also he led them with a cloud, and all the night
with a light of *fire*."[1]   Nergal-Sarezer, the Chaldean chief
of the Magi (Rab Mag), accompanied the Chaldean armies.[2]

Agni, "the Divine Fire," the Hindu deity, is the Sun;[3]
fire and sun being the same.[4]   The sun's heat or fire is as
prominent as light in its influence upon Nature, as a cause
of life.   Hence, while the American Indians are almost
universally sun-worshippers, they worship also the creative
power of fire.   The phrase "Sun my Creator" occurs in the
prayers of the Cherokees.[5]   The fire is to the Persian the
visible symbol of Ormuzd ; the more brilliant, so much the
purer and more deserving of worship.   Ormuzd is Light.
Where fire is, there is light, and, therefore, Ormuzd is in
the fire.[6]

The Assyrian and Persian coins have flaming fire-altars
upon them.   The fire ceremonial among the American Indians was performed by the inhabitants of the cabins at the
lighting of the New Fire.   It was the same in Peru and
Mexico.   In ancient Italy the head of the family performed
the functions of priest.   It was the same anciently among
the Vedic peoples who dwelt upon the Indus.   At the
same time, we find a *high priest* in Mexico, in Peru, among
the southern tribes of the United States,[7] as well as in
Rome, Assyria, Babylon (Rab Mag), and at Jerusalem,
whose office was to preside over the public celebration of
religious rites.   It is said that the Old Canaanites had no
order of priesthood, except where the worship of the fire-god
Moloch existed.[8]   A deity whose idea (image) is the pure,
holy fire, cannot be approached by common men : he requires a priest-caste.   "Now, therefore, why should we die?
for this Great Fire will consume us: . . . for who of all

[1] Ps. lxvii., 14 ; Ex. xiii. 21.   [2] Movers, 70.
[3] Wilson, Rig Veda Sanhita, ii. 143.   [4] Wilson, ii. 133.
[5] Serp. Symb. 68 ; see J. Müller, 108, 116, 117.
[6] Ersch and Gruber, Lex. 329.   [7] Adair, 19, 81.
[8] Movers, 358—360.

flesh has heard the voice of the living Elohim speaking out of the midst of the fire, as we have, and lived."[1]

Ye shall kindle no FIRE throughout your habitations on the Sabbath day.[2]

The Ojibway Indians kept the sacred fire always burning.[3] In Sanskrit, As means "life ;" in Hebrew, Aesh means fire. An Ojibway addressed Tanner thus : In future let no more the fire in thy hut go out. In summer and winter, by day and by night, in storm and calm weather, thou wilt remember that the life in thy body and the fire upon thy hearth are one and the same thing. Let thy fire go out, and at once thy life is extinguished.[4]

> Yea, the *light* of the wicked shall be put out.
> And the *spark of his fire* shall not shine. (Job xviii. 5.)

The same Spirit ("Purusha") which is in the Sun rests also in the heart.[5]

Agni, as Yama, is all that is born ; as Yama, all that will be born.

"Although a man is risen to pursue thee and to seek thy soul, yet the soul of my lord shall be bound in the bundle of the living with Jahoh, thy Elohi (thy God) ; and the soul of thine enemies shall he sling out in the middle of the hollow of a sling.[6]

In living beings slumbers the God (First Cause) under the name Purusha, and under the form of the living soul.[7] In the Hindu philosophy, "The souls issue from the Soul of the World and return to it as sparks to the fire."[8] The Sun is the soul of all things ; all has proceeded out of it, and will return to it.[9]

Man is born unto trouble as the sparks fly upward.[10]

Saturn dwells in the seventh heaven, in a high, well guarded castle, the type of the tower of Babel.[11] He is,

[1] Deut. v. 23, 24, 25, 26.
[2] Exod. xxxv. 3.   [3] J. Müller, 55.
[4] Ibid.   [5] Wuttke, ii. 312 ; Maitraj Upanishad.
[6] 1 Samuel, 25—29. See Movers, 180.
[7] Bhagavat Purana, vii. 14, 37, 38, Wuttke, ii. 328.
[8] Duncker, vol. 2, page 162.   [9] Wuttke, ii. 262.
[10] Job, v. 7.   [11] Movers, 154, 259.

therefore, among the Phœnicians and Chaldeans like Jao (Jah) called "He who is over the seven heavens," just as the Jews related that God had his throne in the seventh heaven in a castle of fire. The book of Henoch says, "I strode forwards until I came to a wall built of stones of crystal. A trembling flame surrounded it which began to inspire me with dread. Into this trembling flame I trod and approached a spacious abode which was also built of crystal. The walls and the pavement were of crystal, as was also the foundation. Its roof had the look of stars moving with impetuosity and with shining lightnings, and under them were cherubs of fire. A flame burned round about the walls, and their portal blazed with fire. As I entered this abode, it was hot as fire and cold as ice.

"And lo! there was *another* spacious dwelling, whose every entrance stood open before me, erected in a trembling flame. Its pavement was of fire, above were lightnings and moving stars, while its roof showed a blazing fire. Attentively I regarded it, that it contained an elevated throne, in appearance like the ring while its circuit resembled the circle of the radiant sun. Below, streams of burning fire poured out from this mighty stream; to look on it was impossible. One Great in glory sat thereon, his garment more brilliant than the sun and whiter than snow. No angel could penetrate to look upon his countenance the Glorious and Beaming. Also could no mortal look upon him. A fire glared round about him. A fire also of great compass mounted continually up from him, so that no one of those about him could approach him among the myriads in his presence.'

Ezechiel and Daniel give the personality of God in a manner that irresistibly leads one to think of the description of Saturn's castle of flame in the seventh heaven. "And I looked, and behold a whirlwind came out of the north, *a great cloud and a fire infolding itself, and a*

' Book of Henoch, 14, v. 10 ff.; Movers, 260.

brightness was about it, and out of the midst thereof as the color of amber, out of the midst of the fire . .. And above the firmament (of the color of the terrible crystal that was over their (the cherubim) heads was the likeness of a throne, as the appearance of a sapphire stone: and upon the likeness of the throne was the likeness as the appearance of a man above upon it. And I saw as the color of amber, as the appearance of fire round about within it; from the appearance of his loins even upward: and from the appearance of his loins even downward, I saw as it were the appearance of fire and it had brightness round about it." [1] "The Ancient of days did sit, whose garment was white as snow, and the hair of his head like the pure wool; his throne the fiery flame, his wheels, burning fire. A fiery stream issued and came forth from before him; thousand thousands ministered unto him, and ten thousand times ten thousand stood before him." [2]

---

[1] Ezechiel i., 4, 22, 26, 27.　　　[2] Daniel, vii. 9. 10.

CHAPTER V.

LIGHT.

The Oumas, a tribe affiliated to the Natchez, believed that the Supreme Being resides in the Sun, and that he deserves to be revered in that vivifying orb as the *Author of Nature*. The Creeks and all the tribes visited by Bartram seemed to believe in a Supreme God or Creator of whom the sun was the recognised symbol. He was called by names which signify "*the All-pervading Spirit*," the Giver and Taker away of breath, the Soul and Governor of the Universe.[1] The Indians of the Upper Orinoco worship a being "who regulates the seasons and the harvest," the office of the Celestial Sun.[2] In Mexico, the heroes who fell in battle or in sacrifice passed at once into the presence of the Sun, whom they accompanied in his bright progress through the heavens. The Mexican heaven was made up of *light*, &c. "The wicked" (comprehending the greater part of mankind) were to expiate their sins in a place of everlasting *darkness*.[3] A remarkable festival was celebrated at the termination of the great cycle of fifty-two years when the sun was to be effaced from the heavens, the human

[1] Serp. Symb. 153.
[2] Ibid. quotes Humboldt, Personal Nar. 273.
[3] Prescott, i. 62, 63.

race from the earth, and the darkness ot chaos was to settle on the world. "The cycle ended in the latter part of December; and, as the dreary season of the winter solstice approached, and the diminished light of day gave melancholy presage of its speedy extinction, their apprehensions increased. On the arrival of the five "unlucky" days which closed the year, they abandoned themselves to despair. They broke in pieces the little images of their household gods in whom they no longer trusted. The holy fires were suffered to go out in the temples, and none were lighted in their own dwellings." On the evening of the last day a procession of priests moved to a mountain two leagues from the capital, carrying with them a victim for the sacrifice, and an apparatus for kindling the New Fire. At midnight, when the constellation of the Pleiades approached the Zenith, the New Fire was kindled by the friction of the sticks placed on the wounded breast of the victim. As the light streamed up to heaven, shouts of joy and triumph burst forth from the countless multitudes who covered the hills, the terraces of the temples, and the housetops, with eyes anxiously bent on the mount of sacrifice. Couriers with torches lighted at the blazing beacon, rapidly bore them over every part of the country; and the cheering element was seen brightening on altar and hearth-stone, for the circuit of many a league, long before the Sun, rising on his accustomed track, gave assurance that a new cycle had commenced its march, and that the laws of nature were not to be reversed for the Aztecs." [1]

The Phœnician and Chaldean worship of Baal and all the host of heaven, the astral worship among the Toltecs and the Peruvian adoration of the Sun, Moon, and the brilliant host of stars as dispensers of light, heat and life, [2] point to the worship of Light. The Creeks, Cherokees, Choctaws &c. worshipped the Supreme Holy Spirit of Fire who resides

---

[1] Prescott, i. 126, 127.　　　　[2] Mexique, 367.

above the clouds, and on earth amongst unpolluted people. He is the author of warmth, light, and all animal and vegetable life.[1]

The Peruvians determined the period of the equinoxes by the help of a solitary pillar or gnomon placed in the centre of a circle which was described in the area of the great temple, and traversed by a diameter that was drawn from east to west. When the shadows were scarcely visible under the noontide rays of the sun, they said that "the god sat with all his light upon the column."[2]

In the Edda, the stars are sparks of fire out of Muspellheim the world of fire and light.[3]

In Mexico, we find the adoration of the Morning Light. Tlavizcalpantecutli was the god of Morning or of the Light, when the sign of the morning twilight or the crepusculum arises, which they say was created before the sun.[4] Tlaviz-calpantecutli is the star Venus, the first created light before the deluge. They say that it was fire, or a star: it was created before the Sun. He is god of the Morning (Lucifer), when it begins to dawn. He is also the Lord of the Twilight on the approach of Night. It was properly the first light which appeared in the world.[5]

Ushas, daughter of heaven, diffuser of light ... at thy rising the soaring birds no longer suspend their flight.

Auspicious Ushas has harnessed (her vehicles) from afar, *above the rising of the Sun:* and she comes gloriously upon man with a hundred chariots (of light).

Bringer of good she lights up the world.

Inasmuch, bringer of good, as thou dawnest, the breath and life of all rest in thee: diffuser of light, come to us with thy spacious car; ... Ushas since thou hast to-day set open the two gates of heaven with light.

Ushas come by auspicious ways from above "the bright," of the firmament: let the purple cows (=clouds, the vehicles of the morning) bring thee to the dwelling of the offerer of the Somajuice.[6]

[1] Serp. Symb. 112.

[2] Prescott's Peru, i. p. 126.

[3] Grimm, Deutsch. Myth. ii. 685.

[4] Cod. Vat. Lord Kingsbor. vi. 204.

[5] Cod. Telleriano Remensis, ibid. vi. 126.

[6] Wilson, Rik Veda.

Thou, Ushas, dispersing the darkness, illuminest the shining universe with thy rays.

Her brilliant light is first seen towards (the east); it spreads and disperses the thick darkness: she anoints her beauty as the priests anoint the sacrificial food in sacrifices: the daughter of the sky awaits the glorious sun.

Aswins, who have sent adorable light from heaven to man, bring us strength.

Ushas, endowed with truth, who art the sister of Bhaga, the sister of Varuna, be thou hymned first:

Mother of the gods, rival of Aditi, illuminator of the sacrifice, Mighty Ushas, shine forth; approving of our prayer, dawn upon us.

Unimpeding divine rites, although wearing away the ages of mankind, the Dawn shines the similitude of the (mornings) that have passed, or that are to be, forever; the *first* of those that are to come . . . .

Born in the eastern quarter of the spacious firmament, she displays a banner of rays of light. Placed on the lap of both parents (Heaven and Earth) filling them (with radiance), she enjoys vast and wide-spread renown.

She goes to the west as (a woman who has) no brother, to her male relatives; and like one ascending the hall (of justice) for the recovery of property: and, like a wife desirous to please her husband, Ushas puts on becoming attire, and smiling as it were, displays her charms . . .

Ushas, dispersing the darkness with the rays of the sun, illumines the world like congregated lightnings.

Of all these sisters who have gone before, a successor daily follows the one that has preceded. So may new dawns like the old, bringing fortunate days, shine upon us with blessed affluence . . .

This youthful (Ushas) approaches from the east: she harnesses her team of purple oxen. Assuredly she will disperse the darkness, a manifest sign (of day) in the firmament: the (sacred) fire is kindled in every dwelling.[1]

The Deity being regarded as the purest Light, received the name of the planet Saturn.[2]

In the eighth century after Christ, the Mahavira Cheritra, a Hindu drama by Bhavabhuti, opens with an address to the Supreme Light, the One and indivisible, pure, eternal and invariable God.[3]

White-shining Agni who is possessed of manifold light, the extinguisher of the dawn.[4]

The golden-haired Agni is the agitator of the clouds when the rain is

[1] Wilson, Rigv. i. 237, 239, 129, 130, 131; ii. 8; i. 300; ii. 10, 13.
[2] Movers, Phön. 271, 317.   [3] Wilson's Hindu Drama, 325.
[4] Wilson, Rigv hymn 69.

poured forth, and, moving with the swiftness of the wind, shines with a bright radiance.[1]

The *thousand-eyed*, all-beholding Agni drives away the Rakshas.[2]

Dissipate the concealing darkness; show us the light we look for.[3]

The divine Savitri travels by an upward and by a downward path: deserving adoration, he journeys with two white horses: he comes hither from a distance, removing all sins.

His white-footed coursers, harnessed to his car with a golden yoke, have manifested light to mankind. Men and all the regions are ever in the presence of the divine Savitri.

Three are the spheres; two are in the proximity of Savitri, one leads men to the dwelling of Yama.

The gold-handed, all-beholding Savitri travels between the two regions of heaven and earth, dispels diseases, approaches the sun, and overspreads the sky with gloom, alternating radiance.[4]

The regal Varuna of pure vigor, (abiding) in the baseless (firmament), sustains on high a heap of light, the rays are pointed downwards, while their base is above; may they become concentrated in us as the *sources of existence*.

Thou who art possessed of Wisdom shinest over heaven and earth and all the world.[5]

Indra's heaven is illuminated by a light a thousand times more brilliant than that of the sun.[6] In the Old Arian religion, the light had its abode *not in the regions of Air*, but *beyond*, in the illimitable space of Heaven. It is not united with the Sun, but independent of him—*an eternal power*. Between this world of light and the earth lies the realm of Air, in which deities govern, in order to keep clear the path of the light to earth, and to assist the running of the heavenly waters which also have their home in the world of light.[7]

Where is the way where the light dwelleth? and darkness, where is the place thereof?

That thou shouldst know the path to the house thereof. (Job xxxviii. 19, 20.)

I form the light, I create the darkness. (Isaiah xlv. 7.)

Thou makest darkness, and it is night.

---

[1] Wilson, i. 402.　　　　　　　　　　[2] Ibid. 204.

[3] Ibid. 223.　　　　　　　　　　　　[4] Wilson, 98, 99.

[5] Ibid. 62, 67.　　　　　　　　　　　[6] Inde, 196.

[7] Roth, Die höchsten Götter der arischen Völker.

Who covereth himself with Light as with a garment.[1]

O Æther, that diffusest thy common Light![2]

This eternal and unapproachable in which the Adityas rest and of which their essence is composed, is the heavenly light. Like the effulgent Æther of the old Greek nature-philosophy, which Aristotle says the ancients prior to his time regarded as something *Divine in its nature*, this Light fills the space of heaven and is *the* life-giving principle which Creation possesses. The Adityas, the gods of this Light, are by no means the same as the heavenly bodies; they are neither sun nor moon, nor stars, nor the morning dawn, but, as it were behind all these visible appearances, the eternal carriers of this Light-vitality.[3]

But do thou, O heaven-born Light, restrain her.　Euripides, Medea, 1257.

King Agamemnon is come, bringing a light in darkness.　Æschylus, Agamemnon, 523.

And the glory of the God of Israel came from the way of the east, and the earth shined with his glory.[4]

God came from Teman and the Holy One from Paran. Selah!

His glory covered the heavens ... And his brightness was as the light ... Before him went the pestilence, and burning coals went forth at his feet.[5]

The Sun and Moon stood still in their *habitations:* at the sight of thine arrows they went and at the shining of thy glittering spear.[6]

Ἐκεῖ γὰρ ὁ ἡλιακὸς κόσμος καὶ τὸ ὅλον φῶς.

For there is the sunworld and the entire light.[7]

And the light dwelleth with him.[8]

Out of Zion the perfection of beauty God hath shined.[9]

The Lord is my light and my salvation.[10]

The Lord came from Sinai and rose up from Seir (Oseir-is) unto them; he shined forth from mount Paran, and he came with ten thousands of saints.[11]

In the later invocations of the Persians is found: "I

[1] Ps. 104.　　　　　　　　[2] Prometheus Bound, 1095.

[3] Roth, Ibid.　　　　　　　[4] Ezech. 43, 2.

[5] Habakkuk, iii. 3, 4, 5.　At the feet of Tezcatlipoca, a serpent and heap of fire were represented.

[6] Ibid. iii.　　　　　　　　[7] Procl. in Tim. 264; Cory, 266.

[8] Daniel, ii. 22.　　[9] Ps. l. 2.　　　[10] Ps. 27.

[11] Deut. 33, 2. Ail-Paran, Gen. xiv. 6. Compare Varna, the Varani, Varuna.

praise the Creator Ahura-mazda the shining." "I praise the Holy Word the very shining!"[1]

> O Jove, our Sire, blast by thy thunderbolt. Thine invincible arrows also,
> O Lord of Light, from the golden-twisted horns of thy bow.[2]
>
> Through the brightness before him were coals of fire kindled.
> Jehovah thundered from heaven and Eliōn uttered his voice.
> And he sent out arrows and scattered them; lightning and discomfited them.[3]
>
> God of the silver[4] bow who with thy power
> Encirclest Chrysa, and who reign'st supreme
> In Tenedos and Cilla the divine,
> Sminthian Apollo! If I e'er adorn'd
> Thy beauteous fane, or on thy altar burned
> The fat[5] acceptable of bulls or goats,
> Grant my petition .... The god
> Down from Olympus[6] with his radiant bow
> And his full quiver o'er his shoulder slung
> Marched in his anger ....
> Gloomy he came as night; sat from the ships
> Apart and sent an arrow ...
> Mules first and dogs he struck, but at themselves
> Dispatching soon his bitter arrows keen,
> Smote them. Death piles on all sides blazed.
> Nine days throughout the camp his arrows flew.—Cowper, Iliad.

The punishments of Varuna are especially sickness and death. The power over these was later given over to Yama. Thus the restless play of the mythus may be traced for centuries.[7]

> Light excelleth darkness.[8]
> While the Sun, or the Light, or the Moon, or the Stars be not darkened.[9]

[1] Duncker, ii. 359; Spiegel, Vendidad, p. 246, 263.

[2] Sophocles, Œd. Tyr. 202. Transl. Buckley.

[3] 2 Sam. xxii.; Ps. xviii. 4.

[4] "of the golden bow," in Pindar, Ol. xiv.

[5] πίονα μηρία; All fat is the Lord's. Levit. iii. 16. Elapol, 1 Chr. viii. 12.

[6] "The *Mount of Assembly* in the furthest sides of the north. Isaiah xiv. 13.

[7] Roth, Zeitschr. der D. M. G. vol. 4; ibid. Die höchsten Götter der arischen Völker.

[8] Eccl. ii. 13.   [9] Eccl. xii. 2.

The Lord is my light![1]
Light is sown for the righteous.[2]
For with Thee is the fountain of life; in thy light shall we see light.[3]

In Babylon the feast of the sun-god was probably celebrated on the first day of the week; for the division into weeks in honor of the Planets was common to the Babylonians, Egyptians, Carthaginians and other ancient nations. The seventh day among the Egyptians and Chaldeans was sacred to Phainōn (the Everlasting, Saturn).[4] The Persian religion and the Hindu Vedas and the Egyptian division into *seven* chief deities are so many additional proofs how wide spread was the notion of Light descending in seven rays to or through the sun, moon and five great planets. The seven Amshaspands of Persia and the Adityas of India have the names of sun-gods. "Next the throne of Ahura-mazda are placed six spirits who sit on golden thrones like himself. They are called the good rulers, the wise, the holy immortals." They are the archangels of the Bible.

The Egyptian Pimander says: "He has then formed seven agents who keep the material world in the circles."[5] "We know from Dion Cassius that the custom of assigning a day of the week to the Sun, Moon and Planets arose in Egypt, where the number seven was held in great reverence."[6] The week was a most ancient division of time taken from the four quarters of the moon. The days were early named after the planets in India, Egypt and Greece. The Therachites had this division; and the account of the Creation in the Bible is written according to it.[7] Among the ancient Egyptians the hierogrammat was required to understand the order of the Sun, Moon and the five

---

[1] Ps. 27. 1.   [2] Ps. 97. 11.
[3] Ps. 37. 9.
[4] Munter, Bab. 66 ; quotes Lydus de Mensibus, 25.
[5] Champollion, Egypte, 141 ; See Lepsius, Berlin. Ak. 1851.
[6] Kenrick, i. 283.   [7] Friedlander, 111, 112.

Planets.[1] The Babylonians worshipped these as superior to the twelve Great Gods. The Jews and Chaldeans believed in seven heavens. Layard says that " the seven disks " on the Assyrian monuments " are the seven great heavenly bodies."

According to the Babylonian philosophy, the divine influence descended from the sphere of light in seven rays in the Sun, Moon and five Planets. These seven planet deities received adoration as the sacred seven highest gods ; and the sacredness of the number remained long after these gods had become archangels, and had waned in the regard of the Hebrews. In Exodus xxv. and Numbers viii. we find a candlestick with seven lamps. In Zachariah we have " a candlestick with seven lamps," and a " stone with seven eyes." "They are the eyes of the Lord which run to and fro throughout the whole earth."[2]

The Egyptian religion was closely connected with the worship of the stars. Upon their sculptures appear figures of personified stars or Spirits of the Stars (a man with a huge star in his middle). All this is found again among the Chaldees. The Sabian idea is that the world is an intermediate kingdom between the realms of light and darkness, ruled by the spirits of the twelve Zodical signs, and the seven (the Sun, Moon, and five Planets).[3] According to the learning of the Egyptians the nature of God is fire, and its first immediate emanation is the ineffable Light, that spiritualized, pure Light, which, in the philosophy of Babylon, was regarded as the First Cause of all things and called " the Father " ($\pi\alpha\tau\dot{\eta}\rho$).

In the Hindu philosophy, the First Cause (Tad) opened his eyes out of which sprung a brilliance of light, and from this light came the sun.[4] Brahma, by whom all

---

[1] Kenrick, i. 276.   [2] Zach. iii. iv ; 2 Chron. xvi. 9.

[3] Gesenius, Jesaia ii. 335, 529.

[4] Wuttke, ii. 295. Thou hast prepared the Light and the Sun.—Ps. 74, 16.

things receive light, who lets the sun and stars shine with his light.[1] The Light was to the reflecting minds of antiquity something higher, subtler, purer, nobler, than the orbs or beings whose essence it was. It was regarded as the *First Light*—the First Cause of all Light, of which the Sun was a *secondary* cause, an inferior agent receiving his powers from the Supreme Light of all light.

"Ἥλιον Θεὸν μέγιστον ἀνέφηνεν ἐξ ἑαυτοῦ πάντα ὅμοιον ἑαυτῷ.[2]

The Sun, the Greatest God, he uttered out from himself, in all things like himself.

The doctrine of the emanation of all creation out of the Godhead is one of the oldest theories of Religion. It is found in all ancient religions in which Sabaism was prominent. Hence all these religions were Light-religions; for the human mind could only picture the Deity to itself as the *purest light*. Not merely the corporeal world, but the world of spirits were considered emanations of the Godhead. Hence the Chaldean must believe the soul to be immortal.[3] The defunct is seen in the Egyptian representations addressing a prayer to the God of Light coming from heaven, whose eyes illumine the material world and dissipate the darkness of the night. In the picture which follows this prayer, souls and men are depicted adoring a luminous disk.[4]

From the sphere of light, the divine influence (Light) descended in seven rays, in the Sun, Moon and five Planets. Iao of the Chaldeans was the Ἑπτάκτις, the seven-rayed God.

In it (the Word) was life, and the *Life* was the *Light* of men.[5]

" He (John) was not the Light, but came to bear witness of the Light. The true Light was that which lighteth every man that cometh into the world."

It was in the world, and the *world was made through it*. And the Light shineth in Darkness, and the Darkness perceived it not.[6]

[1] Wuttke, ii. 324. [2] Julian. [3] Munter, Babylonier, 88. [4] Egypte, Univers pitt. 125. [5] John, i. [6] Ibid.

We have followed mankind in their advance from the worship of the powers of nature and spirits up to a Great Spirit, the Supreme Being whose symbol is the holy fire. While in the preceding chapter *Fire* was "*the life,*" in this "*the Light* is *the Life* of men."

I am the Light of the world.[1]

In the Creed, Christ is called "Light of Light, very God of very God," to denote his con-substance with "the Father." The Word (Logos), the Father and the Holy Spirit have one essence—Light!

[1] John, ix. 5.

CHAPTER VI.

COSMOGONY.

Here dwelt men whom kindred Aiōn saw, sole contemporaries of an eternal world.—NONNUS xl. 430, 431.

IN Florida Aguar was worshipped as the Creator of all things, who dwelt in the heaven whence the water and all good things come.[1]

The Hindus regarded the Sun as the source both of water and light. "From the Sun comes rain."[2] "The Sun pours out water."[3] "The waters are collected in the Sun."[4]

Tanunapat whom the deities Mitra, Varuna, and Agni worship daily thrice a day, render this our sacred rain-engendering sacrifice productive of water.

Those waters which are contiguous to the Sun, and those with which the Sun is associated be propitious to our rite.

I invoke for our protection the Celestial, well-winged, swift-moving, majestic (Sun) who is the *germ of the waters*, the displayer of herbs, the cherisher of lakes, replenishing the ponds with rain.

Agni abiding in the waters......Agni immortal sustainer of the universe...... manifested, as it were, in the womb of the waters.[5]

Jove rained all night.[6]

Iahoh sits king upon the floods.[7]
He waters the hills from his chambers.
Who lays the beams of his chambers in the waters.—Ps. 104.
    "He thrones in the water.

---

[1] Nunez, quoted by J. Müller, 119.   [2] Wuttke, ii. 347.   [3] Ibid. 265.
[4] Wilson, Rigv. i. 57.   [5] Ibid. i. 57; ii. 144; i. 58, 119, 177.
[6] Odyssey, xiv. 457.   [7] Ps. xxix.   [8] Wuttke, ii. 266.

> I would look to El
> And to Elohim commit my cause;
> Who gives rain upon the earth,
> And sends water upon the fields.—Job v. 7, 10.[1]

Covered with watery drops in the heavens and shining with the light of the water-collecting (Sun). Stevenson, Samaveda, p. 278.

All the starry worlds are considered as spirits and gods which have emanated from the original Light, the central Sun of Spirit, the Persian Light-water, Arduisir.[2]

".Descend, O Soma, with that stream with which thou lightedst up the sun; do thou descend and send *water* for the use of man. Become to us the Purifier of the mind, thou that art manifested in a thousand streams."—Stevenson, Samaveda, pp. 188, 224.

Soma, a Life-ocean spread through All, thou fillest creative the sun with beams.[3]

They have termed the five-footed twelve-formed parent Purishin (the Sun as the source of rain).

The even-fellied, undecaying wheel, repeatedly revolves: ten, united on the upper surface, bear (the world): the orb of the Sun proceeds invested with water, and in it are all beings deposited.—Wilson Rigv. II. 129—131.[4]

The smooth-gliding wafters (of the rain, the solar rays) clothing the waters with a dark cloud ascend to heaven: they come down again from the dwelling of the rain and immediately the earth is moistened with water.—Wilson Rigv. II. 143.

The ancients regarded Light as independent of the sun.[5] In the first chapter of Genesis, the light begins three days before the sun is created. Aurora brings the light to immortals and to men.[6]

By what way is the LIGHT parted, the east wind scattered over the earth?—Job, xxxviii. 24.

---

[1] Schmid; Noyes.

[2] Encycl. Americana, vi. 567. Ardisur or Arduisur is the Persian angel of the waters.

[3] Wuttke, ii. 349.   [4] Purisha, " water;" the five feet are the five seasons.

[5] Movers, passim; Roth, Die höchsten Götter der arischen Völker.

[6] Odyssey v. 1.

The winds were the children of Eos.[1] They were thought to begin to blow at sunrise.[2]

Where is the abode of LIGHT, and DARKNESS, where is its dwelling place?

That thou shouldst take it to the bound thereof, and that thou shouldst know the paths to the house thereof?—Job xxxviii. 19, 20.

The sun set and DARKNESS came on.—Odyssey III. 329.

With clouds he covers the LIGHT and commands it not to shine.—Job xxxvi. 29, 30, 32.

And I (Minerva) alone of gods know the keys to the abodes *in which the thunder is sealed up!*—Æschylus, Eum. 827, 828.

Thou didst call in trouble and I delivered thee:

I answered thee *in the secret place of the thunder!*—Ps. 81, 7.

When he made a decree for the rain and a way for the lightning of thunder.

Who has divided a watercourse for the overflowing of waters, or a way for the lightning of thunder?—Job, xxxviii. 25, 26.

Tlaloc, the chief of the rain-gods, and Quiateot, the rain-god in Nicaragua and Mexico, were gods of the thunder and lightning, like Zeus, Jupiter, and Indra.[3]

When the first chapter of Genesis was written, the world was supposed to have been created out of water.[4] Thales considered that all things were formed out of water.[5] It was the first form of primitive matter.

For thy Almighty hand that made the world of formless Matter.—The Wisdom of Solomon, xi. 17.

Later, we find in the Jewish and Egyptian writings, and in St. Paul, the idea of a creation out of nothing.[6]

God calleth things not in being as though they were.—Hebrews, xi. 3; Rom. iv. 17.

The American Indians speak of the earth as firm land in contrast to Water, which is the original element, and existed before the earth.[7] They believed that the heaven

---

[1] Rinck i. 47 ; Hesiod, Theog. 378.

[2] Rinck i. 50.   [3] J. Muller, 496, 500.

[4] Gen. i. 2, 6, 8, 9, 10.   [5] Ritter Hist. Phil. i. 199.

[5] See 2 Maccabees, vii. 28.   [7] J. Müller, 108.

above was the counterpart of the earth with its hills and plains.[1] The Egyptian Book of the Dead reads: "I who have confirmed my land above the heaven."[2] The ancients placed the palaces of the gods overhead on each side of the Milky Way.[3] It was the old opinion that the heaven was solid, framed of brass.[4]

But the Sun having left the very beauteous sea, rose upwards into the *brazen* heaven.[5]

The hard heaven spread out like a molten mirror.—Job, xxxvii. 18.

There is one who hath lighted the lamps of heaven ; One who hath woven the star-covered path (the Milky Way) for his servants the (walking) statues in the house of the Most Holy One; who hath lighted the heavenly lamps for you; who hath woven the star-covered path for you; that is the Most Holy One, your Sovereign![6]

I am the Weaver of the Heavenly Firmament which is the place where walk the mighty gods; I am the Weaver of the lovely carpets which surround the heavenly dwellings. I am the exalted Creator God.[7]

Atlas supports *the heaven* on his shoulders.

And Earth first produced the starry Heaven equal to herself
That it might enclose all things around herself.[8]

And Elohim said, Let there be an expansion in the midst of the waters, and let it *divide the waters from the waters*.—Gen. i.

And Elohim made the firmament, and divided the waters under the firmament from the waters above the firmament.[9]

It is supported on pillars and foundations.—Job, xxvi. 11. It has windows and doors.—Ps. lxxviii. 23; Knobel, Gen. 12.

If I shut up heaven that there be no rain.—2 Chron. vii.

For who can stay the bottles of heaven?—Job, xxxviii. 24.

In the realms of Air are fountains, streams, seas. Trita (Varuna) is the Waterborn in the distant waters of heaven;

---

[1] Schoolcraft, Algic Res. [2] Seyffarth Theolog. Schriften, 13.
[3] Ovid, i. 13, 14; ed. Bohn. [4] Buckley, Transl. Odyssey, 28.
[5] Odyssey, iii. 1. [6] Seyffarth Theolog. Schr. 9 ; Ibid. Chronology, 66.
[7] Ibid, Computationssystem, 135. [8] Hesiod, Theog. 116. [9] Gen. i. 7.

and as the Winds are born there, he enters among the wind gods.[1]

Praise him ye heavens of heavens, and *ye waters that be above the heavens.*[2]
Or who shut up the Sea with doors when it brake forth as if it had issued out of the womb?
When I made the cloud the garment thereof (that is, of the great sea in heaven) and thick darkness a swaddling band for it.[3]

The American Indians have an idea of a sea above.[4] The Persians had their Var, a heavenly sea (Varkash).

The Jove-replenished river.—Odyss. viii. 284.

The Nile and Ganges have their sources in heaven.[5] Plutarch calls the Nile the "outflowing of Osiris." Osiris is the Sun.[6] Osiris is the " Creative Intellect" called Amon.[7] Osiris is the Celestial Nile.[8] The Celestial Nile is called Hap and Oceanus.[9] Ap the Sun in Italy, Egypt, &c., is Ap "water" in Sanskrit. The sun-god Apis (Osiris) is Hap the Nile. Hap is father of the gods.[10] Nero, Anar, is the Sun; Nereus, the old water-god. Varuna, Saturn, having the sun as his eye, is also god of the waters. Bar, or Abar, the Sun, is the River Var, and Vari "water," in Sanskrit. The waters of heaven were diffused by the seven solar rays and the seven rivers.[11] Oceanus is "father of the gods," according to Homer. Ogenos, Ogēn, or Ocean-us, is Akan, Agni, the Sun and water-god.

Associated in the firmament with the moving waters, he assumes an excellent and lustrous form.
He causes the waters to flow in a torrent through the sky, and with those pure waves he inundates the earth.[12]

---

[1] Zeitschr. der D. M. G. ii. 225.
[2] Ps. cxlviii. 4.   [3] Job, xxxviii. 8, 9.   [4] J. Müller, 139.
[5] Wilson, Rigv. i. 248, 249; Duncker, ii. 370.
[6] Kenrick's Egypt, i. 300, 302, 352, 331, 332; Diog. Laert. Proem, 12.
[7] Kenrick, i. 303; Cory, 283.   [8] Champollion, Egypte, 132.
[9] Ibid.; Plut. de Is. xxxiv.
[10] Seyffarth, Theol. Schriften, 36.
[11] Wilson, Rigv. i. 192; ii. 129.   [12] Ibid. i. 249,250.

The germ of many waters he issues from the ocean.[1]

He (Agni) is like a horse urged to a charge in battle, and like flowing waters ; who can arrest him ?

He breathes amidst the waters like a sitting swan ; awakened at the dawn, he restores by his operations consciousness to men; he is a creator like Soma; born from the waters like an animal with coiled up limbs, he became enlarged, and his light (spread) afar.[2]

The gods have placed in this world the delightful Agni in a delightful chariot, the tawny-hued Vaiswanara, the sitter in the waters, the omniscient, the all-pervading, the endowed with energies, the cherisher, the illustrious.[3]

The waters saw thee, O God, the waters saw thee : they were afraid: the depths also were troubled.

The clouds poured out water : the skies sent out a sound : thine arrows also went abroad.

The voice of thy thunder was in the heaven : the lightnings lightened the world : the earth trembled and shook.

Thy way is in the sea, and thy path in "the Great waters," and thy footsteps are not known.—Ps. lxxvii. 16, 17, 18, 19.

The Dogribs and Chippewyans believed that the earth was originally covered with water.[4] It was an ancient opinion that the earth floated in the midst of the waters.[5] The Great Sea surrounded the whole earth. In this all-circling stream of Heaven and the Great Deep the sun-god pursued his way.

Thou visitest the earth and waterest it: thou greatly enrichest it: the RIVER OF GOD IS FULL OF WATER.—Ps. lxv. 9.

"The bark (of the Sun) navigates upon the ocean of heaven, the Aether, which runs like a river from east to west, where it forms a vast basin in which a branch of the river terminates that traverses the inferior hemisphere from west to east."[6]

Beneath the wide-wayed earth flows a branch (keras) of Ocean from the sacred river through black night.—Hesiod, Theog. 786.

[1] Wilson, Rigv. i. 248.   [2] Ibid. ii. 178.   [3] Ibid. ii. 328.
[4] J. Müller, 121.   [5] Ritter, Hist. Phil. i. 199.
[6] Champollion, Egypte, 104.

The Sun also ariseth and the Sun goeth down and hasteth to his place where he arose.—Eccles. i. 5.

He went under the earth by water, and hence was represented with the tail of a fish. His goddess, Aphrodite (Venus), was said to have sprung from the foam of the sea.

To him that stretched out the earth above the waters.[1]

For He hath founded it upon the seas, and established it upon the floods.[2]

Who laid the foundations of the earth that it should not be removed for ever.

Thou didst cover it with the Deep as with a garment: the waters stood above the mountains.

At thy rebuke they fled; at the voice of thy thunder they hasted away.

They go up by the mountains; they go down by the valleys unto the place which thou hast founded for them.

Thou hast set a bound that they may not pass over; that they turn not again to cover the earth.[3]

Unto the place from whence the rivers come, thither they return again.[4]

The ancients believed that Ocean rolls round the whole earth in his unslumbering stream.

Father Ocean that is eddying round the whole earth.[5]

    Circumfluus humor

    Ultima possedit, solidumque coercuit orbem.[6]

With this agrees the passage in Proverbs:

When he prepared the heavens, I was present;

When he *described a circle on the face of the deep;*

When he disposed the atmosphere above;

When he established the fountains of the deep;

When he published his decree to the sea,

That the waters should not pass their bound.[7]

In accordance with this view of the earth as "a circle described on the face of the deep," Homer represents Oce-

---

[1] Ps. cxxxvi. 6.   [2] Ps. xxiv. 2.   [3] Ps. civ. 5–9.   [4] Ecclesiastes, i. 7.

[5] Æschylus, Prometheus, 138–140.   [6] Ovid, Met., 26, 37.

[7] Proverbs, viii. 27–30.—Lowth.

anus as an immense stream encircling the earth from which
the different seas ran out as bays. On the shield of Achilles
the poet represents Oceanus as encircling the rim.

In the ancient cosmogonies the gods form a part of creation. Hence they, with the earth, were once beneath the
mass of waters.

> This great (universe) the Ruler Soma has brought forth, when the Water's
> bosom as yet conceals the gods.—Benfey, Samaveda, 239.

The Egyptian cosmogonies let the gods arise with the world
in the process of its self-formation.[1]

> The race of the immortals was not till Eros mingled all things together;
> But when the elements were mixed with one another
> Heaven was produced and Ocean and Earth and the imperishable race of
>   the blessed gods.[2]

The Babylonians believed that all was originally a watery
chaos.[3] The Hindus said that Brahma created the waters first. "He thought I will let worlds issue from me:
and he let them issue; Water, Light, Perishable Matter, and
the Waters. Water was above the heaven which carries it.
The circle of the air encloses the light, the earth contains
the perishable, and in the deep are the waters."[4] In the
Cosmogony in Manu, "He, the Invisible, the Unfolded, the
Eternal the Soul of all beings, the Inconceivable, streamed
forth in light. He *first* created the Waters."[5] In Genesis,
the Spirit of God moved on the face of the waters.

The Algonquin tribes state that when Michabu made the
earth out of a grain of sand, this displeased the god of the
waters and he refused his assistance. The Mingos had the
same legend.[6] The opposition of water to creation appears
in the numerous flood-legends on the continent which have
no historical, but only a cosmogonial signification—creation

---

[1] Knobel's Gen., 5.   [2] Aristophanes, Aves, 770.
[3] Munter, 37.   [4] Wuttke, ii. 295.   [5] Ibid. 300.
[6] J. Müller, 111.

in spite of the water.[1] The sun-god in America was considered opposed to the watery element. He is Creator wherever the water precedes the Creation.[2] The creation of the earth is regarded as the work of the Creator or Great Spirit, as First Man or sun-god, or in some other shape.[3] The water is the original element, and is represented as opposing the creation of the earth.[4] In the Phœnician flood-mythus, Pontus (the Sea) overcomes Demarus (Adam-Aras; Tamo, the lord of the sun-city),[5] the sun-god or Creator. In the Egyptian myth, Typhon (the Devil) is the Sea.[6] In other cases Typhon is the Evil Principle generally, Moloch the Destroying Fire.

All was originally water.[7] From the hostility of the water a flood occurs, and *a second Creation* takes place.[8] According to a myth of the Canadians, a new earth is made by a second Creator, Messou.[9] New men were created after the Flood, or animals were turned into men. One account says individuals were preserved from the Flood. A dog prophesies the Flood among the Cherokees, a fish among the Hindus. According to the Babylonians, El, the chief god, warns Xisuthrus of the Flood. Noah's name is wanting in the first list of patriarchs.[10] His name (if not Enoch's) is found in Iconium in Asia Minor, where Annakos announces the Flood with useless warning.[11]

The Egyptians tell a myth that, on the *seventeenth day of the month*, Osiris died, which day the *full moon* is most evident. And at the so-called *obsequies of Osiris*, cutting the wood they prepare an ark in the shape of the crescent, because the moon when it is near the sun, becoming crescent-shaped, is concealed.—Plutarch, de Iside, xlii.

On the new moon of the month of Phamenoth (from February 25 to March

[1] J. Müller, 112.   [2] Ibid. 118.   [3] Ibid. 111.
[4] Ibid. 111, 112.   [5] Seyffarth's Computationssystem, 200, 128.
[6] Nonnus, ii. 439; Seyffarth's Chronology, 118.
[7] J. Müller, 111.   [8] Ibid. 112.
[9] Hazard, 437; in J. Müller, 112, who gives many illustrations of this idea amongst the Indians.
[10] Gen. iv. 24.   [11] Bunsen, "Aegyptens Stelle," book v. parts 4, 5, p. 64.

27) they celebrate a festival called the *ingress of Osiris into the* Moon, being the beginning of spring.—Plutarch, de Iside, xliii.

In the six hundredth year of Noah's life, in the second month, *the seventeenth day of the month*, the same day were all the fountains of the Great Deep broken up, and the windows of heaven were opened.[1]

The fountains also of the Deep and the windows of heaven were stopped, and the rain from heaven was restrained.

And the Ark rested in the seventh month, on the seventeenth day of the month (Phamenoth) on the mountains of Ararat.

And the waters decreased continually until the tenth month.[2]

Plutarch says that on the *seventeenth of Athur* in which month Sol passes through Scorpio, Typhon put Osiris in the ark, in the 28th year of the reign of Osiris.[3] Hesiod also mentions the Flood in the time of the Silver Race of mankind :

For a hundred years a boy was reared and grew up beside his wise mother in her house, being quite childish. . . . . Them indeed afterwards Zeus Son of Kronos *buried in his wrath*, because they gave not due honors to the Blessed Gods who occupy Olympus. Now, when earth had ingulfed this race also, they *under the earth* are called Blessed Mortals, second in rank to the gods. But still honor attends these also.—Hesiod, Works and Days, 122 ff.

" Xisuthrus," or " Sisuthrus," is the Sun in the sign of the Waterman in the Zodiac.[4]   He is the lunar Saturn.[5] He is a bisex deity, and regarded as Semiramis.[6]

In the reign of Xisuthrus, tenth King of Babylon, there was a great flood.   Saturn (Kronos) appeared in a dream to Xisuthrus and informed him that mankind would be destroyed by a flood on the 15th of the month Däsios.   He ordered him to write down all the human knowledge and science, and bury it in the city of the Sun called Sipparis,[7] then to build a ship and enter it with his companions, relations, and nearest friends ; to take food to eat and to drink,

---

[1] Gen. vii. 11.   [2] Gen. viii. 2, 4.

[3] De Iside, xviii.

[4] Movers, 165, 589, 634, 384, 645.   [5] Ibid. 674, 164.   [6] Ibid. 674.

[7] Sepharvaim lay on the Euphrates where it separates into two arms, and is probably the city of the Sun, Sippara.—Munter, 27.

and fowls and animals with him; if he was asked where he was going, to say, " to the gods, to entreat grace for men." He built the ship as commanded, five stadia long and two broad. He sends out birds, which, after being sent a third time, did not return. He leaves the ship, *prays to the Earth*, and offers to the gods, and then, with his wife, daughter, and steersman suddenly disappears, but calls to his companions out of the Aether to lead a pious life. They are taken up to dwell with the gods on account of their piety.[1]

After the Flood had been upon the earth and was in time abated, Xisuthrus sent out birds from the vessel, which not finding any food nor any place where they might rest their feet, returned to him again. After an interval of some days he sent them forth a second time, and they now returned with their feet tinged with mud. He made trial a third time with these birds, and they returned to him no more. He therefore made an opening in the vessel, and upon looking out found that it was stranded upon the side of a mountain; upon which he immediately quitted the vessel with his wife, his daughter, and the pilot. Xisuthrus then having constructed an altar, offered sacrifices to the gods.[2]

The Phœnicians placed the flood in which Pontus (the Sea) overcame Demarus (Jupiter), in the thirty-second year of the reign of Saturn, 2,200 years after the creation of the world.[3]

When Jupiter sought to destroy the Brazen Race of men on account of their impiety, Deucalion by the advice of his father made himself an ark, and having taken in provisions entered it with his wife Purrha. Jupiter then poured rain from heaven and inundated the greater part of Greece, so that all the people except a few who escaped to

---

[1] Munter, 119, 120. Coins of Apamea in Phrygia tell this story, and have NO on them.—Munter, Bab. 120.

[2] Priaulx, Quaestiones Mosaicae, p. 201.

[3] Seyffarth, Computationssystem, p. 128.

the lofty mountains perished in the waves. Deucalion was carried along the sea in his ark for nine days and nights until he reached Mount Parnassus. Leaving his ark he sacrificed to " Jupiter who protects flight."

> And Nah built an altar to Iahoh (Ehoh, Ihoh) . . . .
> And Iahoh smelled a satisfactory odor.—Genesis viii. 20, 21.
> Apollo having partaken of the savor of lambs and unblemished goats . . . and the savor involved in smoke ascended to heaven.—Iliad, i. 66, 318.

The mythologists, says Plutarch, inform us that a dove let fly out of the ark was to Deucalion a sign of bad weather if it came in again, of good weather if it flew away.[1] Deucalion is certainly Xisuthrus.[2] Xisuthrus was undoubtedly one of the Babylonian deities, and so were his nine predecessors, kings of Babylon. So were also Oannes, Odacon, &c.[3] There was a temple to Deucalion.[4]

The Egyptians seem to have been in doubt whether all beings, or only a part, were carried away by the Flood. They thought several floods had preceded Deucalion's. The Greeks also thought that several deluges had occurred.[4] The Great Flood is mentioned by Ovid, and the rainbow and the wandering bird seeking for land.

> Quaesitisque diu terris, ubi sidere detur,
> In mare lassatis volucris vaga decidit alis.—Ovid, Met. 19, 20.

The Hebrew and Hindu accounts have a marked preference for " seven " as a sacred number.

In Hindustan, a horned fish (Brahma or Vishnu) prophesies the Flood to Manu, who, with seven sages (Rischis), enters a ship, and ties it to the fish's horn by a cable. One account relates that this cable was a serpent. The ship is finally tied to the peak of the Himālāya, mount Himavan.[6]

In *seven* days, all creatures who have offended me shall be destroyed by a deluge, but thou shalt be secured in a vessel miraculously formed; take,

---

[1] Anthon's Dict.   [2] Munter, Bab. 67 ; Movers, 674.   [3] Munter, 31.
[4] Ovid, Bohn's transl., p. 26.   [5] Knobel's Genesis, 70, 72.
[6] Milman's extract from the Mahabharata.

therefore, all kinds of medicinal herbs and esculent grain for food, and together with the *seven* holy men, your respective wives and pairs of all animals, enter the ark without fear; then shalt thou know God face to face, and all thy questions shall be answered.[1]

The Babylonians had three heavens: the fire-heaven, Aether-heaven and the planet-heaven.[2] The Hindus had three heavens. But the ancients also believed there were seven heavens.

> He made the heavens six in number, and for the seventh
> He cast into the midst the fire of the Sun.[3]

> Where untransitory light is, in the world where the sun-radiance lives,
> There bring me, O Soma, into the immortal, invulnerable world.
> Where the Vivasvat's son (Iama) rules as king,
> Where is the innermost part of heaven,
> Where those Great Waters dwell—
> There let me immortal be!

> In the THREE HEAVENS' arch, where man moves and lives at his pleasure,
> Where are the radiant places,
> O there let me immortal be!
> Where wish and longing stay, where the beaming Sun abides,
> Where happiness is and satisfaction—
> O there let me immortal be.

> Where pleasure and joy is,
> Where delight and enchantment reign,
> Where all desires are fulfilled—
> O there let me immortal be!—Song of Kaçjapa, ix. 7, 10, 7, 8.[4]

To a dead person they call:

> Go to the Fathers, to Jama, with whom is satisfaction of wishes in the highest heaven!
> Go in to the Home, laying aside all imperfection; go (to them) noble in form.[5]

---

[1] Bhagavatgita.   [2] Munter, 104.
[3] Proclus, in Tim. 280; Cory, 265; Nonnus, ii. 347.
[4] Roth, Zeitschr der D. M. G. ii. 225; iv.; Rigv. Book 10th, i. 148; i. 15; Duncker, ii. 26.   [5] Ibid.

CHAPTER VII.

Εὐρώπη λίπε Ταῦρον, ἔα Δανάη χύσιν ὄμβρου.—Nonnus, Dionysiac viii. 302.

STARTING from Trebizond on the Black Sea, and going south-easterly in the direction of Nineveh and the Tigris, the traveller enters a country made up of mountains, soon after leaving the coast. Armenia, where the passes are closed during long periods of the year, must be crossed in its whole extent. This barrier extends along the north from Lake Wan, and stretches away in the direction of the Caucasus and the Caspian Sea. Here the Kasbeck, Alborus, and Ararat rear their stupendous summits. Hemmed in by a frightful country on the north, by the sea and the Arabian Desert on the south, lies Mesopotamia, across which the merchants of the East and the West were in a measure compelled to pass, where the votaries of Mithra and Assar, of Varuna and Osiris, of Adan, Adoni or Adonis, of Nebo, Achad and Ahuramasda, mingled in pursuit of pleasure or philosophy, or in the strife of armed hosts to extend the sway of Assyrian, Persian, Greek or Roman, over the centre of the ancient world.

> Babylon hath been a golden cup in the Lord's hand that made all the earth drunken: the nations have drunk of her wine.—Jeremiah, li. 7.

Sun-worship was the basis, the first principle, of the ancient philosophy. Reared in a profound faith in Abal or Bel, no doctrine of the creation of the world could satisfy a Chaldean's mind that did not found itself in the Sun's influence upon universal Nature. Above his head the angels hung their lamps in the dark vault of the firmament that contained within it the unseen beatific world, the Sun's kingdom and the entire light. In his castle of flame Bel-Saturn sat, the inactive Supreme Light, forever unrevealed to mortals. His minister, the Creative Light, the Demiurgus, the "Idea" and celestial "image" of the glorious orb of the sun, is the moving Power of the world, the sun-god that has created life for untold ages in the plains of the habitable earth. The great Planets move from orb to orb among the glittering host, the interpreters of his will to the angels and herds of the Resurrection.—

While the Babylonians offered sacrifices to the spirits of the dead, and the twelve great gods presided over the months, and the thirty-six gods over the decani of the kalendar; while kedeshim ministered to Bel, and strophe and antistrôphe poured forth praise to this Great King of the gods, the author of rain, the giver of corn, and wine, and fruits, and flax, and oil, of every perfect gift; all-seeing, all-knowing,[1] the only Creator, their Jupiter, their Saturn, the Great Spirit, whose voice is heard in the thunder, whose form is the burning flame, whose symbols are the ram, the bull, the lion, the eagle, and the serpent—the God of the *spirits* of all flesh, from whose bundle issues the life and soul of every being; whose Breath is the Light, the Breath of Life to mortals—the eternity of whose existence was betokened by the ring of the Magi, "that hath neither beginning nor end:" who was worshipped as Baalan (Apellon), Elon, El, Hercules, Oannes, and Moloch-Ariel;—while gods innumerable, portents, prophets, soothsayers, and astrologers perplexed the people, the Chaldeans philosophized in their schools on the causes of things and the modus operandi of Nature and Creation.

As they held, with the Peruvians and other American nations, that the Sun was the Creator, and at the same time

---

[1] "The all-knowing Sun."—Wuttke ii. 263; Creuzer i. 350.

professed the doctrine of the marriage of Heaven and Earth (Ouranos and Ge), it only remained for them to proclaim the principle of the Assyrian and Babylonian priests, that " Bel was both Saturn and Sol." Linguâ punicâ Bal Deus dicitur, apud Assyrios autem Bel dicitur quâdam sacrorum ratione Saturnus et Sol.[1] " Kronos (Saturn) they call Sun."[2]

For Zeus and the Sun were wroth with him, for his companions slew the oxen of the Sun.—Odyss. xix. 275, 276.

O Father Zeus, ruling from Ida, most glorious, most mighty,—and thou, O Sun, who beholdest all things—and ye Rivers and thou Earth, and ye below who punish men deceased!—Iliad, iii.

Xerxes carries the chariot of Zeus in procession, but, at the same time, makes his libation to the Sun.[3]

To sacrifice a boar to Zeus and the Sun.—Iliad, xix. 197.

Jupiter Syrius, or Sol.—Spartianus, Caracalla, c. 11.[4]

Quem Solem alii, alii Jovem dicunt.

Whom some call Sun, others Jove.—Servius ad Aeneid. i. 729.

Saturnum quem et Solem dicunt.

Saturn whom they also call Sun.[5]

'Εν τῷ Ἡλίῳ ἔθετο τὸ σκήνωμα αὐτοῦ.—Ps. xix. 4 ; Septuagint Ver.[6]

In Sole tabernaculum suum posuit.—Ps. xix. 4, Vulgate.

" In the sun he hath set his tabernacle."

Julian calls the Sun God and the throne of God.[7] When Moses speaks of the Sun he means the Divine Logos, the Model of that sun which moves about through the heaven and with respect to which it is said :

The SUN went forth upon the earth and Lot entered into Segor, and the LORD rained upon Sodom and Gomorrah brimstone and fire.

Moreover it appears that Moses has also in other pas-

---

[1] Servius ad Aeneid, i. 733; Layard, Nineveh, 450; Movers, 184, 185.

[2] Diodor. ii. 30; Movers, 186, 187.

[3] Beloe's Herodot. iii. 402, 412, 413, i. 180.   [4] Movers, 182.

[5] Movers, 180, 182, 185.   [6] In Egypt, B. C. 285.

[7] Apud Cyril. 1. ii. p. 69; in Gibbon ii. 326, note 21.

sages taken the Sun as a symbol of the Great Cause.—Philo on Dreams. Yonge, § xv. xvi.

Thus speaks the Lord of the world, the Sun, the Great God, the Lord of heaven, to Rhamses Osymandyas. . . . . —Uhlemann, Thoth, 187.

When we compare with these the Egyptian idea that "Osiris (the Most High God) is concealed in the arms of the Sun,"[1] and the fact that Osiris was the sun-god, we perceive clearly the ancient idea, that the Creator took up his abode in the sun and thence governed the world. As Sol, Bel was Creator (Demiurgus), sun-god and Logos; as Saturn, he was the "God of Heaven," the Father of the gods, the Life-god Iah philosophized into the First Cause of all things, the unknown God, the old Bel of all antiquity who had existed since the memory of man ran not to the contrary, the God especially of the circling years and divisions of time (Aiōn), Chronos Time himself, the Eternal God "who is and will be."

If I lift up my hand to heaven and swear I live for ever.—Deut. xxxii. 40.

As sun-god and God of Heaven his partner was the Earth-goddess, earlier the Moon,—Elioun, God of Heaven (Berith), and his goddess Berouth (Isis),—but in the higher conceptions of him as Lord of all life and sole Cause of all things, he was in himself both male and female. In this view his goddess partially sinks out of sight. In the next step of philosophy she is lost entirely; for the Hermaphrodite separates into Heaven and Earth euhemerized into Adam (Ahoh) and Eve (Hoh). Thus the stages to the One Great King above all gods are passed through, and no goddess remains to impair the aspect of modern Mosaic monotheism.

Zeus is the first, Zeus the Thunderer[2] is the last. Zeus is the head, Zeus is the middle, and *by Zeus all things were made. Zeus is male, Immortal*

[1] Plutarch de Iside, lii.

[2] El-Hachabod thundereth: Iahoh is upon many waters!—Psalm xxix. 3.

10

Zeus is female. Zeus is the foundation of the earth, and of the starry heaven. Zeus is the Breath of all things. Zeus is the rushing of indefatigable fire. Zeus is the root of the sea. He is the sun and moon .... his eyes the sun and the opposing moon; his unfallacious Mind the royal incorruptible Aether. —Orphic Fragments.[1]

The Cabbalists spoke of Adam as hermaphrodite.[2] Phanes is male and female. Eros is twofold in nature.

But any one that cheerfully celebrates Zeus in songs of triumph shall completely attain to understanding; him that leads mortals the way to wisdom, *that places knowledge upon suffering,* firmly to remain.—Æschylus, Agamemnon, 175–178.

But "the God" Zeus gives both good and evil sometimes to one and sometimes to another; for he can all things.—Odyssey, iv. 236.

In the Chaldean philosophy, Bel-Saturn is "the Father" who *rests* or *remains* the First Cause of all things, the One Principle that is never named but passed over in silence by the Babylonians and other Orientals. And they constitute Two Principles, one Male (the Spirit) and the other Female (Matter), corresponding to the Greek Ouranos and Ge, the Roman Cœlum and Terra, Heaven and Earth, the Sun and the Earth-goddess, Bel and Mulitta, Mars and Venus, Apason (the Supreme Light, Taaut, Thoth the Sun) the original Male Potenz and Taauthe the feminine Matter, Baal and Beltis or Astarte, Osiris and Isis, Dionysus and Demeter, Tezcatlipoca and Tonacacihua (in Mexico), Saturn and his wife Ops the Earth-goddess,[3] Adam and Eve, Ormuzd (Adonis) and Tanais (Athena), Elion (Baal-Berith) and Beruth his goddess, the Two First Principles of all things. The same Two Principles are found among the Mexicans.[4] " Let those who fall (in war) be kindly received by the Sun and the Earth who are the Father and Mother of all. .... O Lord most gracious to men, Lord of Battles, All-ruler whose name is Tezcatlipoca, God invisible and imperceptible! we entreat thee that those whom

---

[1] Euseb. Praep. Ev. iii. ; Cory, Anc. Fragm.   [2] Movers, 544.
[3] Niebuhr's Rome, Am. ed. i. 62.   [4] Serp. Symbol, 162.

thou lettest fall in this war may be taken up into the abode of the Sun, that they may be gathered to the heroes fallen in previous wars: there they enjoy eternal pleasures, they celebrate in everlasting songs of praise our ruler, the Sun.[1] The Homeric hymn styles Earth "the Mother of all." The author of Genesis calls Eve "the Mother of all living," and Æschylus invokes "Venus the original Mother of our race."[2] Agni the Fire-Sun (Moloch-Apis) is called "the Steer produced in the bed of waters," that is, in the thunder cloud.[3] The Indians of the New Netherlands placed with the Creator a Woman-power as wife. She was before the Beginning of things. The Earth influenced by the Sun's light and heat, and rendered fruitful by the fertilizing rains, is the cause of vegetable life. The Sun and the Earth are the causes of all things that she bears upon her bosom.[4] The Indian chief Tecumseh declared the Sun to be his Father and the Earth his Mother.

"The Father," he that beholdeth these things, the Sun.—Æschylus, Choephorae, 990.

O King Zeus and Earth and heavenly flames of the Sun, and sacred brightness of the Moon, and all Stars!—Orphic Hymn, i.

O dread majesty of my Mother Earth!

O Aether that diffusest thy common light!—Æsch. Prom. Buckley, p. 35.

O Divine Aether, and ye swift-winged breezes, and ye fountains of rivers, and countless dimpling of the waves of the deep, and thou Earth Mother of all, and to the all-seeing orb of the Sun, I appeal.—Æschylus, Prom. 88–91.

TO AETHER.

O thou that hast the might on high always untired of Zeus, a portion of the Stars and Sun and Moon, all-subduer, fire-breathing, that kindles all that live: Aether that givest light from on high, best rudiment of the world: O shining growth, light-bringing, star-radiant, calling on I beseech thee tempered to be serene.—Orphic Hymn, v.

The Aether is the Spirit and the Spirit is Jupiter and Ammon.[5] For the Egyptians call the "Spirit" Jupiter.[6]

---

[1] J. Müller, 620.   [2] Seven against Thebes, 140.   [3] Duncker, ii. 21.
[4] J. Müller, 112.   [5] Lepsius, Die Götter der Vier Elemente, 189; Heeren, Greece, 56.   [6] Plut. de Iside, 36.

According to the Hindus the Deity in the shape of Aether pervades all things.[1] The Father (Belitan) was regarded as Light-Aether in Phœnicia, and the expressions "Aetherial Light" and "Aetherial dew" are found.[2] In the Egyptian catacombs, the bark of the Sun may be traced, in each of the twelve hours of the day, navigating upon the primordial fluid the Aether, the Cause of all things physical, according to the Old Egyptian philosophy.[3] The Phœnicians regarded the sun-light as a Spiritual Power issuing from "the Father" Bel-Saturn to the sun-god.[4]

"In the Chaldean philosophy the Sun and Moon are the first deities, to which all Stars are subjected: and all Powers of the Planets, of the Zodiac and all the heavenly host go out from the Sun."[5]

And of Ioseph he said, Blessed of Iahoh be his land, for the precious things of heaven, for the dew, and for the Deep that coucheth beneath: and for the precious fruits brought forth *by the Sun,* and for the precious things *put forth by the Moons.*—Deut. xxxiii. 14, 15.

"Iao is the life-giving power in Nature, proceeding from the Sun and given over to the Moon, which in the Chaldean wisdom was regarded both as the physical power of production (Adonis) and also as the Intellectual Light and Life Principle. . . . . The other Planets which lead their dance, circling round the Sun as about the King of heaven, receive from him, with the Light, also their powers; and as their light is only a reflection of the Sun's light, so their powers also are only emanations from the physical and spiritual Life-fulness of the sun-god, who pours them out into the seven heavenly spheres, where they at last are taken up by the Moon who distributes them to Earth. In it participates especially the planet Venus, because he is nearest to the Sun, divides fruitfulness to the Earth and animal vitality to the creatures."[6] Osiris enters the moon. Iao is

---

[1] Wuttke, ii. 261.   [2] Movers, 158, 183.   [3] Champollion, Egypte, 131.
[4] Movers, 554.   [5] Movers, 167.   [6] Movers, 159, 160.

" the Spirit" in the moon.[1] In the opinion of the Phœnicians the productive energy was given out from the sun to
the moon which pours it into the Aether.[2]

When dewy Selene milks the resisting fire of thy parturient beam, drawing
together her bent-forward cow horn.—Nonnus, Dionus. xl. 378.

The Moon is called in the Yasna " the preserver of the
Steer's keim." She takes two-thirds, and the Earth the
remainder.[3] Luna or Hecate gave increase to flocks.[4]

The female deity represents sometimes the chaste goddess the Moon, sometimes the Earth-goddess, sometimes
the Fire-goddess, sometimes the female Sun, the goddess
of Wisdom (Minerva, Onka, Sarasvati, &c). Turning now
to the Phœnician philosophy, we find that its Two " First
Principles" were Spirit and Matter, which correspond to
Sunlight and the Earth, Cupid and Chaos, Eros (Kama)
and Darkness, the Aether and Air of the Phœnicians, the
Babylonian Apason and Taauthe, the Water and Sand of
the Egyptians, the Purusha and Prakriti of the Hindus, the
Yang and Yn of the Chinese. The ideal sun-light was regarded as a Spiritual influence issuing from the Highest
God.[5] In Phœnicia it was called Iao " the light conceivable
only by the intellect" ($\Phi\hat{\omega}\varsigma$ $\nu o\eta\tau\grave{o}\nu$, the Intelligible Light),
" the physical and Spiritual Principle of all things ; out of
which the souls emanate."[6] It was the Male Essence while
the Primitive Matter or Chaos was the Female. This Intelligible Light was personified in Iao. In the Egyptian
philosophy and in Genesis, we find " the Spirit" moving
upon the face of the waters (Chaos).

The universe, according to Confucius, is one animated
system made up of one Material Substance and one Spiritual
Being, of which every living thing is an emanation, and to
which, when separated by death from its particular material

[1] Movers, 549. [2] Ibid. [3] Rinck, i. 72 ; Duncker, ii. 358, quotes Burnouf, 375. [4] Hesiod, Theog. 445.
[5] Movers, 554. [6] Ibid. 269, 554.

part, every living thing again returns.[1] The Platonic philosopher Proclus said, "The Monad is extended which generates Two."[2] So the Chinese: The Tao has produced One, One has produced Two, Two have produced Three, Three have produced all things.[3] This is the Pythagorean Monad from the One, the Duad (Spirit and Matter), the Triad (their union in the World).

All things are governed in the bosom of this triad.[4]

The Chinese and Pythagoreans considered Fire the Principle of life in the world.[5] The ancient Chinese thought (B. C. 550) that the Taiki (the First Principle) is made up both of Mind and Matter. Lao Tseu recognized two natures in his First Principle, the divine and the corporeal.[6] They can no more be separated "than fire from the burning substance." According to the Pythagoreans, "Before the heaven was made, there existed Idea and Matter, and God the Creator (Demiurgus) of the better."[7] The Egyptians said: "The Intelligence is God possessing the double fecundity of the two sexes, Who is the Life and the Light of his Intelligence."[8] The Chinese said, In the midst of Chaos was a subtile Vivifying Principle.[9]

The Tao, the Supreme Reason, the Intelligent Working Power in Nature (the Intelligent Heaven), is everywhere.[10] It is the Igneous Principle of life, the Luminous Principle of Intelligence, the Spirit, the Yang or Male Principle.[11] Before Creation, in its state of immobility, it is nameless like the Babylonian First Cause, who is passed over in silence.[12] The Supreme Tao circulated alone in the void and silent infinitude.[13] The Absolute (Tai-ky, "the highest

[1] Edinburgh Encyc. Art. China, p. 89.   [2] Proc. in Euc. 27.
[3] La Chine, Pauthier, i. 116. ii. 354.   [4] Lydus de Mensibus, 20.
[5] Ritter, Hist. Phil. i. 395; Wuttke, ii. 23.   [6] La Chine, ii. 356.
[7] Cory, Anc. Fragm. 303.   [8] Champollion, Egypte, 141.
[9] La Chine, i. 115.   [10] La Chine, ii. 350; Wuttke, ii. 14.   [11] Ibid. 356.
[12] Ibid. 352.   [13] Pauthier, La Chine, i. 115.

point," the Primal Power) was before any being had separated itself from it; from it proceeded the Resting and the Impulse-giving Principle; all beings spring from it and nevertheless it is in all beings.[1] The Primitive Power (Ly) contains in it the primitive Matter. It is the One which divided itself.[2] In Hindustan the Purusha (the Primitive Spirit) already stands before the Primitive Matter, from whose union springs Mahan Atma the Life-spirit (the Great Soul).[3] The Chinese Two Principles (Spirit and Matter) were the Yang, the Male, and the Yn, the Female Principle. The Yang is the strength, the Primitive Power, the cause of all movement; Yn is the passive, the motionless, and receives movement only through the Yang. The Yang appears most perfect in the Sun.[4] Yang and Yn both arise from the One Primitive stuff.[5] The Divine Essence is duality.[6] But the Hindus say that the Sun is the Soul of all that is movable or immovable. This whole world has emanated from the Sun, it will return to the Sun to find its annihilation in it.[7] This is pantheism.

The Spirit divine which circulates in heaven is called Indra, Mitra, Varuna, Agni, Yama, Matarisvan (the Wind).[8]

Paratma the Soul of the Universe engendered by division of himself the divine Male Purusha who unites himself to Pradhana (Matter).[9]

Nothing existed then, neither visible nor invisible. No region above, no Air, no Heaven. Where was this covering of the world? In what bed were the waters found contained? Where were these impenetrable depths of the Air?

No death nor immortality existed. Nothing announced the day or night. He alone breathed without exhalation shut up in himself. He alone existed.

In the Beginning the Darkness was enveloped in Darkness, the Water existed without Impulsion. All was confused. The Being reposed in the midst of this Chaos, and this great All received birth owing to his piety.

In the Beginning, Love was in Him, and from His "Spirit" issued the first seed . . .

The ray of these sages went forth extending itself above and below. They

---

[1] Wuttke, ii. 14. [2] Ibid. 13. [3] Weber, Akad. Vorles. 213, 214.
[4] Wuttke, ii. 12. [5] Ibid. 19. [6] Ibid. 25. [7] Wuttke, ii. 262.
[8] A Vedic hymn, Baudry, Etudes sur les Vedas, 34. [9] Ibid.

were great; they were full of fruitful seed, like a fire whose flame rises above the hearth that feeds it.

Who knows these things? Who can tell? Whence come the beings? What is this creation? The gods have also been produced by Him. But He, who knows how He exists?[1]

"When the WORD of the LOVING SPIRIT in the kingdom of the Most High created."[2]

One of the Babylonian legends represents Bel as cutting the Woman Omorka (the Nature-goddess, or Primitive Matter) into two halves; of one he makes heaven, of the other earth.[3] Other philosophical accounts make Bel a union of man and woman which separate into Heaven and Earth.[4] Bel is thus the First Cause of the Heaven and Earth, the Winged Globe that flies through eternal space, the Great Serpent bespeckled with stars, the Life-dragon Chronos, the Sun-serpent and Wisdom of the universe, the Everlasting God.

The Lenape tribe of the Shawnees believe that the Sun inspires all life.[5] The same is said of the Persian Ahura (Ormuzd).[6] Chimanitou formed the animals out of clay. The subordinate Manitus looked on and were pleased with the work. In the side of every animal he made an opening through which he entered for several days, and so put life into the animal. If they suited him they were allowed to swim to the continent, and fill the forests: but if he did not like them, he first *drew back the life* from them, and then destroyed them.[7]

If he gather unto himself his "Spirit" and his "Breath,"
All flesh shall perish together and Man shall turn again unto dust.—Job, xxxiv. 14, 15.

The spirits of men were supposed to have been bestowed by the Sun. Their bodies came from the earth.

[1] A Vedic hymn, Baudry, Etudes sur les Vedas, 34, 35.
[2] Benfey, Samaveda, 239.   [3] Munter, Bab. 42.
[4] Movers, 271, 266, 554 et passim.   [5] J. Müller, 117.
[6] Wuttke, ii. 251.   [7] J. Müller, 108, quotes Schoolcraft's Wigwam, 121 ff.

But their life the shining Sun hath taken away.—Homer, Odyssey, Book xxii. line 388.

The Pythagoreans considered all souls an efflux from the Universal Soul.[1] The Hindus said that the Spirit (Purusha), the Cause of being, is Light.[2] Moses calls Iahoh "the God of the spirits of all flesh,"[3] because they are emanations from the Spirit of God.

But there is a Spirit in man; and the inspiration of Sadi gives them understanding.—Job, xxxii.

In whose hand is the soul of every living thing and the Breath of all mankind.—Job, xii. 10.

As he knew not his Maker and Him that breathed into him an active *soul*, and breathed in *a living spirit !*—Wisdom of Solomon, xv. 11.

Then shall the dust return to the earth as it was, and the Spirit to Elohim who gave it.—Eccl. xii. 7.

The soul being a bright fire, by the power of the Father

Remains immortal, and is mistress of life.—Psell. 28 ; Cory, 243.

I the Soul dwell a heat animating all things—

For he placed mind indeed in soul, but soul in dull body.

Proc. in Tim. ; Cory, 243.

Thus saith Hael (the God) Iahoh that created the heavens and stretched them out: he that spread forth the earth and that which cometh out of it; he that giveth Breath unto the people upon it and Spirit to them that walk therein.—Isaiah, xlii. 5.

For thine incorruptible SPIRIT is in all things.—Wisdom of Solomon, xii. 1.

My Spirit shall not always strive with man for that he also is Flesh : yet his days shall be 120 years.[4]

Hesiod says the human mind is God incognito; Orpheus says, One God is present in all. Tully says: Deum te scito, " know that you are God."[5] Eve says :

I have gotten a man who is Iahoh !—Gen. iv. Schmid's Bible.

This is a Hebrew pun (*kai*ni*thi, I have possessed) on the word Kin. Kin (Cain) was one of the names of Iahoh. Iehouah passed with the heathen for Saturn and Typhon.[7]

[1] Ritter, i. 416. [2] Wuttke, ii. 295, 296, 324, 328 ; De Wette, Bibl. Dogm. 433, 84. [3] Numb. xxvii. 16. [4] Gen. vi. 3. The Spirit is here the Life Principle Iao. [5] W. Williams, 42.

[6] Kin is Akan, Iachin, Chon, Agni the Fire-god (Iahoh). [7] Movers, 297.

7*

For Egypt is Adam (man) and not El (God), and his horses are Flesh but not Spirit.—Isaiah, xxxi. 3.

Until the Spirit be poured upon us from on high.—Isaiah, xxxii. 15.

> Dum Spiritus hos reget artus.
>
> While Spirit shall rule these limbs.—Virgil, Æneid, iv. 336.
>
> Spiritus intus alit.
>
> Spirit feeds within us.—Æneid, vi. 726.
>
> Est Deus in nobis.
>
> God is in us.—Ovid.[1]

Iao is the physical and Spiritual Life-principle from which the souls emanate.[2] Like man, all Nature separates into Body and Spirit.[3] According to the Chinese, " in the midst of Chaos there was a *subtile vivifying principle*. This was the Suprême Verité."[4]

And he will give you another Advocate (Paraclete), the "Spirit of Truth." —John, xiv. 17.

The principle of life and motion beyond the material world Anaxagoras called " Spirit," which is " the purest and most subtile of all things, having the most knowledge and the greatest strength." This " Spirit" gave to all those material atoms, which in the Beginning of the world lay in disorder, the impulse by which they took the forms of individual things and beings.[5]

Know ye not that ye are the temple of God, and that "the Spirit" of God dwelleth in you."—1 Cor. iii. 16.

For what man knoweth the things of a man, save "the Spirit" of a man which is in him? Even so the things of God no man knoweth, but "the Spirit" of God.—1 Cor. ii. 11.

With Ahura-masda is mentioned the Spirit of Ahura-masda, the Holy Spirit.[6]

"The Spirit" Narayana desired to create: out of Narayana sprung Brahman, Vishnu, Rudra, the twelve Adityas, the Rudras. " Narayana is all that has been and will be."[7]

---

[1] Williams, 42.   [2] Movers, 269.   [3] Duncker, ii. 66.

[4] Pauthier, La Chine, i. 115.   [5] K. O. Müller, Hist. Greek Lit. 247.

[6] Duncker, ii. 335.   [7] Weber, Ind. Stud. i. 381.

Narayana is adored as Vishnu.[1] Vishnu is later identified with the previously independent existing Narayana, "the Spirit" that life-giving moves over the waters and works creative in them.[2]

The Spirit of God is Fire.[3] In the rite of baptism Water is an emblem of the Spirit.

I indeed baptize you in water . . . He will baptize you in Holy Spirit and Fire.—Luke, iii. 17.[4]

Water as compared with Air is Matter, as compared with Earth it is Spirit. Air is Spirit when compared with Water, but it is Matter when compared with Aether.

Pherecydes, the Syrian, considered that Chronos (Saturn) generated from himself Fire, Spirit and Water, representing, as Damascius supposed, the threefold nature of " That which only the mind perceives." [5]

Moisture is a symbol of the soul (life or Spirit). Plato calls it, at one time, "the liquid of the whole Vivification," at another, "a certain fountain." [6]

Heraclitus, a Greek philosopher who lived about 505 B. C., regarded Fire as Spirit in the fire, as the true Soul of the world.[7] This is the Hindu idea of Agni (Ignis) the Fire as Soul of the world. Heraclitus thought, "that every thing is in perpetual motion, that nothing has any stable or permanent existence, but that every thing is assuming a *new form* or perishing. Fire lives the death of the earth; air lives the death of fire; water lives the death of air; and the earth that of water;[8] by which he meant that individual things were only different forms of a universal substance, which mutually destroy each other. In like

[1] Weber, Ind. Stud. i. 252.

[2] Wuttke, ii. 291; Lassen Ind. Alterthumskunde, 682, 777.

[3] Egypte, 141; Chinese Repository, x. 49; Wuttke, ii. 295; Ovid, Metam. Fable I. 22; 2 Kings, i. 12; Gen. i. 2.   [4] Transl. Griesbach's New Test.

[5] Damascius, in Cory, 321.   [6] Cory, 259.   [7] Weber, Ind. Stud. ii. 382.

[8] Out of the Soul of the world (Atman) sprung the Aether, out of the Aether the Air, out of the Air came the Fire, out of the Fire Water, out of the Water Earth.—Ind. Stud. ii. 217.

manner he said of men and gods, ' Our life is their death ;
their life is our death ; ' that is, he thought that men
were gods who had died, and that gods were men raised
to life."[1] Euhemerus also held that the gods were deceased men : and this view is taken in the Bible, which
turns the old gods into " deceased patriarchs " of the
Hebrew nation. Like Moses, who described God as fire,
Heraclitus considers it the principle of this perpetual destructive transition from one thing into another; though
he probably meant not the fire perceptible by the senses,
but a higher and more universal agent (the Divine Fire).
He conceives the idea of the *igneous principle of life*, like
the *principe igné* of the Chinese philosophers and the
American Indians.[2] "The unchanging order of all things
was made neither by a god nor a man, but it has always
been, is and will be ' the Living Fire ' which is kindled and
extinguished in regular succession. This perpetual motion
is guided and directed by some power, which he called
Fate. Heraclitus considered the original Matter of the
world to be the source of life."[3] Xenophanes (born 556 B. C.)
considered God all Spirit and Mind. Following Xenophanes
the whole philosophy of Parmenides (B. C. 450) rests upon
the idea of Existence, which, strictly understood, excludes
the ideas of creation and annihilation.[4] That the Fire was
regarded as the Spirit issuing from the Unrevealed God is
evident from the Hindu philosophy.

" In the Beginning the First Cause (Tad) existed alone. He thought : I will
let the Worlds issue from me : He let them go forth : Water, Light, Transitory
(Matter) and the Waters (of Heaven). Water was above the Firmament (Heav-
en) which bears it. Then he formed out of the waters the Spirit (Purusha).
He looked upon it and its mouth opened like an egg ; out of its mouth proceeded Speech, and from the Speech, Fire." [5]

Kneph (the Good Daemon the Sun) the Creator brought

[1] K. O. Müller, 244, 245.   [2] J. Müller, 55, 56 ; La Chine, ii. 356.
[3] K. O. Müller, 245.   [4] Ibid. 250, 251.   [5] Wuttke, ii. 295.

forth out of his mouth an Egg from which Ptah sprung.[1]
" The philosophers of later times made him to be an Intellectual Principle ; he was, according to more material conceptions, the element of Water, or the Sun." The Phœnicians represented this god by a serpent.[2] He is Ophion-Uranus the Deity conceived as purest Intelligence, like Ahura-
Mazda (Mazda=the Wise) in Persia. " In the temple of
Osiris at Philae he appears fashioning upon a wheel or lathe
the limbs of Osiris,[3] while the figure of the god Nile stands
by and pours water on the wheel."[4] The Hindus said:

> Then he formed out of the waters "the Spirit" (Purusha).

Purusha also means " a man." The Nilometer was kept in
the temple of Serapis at Canop-us (Kneph). The Nile was
called by many names of the Sun, as Melo, Iaro, Oceam-es,
Ocean-us, Siris (Asar) Osiris, Ap (Hapi), Sihor, Anel (Neleus,
Nilus). Pliny calls it Agathodemon, the Good Daemon (the
Sun-deity).[5]

" Emanations of light and water appear to have been described by similar names."[7] Thus we have iom " day" (sun),
iamim " days ;" iâm (or iŏm) "lake" in Hebrew : Mu "light,"
a god Mu in Egypt ; mû, mŏ " water" in Egyptian,[8] mi " water" in Hebrew ; Nero the shining, the Sun, Nerio " Mars"
(Sol), Nara " the waters," Nereus water-god, Narayana " the
water-moving," the " Spirit" in India, Anar " the Forming
Principle" in the Scandinavian mythology,[9] Ianuar (Ianus)
Anaur-us, a river of Iolcos, Nara a Russian stream ; Abar
or Bar (Var) the Sun, Var the Sun's river, Vari " water" in
Sanskrit, Var " a sea in heaven" in Persia, Varuna " water-
god ;" Adar (Atar) the Sun, Thor the thunder and water-

---

[1] Uhlemann, Thoth, 26, 37.   [2] Kenrick, i. 314.

[3] Adonis, Adam, Apason, Ar, Eros the archetype of light, the Spirit of Elohim in the inundation.   [4] Kenrick, i. 314.   [5] Wuttke, ii. 295.

[6] Williams, 285, 312.   [7] Ibid. 301.

[8] Uhlemann, Handbuch, i. 161; Bunsen, Hist. Phil. ii. 61.

[9] American Encycl. Art. Northern Mythology.

god, H-udōr "water;" Ap the Sun, Ap "water" in Sanskrit ;
Opo or Po, the river; Tag the Sun, Tagus the Sun's water;
Osiris the Sun and Osiris the Nile; Anos the Sun, Anoh
the water-god Nuh or Nah; Anakos the Sun, Anakos or
Noach the Sun and water-god who foretold the Flood in
Phrygia; Ani the Sun and Oannes the god with the fish-
tail; Purisha in Sanskrit "water," Purishin the Sun.[1] Amon
the Sun, Baal-Maeon ; Maon in Arabic is "water;"[2] "As"
the Sun, Ash "fire" in Hebrew, osh "water" in Egyptian ;
Anan or Hanan the Sun, Noun "water" in Egyptian.[5]

And Iahoh came down in a cloud and spake to him (Moses) and took of
the Spirit that was upon him and gave it unto the seventy elders: and it came
to pass that when the Spirit rested upon them they prophesied.—Numb. xi. 25.

And Pharaoh said unto his servants, Can we find such a one as this is, a
man in whom is the Spirit of God?

And Pharaoh said unto Joseph: Forasmuch as Elohim (God) hath showed
thee all this, there is none so discreet and wise as thou art.—Gen xli. 38, 39.

Take thee Iahosha the son of Non, a man in whom is the Spirit.—Numb.
xxvii. 18.

As the light proceeding from the sun is the source of life,
it is considered besides as a Spiritual influence going out from
the Most High God.[4] The Sun is the source of all inspiration and poetical power. .

Apollo with full force rushed on Demodocus.—Il. viii.

He was filled with the Holy Ghost and prophesied.

And God (Theos) has breathed into my mind all sorts of songs.—Odyssey,
xxii. 347.

But Zeus himself made this thought in my mind.—Odyssey, xiv. 273.

Behold I pour out my Spirit upon you.—Prov. i. 23.

The Spirit of Iahoh spake by me and his Word was in my tongue.—2 Sam.
xxiii. 2.

And the Word of Iahoh came expressly unto Iahazakal the priest.—
Ezekiel, i. 3.

The Light-Aether is the Spirit.[5] "With respect to the
soul some say that it is incorporeal, others that it is a body.

[1] Wilson, Rigv. ii. 130.   [2] Williams, 291.
[3] Seyffarth, Gram. Aegypt. 33.   [4] Movers, 554.   [5] Ibid. 281, 282.

Some say that it is made up of atoms; others that it is fire, air, water. Some say it is an *Aethereal body.*"—Aristotle, ed. Taylor.

The Mind of the dead lives not, but has an immortal intelligence, *falling into the immortal Aether.*—Euripides, Helen. 1015, 1016.

It is sown a natural body, it is raised a *Spiritual body.*

If in this life only we have hope in Christ, we are of all men most miserable.

But some will say, How are the ,dead raised up, and with what body do they come?

Fool, that which thou sowest does not produce life, except it die: and that which thou sowest, thou sowest not that body that shall be, but only grain.—Paul, 1 Cor. xv.

The earth is only corruption and generation. All generation proceeds from a corruption.—Livres Hermetiques; Egypte, 140, 139.

It is sown in corruption, it is raised in incorruption.

These doctrines were taught in the Eleusinian Mysteries.[1]

But Elohim will redeem my soul from the hand of Hades; for he will receive me.—Psalm, xlix. 15.

Though I walk in the midst of trouble, thou wilt revive me; thy visitation has preserved my spirit.—Job, x.

Whither shall I go from thy "Spirit," or whither shall I flee from thy presence?

If I ascend up into heaven thou art there; if I make my bed in Hell, behold thou art there.

If I take the wings of the Morning, dwell in the uttermost parts of the sea; Even there shall thy hand lead me, and thy right hand shall hold me.

For *thou hast possessed my reins:* thou hast covered me in my mother's womb.

I will praise thee, for I am *fearfully and wonderfully made:* marvellous are thy works, and that my soul knoweth right well.

He who is, as it were, the Generator of men as well as of heaven and earth, of whom Creation has imbibed life, abides with his glories: HE IT IS WHO ENTERING INTO THE WOMB PROCREATES.—Wilson, Rigveda, ii. 84.

As thou knowest not what is the way of the SPIRIT, nor how the bones grow in the womb of her that is with child.—Eccles. xi. 5.

My substance was not hid from thee when *I was made in secret,* curiously wrought *in the lowest parts of the earth.*[2]—Psalm, cxxxix.

---

[1] See page 213, Chap. VIII. of this work.

[2] A philosophical myth, in Plato, says that the gods formed man and other animals of clay and fire *within the earth.*—Anthon, Art. Prometheus.

Thine eyes did see my substance while it was yet unfinished; and in thy book all my members were written, in continuance were fashioned when as yet no one of them existed.—Psalm, cxxxix.

The Spirit of El hath made me and the Breath of Sadi (Shaddai) gives me life. —Job, xxxiii. 4 ; Hebrew Bible, Schmid.

Adonai Iahoh and his Spirit hath sent me.—Isaiah, xlviii. 16.

There is no man that hath power over the Spirit to retain the Spirit: neither hath he power in the day of death.—Eccles. viii. 8.

The Hindu Vedas say :

Agni, the Sun, the Soul of all that is movable or immovable, has filled (with his glory) the heaven, the earth, and the firmament.[1]

Mahan Atma (the great Soul or Spirit) is the Sun.[2] Mahan Atma is Brahma.[3] The Sun is "the Brahman."[4] "The Brahman" manifests itself externally as Wind (Vayu), internally as Breath of life (Prana).[5] The Atman (Soul of the universe) manifests himself within as Breath of life, externally as the Sun.[6] Adam (in German Odem and Athem, meaning Breath, Athmen "to breathe," the Hindu Atman, the Hebrew Spirit of God or Breath of life) is Narayana "the Spirit" that moves creative on the face of the waters, according to Hindu philosophy. Narayana and the Atman are one and the same.[7] Narayana is Vishnu the Sun.

"The Brahman" (das brahman) is compared with the heart (manas, mens=mind) and the Aether (âkâça).[8] "The

Compare Bacchus and Demeter under the earth.—Egypte, 133; K. O. Müller, 231.

Who descends beneath the hollow earth
Knows the God-given beginning of life.—Pindar, Threnoi. 8.

Dying I go beneath earth whence I came!—Euripides, Hercules Furens, 1247.

"The deities under the earth," to whom God, the leader of all, intrusted the administration of the world filled with gods and men and other living beings, as many as have been made by the Demiurgus according to the best image of a form not begotten, and eternal, and to be perceived by the mind.—Timæus the Locrian, υ. 105, ed. Stallbaum ; Burges, Plato.

[1] Rig Veda Sanhita, Wilson, i. 304.   [2] Mills, Hist. British India, i. 200, 206.
[3] Wuttke, ii. 257.   [4] Weber, Ind. Stud. i. 261.   [5] Ibid. 262.
[6] Ibid. 277.   [7] Weber, Ind. Stud. pp. 8, 9.   [8] Ibid. i. 260.

Brahman" (the neutral Brahma) is the heart of the universe.[1] Akar, Kur, is the Sun; Kar, Kardion, "the heart" in Greek. In India Purishin is the Sun,[2] Purusha "the Spirit," and Pracriti " Matter." Purusha also means " a man" in Sanskrit. So in like manner Adam is the Sun (Adamus or Thammuz). Adam is "the Spirit" and means "man," "a man" in Hebrew. In Egypt Athom, Thom, Tom, Atumu, Atmu, are names of the Sun; in Greek Thumos is " the mind," and Edom a people. The Bible considers every life or soul an emanation from the Spirit of God. " As" means " Sun," " life." In Egyptian, Ash means man (As, Es),[3] in Hebrew Aish means man, and Ash fire (the Spirit). Osh is water.[4] We have also Abas, Busi, the Sun, Abōs the Dawn, Phōs "light," and Phōs " a man" in Greek; Anar, Nero the Sun, Aner " man" in Greek, Nri in Sanskrit, Nere, Nar, Nara " man" in Zend, Ner in Umbrian; Abar, Bar, Avar, Var the Sun; Pur, Feuer (fire), Vir " man" in Latin, vira, vir " man" in Zend, vira " man" in Sanskrit; Amad, Muth the Sun, mat " man," Mata " a Mede," Madai " Medes": Aman the Sun, Amon in Egypt the Demiurgic Spirit or Intellect, Man in English " a living soul," Mēnēs in Egyptian " the Eternal One,"[5] Manas in Sanskrit the Soul of the World (Mens in Latin) the Mind of the universe: Asal, Asel, Azael, Sol, the Sun; Seele "the soul" in German, in English, soul. Am is the Sun (Iama, Iamus, Om, Iom, Ioma) in India, Greece, Palestine, Egypt, Asia Minor and Chaldæa; in Slavonian Oum, um means spirit, soul.[6] Am (Om) in Hebrew means " people," populus, Ham " mankind," ham " man" in Egyptian, hime " woman,"[7] ham " creatus"; homo " man" in Latin, Aham " I," Old Persian. We find Paran (Baran), Varuna (sun-god), and Prana the " Breath of life," phrēn the intellect; Basak

---

[1] Weber, ii. 376.   [2] Wilson, Rigv. Sanh. ii. 130.
[3] Seyffarth, Gramm. Aegypt. 16, 18.   [4] Ibid. 33.
[5] Uhlemann, Handb. i. 161.   [6] Grimm, Berl. Akad. 1854, p. 309.
[7] Seyffarth, Grammar, App. 5.

(Adoni) and Psukē the Soul; Abas (the Sun), Afza the "spirit" in Persian; Adal, Tal the Sun, and Dil the "heart" in Persian (diligo in Latin); Ani, Ianus the Sun and ian "soul" in Persian. Ani is the Sun; Philo says "on" is "mind."[1] An-thropos in Greek means "man" and Iaon-es "men" "Ionians." Anam, Noum were Egypto-Phœnician names of the Sun; anim-us is in Latin "the mind," anima the soul. Anak, Anakos, is the Sun, Anok is "I" in Hebrew. Ak, Ag, Iauk, Ukko, Auges, are sun-names, Ego, Ich are pronouns of the first person. Manu is in India and Asia Minor the Sun; manudscha, mensch, man the sun-born. Abi is the Sun, Iabe God; Bai means "soul" in Egyptian.[2] Ad, or At, is the Sun; Eth (ἠϑ) is "heart."[3] Anos, Anus, Enos are Babylonian and Old Italian names of the Sun; Nous means "mind" in Greek, and Enos in Hebrew means "mankind," "men";[4] Noah the patriarchal "man." Compare Asam, Shem the Sun, Shem "mankind;" Iapet-os, a Titan, the Sun, Abot the Sun, Buddha, Phut the Sun and fire-god, Aphthas, Iephtha, Pthah the fire-god and sun-god, and Iapet "mankind"; Alak, Lukos, Lux, Lukeios (Apollo) the Sun, Logos the Creator-Sun, the Divine Wisdom or Mind,[5] Logoi "souls" in Greek.

> And Lukos guided the course of the maritime horses,
> Conducting the car of his Father.—Nonnus, xxiii. 125.

The term Logos, in Greek, means literally "Word;" the plural Logoi means "words," "ideas," "souls." In philosophy logoi are the archetypes or eternal "images" of things, which existed in the Mind of the Eternal One as "Ideas." They were clothed with Matter by the Efficient Cause (Iao the Demiurg, Creator) to form the existing bodies. This is the old traditional Babylonian and Platonic philosophy of Creation, and is substantially that of the Old and New Testament. The Sankhya school of philosophers in India (B. C. 600) held that the individual souls were eternal and

---

[1] Philo Judæus, ii. 308 ed. Bohn. [2] Uhlemann, Handbuch, i. 160. [3] Ibid.
[4] Philo, ii. 398; Bunsen, Aegyptens Stelle v. 4, 5, p. 65. [5] Movers, 270.

clothed themselves with material forms. The Hindu doctrine of "living atoms or seeds" the archetypes of the senses, placed their origin in the mind, the heart, the interior sense within us (manas, mens). The Heart of the world (Brahm) excited by Love (Kama, Eros) becomes creative, and from it the senses emanate changing the space within the manas (the Divine Mind or Soul) into the external world. The world emanates from Brahm.[1]

The Babylonians pass by in silence the One Beginning of all things, and they constitute Two, Apason and Taauthe, making Apason the husband of Taauthe and naming her the Mother of the gods.[2] Apason and Taauthe are the Spirit and the Matter, Bel and Mulitta, Adonis and Venus, Bacchus and Ceres, Osiris and Isis, Dionysus and Demeter, Adam (Euas) and Eua, the Two Principles of the ancient philosophy celebrated in the Eleusinian Mysteries. We find them also in Hesiod.

> Sing the sacred descent of the immortal gods who sprung from *Earth and starry Ouranos,*
> And murky Night and those whom briny Pontos reared.
> And tell how first the gods and 'Gaia sprung,
> And rivers and boundless Pontos raging with billows.
> Chaos was generated first, and then
> The broad-bosomed Earth the ever stable seat of all
> The Immortals that inhabit the snowy peaks of Olympus
> And the dark, dim Tartarus in the depths of the wide-wayed Earth
> And LOVE, the fairest 'of the Immortal Gods. . . . .
> Then came vast Heaven bringing Night with him
> And eager for love brooded around Earth.—Hesiod, Theogony.

On account of the various fertilizing and animating influences which the Earth receives from the Heaven, the Greeks were led to conceive Earth and Heaven as a married pair, whose descendants form in the Theogony a second great generation of deities. With Zeus, God of the heavens, who dwells in the pure expanse of the Aether, is associated,

---

[1] Weber, Ind. Stud. ii. 376.   [2] Damascius; Movers, 275.

though not as a being of the same rank, the goddess of the Earth. The marriage of Zeus with this goddess (which signified the union of Heaven and Earth in the fertilizing rains) was a sacred solemnity in the worship of these deities.[1]

The Vedic hymns say :

I praise Heaven and Earth for preliminary meditation.[2]

The Heaven is my parent and progenitor; the navel (of the earth) is my kinsman; the spacious Earth is my mother.

The womb lies between the two uplifted ladles, and in it the Parent has deposited the germ of the fruitfulness of the daughter.

Those Two, the divine Heaven and Earth, are the diffusers of happiness on all, encouragers of truth, able to sustain the water (of heaven), auspicious of birth, and energetic: in the interval between whom proceeds the pure and divine Sun for (the discharge of his) duties.

Wide-spreading, vast, unconnected, the Father and Mother, they two preserve the worlds. Resolute as if (for the good) of embodied (beings) are Heaven and Earth, and the Father has invested every thing with forms.

The pure and resolute Son of (these) parents, the Bearer (of rewards), sanctifies the worlds by his intelligence as well as the Milch Cow (Earth) and the vigorous Bull (Heaven), and daily milks the pellucid milk of the sky.[3]

The Chinese said, The Tao (the Reason Supreme) is the Heaven, it is the Life, it is the Spirit.[4]   " The Heaven and the Earth are transported in space and mutually penetrate."[5]

The Chinese philosopher TCHOUANG-TSEU (B. C. 338) said that the Tao, the Supreme Intelligence, gave birth to Heaven and Earth.[6]   This is the Egyptian doctrine that God produced Matter from the Materiality of his *divided* Essence.   The Book of Genesis commences :

In the Beginning Alohim created the Heavens[7] and the Earth (Aras).

The Samaritan version reads :

In the Beginning Alhh (Alahah) created the Heavens (Shomih) and the Earth (Arah).—Samaritan Pentateuch.[8]

---

[1] K. O. Müller, Hist. Greek Lit. 14, 90.   [2] Wilson, Rigv. i. 287.
[3] Wilson, Rigv. ii. 138, 106, 107.   [4] Pauthier, La Chine Mod. 360.
[5] La Chine Mod. 361, univ. pitt.   [6] Ibid. 363.
[7] The Septuagint Version B. C. 285, reads "Heaven."—Gen. i. 1.
[8] The J polyglot : Paris polyglot.

Aben Ezra says, The Samaritans write instead of "*Elohim* created," "*Azima* created." The most learned Rabbins said Azima was a goat. Compare the Mendesian Goat in Egypt and the sun-god Pan with goat's horns. Compare also Baal-SEMES the Sun.[1]

In the Egyptian account, there was an eternal Chaos and an eternal Spirit united with it which arranged the discordant materials and formed the universe. According to Egyptian philosophers, the One Principle of the universe is Unknown Darkness. The Two Principles are Water and Sand (Spirit and Matter.)[2]

The watery element which is the Beginning and Genesis of all things from the Beginning created three bodies first: Earth, Air and Fire.[3]

In Phœnician philosophy the Two Principles were "Tenebrous Air filled with Spirit" and Chaos.[4] According to the Orphic Cosmogony, "the Aether was manifested in Time from the Beginning, and on every side of the Aether was the Chaos." The Aether is the "Spirit" surrounded by the Chaos. It is the Phœnician Light-Aether. "The Earth was invisible on account of the darkness; but '*the Light*' *broke through the Aether*."[5] The Hebrew opinion about Matter would naturally be that of the Phœnicians, for they dwelt together and spoke the same language.[6] We know that the Phœnicians held the doctrine of the "Two Principles," Spirit and Matter, as the causes of all things. Fire or Wind was the material symbol of the Spirit; Water, of Matter. Genesis begins with a description of the creation of *heaven and earth, but not of Water* (the first form of Matter in all the ancient Cosmogonies).

In the Beginning, Elohim created the heaven and the earth. And the earth *was without form and void:* and the Spirit of God *moved on the face of the waters.*

---

[1] Movers, 174.   [2] Damascius; Cory, 321.
[3] Pythagorean fragment: Cory, 321.   [4] Philo's Sanchoniathon, A.
[5] Cory, Anc. Fragm. 297.   [6] Munk's Palestine, 86, 87, 435.

When he prepared the heavens I was present;
When he described a circle on the face of the deep:
When he disposed the atmosphere above.—Proverbs, viii. 27.

And Elohim made the firmament (the heaven), and divided the waters which were under the firmament from the waters which were above the firmament.

And Elohim said, Let the waters under the heaven be gathered together unto one place, and let the dry land appear.—Genesis, i.

Then was the SPIRIT, and Darkness and silence were on every side!

Then thou didst command a fair LIGHT to come forth.

Upon the second day thou didst make the spirit of the firmament, and didst command it to part asunder and make a division betwixt the waters, that the one part might go up and the other remain beneath.—2 Esdras, vi.

He spreads out the heavens like a vault; upon the waters he has founded it.—2 Esdras, xvi. 59.

Thou saidst, LET IT BRING FORTH, and it gave birth: for he fixed the earth
Ever tossed by Tartarus, and sweet LIGHT he himself gave.
Heaven above and the azure sea he spread out.—Eruthræa Sibylla.[1]

We know from Herodotus that the Orphic and Bacchic doctrines and usages were really Egyptian.[2] "Orpheus and Homer transmit the philosopher's mantle and a divine language to Plato."[3] "It is difficult to determine the time when the Orphic association was formed in Greece, and when hymns and other religious songs were first composed in the Orphic spirit. But if we content ourselves with seeking to ascertain the beginning of higher and more hopeful views of death than those presented by Homer, we find them in the poetry of Hesiod. . . . At the time when the first philosophers appeared in Greece poems must have existed which diffused, in mythical forms, conceptions of the origin of the world and the destiny of the soul, differing from those in Homer. About 612 B. C., Epimenides of Crete, an early contemporary of Solon, was sent for to Athens, in his character of an expiatory priest. Damascius ascribes to him a cosmogony in which the MUNDANE EGG plays an important part, *as in the Orphic cosmogonies.* Another and more ex-

---

[1] Boissard, 210; Servatius Gallaeus.   [2] Kenrick, i. 338; Herodot. 2, 81.
[3] Marcellus, Nonnus, Notes to Dionusiac iv.

traordinary individual of this class was Abaris, who, *about a generation later*, appeared in Greece as an expiatory priest, with rites of purification and holy songs. Some fragments of a theogony composed by Pherecydes (about 600 B. C.) have a much closer resemblance to the Orphic poems than to Hesiod. *They show that Orphic ideas were then in vogue.* The god Ophioneus (the Serpent-god, the Divine Wisdom of the Deity), *the unity of Zeus and Eros,* and several other things in the Theogony of Pherecydes also occur in Orphic poems. Plato derived many of his ideas from the Orphic and Pythagorean doctrines." These Orphic priests seem to have had ideas like the Jewish. They dressed in linen like the Phœnician, Hebrew, and Egyptian priests, and promised to release men *from their own sins and those of their forefathers,* by sacrifices and expiatory songs.[1] They had the same regard for the ox as a sacred symbol which the Hebrews evinced. In describing the creation of the world, they usually employed the image of a bowl (crater), in which the different elements were supposed to be mixed in certain proportions, or garment, in which the different threads are united into one web.[2]

Janus (Aion) says:

Me the ancients called Chaos, for I am THE PRISTINE THING.
See, of how long a time I will sing the acts.
This lucid Air, and, what remains *three* bodies,
Fire, waters, earth, were one heap.
When this once separated, by the strife of its own things,
And the loosened mass removed into new homes,
The Flame sought heaven ; a nearer place took Air:

---

[1] K. O. Müller, 235.

Alas! wretched are these sufferings, but from some distant period or other I receive this calamity from the gods, *for the errors of some of those of old.*—Euripides, Hippolytus, 832.

Visiting the sins of the fathers upon the children unto the third and fourth generation.—Second Commandment.

The Hindus held that the misfortunes of this life were owing to sins committed in a former existence of the soul.

[2] K. O. Müller, 237, 232.

In the midst of the bottom earth and ocean sat.
Then I, who had been globe and unformed mass,
Returned into form and members worthy of a god !
Now also, as a little mark of my formerly confused figure,
What is in me seems the same before and behind !—Ovid, Fast. I. 113.

First I sung the obscurity of ancient Chaos,
How the Elements were ordered and the Heaven reduced to bound ;
And the generation of the white bosomed Earth and the depth of the
      Sea,
And EROS (LOVE) THE MOST ANCIENT, self-perfecting, and of manifold
      design,
How he generated all things and parted them from one another.
And I have sung of Kronos so miserably undone, and how the kingdom
Of the blessed Immortals descended to the thunder-loving Zeus.
                                   Orpheus, Arg. 419.

First, the vast necessity of ancient Chaos,
And Kronos, who in the boundless tracts brought forth
The Aether and the splendid and glorious Eros of a two-fold nature,
The illustrious Father of Night, existing from eternity.
I have sung the birth of powerful Brimo (Hecate) and the unhallowed
      deeds
Of the earth-born (Titans) who showered down from heaven
Their blood, the lamentable seed of generation, from whence sprung
The race of mortals who inhabit the boundless earth for ever.
                                   Arg. 12.[1]

Then a second race of men will spring up, huge, terrible, the race of the
earth-born Titans. Who have the same visage, one nature and manner of
body, all will have one species and one voice. They will determine lastly,
hastening to destruction, to fight arrayed against the starry heaven. Then
there will be an overflow of great OCEAN upon them, with raging waters. But
the Great Sabaoth incensed will restrain him, suppressing, that he should not
again undertake to make a deluge upon evil-minded men. But after the Great
God that thunders on high shall have compressed the Sea shut up in its own
bounds within shores and harbors, and shall draw a line of earth about it, then
the SON of Great God shall come in the flesh to men, like to mortals upon
earth ... For eight monads, as many decads in addition to these, and eight
hecatontads will signify to unbelieving men THE NAME. But do you in your
mind recognize Christ Son of Immortal God Most High! He will fulfil the
law of God, he will not abolish it, being an exact IMAGE, and will teach all
things. To him the priests shall bring offerings, proffering gold, myrrh, and
frankincense.—Sibylline Orac. [2]

[1] Cory, 291.   [2] Gallaeus, 175–180.

According to Pherecydes, " Chronos (Time, Saturn), Zeus and Chthonia existed from eternity. Chthonia was called Earth." Here we have Chronos the First Cause, and the "Two Principles" Zeus and Chthonia, like the Babylonian "Two Principles" Bel and Mylitta. Pherecydes next relates how *Zeus transformed himself into Eros, the God of Love*, wishing to form the world from the original materials made by Chronos and Chthonia.' "The Orphic theogony placed Chronos (Time) at the head of all things and conferred upon it life and creative power. Chronos was then described as spontaneously producing Chaos and Aether (the Spirit) and forming from Chaos, within the Aether, a mundane egg of brilliant white. The mundane egg is a notion which the Orphic poets had in common with many oriental systems ; but the Orphic poets first *developed* it among the Greeks. . . . They as well as Hesiod made Zeus the Supreme God at this period of the world. He was therefore supposed to supplant Eros-Phanes, and to unite this being with himself. . . . *The unity of Zeus and Eros* and several other things in the Theogony of Pherecydes also occur in the Orphic poems.² The Orphic poets also described Zeus as uniting the jarring elements into one harmonious structure ; and thus restoring by his Wisdom the unity which existed in Phanes, but which afterwards had been destroyed and replaced by confusion and strife. Here we meet with the idea of a *creation*, which was quite unknown to the most ancient Greek poets. . . . The Orphic poets conceived the world as having been formed by the Deity out of pre-existing matter, and upon a pre-determined plan." ³

First was Chaos and Night, and black Erebus and vast Tartarus ;
And there was neither Earth nor Air nor Heaven ; but in the boundless
  bosoms of Erebus
Night, with her black wings, first produced an aerial egg,
From which, at the completed time, sprang forth the lovely Eros,

¹ K. O. Müller, 241.   ² Ibid. 234.   ³ Ibid. 237.

Glittering with golden wings upon his back, like the swift whirlwinds. ...
The race of the Immortals was not till Eros mingled all things together:
But when the elements were mixed with one another, Heaven was pro-
duced and Ocean,
And Earth, and the imperishable race of all the Blessed Gods.

Aristophanes, Aves, 698.

According to Eudemus of Rhodes, a scholar of Aristo-
teles, the Sidonians set before all, Saturn, Desire and Mist.
Desire is the Babylonian Apason, the LOVE of the unrevealed God. From the union of Desire with Mist are born
Aether and Air, and from these two the egg is formed by
the Intelligible Wisdom.[1]

The Egg the Duad of the natures male and female contained in it... and the
Third in addition to these is the Incorporeal God with golden wings upon his
shoulders, on his head a serpent invested with the varied forms of animals
(the Zodiac ?). This is the Mind of the Triad.—Damascius.[2]

Oulomus would be the Intelligible Mind.[3] The Sun is
the Intelligible Mind.[4] " Metis the first Father and all-de-
lightful Eros.[5] " The Demiurgus is more particularly
Phanes.[6]

Eros, Eros, O Thou that instillest desire through the eyes, inspiring sweet
affection in the souls of those against whom thou makest war, mayst thou
never appear to me to my injury nor come unmodulated: for neither is the
dart of fire or the stars more vehement than that of Venus which Eros THE
BOY OF ZEUS sends from his hands. In vain, in vain, both by the Alpheus
and at the Pythian temples of Phœbus does Greece then solemnize the slaughter
of bulls : but Eros the tyrant of men, porter of the dearest chambers of Venus,
we worship not, the destroyer and visitant of men when he comes... O sacred
wall of Thebes, O mouth of Dirce, you could relate with me in what manner
Venus comes: for by the forked lightning, by a cruel fate, she put to eternal
sleep the parent of the *Jove-begotten Bacchus*, when she was visited as a bride.
—Euripides, Hippolyt. 560.[7]

Eros is the tendency to create. It is "the Spirit."
Hephæstus (Fire) seems to mean the Divine Breath which

---

[1] Damascius, l. c. p. 259 ; Movers, 278.   [2] Cory, 314.
[3] Cory, 320.   [4] Damascius ; Cory, 321.   [5] Proclus in Tim. ii. 102.
[6] Proclus in Tim. ii. 93 ; Cory, 306.   [7] See Buckley's Transl.

inspired the earth-clod with the life-fire, like Chronos the Life-dragon who created the world-egg.[1] Compare the Vedic Pramati, the "Fire on the altar" regarded as Soul of the world, Anima mundi: also Prometheus who stole fire to create men. Pramati is Agni.

And WISE EROS, self-taught, Shepherd of Eternity, having forced the murky gates of original Chaos.—Nonnus, Dionysiaca, vii. 110.

Wisdom says:

I came out of the mouth of the Most High, and covered the earth as a CLOUD. He created me from the Beginning before the world.—Ecclesiasticus, xxiv. 3, 9.

This is the Phœnician doctrine of the Two Principles, Aether and Chaos, Spirit and Matter.

The Spirit (Pneuma) is the primal Male Power (männliche Urkraft).[2] The Book of Wisdom says that "In the Divine Wisdom there is an intellectual Spirit ($\pi\nu\epsilon\hat{\upsilon}\mu\alpha$ $\nu o\epsilon\rho\grave{o}\nu$), holy, Only-begotten, manifold, subtile."

For WISDOM is more moving than any motion: she passeth and goeth through all things by reason of her pureness.

For she is the BREATH OF THE POWER OF GOD and a PURE INFLUENCE FLOWING FROM THE GLORY of the Almighty.—Wisdom of Solomon, vii. 22, 24, 25.

The Platonic philosophers hold that Intellect is the very Life of living things, the First Principle and Exemplar of all, from which by different degrees the inferior classes of life are derived.—Proclus.[3]

But we speak of the WISDOM of God in a mystery, the HIDDEN WISDOM which God ordained before the world.—1 Cor. ii. 7.

But we preach Christ crucified. . . . . Christ the POWER of God and the WISDOM of God. . . . .—1 Cor. i. 23, 24.

Iamblichus and Plutarch regard Amun as the Demiurgic Mind.[4] This is the Logos, the Divine Intelligence.

[1] Rinck, i. 67.　　[2] Movers, 283.　　[3] Taylor, xxi.　　[4] Movers, 268.

We find the Egyptian Amon אָמוֹן, the Demiurg, used in Proverbs viii. 30, to express the Divine Wisdom (the Demiurg) Who created the world.[1]

> I was with him nutritious (Amōn).—Prov. viii. 30 ; Schmid.
>
> Bacchus is the Nutritive and Generative Spirit.—Plut. de Is. xl.

Amun-Khem appears to be really the god whom Plutarch describes as a form of Osiris. . . . The inscription "Amun-Ra," followed by the bull and vulture, is also found over a god with the head of the ram, so that we have here the three gods Amun, Kneph, and Khem, united under one form. Another combination is Amun-Hor with the head of a hawk, the bird especially consecrated to Horus ; and on the Kosseir road is a tablet in which the god Khem is repre-sented as a hawk with human legs, holding up the flagellum, and with the plumes of Amun.—Kenrick, i. 318 · Wilkin-son, M. and C. 4. 265.

> The doctrine of the Egyptians concerning the immaterial archetypes incul-cates the origin of all things from the One with different gradations to the Many ; which again are held to be under the supreme government of the One. And God produced Matter from the materiality (the physical part) of his divided essence, which (Matter) being of a vivific nature the Demiurg took it and made from it the harmonious imperturbable spheres : but the dregs he used in fabricating the generated and perishable bodies.[2]

> Thus spake the Creator and again into the same bowl in which he had by mingling tempered the Soul of the World, he poured what was left of the for-mer mixture, but not so pure as the first, less so by two or three degrees. And after having thus framed the universe he allotted to it souls equal in number to the stars, and distributed each soul to each star.—Stallbaum's Plato, Timaeus, p. 180.

> For the Creative Intellect when it proceeds to production, and leads forth into light the invisible power of the hidden archetypes (" causes," " images," " ideas," " souls," λογων), is called Amon : and when it perfects all things unerringly and according to art with truth, it is called Phtha : but the Greeks change Ptha into Hephaistus, attending only to the technical. And, as being a Producer of *good* things, it is called OSIRIS, and has other names in virtue of other powers and operations.[3]

Ptah as Fire and Light god is the creating Artificer, the

---

[1] Rinck, i. 164.   [2] Hermetic Fragments ; Cory, 285.

[3] Cory, 284; Kenrick, i. 308.

Power of the sunlight. Osiris-Ptah is Lord of life.[1] The first Chinese symbol —— represents at the same time the First Male Principle Yang, the Sun, light, heat, movement (Energy) and power. The second —— —— represents the Female Principle Yin.[2]

The Egyptians esteem the Sun to be the Demiurgus.[3] The Sun is the emblem of the Divine Intelligence when it goes forth to production. This Divine Reason or Intelligence is personified in the Egyptian Amon, Osiris and Thoth the Supreme Wisdom, called by the Father "Soul of my Soul and sacred Intelligence of my Intelligence." This Demiurg (Creator) Thoth is the Logos of Plato, the Divine Wisdom of Jesus Sirach and Philo, the "Word" of St. John, the Wisdom and Power of God mentioned by Paul. Plato's Logos is the Divine Reason; and was conceived in two ways —first as quiescent in God; second, as going forth to production. In like manner the Egyptian Thoth is conceived in two modes, Thoth 1st and Thoth 2d—another symbol of the Sun (Phre)—the incarnation of the First Thoth who delegated to him the government of the earth, moon and a superior ministry in the hells.[4]

In the Egyptian dialogue between Pimander (the unrevealed Intelligence of the First Cause) and Thoth, the Divine Wisdom manifested, we find a more philosophized expression of the same conception.

"I am Pimander, the 'THOUGHT' of the POWER Divine. . . . . He changed form and suddenly revealed to me All. I had then before my eyes a prodigious spectacle; all was converted into Light, an appearance wonderfully agreeable and attractive; I was enchanted. Shortly after, a terrible cloud, which terminated in oblique folds, and was clothed with a humid nature, was agitated with a

---

[1] Uhlemann, Thoth, 45, quotes Book of the Dead, 142, 15.
[2] La Chine, ii. 346. , [3] Cory, 287, from Chaeremon.
[4] Champollion, Egypte, 125; De Wette, Bibl. Dogm. p. 127.

dreadful crash.   A smoke escaped from it with noise:
from this noise went out a voice; it seemed to me the
voice of the Light, and 'THE WORD' proceeded out of
this VOICE of the Light.

"This 'Word' was borne up on a humid principle (the
waters) and from it proceeded the fire pure and light, which
elevating itself, became lost in the airs.   The Air, light like
the Spirit, occupies the midst between the water and the
fire; and the earth and the waters were so mingled together
that the surface of the earth enveloped by the waters did
not appear at any point.   They were both agitated by the
Word of the Spirit since it was borne above them. . . .
Pimander says: This Light is me.   I am the Intelligence, I
am thy God and am much more ancient than the Humid
Principle. . . . I am the germ of the thought, the resplendent Word the Son of God.   Think that what thus sees and
perceives in you is the Word of the Master, it is the
THOUGHT which is God the Father; they are not at all
separated, and their union is life. . . .

" I prayed Him to turn his face to me.   When he had
done so, I immediately perceived in my thought a Light,
environed with innumerable POWERS, brilliant without
limits, the fire retained in a space, by an invincible force,
and maintaining itself above its own proper base. . . . . .
I demanded of him whence the elements of nature emanate.
From the Will of God, said he, which having taken its
own perfection has adorned with it all the other elements
and vital seeds (principles of life) which he has created;
for the INTELLIGENCE is God, possessing the double
feeundity of the two sexes, which is the LIFE and the
LIGHT of His Intelligence; He created with His Word another operative Intelligence (operating as creator); He is
also God the Fire, and 'God the Spirit.'

" The Operative Intelligence and the Word enclosing in
them the Circles, (7), and turning with a great velocity, this

machine moves from its commencement to its end without having either beginning or end."—Books of Hermes.[1]

In the cosmogony of Diodorus (borrowed partly from the Egyptians) Heaven and Earth had but one form, Chaos. Then the bodies separated from one another, and the universe received its arrangement because the Air was in constant motion. The fiery element ($T\grave{o}$ $\pi\upsilon\rho\tilde{\omega}\delta\epsilon\varsigma$) elevated itself into the upper regions and formed the sun and the other stars. The clay and earthy matter sunk by mixture with the Moisture. Later, by degrees the Water and Earth were divided by the constant internal movement and formed the sea and the firm land. By the fire which streamed from the Sun were formed bubbles in which the animals created were nourished and developed by the night-mist and the day-heat of the Sun.[2] According to the Egyptians, The One Principle of the universe is celebrated as Unknown Darkness. The Two Principles are Sand and Water, from whom the First Kamephis is generated. . . . . But the more modern Heraiscus says that the Third, who is named Kamephis from his father and grandfather, is the Sun, equivalent in this case to the Intelligible Mind.[3] In Egypt the Sun was the image of the Creator (Demiurg).[4]

In the Egyptian-Phœnician Cosmogony at the commencement of Sanchoniathon the Divine Male is not yet developed so far as to become Light or Ligh-aether. "He places," says Philo, "as original Beginning, a cloudy Spiritual Breath, or the Breath of a cloudy Air and a gloomy Chaos. These are endless and boundless." In him there exists a masculine potenz as Spirit. He knew not yet his own creation. According to the Egyptian view, the Supreme Being in this incomplete state is Amun, living in his own solitude—later, the Divine *Mind* (Nous) *and Logos* (the Creative Intellect) goes forth to create.[5]

---

[1] Champollion, Egypte, 141.   [2] Uhlemann, Thoth, 31.

[3] Damascius; Cory, 321.   [4] Seyffarth, Theolog. Schriften, 13.

[5] Movers, 284.

Tenebrous Air filled with Spirit, and Chaos are the Two Principles in the Phœnician Cosmogony of Sanchoniathon.[1] Saturn-Kosmos is the God Ophioneus, the Divine Wisdom. The Orphic poets endow Zeus with the Anima mundi the Life of the world.[2] Pherecydes relates how Zeus transformed himself into Eros, wishing to form the world from the original materials formed by Chronos and Earth.[3]

And when the Air began to send forth Light.—Sanchoniathon's Phœnician Cosmogony.[4]

And the Spirit of God (the Love of the Unrevealed God, the Source of light) moved on the face of the waters : the earth was without form and void. And God *said*, Let there be Light !

The Principle of all things existing is God and the Intellect (the Demiurgic Logos) and Nature; and Matter and Energy and Fate and Conclusion and Renovation. For there were Boundless Darkness in the Abyss, and Water and a subtile Spirit intellectual in power existing in Chaos. But the Holy Light broke forth and the elements were produced from among the Sand of a Watery Essence.—Serm. Sac. liber iii.[5]

Plato and the first chapter of Genesis both regard the Deity *in the same point of view*. Both make God the Demiurg or Creator of the world, and both make him *rest* after he has done creating.[6] The world is created by the Divine Wisdom (Logos) according to Plato, and by the " Wisdom," " Word ". and " Spirit," according to the Old Testament.

Genesis opens with the nature of God as Uncreated Light, His Word as the Logos-Creator, and His Spirit as a co-operative, life-bestowing agency. This is exactly the Egyptian doctrine of the Pimander Dialogue. As the sunlight is a creative power giving life to the vegetable world, and was even held to be the life or cause of life in men and animals, the Hebrew philosopher very naturally laid down the first appearance of light as the moment when creation began. This Light proceeded as the Holy Spirit forth from God at

[1] Philo's Sanchoniathon, A.   [2] K. O. Müller, 236.   [3] Ibid. 241.
[4] Cory, 4.   [5] From the Modern Hermetic Books ; Cory, Anc. Fragm.
[6] Timaeus, ed. Stallbaum, 43, A.

his Word of Command, and the dark mass of chaotic waters received from the Light-influence, the seeds of life. Light comes from the Light-Principle in seven streams through the sun, moon and five planets, else he would not have let Light appear three days before God made the sun. The Light-Principle is "Iao the Light and Life-Principle,"[1] the Logos, "the Word of Life."

For the Life was manifested, and we have seen and bear witness and show unto you that ETERNAL LIFE (the Logos) which was with the Father, and was manifested to us.—John, Epist., i. 1.

He is the Spiritual Light-Principle from which, in the Chaldean doctrine, all spiritual beings (souls) emanated.[2]

No one has seen the First-born with his eyes
Exeept the sacred Night alone : all others
Wondered when they beheld in the Aether the unexpected Light
Such as the skin of the Immortal Phanes shot forth.—Orpheus.[3]

"The Earth was invisible on account of the darkness but the Light broke through the Aether. The Light was the Demiurgus (Creator) a Being Supreme above all others, and its name is Metis, Phanes, Erikapaeus. These three powers are the three names of the ONE POWER and STRENGTH of the Only God whom no one ever beheld. By this POWER all things were produced, both the incorporeal Beginnings (Αρχαι) and the Sun and Moon and their influences. And man was formed by this God out of the earth and endued with a reasonable soul as Moses has revealed."[4]

Dwelling of the God who separated the mass of the earth and the water, who surrounded the earth with water.[5]

Ahura-mazda has perfected the creation of the world in 365 days. First, he made the heaven, working with the holy immortals zealously for 45 days: next, he in 60 days

---

[1] Movers, 265.　　[2] Ibid. 550.　　[3] Hermias in Phaed. ; Cory, 296.
[4] Orpheus; J. Malala, 89, in Cory, 297, 298.
[5] Seyffarth, Theol. Schr. der Alten Aegypt. 36.

12

created the waters—then in 75 days the earth, in 30 days
the trees, in 80 days the animals, and finally in 75 days he
made man. In these six periods Ahura-mazda made
"Heaven and Earth," corresponding to the six days of the
Mosaic account of the Creation. King Darius and his successors name Ahura-mazda, in their inscriptions, "the
greatest of the gods," or "the chief of the gods, who has
created Heaven and Earth."[1] The Persians said that the
Creation took place when Ormuzd spoke "the Word Honover" the "Light-Word." The Brahmans held that Brahm,
the Soul of the world, shone forth in person : that, pronouncing the Word OM, the Mighty Power became half
male half female.

He framed the Heaven above and the Earth beneath ; in the midst he
placed the subtile Aether, the eight regions and the permanent receptacle of
the waters.—Asiatic Res. vol. v.

Pythagoras taught that God is the *Universal Mind diffused through all things*, the Source of all life, the proper
and intrinsic Cause of all motion, in substance similar to
Light, in nature like truth, the First Principle of the universe, incapable of pain, invisible, incorruptible, and *only
to be comprehended by the mind*. Cicero remarks that Pythagoras conceived God to be a Soul pervading all Nature
of which every human soul is a portion. He taught the
transmigration of souls, which doctrine was common to
India and Egypt where Pythagoras probably derived it.
He also believed that certain "intelligent forms" subsist in
the Divine Mind (Logos).[2] These are the archetypes or
causes, the links which communicate between the Divine
Mind, and Matter. The Peruvians had an idea that every
thing on earth had its "archetype" or "idea," its "mother"
as they emphatically styled it, which they held sacred as,
in some sort, its spiritual essence.[3]

[1] Dunker, ii. 360; Bundehesh, chapter i. by Spiegel.
[2] Anthon.   [3] Prescott, i. 94.

The Beginnings (causes) are the spiritual or ideal forms before they are clothed in visible works and bodies. They are the Principles which have understood the ideal works of the Father.[1]

All things are the progeny of One Fire. The Father perfected all things and delivered them over to the Second Mind whom all nations of men call the First.[2]

God the FIRST CAUSE, according to Aristotle, induces a movement in the universe, without being moved himself.[3] This is the Oriental idea of the First Cause in a state of rest, inaction, complete in himself, like Brahm before Eros or Kama stirs "IT" to production. Aristotle's CAUSE is INTELLIGENCE (Logos).[4] This is the Logos that was in the Beginning, the Logos *remaining in* the Deity before it goes forth to production.

Such is the Mind which is there energizing before energy, that it has not gone forth but abode in the paternal depth and in the adytum according to divinely nourished silence.—Proclus in Timaeum.[5]

Before all things that actually exist, and before the whole "Ideal forms" there is One God prior to the *First God and King*,[6] remaining immovable in the solitude of his unity. For neither is "the Ideal" mixed up with Him nor any other thing. He is established the *exemplar* of the God who is the father of himself (meaning that He is the exemplar of Iao the Demiurg, the Son): self-begotten, the only Father—and who is truly Good. For He is something greater and the First; the fountain of all things, the ROOT of the first "forms" existing as "Ideas" in the Divine Reason ("Intelligible existing forms"). And from this One the Self-originated God (the Son) caused himself to shine forth; for which reason he is his own father and self-originated. For he is both an *Αρχη* (a "Beginning" or Soul) and god of gods, a Monad from the One, prior to substance and the be-

[1] Dam. de Princip. ; Cory, 254. [2] Psellus, 20 ; Pletho, 30 ; in Cory, 242.
[3] Cousin, Lectures, i. 421. [4] Ibid. [5] Cory, Anc. Fragm
[6] IAO the Efficient Cause.

ginning of substance. . . . He is called the Beginning of
the Intelligibles.[1]

Under Two Minds the Life-giving Fountain of souls is comprehended.[2]
The Principal of the incorporeals is their basis (" underlies" the souls).[3]

In the 5th volume of the Asiatic Researches is the following Hindu Cosmogony :

This Universe existed only in the first divine idea, yet unexpanded, as if
involved in darkness, imperceptible, undefinable, undiscoverable by reason
and undiscovered by revelation, as if it were wholly immersed in sleep.

When the sole self-existing Power, himself undiscerned but making this
world discernible, with five elements and other principles of nature, appeared
with undiminished glory, expanding his idea or dispelling the gloom.

He whom the mind alone can perceive, whose essence eludes the external
organs, who has no visible parts, who exists from eternity, even he, the Soul
of all beings, whom no being can comprehend, *shone forth* in person.

He having willed to produce various beings from his own divine substance
first *with a thought* created the waters.

The waters are called nara, because they are the production of Nara, the
Spirit of God ; and since they were his first ayana, or place of motion, he
thence is called Narayana, or " moving on the waters." [4]

From that which is, the First Cause, not the object of sense, existing
everywhere in substance, not existing to our perception, without beginning or
end, was produced the Divine Male.

He framed the heaven above, and the earth beneath : in the midst he
placed the subtile Aether, the eight regions, and the permanent receptacle of
waters.

He framed all creatures.

He too first assigned to all creatures distinct names,[5] distinct acts, and
distinct occupations.

He gave being to time and the divisions of time, to the stars also and to
the planets, to rivers, oceans and mountains ; to level plains and uneven
valleys.

For the sake of distinguishing actions he made a total difference between
right and wrong.

[1] Kenrick, i. 303 ; Cory, Anc. Fragm.   [2] Damascius, de Prin.; Cory, 60, 61.
[3] Dam. in Parm ; Cory, 60, 61.   [4] The Indogermanic Nerio and Neriene
(Nariana ; Sanskrit Narayana " water-movement " or " water-way ") Sol-Mars
and his wife. Nara is a Russian stream. Narayana is old Nereus, the Sun
considered as the source of the waters.

[5] Adam does this in Genesis. And whatsoever Adam called every living
creature, that was the name thereof.—Gen. ii. 19.

Having divided his own substance, the Mighty Power became half male, half female.

He whose powers are incomprehensible, having created this universe, was again absorbed in the Spirit, changing the time of energy for the time of repose.[1]

He, that Brahma, was all things, comprehending in his own nature the indiscrete and discrete. He then existed in the forms of Purusha and Kala.[2] The One Supreme Being is Brahm in the neuter gender. When the Divine Power is conceived as *exerted in creating*, he is called Brahma. The Mind (Manas, Mens) incited by the Love (Kama, Eros) becomes creative. The neutral Brahma is personified, becomes through emanation Brahma the Creator of the world.[3]

There were born to Kronos, in Peraia, three boys, Kronos named like his Father, and Zeus-Belus and Apollon.—Sanchoniathon, p. 32; Movers, 186.

"There were two Bels: the first, Saturn; the second, Sol."[4]

First is Belus who is Kronos; from him are Belus and Canaan; and this Canaan bore[5] the father of the Phœnicians. And from him was born a son Choum who is called AsNOLOS by the Greeks.—Alexander Polyhistor.[6]

"This is the order of the series: Jupiter Epaphus, Belus priscus, Agenor, PHŒNIX, Belus minor who is Methres."—Servius ad Æneid, i. 642, 343.

> Ogugia calls me Bacchus;
> Egypt thinks me Osiris;
> The Musians name me PHANAX;
> The Indi consider me Dionysus;
> The Roman Mysteries call me Liber,
> The Arabian race Adonis!—Ausonius, Ep. 30.

"The Father (das Urgute) produced the Intelligible (Invisible) Sun, which in the Chaldean doctrine is Iao, the Intelligible-Light and Spiritual Principle of life."[7]

---

[1] Edinburgh Encycl. [2] Vishnu Purana, 9. [3] Weber, Ind. Stud. ii. 876.
[4] Movers, 186. [5] The Phoenicians (Phoinix) were Canaanites.—Genesis x. 15, 19, 18; Movers, 2. [6] Ibid. 186; Eusebius, praep. ev. ix. 17. [7] Movers, 265, 266.

Salve vera Deûm facies vultusque paterne!
Hail! true Form of the gods and Face of the Father!

Martianus Capella de Nupt. Phil.[1]

Father-begotten Light! for he alone having gathered the strength of the Father, the flower of Mind, has the power of understanding the Paternal Mind.—Proclus in Timaeum, 242.[2]

"This Primal Father of all has an Only-begotten Son who is in every respect like him, and therefore is himself again, and in the Trinity takes the first place: he is the Creator (Demiurg) Bel, the revealed Saturn, the mystical Heptaktis (7 rays) or Iao of the Chaldean philosophy. . . . In the Chaldean oracles of the two Julians, father and son, the two Bels the Older and the Younger, divested of their mythic personality, were hymned as the Old and New Eternal Time (Kronos).—Proclus in Tim. iv. 251. According to the Emperor Julian, the Highest Deity, the Supreme Goodness, has brought forth out of itself the Intelligible Sun, of which the visible sun is only an image, and which in the Chaldean doctrine is the Intelligible-Light and Spiritual Life-principle Iao, like to Himself the Original Being, in all respects." [3]

The Chaldeans call the god Iao, instead of φῶς νοητὸν=Intelligible Light. —Lydus de Mens. iv. 38, p. 74.[4]

The Sun the greatest god He has caused to appear out of Himself, in all things like Himself.—Julian, l. c. p. 132.[5]

Behold, at the door of the temple of Iahoh, between the porch and the altar were about five-and-twenty men (the High-priest and twenty-four priests) with their backs towards the temple of Iahoh and their faces towards the east; and they worshipped the Sun towards the east.—Ezekiel, viii. 16.

ORPHIC HYMN TO THE SUN.

Titan of golden lustre, moving above, Heavenly Light, self-produced, ... fiery, food-bringing, fruitful Paian: glowing, pure, Father of Time, immortal Zeus, serene, visible to all, the circumambient Eye of Kosmos, Eye of righteousness, Light of life.—Orphic Hymn, xi. ed. Hermann.

Shining Zeus, Dionysus, Father of sea, Father of earth,
All-producing Sun (Heli) all-radiant, golden-lustred!—Macrobius,
Sat. i. ch. 23.

[1] Movers, 266.   [2] Cory, Anc. Fragm.   [3] Movers, 265.   [4] Ibid.   [5] Ibid.

CHAPTER VIII.

THE LOGOS, THE ONLY-BEGOTTEN AND THE KING.

Unto you it is given to know the Mysteries of the Kingdom of God.

Luke, viii. 10.

The hidden belong to Iahoh, but the revealed to us.—Deut. xxix. 29.

Whence first appeared the festivities of Bacchus with the dithyramb that gains the bull as prize ?—Pindar, Olympic Ode xiii. Before Christ 464.

Dionysus a joy to mortals. . . . . Demeter the fair-haired queen.

Iliad, xiv. 325, 326.

God is the Cause, the Logos the instrument, and Matter the material, the element of Creation.[1]

The Monad is there first, where the Paternal Monad subsists.—Proclus in Euclid, 27.[2]

The Monad is extended which generates Two.—Proclus, in Euc. 27.[3]

The Maternal Cause is double, having received from the Father Matter and Spirit.

·For the Duad sits by this and glitters with intellectual sections to govern all things and to arrange each.—Proc. in Plat. 376.[4]

The Mind of the Father said that all things should be cut into three. His Will assented, and immediately all things were cut.—Proc. in Parmenides; Proc. in Tim.

The Father mingled every Spirit from this Triad.—Lydus de Mensibus, 20.[5]

All things are governed in the bosom of this Triad.—Lydus de Mens. 20.

For in the whole world shines a Triad over which a Monad rules.—Chaldean Oracles, Damascius in Parm.[6]

Pherecydes said that the Beginnings (First Principles) are Zeus, Chthonia and Kronos (Saturn); Zeus the Aether, Chthonia the Earth, and Kronos (Time, Sun).—Hermia, 6.[7]

---

[1] De Wette, Bibl. Dogm. p. 136.   [2] Cory, 241.   [3] Ibid. 245.   [4] Ibid.

[6] Taylor ; Cory, 245.   [6] Ibid. 246.   [7] Opera omnia Patrum Graec. iii. 432, 433. Wirceburg, 1777.

"Plato saying that the Beginnings (Αρχας) are God and Matter and Model" (Soul of the World).—Hermia, 5.

On the temple of Neith (Anaitis, Athena, Isis) at Sais in Egypt was the inscription :[1]

I am that which has been, is and will be, and no one of mortals has ever lifted my robe : the fruit which I brought forth became the Sun.

Who knows Mitra and Varuna, that it is your doing, that the footless dawn is the precursor of footed beings; and that your Infant (the Sun) sustains the burden of this (world): he diffuses truth and disperses the falsehood.[2]

"Type the Woman, Mother of the Sun" was represented "surrounded by innumerable stars." She was the Heaven.[3]

O Calliope, Child of Zeus, again begin to hymn the shining Sun whom large-eyed Euruphaessa bore to the Son of the Earth and the starry Heaven.—Homeric Hymn to the Sun.[4]

And Theia overcome by the love of Huperion bore great Helios.—Hesiod, Theog. 371–374 ; Pindar ; Catullus.

Whom spangled Night as she dies away brings forth and again lulls to sleep,—the Sun, the blazing Sun! Sophocles, Trachiniae 94–96.

The sun-god Ra is represented on the Egyptian monuments as a child with the disk and Uraeus on its head, carrying its finger to its mouth, sitting upon a lotus flower which rests upon the symbol of water. In the inscription before him he is named Ra of Edfu, the Sun-Horus of the two spheres.

In the Egyptian valley of Biban el Molouk in one of the tombs of the Pharaohs, the heaven was represented as the body of the Celestial Venus variegated with stars.[5] In the East, the Sun issues from her womb. He is born from the bosom of his divine mother Neith under the form of a little child putting its finger to its mouth.[6] This is "Eros

---

[1] Plutarch de Iside, ix.; Kenrick, i. 327, quotes Proclus in Tim. 30.

[2] Wilson, Rigv. ii. 91.   [3] Seyffarth, Computationssystem, 160.

[4] Buckley.   [5] Lepsius, Berlin Akad. 1856, p. 191. The lotos flower as the representation of the creative power in Nature is the symbol of Lakshmi (Venus) in India.—Wuttke, ii. 272.   [6] Champollion, Egypte, 104.

(Sun) the primitive Ruler of generation,"[1] or Cupid the Love of the Unrevealed God, Apason as he was called in Chaldea, Desire in Phœnicia, Erō in Egypt. Erō (Ar the Fire, Ares, Mars the fiery) is the eleventh sign of the Zodiac "the Bull." Neith is called "the Great Cow the Engenderer of the Sun."[2] Neith was called Isis.[3] We find "the sacred Cow of Hathor" (Venus the Earth-goddess).[4] Isis was called Athuri.[5]

In the Northern Cosmogony, Melted Ice was the first existence, whence sprung the giant Ymer (Amar, the Sun) and the cow Audumbla.[6] Their three sons killed their father and formed the heaven of his skull, the clouds of his brain, of his body the earth, of his blood the water, of his bones the mountains.[7] It is said that the Finns possessed the idea of the World growing as a living being from the Egg, and the notion of "the Word" as a Spiritual Potenz.[8]

Horus, the Sun, "the Shepherd of the peoples"[9] was born of Osiris and Isis the "Two Principles." Plato says the "World" is the Son of Thought the Father and Matter the Mother. In Egypt the Divine Intelligence, personified as Pimander, calls himself "the Thought of the Power Divine."[10] Horus is the Soul of the World.

Orus is the terrestrial World noways free from decay nor from birth.[11]

Female and Father is the mighty God Erikapaeus.—From the Ancient Theologists.[12]

Night and Heaven reigned and *before* them Erikapaeus their most mighty Father, who distributed the world to gods and mortals, over which he first reigned the illustrious Erikapaeus.[13]

Phanes the Man-woman is Saturn, the Son as the Soul of the World that, later, separates into Heaven and Earth, Adam and Eve. Metis (Mind), Phanes, Erikapaeus are all

---

[1] Nonnus, xli. 129.   [2] Kenrick, i. 327, 324.   [3] Ibid.
[4] Egypte, 126; Kuhn's Zeitschr. iv. 112, 113.   [5] Plutarch de Iside, lvi.
[6] The Earth, in India.—Kuhn, Zeitschrift, iv. 113.   [7] Rinck, i. 73.
[8] Castren, Finn. Mythol. p. 291.   [9] Egypte, 119.   [10] Ibid. 141.
[11] Movers, 268; Plutarch, de Is. xliii.   [12] Cory, 299.   [13] Ibid; Cory.

three the One Power and strength of the Only God.[1]   Bel,
who was both male and female in himself separated into
Heaven (Adam Epigeios) and Earth.[2]   Some of the systems
make Saturn to be Kosmos before he is thus separated.[3] He
is the Intelligent Life (Noera Zoē).   He is Hercules as the
impersonation of time, the winged Kosmos.[4]   The dragon is
his emblem.   Among the Egyptians the serpent was the
symbol of fruitfulness and the life-giving Power in Nature.[5]
Saturn is the Divine Wisdom, Kadmus, Ophion-Uranus.
The serpent-god is the symbol of the Soul of the World.[6]
Damascius calls Iao (the Son) the Soul of the World as the
Newplatonists call the Bel-Iao of the Chaldeans.[7]

The Incorporeal world then was already completed having its seat in the
Divine Reason.[8]

The Egg, the Duad of the natures male and female contained in it, ...
And the Third in addition to these is the " Incorporeal god " (the Soul of the
World).[9]

Plutarch says the better and diviner nature consists of *three*,
" What the Intellect perceives," Matter, and their offspring
Kosmos or Horus the Son.[10]

Before the heaven existed there were, through Logos,[11] Idea and Matter
and the God who is the Creator (Demiurg) of " the better."   The Deity made
this world out of the whole of Matter, One, Only-begotten, perfect, endued
with soul and with reason, and of a spherical body.   He made it a deity
created, never to be destroyed by any other cause than the God who had put it
together.   And it is the best of created things, since it has been produced by
the best Cause. . . . .[12]

He has united the Soul of the World with the centre of the world and led
it (the Soul) outwards (towards the circumference) investing the world wholly
with it.[13]

[1] Cory, 297, 299.   [2] Movers, 271, 554.   This is Iao.
[3] Movers, 554, et passim.   [4] Ibid. 556.   [5] Munter, Bab. 103.
[6] Movers, 504.   [7] Ibid. 555.   [8] Philo, On the Creation, x.; Migration
of Abraham, xxxv.   [9] Damascius ; see Cory Anc. Fragm.   [10] Plutarch de Is. lvi.

   The mind alone beholds God the eternal, the Chief-ruler of all things and
their Creator.—Timaeus Locrius, 96.

[11] The Divine Wisdom or Intelligence as Cause of all.
[12] Timaeus Locrius, 94.   [13] Plato, Timaeus, ed. Stallbaum, p. 133.

This heaven was produced according to an eternal pattern, the "Ideal World."[1]

The Primal Being is the Demiurgic Mind (Nous) who includes (encloses) the "Idea" of the "to be created world" within himself, and produces it out of himself.[2] The WORLD was considered a living being with a soul.[3] The Greeks of the time of Homer and Hesiod regarded the world as an organic being which was continually growing to a state of greater perfection.[4]

The SOUL OF THE WORLD is the Best of Eternal Intelligences and partakes of Reason.—Plato.[5]

This "World" (Kosmos) is thus become a visible animal containing things visible, a visible god the image of the invisible, the greatest, best and most perfect—this one Heaven, being Only-begotten.—Plato, Timaeus, 92; ed. Stallbaum.

Call it the World or Olympus or Heaven.—The Epinomis, c. 3.

When therefore that God who is a perpetually Reasoning Divinity cogitated about the god who was to subsist at some certain period of time, he produced his body smooth and equable.—Plato, Timaeus.[6]

The works of Nature coexist with the intellectual Light of the Father. For it is the Soul which adorned the great heaven and which adorns it along with the Father.—Chaldean Oracles.[7]

For after fire let us place Aether; and let us lay down that from it the Soul moulds animals . . . . and that Soul moulds after the Aether, from Air another genus of animals and a third from water. And it is probable that Soul, after it had fabricated all these, filled the whole of heaven with living matter by making use to the best of its power of all genera.—The Epinomis, § 7.

According to Plato the Divine Nature consists of Three

Thought (the Father)   Matter (the Mother)

"THE SON"=Kosmos, the Ensouled World.

The Reason of God is the seat of the Ideal or Intelligible World. The Soul of the World is a third subordinate na-

---

[1] Timaeus Locrius, 97.   [2] Movers, 268.   [3] Ritter, Hist. Phil. i. 199 ff.
[4] K. O. Müller, Lit. of Anc. Greece, 237.   [5] Timaeus, xiii. ed. Davis.
[6] Taylor, 483.   [7] Cory, 243.

ture proceeding both from God and from Matter and therefore is the Son of God.[1]

In the theogony of Mochus, "The Aether was the first
and the Air: these are "the Two Principles;" from them
Ulom[2] the "Intelligible god" was born.[3] The Light-Aether
is here the type of Belitan (the Father) but the Air is the
first form of the Naturegoddess, from whose union springs
Ulom the Aiōn, a new modification of the idea of Belitan.[4]
According to Mochus, Ulom "the Highest of the Intelligibles"
springs from the Two Principles Spirit and Matter. Being
both male and female, he produced out of himself the first
Chusorus the Intelligible (Incorporeal) Power, the Opener of
the egg, then an egg (the World-egg).[5] Megasthenes states that
the Brahmans asserted that the world was created, is transitory, and formed like a ball; and that the God who created
and rules it, pervades the whole.[6] The Orphic Eros-Phanes
springs from the egg which the Aetherial winds impreg-
nate.[7] The Orphic poets conceived this Eros-Phanes as a
Pantheistic being: the parts of the world forming as it were
the limbs of his body: and being thus united into an organic whole. The Heaven was his head, the earth his foot, the
sun and moon his eyes, the rising and setting of the heavenly bodies his horns.[8]

The thirtieth day of the month Epiphi the Egyptians celebrate the birth-
day festival of the Eyes of Horus, when the sun and moon are in one straight
line, since they consider not only the moon but the sun the eye and light of
Horus.—Plutarch, de Is. lii.

"He who generated all things says to them: Gods of
gods, of whose works I am Creator and Father,[9] I will deliver to you the seeds, making a beginning, and, for the rest,
do you weave together the mortal and immortal nature,
constructing and generating animals.[10] Thus spoke the

[1] Plutarch, de Is. lvi.   [2] Sun, Time.   [5] Movers, 282.   [4] Ibid. 283.
[6] Movers, 282; Cory, 321.   [6] Duncker, ii. 271.
[7] K. O. Müller, 236.   [8] Ibid.   [9] Timaeus, 41.
[10] Plato's Timaeus, ed. Stallbaum, p. 180.

Demiurg, and into the same bowl[1] in which by mingling he had tempered the Soul of the Universe." According to Proclus, Bacchus is the Creator[2] (in the Orphic views) analogous to the One Father who generates total fabrication.[3] According to Plato, " One is the Cause of all;" he calls it " the Good," and demonstrates that it is the Fountain which unites Intellect and the Intelligibles.[4] " The One" is neither " Intelligible" nor intellectual, nor, in short, participates of the power of being.[5] In the Chaldean learning the Supreme Being is conceived as the world-creating WISDOM (demiourgikos Nous) which contains the " Idea" of the future WORLD and produces it out of itself. The Supreme Being is Saturn-Kosmos (the First Thoth, Ophion-Kosmos; or, according to Plato, the Divine Reason, the seat and origin of the " Idea" of the world). From this is born the Second Horus, the " existing," " ensouled" world. It is the realized " Idea," which before lay dormant in the mind of Saturn-Kosmos, now brought to light and clothed with material form. The Youthful Horus is the son of Osiris (the Spirit of God; Thought) and Isis (Matter). In like manner Plato calls the " Kosmos" " the Son" of the Father and Mother (Thought and Matter).[6] Saturn-Kosmos is found in the Babylonian, Phœnician and Hindu Philosophy. From the union of the " Two Principles," Spirit and Matter, is born the Phanes of Phœnician, the Mahan Atma (Brahma) of some of the Hindu systems. " In the Kathakopanishad, the Spirit (Purusha) already stands before the Original Matter, from whose union springs the Great Soul of the world (Mahan Atma, Brahma) the Spirit of life."[7] Esmun is Kosmos, and corresponds to Pan.[8]

The Egyptians distinguished between an Older and Younger Horus, the former the *brother* of Osiris; the latter

[1] The Vivific goddess Juno—Taylor's Plato, Timaeus, p. 505.
[2] Demiurg.   [3] Taylor's Plato, p. 484.   [4] Taylor's Proclus, p. 120.
[6] Taylor, p. 118.   [6] Plut. de Is. lvi.   [7] Weber, Akad. Vorles, 213, 214.
[8] Movers, 332.

the *Son* of Osiris and Isis. The first is the "Idea" of the World remaining in the Demiurgic Mind, "born in darkness before the creation of the world." The second Horus is this "Idea" going forth from the Logos, becoming clothed with Matter and assuming an actual existence.[1] The First Horus is Apollo (Bel) the sun-god, like Osiris himself.

The Mundane God, eternal, boundless, young and old, of winding form.— Chaldean Oracles.[2]

The sun-god was considered the heart or life of the world and the "Invisible" and "Celestial" Sun was both Kosmos and Logos ("a soul"). Moumis is the Son of Apasson and Taautha, Adonis and Venus. Moumis is the "Idea" of the future world, proceeding from the Two Principles.[3] He is the first movement of life in dead Chaos; he is the "First-born" of Sanchoniathon, the Ialda-Baoth of the Valentinians, and Logos; or the first revelation of Iao and Iao himself.[4] Iao is, according to Macrobius, Sol and Dionysus.[5]

On a seal in Dr. Abbot's Egyptian museum, in New York, is a representation of Horus (the Power of God) with the Lion's head, the ansated cross in his right hand, a sceptre in his left, and the Sun's disk surrounded by the snake Uraeus on his head.[6] Underneath is the word Ammonio, "To the Creative God" or Logos. The inscription is as follows:

[1] Movers, 268; Kenrick, i. 323, 343; Uhlemann, Drei Tage, 163.
[2] Cory, 240.   [3] Movers, 275.   [4] Movers, 285.   [5] Ibid. 540.
[6] Horus is Phoebus the far-darting god of light. He often appears with the head of a hawk and the Sun's disk, the Uraeus-serpent, the scarabaeus.— Kenrick, i. 328.

This inscription has been twice translated by Prof. Seyffarth—in the Evang. Review, July, 1856, p. 104, and in his Chronology, p. 204.

The seal of IAR with the LION'S HEAD.

MISI MΓ ΕΡΗΕΡΠ.

AMMWNIW
WCOYEIPMIWCΦPH
TOΦWCΠVPΦΛOϟ
MIWCMIWCIAPMI
CIMIEΦEΦNOV
EIΛEWC
KAVΘIMOI
ΘENΛEONTWΠO
ΔITHNKATOIKIANK
EKΛHPWMENOCOE
NTWAΓIWCHKWENI
APYMENOCOAETPAΠ
TWN KAIBPONTWN KA
ΓNOΦOV KAIANEMW
NXVPIOCOTHNENΘ
YPANIONTHC EWN
IOVΦVCEWCKEKΛ
HPWMENOCA
NANKHN
CVIOTAXVEE^EOCΘENHKOOCΘEOCOMETA
ΛOΔOϟOCΛEONTOMOPOΦOCO NMʌ`ΛAC
ΘI

ΑΜΜΩΝΙΩ.

*ΩΣ ΟΥΣΙΡ ΜΙΩΣ ΦΡΗ ΤΟ ΦΩΣ ΠΥΡ ΦΛΟΞ
ΜΙΩΣ ΜΙΩΣ ΙΑΡ ΜΙΣΣΙ ΜΙ ΕΦΕΦ ΝΟΥ ΕΙΛΕΩΣ.
ΚΑΥΘΙ ΜΟΙ Ο ΕΝ ΛΕΟΝΤΩΠΟΔΙ ΤΗΝ ΚΑΤ-
ΟΙΚΙΑΝ ΚΕΚΛΗΡΩΜΕΝΟΣ Ο ΕΝ ΤΩ ΑΓΙΩ ΣΗΚΩ
ΕΝΙΑΡΥΜΕΝΟΣ Ο ΑΣΤΡΑΠΤΩΝ ΚΑΙ ΒΡΟΝΤΩΝ
ΚΑ ΓΝΟΦΟΥ ΚΑΙ ΑΝΕΜΩΝ ΧΥΡΙΟΣ Ο ΤΗΝ ΕΝ-
ΟΥΡΑΝΙΟΝ ΤΗΣ ΕΩΝΙΟΥ ΦΥΣΕΩΣ ΚΕΚΛΗΡΩΜΕ-
ΝΟΣ ΑΝΑΝΚΗΝ.
ΣΥ Ι Ο ΤΑΧΥ ΕΕΛΕΟΣΘΕΝ ΗΚΟΟΣ ΘΕΟΣ Ο
ΜΕΓΑΛΟΔΟΞΟΣ ΛΕΟΝΤΟΜΟΡΟΦΟΣ Ο ΕΝΜΟΛΑΣ
ΟΙ.*

AMMONIO.[1]

Great is Osiris,. greater Phrè (Sun) the Light Fire Flame,
but the greatest is Iar [2] born in [3] (the month) Epiphi, now
very luminous !

Hear me (Thou) who in Leontopolis hast the dwelling,
who in the holy enclosure [4] art invoked, the Lord of lightnings and thunders and storm and winds, who hast the
heavenly control of eternal Nature.

Thou art the God swift-coming from the sun, the great-
ly-glorious, lion-shaped, the very white forever ! [5]

Many of the titles attributed to Horus in the inscriptions
indicate his relations to the Sun.[6] Horus is the seminal
Principle, the Principle of regeneration, the Demiurg. This
is Iao who is over the seven heavens, who received the.
light from the First Cause and poured it out upon the

---

[1] Ammon is the Demiurgic Mind.—Movers, 268.

[2] Ar, Har, Iar, Horus, Orus, the Spirit, the Nile, the Son of God, the Logos
or Word. Ares is Baal.—Movers, 187. Iaro is the Nile. Eiar, Spring, in Greek.

[3] From the beginning of Epiphi. In Coptic, hm=in. In Hebrew, Mi Min
mean "from," "ab initio." Gesenius Thes. p. 806 ; Rödiger's Gesen. Grammar, §§ 100, 151, b.   [4] Holy of Holies ; where the *statue* stood.

[5] The Egyptians called Horus λευκòς (albus) white.—Plut. de Is. xxii.

[6] Kenrick, i. 353.

world. Among the Egyptians the serpent was the symbol
of the fruitfulness and life-bestowing Power of Nature.[1]
The Nile overflows when the Sun passes through the sign
of the Lion in the Zodiac.[2] From Horus (Iar; Iaro=the
Nile) flows the Celestial Nile, "the Outflowing of Osiris,"
the source of life and of Egypt's fruitfulness. It is not until
the *last days of June or the beginning of July* that the rise
of the Nile begins to be visible in Egypt.[3] "The 30th of the
month Epiphi ("Epep," according to Lepsius:[4] Epiphi
begins June 25th),[5] they solemnize the feast of the eyes of
Horus when the sun and moon are in the same straight
line, estimating the sun and moon to be the eyes of Horus."[6]
It is to this that the words "Born in Epheph now very
shining" appear to have reference in the above inscription.

Some words then said the Lord of Fire, Hyperion: On the third table
whence will be the ripening of the grape, you will know where are the
Lion and Virgin.—Nonnus, Dionys. xii. 37, 38.

Where was the Light-bringing Lion; where the Virgin herself was
embroidered glittering in borrowed form.—Ibid. xii. 93, 94.

Now the "Virgin" returns, the Saturnian reigns return.—Virgil,
Ecl. iv.

"Hymn to Ra the shining King of the worlds . . . . Creator, Producer and
Governor of the other gods, the Lord of the heavenly hosts, Prince of the
star-house."[7]

On a stele, at Berlin, he is called "First-born of the Heaven
ly Ones, Producer of time, Cause of life."[8]

Orus, Offspring of the Lord of Lords (efte pe Neb Neb).[9]
The illustrious Orus Son of Atamu (efte Tmo).[10]

Amon-Horus or Horammon is the active and generative
Spirit.[11] Horus, the "Idea" of the pure Light-Aether, has

---

[1] Munter, Bab. 103.　　[2] Plutarch, de Is. xxxviii.; Ibid. Quaest. Conviv.
lib. iv. 5.　　[3] Kenrick, i. 70; Uhlemann, Drei Tage, pp. 193, 163.
[4] Lepsius, Einleitung, 141; Wilkinson, Sec. Series, i. 378.
[5] Kenrick, i. 277. Note.　　[6] Plut. de Is. lii.　　[7] Uhlemann, Thoth, 41.
[8] Uhlemann, Thoth, 41.　　[9] Seyffarth, Theolog. Schr. 91.　　[10] Ibid. 88.
[11] Champollion, Egypte, Univ. pitt. p. 245.

his eye in the sun.[1]   He was the Anima Mundi (Life of the world) like Zeus and Pan.   Iao is the First-born, the Only-begotten Son, called also Zeus-Bel, Mithra, Intelligible Sun, Intelligible Light.   He is related to Moumis, Ulom, Aiōn, Erikapaeus and Phanes.   Damascius calls Iao Intelligible World (Soul of the World) as the Newplatonists call the Bel-Iao of the Chaldeans.[2]   The Chaldee-Persian Logos is the " Idea of the world" going forth from the Demiurgic Mind and realizing itself in actuality, " the Only-begotten of the Father" in the Cosmogony of the Babylonians according to Eudemus.[3]

Horus has taken the place of Osiris and is here " Iao, the highest of all the gods."   He is the Demiurgic Mind. He contends with Typhon (the Devil) for the crown of Osiris. He is like Dionysus and Milichus " the Son of the Father."[4] Earlier we find Osiris, the Good Principle, contending with Typhon who is called " Set," (Sat, or Satan).[5]   Typhon is said in one myth to have conspired against Osiris with seventy-two men and the Egyptian queen Aso. Having persuaded Osiris to get into a box, he pegs and solders him down and sets him afloat on the Nile. Isis cuts off her hair and puts on mourning when she hears the news, and institutes a search until the body is found. Then Typhon comes in the night and cuts the body into fourteen pieces. Finally Osiris returns from Hades and assists Horus to overthrow the power of Typhon, who is vanquished in two battles.[6]

> We invoke Bhaga, the Vanquisher of the morning,
> The strong Son of Aditi ; the Preserver,
> To whom trusting, the poor, the sick
> The king himself speaks : Give thou to me my part !—
>
> Vasishtha, vii. 3, 8, 2.[7]

---

[1] Movers, 411 ; Plut. de Is. lii. lv.   [2] Movers, 555.   [3] Ibid. 268.
[4] Movers, 268 ; Lepsius Einleitung, p. 253.   [5] Lepsius, Berlin Akad. 1851, p. 187 ; Kenrick, i. 351 ; Bunsen, Egypt's Place, i. 69.
[6] Plutarch ; in Kenrick's Egypt, i. 344, 345.   [7] Zeitschr. der D. M. G. vol. vi.

13

In Sclavonia, Media, Persia and India, Bog and Baga were names of the Sun. In Egypt Bak meant " light." [1]

"In Thrace also we learn that the same was considered the Sun and Bacchus; whom they call Sebad-ius (Sebaoth) and celebrate with remarkable worship."—Macrob. 300; ed. Bipont.

The Sun, the King, the Son of Him that journeys on high.—Odyssey, xii.

The King Sun, the glorious Son of Hyperion.—Homeric Hymn to Ceres.

> The assassin that Asopus found in Jupiter the Father,
> Hydaspes finds in Bacchus the Son.—Nonnus, xxiii. 287, 288.

Honoring the Sun and Bacchus and at the same time Zan (Zeus).—Nonnus, xxiv. 67.

> Bringing Zeus who is, after (with) Bacchus, the Father of all the race.—
> Nonnus, xxii. 338.

> Let not Athens hymn the New Bacchus,
> Let him not obtain honor like the Eleusinian Bacchus,
> Let him not change the Mysteries of the former Iacchos,
> Nor dishonor the basket of the autumnal fruits of Demeter.
> Nonnus, Dionysiac, xxxi.

For you have sprung from the heart of the FIRST-ANCESTOR hymned Dionysus.—Nonnus, xxiv. 49.

ZAGREUS, called the FIRST-ANCESTOR Dionysus.[2]—Nonnus, xxvii. 341.

" Physicians have called Bacchus the Mind of Zeus (God) because they said the Sun was the Mind of the world. But the "World" is called Heaven, which they name Jupiter."—Macrobius, 301.

" Orpheus manifestly pronounces the Sun to · be Bacchus in this verse:"

> Helios whom they call by the appellation Bacchus.

" And indeed this is a more positive verse; but that of the same poet is more effective:"

> One is Zeus, One is Hades, One is Helios, One Bacchus.

---

[1] Seyffarth, Theolog. Schriften, 4.

[2] The name Kadmus signifies in Hebrew the Ancient or the Ancestor.— Seyffarth's Chronology, 101. He was perhaps Yama or Pluto.

That is, Zeus, Hades, Helios and Bacchus are one.

"Also Orpheus, demonstrating that Bacchus and Sol are one and the same god, thus writes about his adornment and dress in the sacred festival of Bacchus."—Macrobius, p. 302.

The Intellectual Sun,—we collect his Demiurgic and prolific Power from the mutation of the universe.—Julian, in Proclus, ed. Taylor.

Iao is the physical and Spiritual Life-principle.[1] Iao is the Spirital Light Φῶς νοητόν.[2] Bacchus is the generative and nutritive "Spirit."[3] Iao is Bacchus.[4] Iao is the sun-god.[5] Bacchus is Bel the Younger.[6] Damascius calls Iao Intelligible World (Kosmos Noētos) as the Newplatonists call the Bel-Iao of the Chaldeans. The "Father" is the Intelligible World, Bel-Saturn, from whom the seven planet-rays go over to the sun-god.[7] Bel-Mithra (Zeus-Belus) is the "Son" who goes above and raises up the souls to the Intelligible World.[8]

> Belus Minor qui et Metres.
> Bel the Younger who is also Mithra.
> Servius ad Æneid, i. 642.[9]

Iao is first the sun-god at the different seasons of the year *with the predominating idea* of Adonis as *autumnal God*, but generally a complex of Nature-deities whose essence he unites in the meaning of his mysterious name which was, according to Sanchoniathon, already taught by the oldest Phœnician hierophants in the priestly Mysteries. Second, as Adonis-Eljon, he is the Primitive Being with the feminine Nature-goddess, from whom the Bi-sex Uranos-Ge is born that divides itself into Heaven and Earth. Third, his name had come to Greece with the Bacchic Mysteries under various forms. Fourth, it was in the wisdom of the Chaldeans an appellation of the Spiritual Light and Life-Prin-

---

[1] Movers, 265.   [2] Ibid.   [3] Plutarch de Iside, xl.
[4] Movers, 550; Lydus de Mens. 38, 74.   [5] Movers, 541.   [6] Ibid. 267.
[7] Movers, 555, 554.   [8] Ibid. 554; Julian, Orat. in Solem, p. 136.
[9] Movers, 181.

ciple, where he seems to be now the Highest Life-Principle (Bel-Saturn), now his Emanation and Image (Bel-
Mithra).[1]

> All shall shout at the resounding table Bacchus the ally of the human race,
> and the god shall twist as crown around his hair a reptile lying upon the dark-
> colored ivy of the vines, having as a testimony of his youth a snaky mitre.
>
> Nonnus.[2]

> The snake-haired Bacchus.[3]
> Bacchus in the thigh of Jupiter!
> Bacchus in the form of a bull.[4]

Phanes is " the First-born." He is Eros, the universal
Creator.[5] Phanes, the first-born of every creature, is one
of the names of Bacchus.

> Therefore they call him both Phanes and Bacchus.—Diodorus, Sic. Book I.

> Eros stood near HAVING THE THYRSUS.—Nonnus, Dionusiaca, xi. 353.

> O Boy, most worthy to be believed
> To be Deus ; whether thou art Deus, thou canst be Cupido!
>
> Ovid, Metam. iv. 320, 321.

> Sing the conductor of Jupiter's burning beam the thunder's heavy breath
> giving by the nuptial spark painful delivery, the Lightning waiting in the bed-
> chamber of Semele. Sing the birth of twice-born Bacchus whom having taken
> wet from the fire. . . . —Nonnus, i.

> Having broken a part of the earth-encircling Aether, he placed Dionysus
> in it.—Euripides, Bacchae, 293, 294.

Bacchus was the Productive Principle which imparts its
animating and fertilizing influence to every thing around.[6]
According to Proclus, Bacchus is the Demiurg (in the Orphic views), analogous to the One Father who generates
total fabrication.[7]

> O LEADER OF THE CHOIR OF FLAME-BREATHING STARS, Director of the voices
> that sound by night, Youthful god, SON of Jove!—Sophocles, Antigone, 1149.

[1] Movers, 554, 555.   [2] Ed. Marcellus, p. 65.   [3] Ibid. p. 95.
[4] Ibid. Dionusiac, ix.   [5] Marcellus, note to Nonnus, Dionys. xii. 34.
[6] Anthon's Classical Dict. Art. Orpheus.   [7] Taylor's Plato, 484.

But this god is a prophet—for Bacchanal excitement and frenzy have much divination in them.—Euripides, Bacchae, 298.

For when THE GOD (Bacchus, holy "Spirit") comes abundant into the body, He makes the raving tell the future!—Bacchae, 300.

Bacchus will not compel women to be modest but in his nature modesty in all things is ever innate. This you must needs consider, for she who is modest will not be corrupted by being at Bacchic revels.—Euripides, Bacchae, 318.[1]

And I hear that she this third day keeps her body untouched by the fruit of Ceres, (which she receives not) into her ambrosial mouth wishing in secret suffering to hasten to the unhappy goal of death. For heaven-possessed O lady, or whether by PAN or by Hecate, or by the venerable Corybantes, or by the MOTHER WHO HAUNTS THE MOUNTAINS, thou art raving.—Euripides, Hippolytus, 144.[2]

I am desirous to address my prayer to the MOTHER OF THE GODS, the revered goddess whom, along with PAN, the maidens by my porch often celebrate in song by night.—Pindar, Pyth. iii. B. C. 486–474.

The Sidonian Mustis instituting the nocturnal rites of Bacchus the wakeful.
Nonnus, ix. 114.

IO IO Pan Pan
O Pan Pan, thou ocean-wanderer, show thyself from the craggy ridge of snow-beaten Cullane, thou King of the Gods that leadest the dance!
Sophocles, Ajax, 694–700.

Euripides, in Licymnius, signifying that Apollo and Bacchus are one and the same god, writes:

O Lord that lovest laurel, Bacchus, Paian, Apollo of the excellent lyre.[3]

Adonis is Paian and the beautiful Phaon whom Venus hid in the lettuce.[4] Bacchus was called "Evan" (Aban, Pan, "Avan" as the husband of Venus).[5] Pan was the Anima Mundi the Life of the world.[6] Bacchus and Ceres are Adonis and Venus.

In Rhodes Jupiter was called Paian.[7] Pan appears to be the Egyptian Oben-Ra, Aban the Sun, the Persian

---

[1] Transl. Buckley.   [2] Born 480 Before Christ.

[3] Macrob. p. 299; Buckley's Euripides, vol. i. 93, note 17; Plato's Symposium, Burges, §17.   [4] Movers, 227.   [5] Eschenburg's Manual, 426.

[6] Eschenburg's Manual, 434.   [7] Movers, 26, quotes Hesychius, S. V.

Avan : Phanes is the First-born, and is Kosmos the Soul of
the world.[1]   Ulom is also the Intelligible Kosmos the Soul
of the world.   Ulom is Aion (Aeon) the Celestial Sun.[2]
Phanes is Dionysus and sun-god.[3] Dionysus passed also for
Adonis and Attes.[4]   Adonis is the Sun and lives with
Venus.[5]

For the Nature-philosophers worship the upper hemisphere of the
earth which we inhabit, as Venus ; but they called the lower hemisphere
Proserpine.—Macrobius, Sat. i. 21.

Adonis and Venus are Avan (Evan, Havan, Phanes, Pan)
and Venus; which accounts for the identity of the Pan and
Bacchic rites.   Bacchus is called Evan, whence the name
of the Ox-god Dionysus-Ebon is explained.[6]   In some monuments Bacchus appears bearded, in others horned (the
Bacchus-Sebazius), whence in the Mysteries he was identified with Osiris and regarded as the Sun.[7]   Bacchus is
Melech, or Milichus (Moloch).

Milichus indigenis late regnarat in oris,
Cornigeram attollens Genitoris imagine frontem.
Silius, Pun. iii. 104, 133.[9]
Satisfy with delight that Indra who assumed the shape of a ram.
Worship the Ram who inhabits heaven !—Stevenson, Samaveda, 72, 73.

"The Father is here a horned Satyr, as Amun the
oldest God in Egypt is named Pan because of his goat-
form."[9] "This horned Milichus, the Son of the Ram-god
Ammon, is the Ox-god Bacchus who was considered horned by the Libyans because his Father Ammon naturally
had horns to his temples."   Dionysus is Belus Minor.[10]
Dionysus-Zagreus was a Son of Zeus whom he had begotten
(in the form of a Dragon) upon his daughter Cora-Persephone before she was carried off to the kingdom of shadows
by Pluto.

[1] Movers, 532.   [2] Ibid. 282, 283.   [3] Ibid. 556.   [4] Ibid. 25, quotes Euseb.
H. E. iii. 23.   [5] Ibid. 207.   [6] Ibid. 547, and the authorities there quoted.
[7] Anthon, quotes Keightley, Mythol. 212.   [8] Movers, 268, 326.
[9] Movers, 326.   [10] Ibid. 268, 267.

The Sun the Great God of the regions above and the realms below.

Rosetta Inscription, line 3 ; Munter, 13.

In Greece the Oldest Dionysus appeared as the fire- and pillar-god Moloch.[1]   The Egyptians worshipped Saturn under the symbol of a pillar.[2]   Jacob set up a pillar, because he had seen God.   Dionysus is Moloch, the Dionysus Milichus with the ox-head, the fire-god worshipped under different names and forms in the religions of Western Asia.[3]   Dionysus from Asia Minor is the Phrygian and Thracian Sabos the Arabian Sabi and the Egyptian Seb (Sev) who is Saturn.[4]

With wandering wine-colored chariot Bacchus passed over the Assyrian soil.—Nonnus, xviii. 328.

Not with ten tongues shall I (be able to) sing as many races,
Nor with ten mouths, pouring a brazen sound,
As Bacchus brandishing the spear assembled.—Nonnus, xiii. 47–49.

And the God led, bearing on his shining face
A HEAVENLY RAY THE HERALD OF THE SON OF DEUS !
But around the Ludian chariot of Bacchus the Giant-killer
Were thyrsus-bearing ranks : and he was girded with warriors,
Radiant on all sides, and he lightened back to Olympus :
And in beauty he eclipsed all : and seeing him you would soon say
Burning EELI (Sun) among the wide-spread stars !—Nonnus, xvii.

But when the throng of infantry of Bacchus reached
The passage of the sandy river where in a deep gulf the Indian
Hydaspes like the Nile discharges navigable water,
Then indeed the feminine hymn of the Bassarides was sung
Which begins the Trojan kōmos to the nightly Luaios,
And the chorus of hairy satyrs chanted with mystic voice.

Nonnus, xxii.

---

[1] Movers, 372, 374, 376, 361.   [2] Ibid. 298.

[3] Movers, 372. Dionysus was the son of Zeus by Semele. Semele is the feminine of Samael (Moloch) who is Satan.   Moloch (Typhou) is Pluto in the Egyptian mythology ; therefore Samael-Satan-Typhon-Moloch-Pluto is Zeus the husband of both Semele and Cora-Persephone.

[4] Movers, 23, 495 ; Lepsius, Berlin Akad. 1851 ; Champollion Egypte, 253, 125.

Let me not see the Phrygian kōmos nor swing with my hands the
    cymbals,
I will not celebrate the sportive rite nor know
Maionia, nor see Tmolos nor the home of Luaios (Aloah).
                              Nonnus, xl. 154.

Not bearing the kettle-drums and the Evian cymbals of Rhea
She celebrated the orgies of couchless Luaios (Aloæus).
                       Nonnus, xxxiii. 239 ; Iliad, v. 386.

O Thou, who art hailed by many a name, glory of the Theban
nymph and Son of deeply-thundering Jove, who swayest renowned
Italia, and President o'er the rites of Ceres in the vales of Eleusis
open to all ! O Bacchus, who dwellest in Thebe, the mother city of the
Bacchanals, by the flowing streams of Ismenus and the fields where the
teeth of the fell dragon were sown ; Thee the smoke beheld as it burst
into flame above the double-crested rock, where roam the Corycian
nymphs the votaries of Bacchus, and the fount of Castalia flows ; and
Thee the ivy-crowned steeps of the Nusian mountains and the green
shore with its many clusters triumphant send along amid immortal
words that hymn thy " Evoe," to reign the guardian of the streets of
Thebe !—Sophocles, Antigone, 1125.[1]

When also the starry-visaged Aether of Jove is wont to dance and
the Moon dances and the fifty daughters of Nereus, which in the sea and
in the eddies of eternal rivers celebrate in choir Cora with her golden
crown and her hallowed Mother [Ceres] : . . , —where the Bacchic fire of
the God leaps forth !—Euripides, Ion.[2]

Night-shining Dionysus, having a bull's form,
With dusky feet entered the houses of Kadmus (Pluto)[3]
Brandishing the Kronian frenzied whip of Pan.—Nonnus, xliv. 280.

Harmless Cerberus saw thee decorated
With golden horn ; mildly rubbing his
Tail against and touched with his three-tongued mouth
    The feet and legs of thee retiring.—Horace, ii. Carm. 19.

I Son of Deus am come to this land of the Thebans, Bacchus,
whom formerly Semele the daughter of Kadmus brings forth. being delivered by the lightning-bearing flame : and *having taken a mortal form
instead of a God's* I have arrived at the fountains of Dirce and the water

---

[1] Buckley.   [2] Ibid.
[3] The Devil is called Kadmon.—Movers, 517, 273.

of Ismenus. But I praise Kadmus who makes this place holy, his daughter's shrine : and I have covered it around with the cluster-bearing leaf of the vine. And leaving the very wealthy lands of the Ludians and the Phrygians and the sun-parched plains of the Persians and the Baktrian walls and the stormy land of the Medes, coming upon Arabia Felix and all Asia which lies along the salt sea, having fair-towered cities full of Greeks and foreigners mingled together ; I came first to this city of the sons of Hellen, having danced there also and established my Mysteries that I might be a Lord manifest to mortals. And in Thebes first of the land of Greece, I have raised my shout.... For this city must know, even though it be unwilling, that it is not initiated into my Bacchic rites, and that I plead the cause of my mother, appearing to mortals a God whom she bears to Deus.—Euripides, Bacchae.[1]

And now here and there through the city flew a rumor
Self-proclaimed messenger of Dionysus rich in vines
Wandering to Atthis : and fruitful Athens
Was aroused to the chorus of sleepless Luaios.
And many a komos thundered : and gathered citizens
With variegated garments covered up the streets
With thickly-strewn hands, and Athens spontaneously was
Crowned with leaves of vines of Bacchus who causes plants
To grow : and, between their breasts clothed with iron, women
Girded phalli to their breasts, solemnizing Mysteries ;
And young girls danced : and crowned their Athenian
Braided hair of their temples with the flower of ivy.
And Ilissus rolled about the city inspired water
Honoring Dionysus : and with emulous dancing
The shores of Cephissus clashed the Euion hymn !

With alternate responding feet the laborer of the vineyard bounded
Shouting to Dionysus the Evian hymn of ZAGREUS.
And on the old tiller of the soil the God of young plants bestowed
Vine branches producing grapes, phil-Evian gifts of the banquet :
And the KING taught him, by a certain plant-growing art,
To prune and dig the trench, and to deposit the vines in pits.

Nonnus, xlvii.

It was the time when the Sithonian women are wont to celebrate
The Trieteric Mysteries of Bacchus : Night a witness to the rites.
Rhodope sounds with the clashings of acute brass by night.

Ovid, Met. vi.

---

[1] Lines 1–40 ; Buckley's Euripides, ii. pp. 249, 250.

They give incense and call " Bacchus" and " Bromius" and " Luaios"
To these is added " Nuseus" and " unshorn Thuoneus"
And, with " Lenaius," " Inventor of the genial grape"
And " Nuctelius" and " parent Eleleus" (Eliel) and " Iacchus" and
    " Evan"
And many other names besides which thou hast, O Liber,
Among the Grecian nations!—Ovid, Met. iv.

CHORUS.

 IO ! IO ! Lord, Lord ! come now to our company.
 O BROMIOS ! BROMIOS ! Shake the plane of earth O holy Demeter !
 BACCHUS is in the halls. Worship him !

SEMI-CHORUS.

 WE WORSHIP, O !   Bacchae, 590.

CHORUS.

Coming from the land of Asia, having left the sacred Tmolus, I dance
to BROMIUS, a sweet labor and a toil easily borne, celebrating the god
Bacchus. Who is in the way ? Who is in the way ? Who is in the
halls ? Let him depart ! And let every one be holy as to his mouth
shouting in praise: for I will ever hymn Dionysus according to the
established usages !—
 O Blessed is he whoever being favored knowing the Mysteries of the
gods hallows his life and has his soul initiated into the Bacchic revels,
dancing in the mountains with holy purifications, reverencing the orgies
of the GREAT MOTHER KUBELE and, brandishing the thyrsus, being
crowned with ivy, worships Bacchus. Go Bacchae, Go Bacchae, bringing
" Bromius Boy God of God Dionysus" from Phrygian mountains to the
broad streets of Hellas : Bromius ! whom formerly, being in the pains of
travail, the thunder of Zeus flying upon her, his mother cast from her
womb, leaving life by the stroke of the thunderbolt. And immediately
Zeus, the Son of Saturn, received him in a chamber fitted for birth : and
covering him in his thigh, shuts him with golden clasps hidden from
Juno. And he brought him forth when the Fates had perfected the bull-
horned God and crowned him with crowns of snakes, whence the thyrsus-bearing Mænads are wont to cover their prey with their locks.
 O Thebes, Nurse of Semele, crown thyself with ivy, flourish, flourish
with the verdant yew bearing sweet fruit, and be ye crowned in honor
of Bacchus with branches of oak or pine, and adorn your garments of

spotted deer-skin with fleeces of white-haired sheep, and sport in holy games with the insulting wands; straightway shall all the earth dance. Bromius, who leads the bands to the mountain, to the mountain, where the female crowd abides away from the distaff and the shuttle, driven frantic by Dionysus. O dwelling of the Curetes and ye divine Cretan caves parents to Zeus where the Corybantes with the triple helmet invented for me in their caves this circle o'erstretched with hide; and with the constant sweet-voiced breath of Phrygian pipes they mingled Bacchic sounds and put the instrument in the hands of Rhea resounding with the sweet songs of the Bacchae. And, hard by, the raving satyrs went through the sacred rites of the Mother Goddess. And they added the dances of the Trieterides in which Dionysus rejoices, pleased on the mountains when after the running dance he falls upon the plain, having a sacred garment of deer-skin, seeking a sacrifice of goats, a raw-eaten delight, on his way to the Phrygian, the Ludian mountains. And the leader is Bromius, Evoe! But the plain flows with milk, and flows with wine, and flows with the nectar of bees, and a smoke as of Syrian frankincense. But Bacchus having a flaming torch of pine on the top of his thyrsus darts arousing to the course the wandering Choruses and setting them on with shouts, casting his luxurious hair loose to the Aether. And at once with cries he shouts thus: O go Bacchae, O go Bacchae, delight of gold-flowing Tmolus, Sing Dionysus with deep-thundering drums, Evoe! celebrating the God Evius in Phrygian cries and shouts. When the sweet-sounding sacred pipe sounds a sacred playful sound suited to the frantic wanderers, to the mountain! to the mountain!—and then the Bacchante rejoicing like a foal with its mother at pasture stirs her swift-footed limb in the dance.—Euripides, Bacchae.[1]

The third day after the Ides is consecrated to Bacchus.—Ovid, Fast. iii.
Paean is consulted; and "Summon the Mother of the gods"
    He says: "she is to be found on mount Ida!"—Fast. iv.

Thrice let the heaven be turned on its perpetual axis,
Thrice let Titan yoke and thrice unharness the horses:
Then the Berekuntian pipe with bent horn
Shall sound and there will be the festival of the Idean Parent.
The semimales shall march and beat the hollow drums
And cymbals repelled by cymbals shall give forth clanging.
She herself sitting, on the soft neck of her attendants will be borne
Proclaimed with shouts through the midst of the streets of the city.
                                                    Ovid, Fast. iv.

[1] Transl. Buckley, ii. 251, 252; also, ed. Aug. Witzschel, lines 1–170.

Clamor and the Berekuntian pipe with inflated horn,
And drums and clapping of hands and the shouting of Bacchus!
Ovid, Met. xi.

Deservedly has Terra obtained the name Mother
Since from Terra ('Athor) all things were created . . .
The human race and every animal which wanders everywhere
On the mountains she poured forth almost at a fixed time
And the birds of air, at the same time, with varying forms.
Then first Terra gave the mortal races.
Lucretius, v. 794, 820ff, 803.

EARTH was called Great Mother of the gods and mother of beasts and
    Genetrix of our body!
Her various nations according to the ancient custom of the rites
Vociferate as the Idaean Mother, and give her Phrygian bands
Of women as attendants . . .
With their hands the braced drums thunder and the hollow
Cymbals around, and horns threaten with hoarse music,
And with Phrygian measure the hollow pipe excites the minds . . .
With brass and silver they strow all the way of the streets . . .
With flowers covering the Mother and her bands of companions.
Lucretius De Rer. Nat. ii. 598, 610, 620ff.

Invoking Dindumia the very venerable Mother inhabiting Phrygia.
Apollon. Rhod. Argonaut. i. 1117.

"Maut, Muth (Isis) the *Mighty Mother* of the Mysteries." [1]

Adam and Eve are here the Dionysus and Demeter, the Bacchus and Ceres of the Greek, Egyptian, Phœnician, Syrian, Asia Minor and Persian races. Isis is Eve "Mother of all living," the Naturegoddess. Hence the inscription on her temple:

I am all that has been, is, and will be: and my robe no one of mortals has ever uncovered.—Plutarch de Is. ix.

The Great mundane divinity the Earth.—Earth then proceeds primarily from the Intelligible (Invisible) Earth, which comprehends all the intelligible orders of the gods and is eternally established in the Father. It is not the soul of the Earth, but an animal consisting of a divine soul and a living body. . . . . Some animals are rooted in it and others about it.—Proclus.[2]

Herodotus observes that "all the Egyptians do not wor-

<hr>

[1] Kenrick, i. 320, 321.   [2] Taylor's Proclus.

ship the same gods in a similar manner except Isis and Osiris, the latter of whom is said to be Dionysus; *these all worship in a similar manner.*" "Isis is called in the Greek tongue Demeter or Ceres." [1] Here we find the Mysteries in the time of Herodotus already old, and underlying the myths or "sacred stories." "Euas" (Bacchus) and "Eua" (Eve) are the Adam and Eve of the Mysteries ; or Amadios (Dionysus) and Maut (Isis); the Samaritan Iabe (Ab) and Eba (Eve),[2] the "Iasius and Demeter" . . . the "Zeus Chthonios and holy Demeter" of Hesiod,[3] the "Zeus Infernal and dread Proserpine . . . the Pluto and dread Proserpine" of Homer,[4] the Chthonios and Venus of Nonnus,[5] the Eanus (Janus, Ani : Mars Mamurius) and Anna perenna of the Romans.[6]

> On the Ides is the genial Feast of Anna perenna
> Not far, traveller Tiber, from thy banks.
> The people comes, and, scattered everywhere among the green
>   stalks,
> Imbibes, and each reclines with his female associate.
> Part remain in the open air, a few set up TENTS :
> Some out of branches have made a leafy hut.—Ovid, Fast. ii.

SOUCHI [7] (Saturn) is the Lord of the harmony of the spheres in the land of holiness with my farmfield. It lies in the land of holiness upon the Firmament.—Book of the Dead ; Seyffarth, Theolog. Schriften, 33.

The Sakæ, the Ludians and the Assyrians in common with the Persians and Babylonians celebrated the SAKAIA, the great festival of Anaitis (Isis).[8] The annual Sakæan festivals were probably named after the Carian god OSOGO

---

[1] Herodot. ii. 42, 59 ; Kenrick, 334.   [2] Movers, 547.
[3] Hesiod, Theog. 969 ; Works and Days, 435.   [4] Iliad, ix. 455, 563
[5] Nonnus, xlviii. 21.   [6] Movers, 484.
[7] Asôchi. Socho is the name of a Hebrew.—1 Chron. iv. 18.
[8] Movers, 70, 480 ; Herodot. ii. 59. Anait is Neith, Neith is Isis. See p. 185 of this volume.

The Sakae occupied Baktria and Armenia. They built the temple of ANAITIS and that of the gods Oman and Anandat (Ananadad), Persian deities who shared the same altar : and they solemnized the public festival, each year

(Asak) as the ONLY-BEGOTTEN. The god SICHÆ-US[1] or SUCHOS, and Succoth, the goddess, would be Adonis and Venus; and the Sakaia would be the Persian Adonia, the weeping for Thammuz or Ieoud (Ad, Aud, At, Attes), or the lament for Hadad-Rimmon, Maneros, Linus, Bacchus, the many forms of Adonis.[2]

Aisak the hard Drinker.—Nonnus, xiv. 190.

Asak was god of the Sacæ who were Scythians. The Persian Adonia were celebrated *in tents* and were named "Scythian" (Sakaia).[3]

The herdsmen of Gerar quarrelled with the herdsmen of Isahak (IZHAK) saying: This is our water; whence he called the name of the well ESEK (Asak) because they *contended* with him.—Gen. xxvi. 20.

Asakar Issachar ZAGRE-us [4] is the name of the god Bacchus and a Hebrew or Arabian tribe. Segor was his city.

Add too that Bacchus is the source of joy, who is said to obtain a common kingdom with the Sun. But why should I here mention the epithet Horus, or other names of the gods, all of which correspond with the divinity of the Sun?—Julian.[5]

The Carians gashed their foreheads in the Mourning for Osiris.[6] The Phrygians believe the god in winter sleeps and in summer wakes. The Paphlagonians say he is bound in winter and freed in summer.[7] The Mexicans had a ceremony corresponding to the death of Adonis or Attes. At

kept holy, the SAKAIA.—Strabo, xi. § 4. This is the festival of Artemis-Diana among the Lydians.—Pausanias, iii. cap. xvi.; Movers, 675. It was a festival of Bacchus and Anaitis.—See Higgins, Anacal. p. 319; he quotes Hoffman, voc. Anaitis; Jameson, Herm. Scyth. p. 136.

[1] Movers, 232, 616, 484.
[2] Movers, 480–484, 234, 249, 252, 302, 303; Zachar. xii. 10, 11; Univ. Hist. v. 155, 156.   [3] Movers, 480, 482; See ESHEK 1 Chron. viii. 39, Iah-AZAK-iaho (Hezck-iah), Ich-EZEK-AL (Ezeki-EL).
[4] Compare Zakar, "male," in Hebrew.   [5] Taylor's Proclus, ii. 51.
[6] Kenrick's Phoenicia, 89; Herod. ii. 59; Deut. xiv. 1.
[7] Plutarch de Is. lxix.

the end of December the god Huitzlipoctli with the vegetation dies. The priests made an image of the god Huitzlipoctli of all sorts of seeds which were baked with the blood
of sacrificed children. A priest of Quetzalcoatl then shot an
arrow at the image and pierced the god. His heart was
cut out and eaten by the king. At the end of December
the god with the vegetation dies. The sun-god is then
born and Tezcatlipoca takes new power.[1]

O daughter of my people, gird thee with sackcloth and roll in ashes,
make to thee MOURNING of the ONLY-BEGOTTEN, bitter lamentation.
Jeremiah, vi. 26.

That they look upon Me whom they have pierced: so that they
mourn over him as the Mourning for the ONLY-BEGOTTEN, and bitterly
lament over him as they bitterly mourn the FIRST-BORN.

In that day mourning shall increase in Ierusalem as the Mourning
for HADADRIMMON (the Autumnal Sun) in the valley Megiddon.
Zachariah, xii. 10, 11.[2]

Bruma (Abram) is the first of the NEW and the last of the OLD SUN:
Phoebus and Annus take the same commencement!
Ovid, Fasti, i. 165, 166.

They give incense and call Bacchus, and BROMI-us and Lyaeus.
Ovid, Met. iv. 11.

The Phœnicians every year sacrificed the loved and only-
begotten children to Kronos. Heliogabalus introduced this
custom into Italy : he chose for the offerings to his Saturn-
Mithra or Elagabal boys out of the first Italian families. In
Phœnicia several children were taken out and it was then
determined by lot which should be offered.

Urna reducebat miserandos annua casus.—Silius, iv. 770.[3]

It is best for us that one man should die for the people, and not that the
whole nation perish.—John, xi. 50.

Kronos, named Israel among the Phœnicians, a king of the

---

[1] J. Müller, 605, 623.   [2] Movers, 206 ; Rimmon is Adonis.—Movers, 184.
Rimmon was a Syrian sun-god worshipped in Damascus.—Movers, 197 ; 2
Kings, v. 18. Hadad was a Syrian sun-god.—Movers, 308.   [3] Movers, 304.

country, had an Only-begotten Son called Ieud AS THE ONLY-
BEGOTTEN IS STILL CALLED BY THE PHŒNICIANS. When very
great dangers in war threatened the country he had his
Son adorned with the royal dress and offered him up.[1]

Kronos whom the Phœnicians surname EL, a ruler of the land and
later translated after his death as God into the star of Kronos (Saturn),
had, by a native nymph named Anobret, an ONLY SON whom they
therefore named YEUD (Aud, Ad).—Philo, On the Jews.[2]

Above the stars of AL (El) I will exalt my throne and will sit on the mount
of assembly (moud) in the sides of the north. Isaiah, xiv. 13.

Nor did Maron describe with eloquent delineation the Titan tribe
Nor (did he describe) Kronos, or Phanes more ancient; nor the origin
Of the Titan EELI (Sun) which is contemporaneous with the coeval world.
Nonnus, xix. 204.

Such laments were made for the death of Adonis, Osiris,
Dionysus, Linus, Attis and Maneros.[3]

The Apollonian Linus.—Nonnus, xli. 371.

I am the servant of Bacchus not of Phœbus ; and I have not learned
to sing AILINA such as KING Apollo chanted among the Cretans when
he wept charming Atumnios (AtAmonios, Atman, Dominus, Adam,
Autumnus) : and of the Heliades I was guest, a foreigner of the Eridanus,
I am the bastard of Phaethon the perished charioteer.—Nonnus xix. 180.

Holding the boy as Phœbus (held) Atumnios.—Nonnus, xxix. 31.

ELEEINA in concert groaned the women
Whose boy, whose brother died, whose fathers
Or spouse youthful untimely . . . And about the dead
The pipe of Mugdonis with varied song sounded AILINA
And Phrygian flutists interwound the manly molpe,
With sad faces : and the Bacchae danced to
Ganuktōr singing beautifully with Evian voice :
And under the mouth of Kleocus the Berekuntian double flutes
Roared the frightful Libyan wail . . .
Nonnus, xl. 158 ; 223.

---

[1] Movers, 303 ; quotes Euseb. Praep. Ev. i. 10.   [2] Bunsen, Aegyptens Stelle,
v. 376.   [3] Rinck, i. 341, 342 ; Movers, 244, 245, 251.

AILINON AILINON sing, let this well prevail!
Aeschylus, Agam. 120.

We find Illinos among the twelve gods in the Babylonian Cosmogony,[1] the Phœnician god Elon, the Greek Hellen, and the Hebrew Elion, the Most High God.

And this was a perpetual custom, that each year on the beginning of the first day of the month Tammuz they mourned and wept for Tammus.
More, Neb. iii. 20.[2]

And the priests sit in their temples having their clothes rent and their heads and beards shaven and nothing upon their heads.

They howl and cry before their gods as men do at the feast when one is dead.—Baruch, vi. 31. 32.

" Because, according to the Gentile fable, in the month Junius the Lover of Venus and a very beautiful Youth was slain and afterwards is related to have lived again." [3]

In Egypt the sons of kings were mourned as in the Mourning for the ONLY-BEGOTTEN. Josiah was perhaps mourned in the same way.[4]

They shall not lament for him " Ah my brother," or "Alas sister." They shall not lament for him, saying " Hoi ADON," or, "Alas his glory !"
Jeremiah, xxii. 18.

Thus they shall make a burning for thee and shall lament for thee Hoi ADON !—Jeremiah, xxxiv. 5.

Diving headlong THE DANCE OF DEATH, to Luaios (Aloah).
Nonnus, xliii. 157.

Autonoë let us speed where is the dance of Luaios
And the mountain-wandering sound of the familiar flute is heard
That I may compose a phil-Evian song, that I may know ...
Who has surpassed any one in being Bacchic priest to Luaios.
Nonnus, xlvi. 165.

Dios (Deus) was the husband of Venus and Ceres who is " Daö, Mother of all life." [5]

The Orphic priests (B. C. 500–550) dressed in linen

---

[1] Movers, 276.   [2] Ibid. 210.   [3] Hieronymus, l. c. p. 750; Movers, 210.
[4] Movers, 248, 249, 252; 2 Chron. xxxv. 25. [5] Nonnus, xix. 81; v. 611, 620.

14

like the Hebrew priests.   David danced before Iahoh with
all his might and David was girded with a linen ephod.
" The foundations of the Mysteries must have been ordinary
religion, for the priests instituted them."[1]

> Orpheus showed forth the rites of the hidden Mysteries.
> > Euripides, Rhaesus, 942.

> The Orphic, called the Bacchic rites.—Herodot. xi. 81.[2]

The emblems of Osiris are those of Bacchus. The Egyptian
priests affirm that Orpheus borrowed from them the
Mysteries which he instituted in honor of Bacchus and
Ceres who are Osiris and Isis.[3]

> In the soul, therefore, the mind and Logos, the Leader and Lord of
> all that is best, is Osiris.—Plut. De Is. xlix.

> But when they (the souls) are liberated from the body and pass into
> the invisible impassive and pure region, this God (Osiris) is then their
> leader and KING from whom they depend, insatiably beholding him and
> desiring to survey that beauty which cannot be expressed or uttered by
> men; which Isis (as the ancient discourse evinces) always loving, pursuing
> and enjoying, fills such things in these lower regions as participate of
> generation with every thing beautiful and good.—Plutarch, De Iside,
> lxxviii.; Taylor's Proclus, p. xxxix.

> > O Divinities of the WORLD PLACED BENEATH THE EARTH,
> > Into which we fall again whatever mortal we are created!
> > > Ovid, Met. x.

> A blackened sun-burnt race to ZAGREUS the many-guest-receiving Zeus of
> the dead.—Æschylus, Suppliants.[4]

> And this which the present priests reveal with caution, abominating
> and concealing it, that this God (Osiris) rules and is KING over the dead,
> and is he whom the Greeks call Hades and Ploutōn, it not being per-
> ceived how it is true, disturbs the common people who question if the
> sacred and holy Osiris really dwells in the earth and UNDER THE EARTH
> where the bodies of those are concealed who seem to have come to an
> end.   But he indeed is at the furthest possible distance from the earth.
> —Plutarch, De Iside, lviii.

---

[1] Cousin, Hist. Mod. Phil. i. 404.　　[2] K. O. Müller, 231.
[3] Champollion, Egypte Univ. pitt. 120, b.　　[4] Buckley, Transl. p. 213.

Amestris, the wife of Xerxes, commanded fourteen Persian children of illustrious birth to be interred alive in honor of that deity, who, as they suppose, exists UNDER THE EARTH.[1] Pindar says " that the lawless souls of those who die here forthwith suffer punishment: and SOME ONE BENEATH THE EARTH, pronouncing sentence by stern necessity, judges the sinful deeds done in this realm of Zeus; but the good enjoy the sun's light both by day and by night . . . while those who through a threefold existence in the upper and lower worlds have kept their souls pure from all sin, ascend the path of Zeus to the castle of Chronus where ocean-breezes blow round the Islands of the Blessed and golden flowers glitter, some on the ground and some on resplendent trees, and the water feeds others." In his laments for the dead Pindar more distinctly developed his ideas about immortality, and spoke of the tranquil life of the blessed in perpetual sunshine, among fragrant groves, at festal games and sacrifices; and of the torments of the wretched in eternal night. " Those from whom Persephone receives an atonement for their former guilt their souls she sends in the ninth year to the SUN of heaven." [2]

Between the time of Homer and Pindar a great change of opinion had taken place. All the Greek religions poetry treating of death and the world beyond the grave refers to the deities whose influence was supposed to be exercised in *the dark region at the centre of the earth. The Mysteries of the Greeks were connected with the worship of these gods alone.* That the love of immortality first found a support in a belief in these deities appears from the fable of Persephone the daughter of Demeter. Every year at the time of harvest, Persephone was supposed to be carried from the world to the dark dominions of the invisible King of Shadows, but to return every spring in youthful beauty to the arms of her mother. When the goddess of inanimate Nature had become the queen of the dead, it was a natural

---

[1] Herodot. vii. 114.   [2] K. O. Müller, 230.

analogy which must early have suggested itself, that the return of Persephone to the world of light also denoted a renovation of life and a new birth to men. The Eleusinian Mysteries early acquired great renown. "The endeavor to attain to a knowledge of divine and human things was in Greece slowly and with difficulty evolved from the religious notions of a sacerdotal fanaticism; and it was for a long period confined to the refining and rationalizing of the traditional mythology, before it ventured to explore the paths of independent inquiry."

The Orphic associations dedicated themselves to the worship of Bacchus (as Osiris or Iacchos) in which they hoped to find satisfaction for an ardent longing after the soothing and elevating influences of religion. The Dionysus to whose worship these Orphic and Bacchic rites were annexed was the Chthonian deity, Dionysus Zagreus, closely connected with Demeter and Cora, who was the personified expression not only of the most raptuous pleasure, but also of a deep sorrow for the miseries of life. The Orphic legends and poems related in great part to this Dionysus, who was combined as an Infernal deity with Hades,[1] and upon whom the Orphic theologers founded their hopes of the purification and the ultimate immortality of the soul. When they had tasted the mystic sacrificial feast of raw flesh torn from the Ox of Dionysus, they partook of no other animal food. They wore white linen garments like Oriental and Egyptian priests, from whom, as Herodotus remarks, much may have been borrowed in the ritual of Orphic worship. The Orphic worshippers of Bacchus did not indulge in unrestrained pleasure and frantic enthusiasm, but rather aimed at an ascetic purity of life and manners.[2]

The Mysteries of Demeter and especially those celebrated at Eleusis inspired the most elevating and animating

---

[1] A doctrine given by the philosopher Heraclitus as the opinion of a particular sect. Ap. Clem. Alex. Protr. p. 30. Potter. K. O. Müller, Hist. Greek Literature, pp. 231, 232.   [2] Ibid.

hopes with regard to the condition of the soul after death. "Happy (says Pindar of these mysteries) is he who has beheld them, and descends beneath the hollow earth; he knows the end, he knows the divine origin of life."[1]

All generation proceeds from a corruption. — Livres Hermetiques; Egypte, 139.

It is sown in corruption, it is raised in incorruption.—St. Paul.

"The return of the fallen to the heavenly light of the gods is pictured in the journey of Persephone to heaven. Hermes as 'the leader of souls and angel (of death) takes the goddess at Jove's command from the arms of Pluto to the gods of the upper world. Her existence is divided between two worlds; a third part of the year she passes in the Depth (Tartarus) and two thirds above with the Immortals. The goddess, returned in Spring as the growing up, fruit-bringing seed, is also an image of men directing their course to the day of the spirit-world, from the prison to freedom. The ears which Demeter gave to Triptolemus at Eleusis mean not merely agriculture, which she taught him, but are at the same time an emblem that recalls the idea of Persephone returned to the upper world, who as child of humanity will draw after her all the initiated. They remind us of Jesus who fell as a kernel of wheat into the earth, was raised again and brought forth fruit for all mankind. When the Heathen found in the ear of wheat a reminder to mount with it (or with Persephone) from death to spiritual life, from night to day, from Hades to the heavenly gods, there lay in such a belief a glimmering of the Confession 'we are buried with Christ through baptism, and risen together with and in him through the faith which God works who has raised him from the dead.'"[2]

Man that is born of woman is of few days and full of trouble.

[1] K. O. Müller, Hist. Greek Lit. 231, 233.

[2] Rinck, Relig. der Hellen. i. 156–158, quotes John, xii. 24; Luke, viii. 5; Coloss. ii. 12. See K. O. Müller, Hist. Greek Lit. 231.

Like a flower he goes forth and is cut down: and escapes like a shadow and continues not.[1]

There is hope for a tree; if it is cut down it renews itself again.

But man dies and wastes away; and man expires and where is he?

Waters depart from the sea, and a river is dried up and disappears,

And man lies down and arises not, *until the heavens are no more* they awake not nor are aroused from their slumber. . . .

If a man dies will he revive? In all the days of my sojourning I shall await until my change comes. . . .

Waters wear away stones, the dust of the earth extends its own germs: wilt thou then make the hope of man to perish?

Wilt thou perpetually press him till he dies, changing his countenance until thou cast him away?

His sons shall be honored and he will not know it, they shall be brought low and he will not attend to them.

But his flesh upon him shall have pain and his soul in him shall mourn!

Job, xiv.

But man in honor will not remain; he is assimilated, just as the beasts are destroyed.

This is the way of them, they hope: and those after them approve with their own mouth, Selah!

As cattle, they shall be placed in Saol (Sheol), death shall feed on them and the just shall have dominion over them in the morning: and their beauty shall consume, hell shall be its abode.

But Alahim will redeem my soul from the hand of Shaul (Sheol), for he will receive me.—Psalm, xlix.

I know that my Redeemer lives and that he shall stand at the END upon earth. And after my skin these shall be covered and from my flesh I shall see Aloh (Allah).—Job, xix. Hebrew Bible, Schmid.

For I know that he is eternal who will redeem me upon the earth, will raise up my body which performs these things laboriously: for by the Lord these things were accomplished for me; which I know thoroughly, which my eye has seen and not another; all things have been accomplished to me in the bosom.

Septuagint Version, Tischendorff.

The dead shall arise, and those in the remembrances shall be raised up, and those in the earth shall be cheered: for thy dew is a restorative to them, but the earth of the impious shall fall.—Isaiah, xxvi. 19. Septuagint.

They shall live, your dead (*plural*) my dead body; they shall arise! Awake and rejoice ye that inhabit dust; for a dew of the plants is thy dew (O God) but the earth of Rephaim thou wilt make to fall.—Isaiah, xxvi. 19. Hebrew Bible, Schmid.

Adoni, thou wast our dwelling from generation to generation!

---

[1] Mortals wretched, who like leaves at one time are very blooming, feeding on the fruit of the soil, and, at another, perish lifeless (akērioi)! Iliad, xxi. 464, 465.

Before that the mountains were born and the earth was formed and its circle ; and from eternity to eternity thou art AL (El)!

Thou reducest man even to dust, and sayest, Return, sons of man!—Ps. xc.

Then shall the dust return to the earth as it was, and the "spirit" to Elohim who gave it.—Eccl. xii. Before Christ, 350.

'Tis thine to speed to the Father's light and glory: for as the soul is a FIRE glowing with the Father's virtue, it continues immortal and is mistress of life.—Ammian.[1]

Thoth desires to know what will happen after the ascension of the soul to the Father. The Divine Intelligence replies : " The material body loses its form, which is destroyed with time ; the senses which have been animated return to their source, and will one day resume their functions ; but they lose their passions and their desires, and the ' spirit ' mounts again to the heavens to find itself in harmony. In the first zone it loses the faculty of increase and decrease ; in the second, the power of evil and the deceptions of idleness ; in the third, the illusions of desire ; in the fourth, insatiable ambition ; in the fifth, arrogance, audacity and temerity ; in the sixth, the wicked fondness for riches mal-acquired; in the seventh, falsehood.

" The Spirit thus purified by the effect of these harmonies returns to the state so much desired, having a merit and force that are its own, and it dwells with those who celebrate the praises of the Father. They are then placed among the Powers (of the heavens) and thereby partake of God. Such is the supreme good of those to whom it has been given to have knowledge, they become God."

" Having thus spoken, Pimander (the Divine Intelligence) returned among the divine Powers, and I, I set myself to counsel to men piety and Wisdom :

" O men, live soberly, abstain from gluttony. Why do you precipitate yourselves towards death, since you are capable of obtaining immortality ? Fly the darkness of ignorance, withdraw from the light that is obscured, escape from corruption, acquire immortality. Conductor and

[1] Chaldean Oracles; Cory, p. 243; Williams, Prim. Hist. 47.

chief of the human race I will show it the ways of salvation and will fill its cars with the precepts of wisdom !"—Books of the Thrice Greatest Hermes. Champollion, Egypte, 143.

Alas, alas, torch-bearing Day and thou Light of Deus, another, another life and destiny shall we inhabit.—Euripides, Iphigeneia in Aulis, 1505.

The whole life of men is full of grief, nor is there cessation of labors: but whatever else is dearer than life darkness enveloping hides it with clouds. We appear to be in love with this (life), because this is bright on earth, through inexperience of another life and because *things beneath the earth* are not divulged : but we are led astray by fables.—Euripides, Hippolytus, 190–197.

In the Zoroastrian religion, after soul and body have separated, the souls, *in the third night* after death, as soon as the shining Sun ascends, as soon as the victorious Mithra sets himself in pure radiance on the mount, come over the Mount Berezaiti upon the bridge Tshinavat which leads to Garonmana the dwelling of the good gods.[1]

The ghost of Polydore says :

> Being raised up this third day-light,
> Having deserted my body !—Euripides, Hecuba, 31, 32.

> The third day he rose from the dead!

The image of the corpse of Adonis (-Osiris) was washed, anointed with spices and wrapped in linen and wool.[2]

> Mit Spezereien
> Hatten wir ihn gepflegt,
> Wir seine Treuen
> Hatten ihn hingelegt ;
> Tücher und Binden
> Reinlich umwanden wir,
> Ach ! und wir finden
> Christ nicht mehr hier.

> " Attes lives !! "[3] Ades lives ! Deus lives !
> Christ is arisen,
> Blest is the Loving One !
> Adonis lives and is ascended !

---

[1] Duncker, ii. 326.   [2] Movers, 202, 203.
[3] Movers, 205, and authorities there quoted.

First they offer to the manes of Adonis as to one dead, and the day after the morrow they tell the story that he lives, and send him to the Air.—Lucian, de Dea Syria, l. c. § 6.[1]

Osiris dies on the seventeenth of the month, on the nineteenth *in the night* he is said to be found.—Plutarch, De Iside. xxxix.

Bacchus having the END OF HIS LIFE THE AGAIN RESUMED BEGINNING Was fashioned of another nature receiving in turn multifarious forms Sometimes such as cunning young Kronides (Zeus) shaking the aegis, Sometimes as old heavy-kneed Kronos lancing rain!—Nonnus, vi. 175, ff.

The Earth becomes fruitful through the Sun's light and water. The Sun's essence enters the fruits, the bread and the wine. In the Bacchanalian Mysteries a consecrated cup was handed round after supper called the "cup of the Agathodaemon" (the Good Divinity). In the Mysteries, bread is used in the worship of Saturn in the form of a serpent. A hymn was sung to Python at Delphi on every *seventh* day.[2] Orpheus was the founder of the Mysteries. The foundations of the Mysteries must have been ordinary religion, for the priests instituted them.[3] The use of bread and wine was continued in the Christian mysteries.

> Quid est, quod arctum circulum
> Sol jam recurrens deserit?
> Christusne terris nascitur,
> Qui lucis auget tramitem.—Aurel. Prudentius.[4]

Christmas, the birth of Christ, takes place just at the time of the winter solstice when Huitzilopoctli dies and Tezcatlipoca is born. The days are shortest. From this time however the Sun's power begins to increase. The Sun is, as it were, born anew. The Easter festival is the commencement of spring. It is Nature's resurrection. "Christ has arisen." "As the seed freed from its covering sends forth to the light of the sun a young shoot of life, so will man divested of this mortal coil, press forward to the light of a new life like the risen Redeemer."

---

[1] Movers, 548, 205.   [2] Deane, Serpent Worship, 88, 89.
[3] Cousin, Lect. on Mod. Phil. i. 404.   [4] Cathemerin. Hymn. xi.

Salve festa dies toto venerabilis aevo,
Qua deus infernum vicit et astra tenet.
Ecce renascentis testatur gratia mundi
Omnia cum Domino dona redisse suo.

Venantius Honorius.

For everywhere the grove with leaves, the fields with flowers favor
Christ triumphing after sad Tartarus.

The laws of hell having been suppressed, God, light, heaven, fields,
sea, duly praise him going above the stars.

Lo the God who was crucified reigns over all things, and all things
created give to the Creator prayer!—Venantius Honorius.

Pentecost is the "noblest workings of the ascended Re-
deemer," the fruits, the beginning of the harvest.[1]	Hier-
onymus (A. D. 331–420) relates that in the place where the
Redeemer cried in the manger, the lament of women for
Adonis has been heard even in later times.[2]	Hieronymus
describes the Adonia as existing in his time.[3]	In the fourth
century after Christ, Macrobius says:[4] "Among the Assyrians formerly the worship of Venus Architis and Adonis
especially flourished, which the Phœnicians now preserve."

And when from the Aether on high she beheld him lifeless, and his
body lying in his own blood, she sprang down and immediately tore her
bosom and at the same time her hair, and beat her breasts with
rough hands: and complaining of the Fates says: But still not all shall
be yours; the monuments of my grief, O Adoni, will always remain:
and a repeated image of death shall complete our yearly imitations of
grief. But the blood shall be changed to a flower.—Ovid, Metam. x. 720 ff.

Ezekiel found the women in the temple mourning for
Thammuz (Adonis-Adamus).[5]	The festival called Adonia
or Adoneia by the Greeks lasted in the Orient *seven* days;
for it was the ancient custom of the Israelites, Egyptians
and Syrians to mourn the dead so long.[6]	The Titans tore

[1] Creuzer, iv. 742.	[2] Epist. 49, ad Paulin. Tom. iv. part ii. p. 564, ed.
Martianay; quoted by Movers, 193.	[3] Movers, 210.

[4] Macrobius, Sat. i. 21.	[5] Ezekiel, viii. 14.	[6] Gen. l. 10; 1 Sam.
xxxi. 13; 1 Chron. x. 12; Judith, xvi. 29; Heliodor. Aethiop, vii. 11; Lucian
de Dea Syria, § 52, 53; quoted in Movers, 209.

Bacchus into *seven* pieces. Noah also, as Sisuthrus, Demarus, Adam, Orus, the Good Principle, Manu (Amon, Amanus), Bacchus or Osiris in the moon, is connected with the number *seven*, in reference to the weeks or quarters of the moon.

Sabaoth (Seven) the Demiurg, for thus the Demiurgic number is called by the Phœnicians.—Movers, 550; Lydus de Mens. iv. 93, p. 112.

> Best of all things is WATER!—Pindar, Olymp. I.
> The tender Adonis wanders distressing Aphrodite. . . ,
> And then Deukalion, cleaving the water elevated on high,
> Was a navigator not to be reached, having an air-wandering voyage.
>   Nonnus, vii. 365.
> Thus they place the power of Osiris in the moon.—Plutarch de Is. xliii.

"It has been ascertained that the Egyptians reckoned from the beginning of time to the *death of Osiris* by Typhon, i. e. to the Deluge, thirty thousand lunar-months, hence 2,424 years."[1] "The bull was among the Egyptians an emblem of the Sun; the apis-bull, however, representing as it did at the same time also the moon and the conjunction of sun and moon on the first of Thoth, required to have marked upon it the symbolic signs of the moon. The Egyptians therefore selected for the worship of Apis (who according to Plutarch was to them a living image of the Divine Wisdom, of the soul of Osiris) a black bull which had *a crescent on its side* and a wart in the shape of a beetle (which likewise designated the moon) under the tongue." "*The mooncrescent on the side of the apis-bull*" is mentioned.[2] "Apis is the animated image of Osiris, and is born when the Generative Light descends from the moon and comes to touch the eager Cow" (Earth).[3] Osiris is Bacchus.[4] Osiris was the Nile and Humid Principle generally as the source of production.[5] The Nile overflows when the Sun passes through the sign of the Lion in the Zodiac. In the sacred hymns of Osiris, they invoke him who rests between the

---

[1] Seyffarth's Chronology, 118.   [2] Ibid. 81, 82.   [3] De Iside, xliii.
[4] De Iside, xxxv.; Kenrick, i. 335, 337.   [5] De Iside, xxxv. xxxvi.

arms of the Sun.[1] Osiris wears the emblems of Bacchus.
Bacchus is the Generative and Nutritive Spirit.[2] According
to Proclus, Bacchus is the Demiurg, analogous to the One
Father who generates total fabrication.[3]

Many Greeks make bull-formed images of Bacchus,
but the women of the Eleans also call upon (him) praying
the God to come to them ox-footed. And by the Argives
he is called ox-born Dionusos: but they evoke him with trumpets *from the water*, casting into the abyss a lamb for the
janitor, but the trumpets they hide with thyrsi.[4]

Dionysus went under the wave of the sea.—Iliad, vi. 135.
All things are born from Kronos and Venus.—Plut. de Is. lxix.
Every one of the barbarians (foreigners) dances these Sacred Orgies !
                                                   Euripides, Bacchae, 482.
And they at the appointed hour shook the thyrsus in the Bacchic ceremonies,
calling "Iakchos, the SON OF DEUS, BROMIOS ! "—Bacchae, 724.
She and the women with her crowned themselves with olive and she pre-
ceded in a chorus (dance) all the people leading all the women; and all the
men of Israel followed in armor with garlands, and hymns in their mouth.
                                                   Judith, xv. 13.
Begin to my God with drums, sing to my Lord with cymbals, adapt for
him a new psalm, exalt and call on his name !—Judith, xvi. 1.

When the Elohim helped the Levites (Eloim, Leuitas) carrying the
Ark (Arōn) of the covenant of Iahoh, they sacrificed *seven* bullocks and
seven rams.—1 Chron. xv. 26.

On the fifteenth day of the *seventh* month the Feast of Tabernacles
was celebrated, lasting *seven days*. It was the close of the harvest.
Plutarch considered it a festival of Dionysus. "The time and manner
of the greatest and most perfect festival among the Jews suits with
Dionysus. For, as to the so-called fast, in the height of the harvest
they set out tables of all sorts of fruits under tents and huts woven together mostly of branches and ivy; and the anterior they name Tabernacle of the Feast. And a few days afterwards they celebrate another
festival, not with enigmas, but BACCHUS BEING DIRECTLY CALLED UPON.
There is also a certain garland-bearing and thyrsus-carrying festival[5]
among them in which having thyrsi they enter the temple: but entering,

_____

[1] De Is. lii.   [2] Ibid. xl.   [3] Taylor's Plato, 484.   [4] Plut. de Is. xxxv.
[5] Bag-o, 1 Esdr. vii. 40, Bac-chur, ix.; Bak-Bak-kar, a Levite, 1 Chron. ix.
The festival of the sacred moon, in which it is the custom to play the

what they do we know not: but probably the performances are the Feast of Bacchus: for they use little trumpets, just like the Greeks in the Bacchanalia (in) calling upon the God: and others march playing the harp, whom they call Leuites, so called either from the word Lusios or rather from the word Euios. But I also think that the festival of the Sabbata is not wholly without relation to the festival of Dionysus. For even now many call the Bacchi Sabbi, and they utter this word when they celebrate orgies to the God: the evidence of which certainly can be taken from Demosthenes and Menander. And very apropos one might say that the name was made from a certain pompous movement which possesses those celebrating the Bacchic rites. And themselves bear testimony to this remark when they honor the Sabbath inviting one another to drink and get drunk; and when any thing greater interrupts, making a usage universally indeed to taste strong (drink). And perhaps some one might say these things are conjectural (εἰκότα): according to the force in them, first indeed the high-priest confutes (this idea) going forth mitred at these festivals and clothed in a gold-embroidered fawn-skin and wearing a tunic reaching to his feet, and buskins: and many bells depend from the dress resounding at every step. And, as among us, they make use of hollow sounds at the nocturnal rites and call upon the brazen—(. . .   ) nurses of the God: and the thyrsus incarved, shown on the opposite (sides) of the over-head, and the drums: for these surely suit no other god than Dionysus." "The Arab festival Ashurah, like the Feast of Tabernacles, fell in September. The Arab legend connects with this festival the weightiest events of the Bible and Koran history, Noah's leaving the Ark," &c.[1]

These are the sons of Zabaon; both Aiah and ANAH. This is "the ANAH who found the mules in the desert when he was feeding asses for his father Zebaon."—Gen. xxxvi. 24.

These are the generations of Aso (Oso) who is Adom. Oso took his wives from the daughters of Kanon. Adah daughter of Ailon the Achatian, and Aholibamah daughter of ANAH the daughter of Zibeon the Hivite.—Gen. xxxvi.

NAH (Noah) and Anah (in the feminine) would be trumpet in the temple at the same moment that the sacrifices are offered. From which practice this is called the true Feast of Trumpets.

Philo, On the Eighth and Tenth Festivals.

Your New-moons and your stated Sabbaths!—Isaiah, i. 14.

The Bacchic BRANCH mighty through Greece!—Euripides, Bacchae, 308.

He shall sing Euion to garland-bearing Dionysus.—Nonnus, xv. 131.

[1] Creuzer, Symb. iv. 750, 751, note, 752; Plutarch, Quaest. Conviv. iv. 671, 746, 745. Anos, Anoh, Noh, Ianus, Anus (Time).

Noah and the Anna perenna (the Nature-goddess) of the Romans, Ianus (Bacchus) and Anna (Ceres).[1]

And Nah began, a man cultivating the earth, and he planted a *vineyard.*
And he drinks of the wine and was drunken.—Gen. ix. 20, 21.

They slew their children in sacrifices or used *secret Mysteries* or celebrated frantic komuses of strange rites!—Wisdom of Solomon, xiv. 23.

I am He who made the VINE, corn, sheaves, the threshing-floor and flour in the territory of the king of noble Egypt!
Book of the Dead, Chapt. 1st.[2]

I am the true VINE and my Father is the husbandman.

The young Bacchus, the Principle of fertility, revered by the common people as the God of the vine could well serve the Orphic poets and philosophers as the impersonation of the Life-giving Spirit that, as Son of Jupiter, inspires the dead Matter with life. He could, as Osiris, represent the active Deity the Creator-Sun, the active Power of the Unknown God. As the source of production he was the POWER of his Father Zeus.

Dionysus (Bacchus) is called the POWER of fruit-trees and things planted.—Eusebius, Præp. Ev. 3, 11.

Bacchus the SON OF GOD!—Euripides, Bacchae, line 1.

O KING Bacchus you appear a great God!—Bacchae, 1032.

Bromius Boy God of God Dionysus![3]

Maid of Adonis you have the THYRSUS!—Nonnus, xlii. 420, 421.

For now the general festival of Kupris (Venus) came,
Which throughout Sēstos they keep to Adonis and Kuthereia:
All together they hastened to come to the holy day
As many as dwelt in the remotest parts of the sea-girt islands:
Some from Haimonia and others from Cyprus on the sea;

---

[1] Compare the names of the prophetess Anna and the priest Annas (Nas, Nah, Nissi, Nuseus).—Luke, ii. 36; iii. 2. The priest bore the name of his God throughout the Orient.   [2] Seyffarth.
[3] Bromion Paida Theon Theou Dionuson.—Bacchae, 83–85.

Nor did any woman remain in the cities of Cythera:
And dancing on the summits of blazing Lebanon
Not one of the neighbors then was away from the festival,
Neither dweller of Phrygia, nor citizen of the near Abydos.

Musæus, Hero and Leander, 42, ff.

Therefore in fires (AR-im) honor Iahoh, in the Isles of the Sea the name Ihoh Alahi Isral.—Isaiah, xxiv. 15.

I was wrong. You saw not the stream of Adonis nor the soil of Bublos
Beheld, where is the home of the Graces, where dances
Assyrian Kuthereia and not the bed-shunning Athena.

Nonnus, iii. 109, ff.

But hear Aphrodite sung by the women of Byblus.

Nonnus, xxix. 351.

Ascend the Labanon (Mount Libanus) and cry aloud!

Jeremiah, xxii. 20.

They shall flower like the VINE: his memory as the WINE OF LEBANON!—Hosea, xiv. 8.

And, bringing to light the
Euia of the Egyptian Bacchus the orgies of raving Osiris,
He taught the initiations at night of the mystic usages,
And with furtive voice to the Bacchante raised the Magian hymn
making an acute wailing.—Nonnus, iv. 273.

For this charming Youth is from Libanos where Venus dances.
I am wrong: not easily has a mortal form borne Kadmus.
But he is the Offspring of Deus and has concealed his origin.
Not falsely is he hymned Kadmilos ; for his celestial
Form he alone changed and still Kadmus hears.—Nonnus, iv. 82, ff.

Kadmus was a Phœnician god, called also Kadmiel, and is the Creative Wisdom, the Demiurg.[1] The Cabbalists considered Adam Kadmon the oneness of the powers which emanate from God.[2] "Adam Kadmon is the figure of a man which hovers above the symbolic animals of Ezekiel. From him the creation emanated in four degrees or four

---

[1] Movers, 513, 514, 515.   [2] J. Müller, 135, 124.

worlds." [1] Adam Kadmon is the Sun as the Demiurgic Wisdom or Logos. Kadmus-Hermes stands by the Demiurg in his contest with Typhon. [2]

> O Kadmus, Auxiliary in the war of Deus the Giant-killer
> Fearest thou seeing one serpent only ? But in the wars,
> Obedient to thee, Kroniōn hurled down Typhon. Nonnus, iv. 393.

> Hail Attis, the Assyrians call thee thrice-desired
> Adonis, the Samothracians Adam the Holy !

Zeus DEM-arus is the Son of Saturn, just as Adam is the First-created of Jehovah. [3]

"In the Jewish Cabbala the word Maschia (Messiah) composed of mem (40), schin (300), yod (10), heth (8), gives the numerical value 358 ; the same is the case with the word Nahash (serpent) composed of noun (50), heth (8), schin (300). From this the Cabbalists conclude that the Messiah will conquer Satan represented under the image of a serpent, and that he will destroy sin and the death of the Spirit. The Cabbalists taught that the three letters of the word Adam (ADM) form the initials of the three names Adam, David, Messiah; which indicates that the soul of Adam must appear by transmigration in the bodies of David and the Messiah." [4] The Cabbala had its first origin in Babylon during the exile, but the whole system entire could only be formed later in the Jewish schools of Alexandria where the doctrines of Pythagoras and Plato were combined with certain doctrines of the Oriental philosophy,—a mixture of profound speculations and superstitious notions, of wisdom and extravagance. In pronouncing certain words of Holy Writ it was supposed that the sick could be cured, fires put out and all sorts of miracles performed. [5]

Adam is the FIRST-BORN like Phanes, Evan, Iao and Adonis. Deucalion was also the First-born. [6] "For Adonis

---

[1] Munk, Palestine, 523 ; Ezekiel, i. 26.   [2] Movers, 273.
[3] Movers, 144, 287 ; Sanchoniathon, vii.
[4] Munk, Palestine, 521.   [5] Ibid. 520, 523 ; See Plato, Tim. 139, ed. Stallbaum.   [6] Pindar, Olympic Ode, ix. 41, 43, 44.

was named Ao."[1]   Iao is Adonis and Osiris.[2]   Aos is Iao.[3]
"Iao the God of Moses."[4]   Iao is therefore Iahoh or Jehovah (Adoni).[5]

Non sicut Tu inter deos Adonai [ADNI]
There is none like Thee among the gods, Adonis!—Psalm lxxxvi. 8.

And Abram said, Adoni Ihoh [My ADON, Jehovah]!—Gen. xv. 2.

Ἄδωνις δεσπότης ὑπὸ Φοινίκων καὶ Βόλου ὄνομα.
Adonis "lord" with Phœnicians, and Bel's name!—Hesychius.[6]

Jehovah is called Alahi Alahim O-Adoni H-Adonim, God of
Gods and Lord of the Lords.[7]

Vivit Dominus Adonai, Dominus exercituum!
Pseudo-Matthaei Evang. xii.

And the Thunderer on high Sabaôth Adônaios shall sit
On his throne in heaven and shall fix a great pillar
And Christ himself eternal shall come in a cloud
To the ETERNAL, in glory with his good angels.
And he shall sit on the right on a high throne judging
The life of the pious and the ways of impious men.
Moses also shall come the great friend of the Highest
God . . . . And the great Abraam himself shall come
Isaak and Iakôb, Iasous and Daniël, Elias
Ambakaoum, and Iônas and those that the Ehrews slew
Those with Eremeias.—Sibylline Books, Gallaeus, 278.

יהוה Ihoh, Iahoh (Ahoh) is the name of the sun-god Diony-
sus or Bacchus.[8]   He was also called Iaō, Ieuō and Euas.[9]
Evius is another of his names.   Eve is called Eua in the
Sibylline Books.[10]   Thus Eua is the feminine of Dionysus-
Bacchus.   Bacchus is called Huas and Euimos.[11]   Eve is
called Eoua and Euea.[12]

---

[1] Etym. Magn. Movers, 229.   [2] Movers, 542, 544.   [3] Movers, 285, 550.
[4] Gesenius Thes. 577; Diodor. Sic. i. 94.   [5] Movers, 546, 544, 8, 9.
[6] Movers, 195.   [7] Deut. x. 17.   [8] Movers, 545, 546, 548, 549, 25.
[9] Movers, 547, 548, quotes Euseb. Praep. Ev. l. x. 9; Diodor. Sic. I. 94;
Gesenius Thes. 577.   [10] Servatius Gallaeus, 44.
[11] Scholia ad Aristophanes, Aves, 583.   [12] Movers, 547, and the authorities
there quoted.

Osiris-Adonis-Apasson is the Male and Isis-Venus-Taautha the Feminine Principle. From these two proceeds an ONLY-BEGOTTEN SON, Horus, Phanes (Pan), Bacchus, Moumis, Ulom.[1] "The Spirit unites with Matter as a husband with his wife." This Spirit is termed "the Father."[2] The Platonic philosophers hold that Intellect is the very Life of living things, the First Principle and Exemplar of all, whence by different degrees the inferior classes of life are derived.[3] The Hawk-headed serpent was the Egyptian emblem of the Divine Mind.[4] To the Serpent the beauty and harmony of the universe is ascribed.[5]

For the venerable and incorruptible Kronos was held in the former hypothesis to be the Father of Aether and Chaos; but in this he is passed over and a Serpent substituted; and the three-fold Aether is called *intellectual* . . . .

Saturn is born this Serpent![5]

A Great Serpent was the emblem of Zeus in the Mysteries.

For the Egyptians call the "Spirit" Jupiter.—Plutarch, de Is. xxxvi.

According to an Orphic theogony mentioned in Athenagoras, a Serpent (Saturn) was born from the Two Principles. This creature was Hercules (the Celestial Sun). This Hercules bore an egg which he cut in halves and of one formed the heaven, of the other the earth.[7] Hercules is the "Spirit of God" (πνευμα) like Bacchus and Ammon. —Plutarch, de Iside, xl.

Thou the seed of a Divine Mind art sprung from Hercules.
Euripides, Heraclidae, 541.

VIRGIN PERSEPHONEIA, you found no escape from marriage
But you were wived in a Dragon's hymeneals,

---

[1] Movers, 264, 282.　　[2] Philo, Cain and his Birth, xiii. xvii. ; Munter, Bab. 46.　　[3] Taylor's Proclus, p. xxi.　　[4] Deane, Serp. Worship, 145.
[5] Movers, 109.　　[6] Damascius ; Cory, 313. This is Ophion-Saturn.
[7] Movers, 447.

When Zeus very coiled, his countenance being changed,
A Dragon-bridegroom circled in love-inspiring fold,
Proceeded to the sanctum of the dark VIRGIN
Agitating his rough beard . . . . Through the Aetherial Dracontean
    nuptials
The womb of Persephone was agitated by a fruitful young,
Bearing ZAGREUS the horned Child.—Nonnus, vi. 155, ff.

In the third century, Mani said that the Great Serpent (Saturn the Dragon of Life, the Father, "the Good Divinity") had glided over the cradle of the infant Mary.—Deane, Serpent-worship, 89, 90.

Conceived by the Holy Spirit, Born of the Virgin Mary.
                                Creed; Matthew, i. 20.

The Holy Spirit the Lord and Giver of Life is God the Father, Who acts only by his Spirit and his Word.—De Wette, Bibl. Dogm. p. 84. § 111.

Then the Saviour himself says "Now my mother the Holy Spirit took me."—Apocryphal Evangelium Ebraer.[1]

Fear not, Mary, for you have found favor before the Lord of all, and will conceive from his Logos (Spirit).
The "POWER" of the Lord shall overshadow thee; wherefore that Holy Thing born of thee shall be called the Son of the Highest.
                        Protevang. Iacobi, xi. ed. Tischendorf.

Holy Ghost shall come upon thee and the "POWER" of the Highest shall overshadow thee: therefore also that Holy Thing which shall be born of thee shall be called Son of God.—Luke, i. 35; Evang. de Nat. Mariae, ix.

For that which is conceived in her is from the Holy Spirit.
                                Matthew, i. 20.

For the MIGHTY ONE did great things unto me and holy is his name.
                                Matthew, i. 49.
Τὴν δὲ ζωὴν ἐν πυρὶ καὶ πνεύματι.
But the Life is through Fire and Spirit.
                        Plato, Timaeus, 77, ed. Stallbaum.
He will baptize you in Holy Spirit and Fire.—Matthew, iii. 11.

[1] Creuzer, Symb. i. 341.

The Spirit and Matter philosophy of the Old Testament is perpetuated in the New. In the Egyptian philosophy we find the expression " Word of the Spirit," as if " the Word " were a part of, an emanation from "the Spirit." In the same style of thought Christ is conceived as an Emanation from the Holy Ghost, according to Matthew.

Epimenides affirms that the Two First Principles are Air and Night: whence it is evident that he reverences in silence the One Principle which is prior to the Two.[1] But the Babylonians like the rest of the Barbarians pass over in silence the One Principle of the universe, and they constitute Two, Tauthe and Apason ; making Apason the husband of Tauthe and denominating her the Mother of the gods. And from these proceeds AN ONLY-BEGOTTEN SON, Mōumis, which, I conceive, is no other than the INTELLIGIBLE WORLD proceeding from the "Two Principles."[2]

The WORLD appears to them (the Egyptians) to consist of a *masculine and feminine nature*. And they engrave a scarabaeus for Athena (Minerva) and a vulture for Hephaestus. For these alone of all the gods they consider as both male and female in their nature.[3]

Athána springing upwards shouted with AN EXCEEDING GREAT CRY: and Heaven and Mother Earth shuddered at her.—Pindar, Ol. vii.

Doth not Wisdom CRY ? . . . .

Iahoh possessed me the Beginning of his way before his works, from which (time) :

I was effused from Oulom, from the Beginning, from the earliest times of the earth.

When there were no Depths I was born.

When he prepared the heavens there was I, when he described a circle on the face of the Deep.

I was with him Amon (the Demiurgic Nous) and I was his delight day by day.—Proverbs, viii.

The WISDOM, the daughter of God, is both male and Father.

Philo, de Profugis, 458.[4]

---

[1] Damascius ; Cory, 317.   [2] Ibid. 321.
[3] From Horapollo ; Cory, 286.   [4] De Wette, Bibl. Dogm. p. 142.

" The Word is the Active 'POWER' of Brahma, proceeding from him. She speaks a hymn in the Vedas in praise of herself as the Supreme and Universal Soul." [1] The goddess Neith formed but one whole with the Creator Amon before the creation of the souls and the physical world. Absorbed in the Supreme Being, the Egyptians said that she was both male and female. As the world contains germs male as well as female principles, both must have existed in the God who was their Author. He smiled and ordered that Nature should exist: and instantly a perfectly beautiful female (Nature, Neith) proceeded from his voice and the Father of all things rendered her fruitful. This is the Athena who sprang from the head of Zeus. [2]

Kaiomorts, the FIRST MAN (in the Persian mythology), left behind him at his death a seed from which a bi-sexed tree grew up in which two were united in the closest union. This, having been formed by Ormuzd into a double-man, bore instead of fruits ten human pairs. From Meshia and Meshiane, the first pair, the entire human race is descended. [3] Plato mentions the double-man, and the Bible hints at this idea when it forms the first woman from a rib of the Adam (double-man). Plato says: The male kind was the produce originally of the Sun, the female of the Earth, and that which partook of the other two, of the Moon; for the Moon partakes of both the others (the Sun and the Nature-goddess). The Chaldeans believed that in Chaos there were bi-sex human beings. [4]

Phtha is the active creative " Spirit" the Divine Intelligence. [5] Ptah (Hephaestus) has two sexes.

> The Mighty POWER became half male half female.
>
> Hindu Cosmogony. [6]

---

[1] Milman, Hist. Christ. 46; Colebrooke, Asiatic Res. viii. 402.
[2] Champollion, Egypte, 255, Univ. pitt.   [3] Knobel, Gen. p. 33; See Plato's Sympos. Burges, p. 509: Compare Genesis, i. 27; ii. 23.
[4] Munter, Bab. 38.   [5] Egypte, 255. Champollion.
[6] This is " Eros of two natures."

Kneph, the Good Divinity, the Creator, brought forth out of his mouth an
Egg from which Ptah sprung.—Uhlemann, Thoth, p. 26.

Kneph, who has no beginning and no end, is the First Cause.
Plutarch de Is. xxxi.; Movers, 267.

In the Old Testament God creates by his Word, his
Spirit and his Wisdom (Thoth or Athena-Minerva). The
Egyptian philosophy makes Thoth 1st (Trismegistus) the
Divine Wisdom personified, and Thoth 2nd (the Sun) an
emanation from Thoth 1st. He is the Demiurg. Saturn
creates by the aid of Thoth, Ophion, the Agathodemon, the
Bel-serpent, Surmobel; also by the aid of Minerva and
Mercury.[1] Thoth 1st is only called by the Superior Deity
" Soul of my Soul and sacred Intelligence of my Intelligence." He delegated to the Second Thoth the government
of the earth, moon and hell.[2] Thoth is the Syrian sun-god
Adad, Adodus, the Phœnician Tat, Taaut (Hermes). The
emblems of Osiris as well as " Thoth with the ibis-head " are
enclosed in a circle formed by a serpent biting his tail, an
emblem of eternity. Thoth the companion of Osiris never
abandoned him in hell.[3] He is Ophion-Uranus.

The Divine Wisdom was conceived of in two ways;
first, as being *at rest*. Thus after Elohim had created the
world, *he rested* the seventh day. Again it was conceived
of as *active*, creating the world, the Demiurg or Creator. In
this second stage it is called " the forth-going Word " or
Wisdom.

For Intellect is the fountain of words, and speech is its mouthpiece.
Philo, Cain and his Birth, xiii.[4]

" The Logos of Philo has unquestionably flowed from the

[1] Movers, 109, 141, 161, et passim.   [2] Egypte, 135.   [3] Ihid. 126, 129.
I am Thotho-mone (Thoth-Amon ?) who measures and weighs;
Bak who confounds homicides.—Book of the Dead.
See Seyffarth, Theolog. Schr. 4; Proverbs, vii.; Hebrew Bible.
The consonants of Taautha or Thotho-mone agree with Thoth-Amon, and
the sense also would favor this reading of the Hieroglyphics.
[4] Ed. Yonge.

Chaldean Logos."[1] They are one and the same. Philo says: "God is the Mind of the universe," "the Mind of the universe created the universe."[2] God used the Logos as his Instrument by whom he made the world.[3]

> Ihoh by WISDOM has founded the earth: by Intelligence he has prepared the heavens.—Prov. iii. 19.

The Hebrew considers God active in Nature as "Spirit." The "Spirit" of God is the impulse-giving and the fruitful Principle. In man the Spirit of God is the Principle of all powers, abilities, talents, inspiration. It is the "Wisdom." The highest quality of God as Creator and Governor of the world is the Reason (Logos). This is double since it both remains in God and acts upon the world. The first is the Logos Endiathetikos (the "Wisdom at rest" in the mind), the second is the Logos Proforikos (the "Wisdom that goes forth" to create).

> I (WISDOM) came out of the mouth of the Most High and covered the earth as a Cloud. He created me from the Beginning before the world.
> > Ecclesiasticus xxiv. 3–9.
> For from God I came forth.—John, viii. 42.
> I am the Living Bread that came down from heaven. For the Bread of God is that which cometh down from heaven and giveth life to the world.
> > John vi. 51, 33.

This last is the manifestation, the Type and the exact Image of God in the world. God used this his Oldest and First-born Son as the Instrument of his creation.[4] Philo calls this Logos, who self-created stands next God above every thing that is created, "A God" "the Second God;" he thinks him also the Archetype of humanity. With this Logos he interchanges "the Wisdom."[5] This Wisdom appears clearly as substance in the Book of Wisdom. She proceeds out of God before the Creation, is a Reflection of

---

[1] Movers, 553.   [2] Philo, On the Migration of Abraham, xxxv. Yonge.
[3] Philo, Cain and his Birth, § xxxv.   [4] De Wette, Bibl. Dogm. 127, 128.
[5] De Wette, Bibl. Dogm. 128; Eusebius, Praep. Ev. viii. 13.

the Supreme Light, the exact Image of the Godhead, of divine nature and qualities, is Creator of the world.[1]

For She is the Breath of the POWER of God, and a pure Influence flowing from the glory of the Almighty.

For She is the Brightness of the Everlasting Light, the Unspotted Mirror of the POWER of God and the Image of his goodness.

Book of Wisdom, vii. 25, 26.

He hath made earth by his POWER, he has established the world by his WISDOM and has stretched out the heaven by his Understanding.

Jeremiah, li. 15.

That "the Word" and "the Spirit" of God (the Holy Ghost) interchange with one another, and are very much the same idea is evident from the doctrine of the "Christians of St. John" that Christ is the Spirit and Word of the Eternal Father.[2]

By his SPIRIT he hath garnished the heavens.—Job, xxvi. 13.
By the WORD of Iahoh were the heavens made.—Ps. xxxiii. 6.

That they are the same as the "Wisdom of God" appears from Psalm cxxxvi. 5.

To Him that by WISDOM made the heavens.

Having willed, he brought forth us by means of the "Word (Logos) of truth."—James i. 18.

It is evident that the reluctance of the later Jews and Samaritans to consider God as immediately active in creation extended also to the Egyptian, Babylonian, Hindu and Persian philosophers, and even to Plato who had his Efficient Cause and his Logos the Divine Wisdom. This doctrine of Philo came after the Platonic doctrine of the Soul of the World and the Divine Reason; and was preceded by the idea of the "Word of Creation" among the Hindus, Persians and Jews and the Kabbalistic doctrine of the First Man. The later Jews and Samaritans were reluctant to make God immediately active in the corporeal

---

[1] De Wette, Bibl. Dogm. 136.   [2] Adams, View of Rel. 118.

world; on which account the Speaking of God was conceived and this made the *acting* Person where in the Old Testament Jehovah is represented as acting personally. Wherever God is mentioned as personally appearing, the Word or the Angel of the Lord is meant.[1] Adonai is the "Spirit" and the Word.

The WORD is Light in the Persian Light-Word Honover, in the Egyptian "WORD of the Spirit" and in the Hebrew LOGOS or WISDOM. Both the "WORD" and the "WISDOM" appear as a Being, the Second God,[2] the Demiurg, the active Agent of the First Cause in the creation of the world. The Logos is the Revealed, the Second God, the Mediator between God the Father and Creation.

He is called the Oldest and FIRST-BORN Son of God, the ONLY-BEGOTTEN, Monogenes and PRŌTOGONOS.[3]

For the LOGOS is the oldest IMAGE of God.—Philo, de Confus. Ling. 341.

Bel-Saturn was regarded as Boundless Time before the Creation. Second, he was the Unrevealed Primal Being withdrawn into himself, out of whom the "Second Bel" as Creator (Demiurg) proceeds together with two other Persons of the divine trinity, Zeus-Belus and Baal-Chom or Apollo Chomaeus. In the younger Chaldean Oracles the doctrine of a First Being, the Father of All, the Great Father of the Logos, of the Only-begotten, of Iao the Demiurg, is plainly stated. But the traces of it go back to a higher antiquity. ... This Primal Father of All has an Only-begotten Son who is like him in all things and therefore is himself again and takes the first place in the triad; he is the Demiurg Bel, the Saturn revealing himself, the mysterious Heptaktis or Iao in the Chaldean learning. According to the Emperor Julian, the Highest Deity, the Primal Goodness,

[1] De Wette, pp. 127, 128, 131, 132, quotes Kleuker, Natur und Ursprung der Emanationslehre b. d. Kabbalisten, S. 8 ff.

[2] Philo, Quaest. et Solut. : See De Wette, Bibl. Dogm. p. 130, note *m*.

[3] De Wette, § 156, note.

brought forth out of itself the Intelligible Sun of whom the sun's disk is only a picture; this Sun is, in the doctrine of the Chaldeans, the Intelligible Light and Spiritual Life-principle Iao.

The Chaldeans call the God Iao instead of Light Intelligible.

Lydus, de Mensibus, iv. 38, p. 74.

The Son, Zeus-Belus or Sol-Mithra, is an image of the Father, an Emanation from the Supreme Light (das Ur-licht).[1] Speaking of Bel-Mithra, Movers says: This Bel of the Chaldean-Babylonian Magianism, so often interchanged with the Mithra of the Persian doctrines, usually named Zeus-Belus and already shown by us to be Mithra, appears in the Mithras-grottoes in the symbol of Aiōn and like the Old-Bel passed for Creator.[2]

Among the Orphic theologers the worship of Dionysus was the centre of all religious ideas, and the starting point of all speculations upon the world and human nature. In the same system Dionysus was also the god from whom the liberation of souls was expected; for, according to an Orphic notion, more than once alluded to by Plato, human souls are punished by being confined in the body, as in a prison. The sufferings of the soul in its prison, the steps and tran-sitions by which it passes to a higher state of existence and its gradual purification and enlightenment were all fully described in these poems.[3] "The souls are carried up by the Intermediate Being who is usually called Bel-Mithra, Zeus, namely Zeus-Belus, or "Sun-Intelligible," Logos, Only-begotten, and is merely the other self of Bel-Satnrn (the Father); just as in the case of Philo's Logos whose theology has certainly flowed from the Chaldean."

And the theologians proclaim the Intelligent Life Saturnian but not Jupiterian (Δίϊον), for through the Great Zeus (Dios) is the way up (to heaven). But just as Zeus filled with his own Father and born up into

---

[1] Movers, 262–265.   [2] Ibid. 390.   [3] K. O. Müller, 234, 238.

Him as (to) his own Intelligible (pattern, image) carries also with him what is with him, just so indeed the souls with Zeus make their ascension !—Proclus, in Plat. Alcib. Tom. iv. p. 96.[1]

That I should raise him up at the *last day*.—John, vi. 41.

Aiakos (Eacus, Iacchos) Creative . . . bestowing fruit upon the glebe.
>   Nonnus, xxxix. 146.

Adonis was called Gauas ; Bacchus was called Guēs.[2]   Iao is Adonis and Bacchus,[3] Iao is the Raiser up of souls to heaven.[4]

Agni the Hindu Sun, the Fire of life, is Pramati, the " Fire on the altar" regarded as Soul of the world. This Vedic Pramati, like the Greek Fire-spirit Promethe-us, is the Principle of civilization among the most ancient shepherds and cultivators of the earth[5] and coincides with Prometheus as Creator of men. Fire or ordinary sacrificial fire is called by Homer " the flame of Vulcan." [6] Vulcan, Iapet (Phut, Ptah) and Prometheus are mentioned together by Nonnus.[7] The Fire is the Primal Principle, the neutral World-soul, the highest Atman (Adam) or the Brahma (Brahm in the neuter gender).[8]

>   Fire stolen from the highest part of heaven Prometheus
>   Gave to the lands.—Juvenal, xv. 85.

The Sun is all-knowing in Homer, and is the visible symbol of the Divine Intelligence or Logos. This is Bel Minor, Iao the Life of the world, Zeus or Pan as the Anima mundi, Baga or Bacchus the Life-giver. The Orphic Hymn (xiii. 8) calls Saturn (Kronos) Prometheus.[9] He was regarded as the Creator of the human race. Plutarch says that Anticlidas makes Isis the daughter of Prometheus and wife of Bacchus.[10] But Aristo related that Bacchus was the Son of Jove and Isis.[11] Zeus ordered Prometheus and Minerva to

---

[1] Movers, 553.   [2] Ibid. 545, 547.   [3] Ibid. 542, 543, 554, 547.
[4] Movers, 551, 552, 553.   [5] Weber, Ind. Stud. ii. 380 ; Wuttke, ii. 244.
[6] Iliad, xxiii.   [7] Nonnus, Dionus. ii. 295 ff.   [8] Weber, ii. 378.
[9] Movers, 261.   [10] De Iside, xxxvii.   [11] Ibid.

make men of clay. Minerva, the Wisdom of God, then breathed into the clay and made the images alive.[1] Another legend said that Jupiter caused the winds to blow upon them and thus gave them life.[2] The Greeks said Zeus had swallowed Metis (Mind). Minerva sprung from the head of Jove. The Egyptian Thoth, the Active Intelligence, is the Phœnician Ophion-Kadmus.[3]

"The Orphic philosophy placed Time (Chronos)[4] at the head of all things and endued it with life and creative power. That is, Time is God. From Him emanate Chaos and Aether. Chronos makes an egg of the Chaos surrounded by the Aether and from this springs the golden-winged Eros-Phanes, the Soul of the world.[5] Zeus according to the Orphic poets is the Soul of the world. The unity of Zeus and Eros is mentioned in Pherecydes and the Orphic poems; nevertheless the universe stands in different relations to Zeus and to Eros."[6] It is as difficult to distinguish between God and the Spirit of God as it is between Chronos-Zeus and Eros-Zeus.

The Father is in me and I in him.—John, x. 38.

He that hath seen me hath seen the Father; and how sayest thou show us the Father?

Dost thou not believe that I am in the Father and the Father in me? Believe me that I am in the Father and the Father in me.

John, xiv. 9, 10, 11.

As Matter was "the Mother," and "the Spirit" "the Father," it follows that "the Son" was "the Father."

[1] Stephan. Byzant. 810, Berkelius; Williams, 32, 41; Lucianus, in Prometheus. [2] Anthon; quotes Etym. Magn. et Steph. Byz. s. v. IKONION.

[3] Movers, 518. [4] Kronos is the Sun. Compare Aiôn, Annus, Eanus, Ianus. Compare Ovid, Fast. i. 88, 89, 102.

[5] So Brahma (the Sun) is born of the Aether in the shape of an egg.— Weber, Ind. Stud. ii. 382. Brahma is the Soul of the world.—Mill's India, 200, 206, 239, 241; Wuttke, ii. 293. Timaeus Locrius and Plato give us a Soul of the World different from the usual one. The former is the Son of Spirit and Matter (the Father and the Mother); but generally the Soul of the world is the Spirit = the Father and Son as the Life of the world (Anima mundi).

[6] K. O. Müller, 234, 237.

In the Beginning was the LOGOS (the Power of God, the Divine Wisdom); and the LOGOS was with THE GOD [1] and GOD was the LOGOS.

John, i. 1.; 1 Corinth. i. 23, 24.

What he here calls God is his most Ancient WORD.

Philo, de Somn. xxxix.

On each side are those most Ancient Powers which are always close to the Living [2] God, one of which is called his Creative Power ... And the Creative Power is God; for it is by this that he made and arranged the universe.

Philo, On Abraham, xxiv. xxv.; de Confus. Ling. xxvii. xxviii.

For by him were all things created.—Paul, Coloss. i.

The Chaldean Saturn had his Sun or Logos.[3] The Logos of Philo is taken from the Chaldeans.[4] The sun was the symbol of the Logos.[5] "The central Sun of the world's history rose. The Word (Logos) was made flesh. The Eternal Life (of the Invisible Sun-god, the Helios Noetos) appeared in personal union with human nature." [6]

That Eternal Life which was with the Father and was manifested unto us. The Logos of Life which was from the Beginning!—John, Epist. i. 1.

" Cudworth I. 4 writes that Heraclius held that ' All things were made by the Eternal Logos who was with God and was God.' Even Julian allowed that the Primary Cause produced an intellectual Sun who formed the material sun. The intellectual Sun is the Phanes of the Greeks, the Mono-genes of Orphic philosophy. Empedocles held a Sun the Original of the visible sun. He is Mithras the Mediator." [7]

---

[1] For THE GOD (ὁ Θεος) if he be truly GOD (Θεος) lacks nothing.

Euripides, Hercul. Furens, 1345.

For GOD (Θεος).—Aeschylus, Persians, 772. THE GOD (ὁ Θεος).

Euripides. Ἱκετιδες, 214, 215.

Zeus is the dispenser of various fates in heaven. . . . GOD (Θεος) has brought to pass things unthought of.—Medea, 1419.

[2] We find the "Intelligent Light" (νοερον φεγγος) and the "Intelligent Life (νοερα ζωη) of the Father" in the Chaldean learning.

Movers, 553; Cory, Anc. Fragm. 243.

[3] Movers, 553; Servius ad Aeneid. i. 733.   [4] Ibid.

[5] Philo, Who is Heir, liii.; De Vita Mosis, xxxix.; de Somn. xiii. xiv.; Gibbon's Rome, ii. 326; quotes Julian's Epistles, xli.

[6] Schaff, Hist. Apost. Ch. 185.   [7] Williams, Prim. Hist. 31.

This wealth- and prosperity-conferring Soma, the Lord of all, the Soul of the world in the person of the Sun, enlightens the heaven and the earth.

Stevenson, Samaveda, p. 102.

This Soma like the Sun, the surveyor of all things, runs into thirty vessels at the mid-day sacrifice, and like the seven rivers has his source in the heavens. As the divine Sun, so is this Soma placed above all worlds.

Stevenson, Samaveda, p. 126.

Horus is the Celestial Sun, the Source of the Nile.[1] The Alexandrian Philo says : Moreover it appears that Moses has taken the sun as a symbol of the Great Cause of all things. But according to the *third* signification, when he speaks of the *Sun*, he means the Divine Word, the Model of that sun which moves about through the heaven.[2]

For in good truth the continual stream of the Divine Word, being borne on incessantly with rapidity and regularity, is diffused universally over every thing, giving joy to all.—Philo, de Somniis, xxxviii.

The "Word" of God and the Divine Reason from which flow all kinds of instinctive and everlasting wisdom.—Philo, on Fugitives, xxv.

And the Divine WORD like a river flows forth from WISDOM as from a spring, in order to irrigate and fertilize the celestial and heavenly shoots and plants of such souls as love virtue, as if they were a paradise.

Philo, de Somn. xxxvii.

Since that country is not irrigated by rain as all other lands are, but by the inundations of the River which is accustomed every year to over-flow its banks, the Egyptians in their impious reason make a god of the Nile, as if it were a copy and rival of heaven.

Philo, de Vita Mosis, xxiv.

O God of my fathers and Lord of mercy, who hast made all things with thy WORD.—Wisdom of Solomon, ch. viii. v. 1.

The WORD of God Most High is the fountain of Wisdom.

Jesus Sirach, i. 5.

When the Enlightener of the mind, the WORD of the Ancient One, the Establisher of heaven and earth, first of all produced the illustrious venerable lord Soma, he led him to the sacred receptacle of the inebriating waters.—Stevenson, Samaveda, p. 100, 101.

[1] The Peruvians considered the Sun the only Creator.—Laeroix, Perou, 369.

[2] Philo, On Dreams, xvi. xv. Socrates addressed a prayer to the Sun.

Honover, "the WORD," in Persia, is the Spirit of life and light.[1]

When the WORD of the LOVING SPIRIT created him, in the realm of the Most High.—Benfey, Samaveda, 239.

The WORD Ahû (Aum, Om) indicates both the world and its Creator, merely as existence (Seiendes).[2]

In the Persian Liturgy, Zoroaster asks:

O Ormuzd wrapped in glory, just Judge of the pure world which thou carriest—what is the Great WORD, by God created, the WORD of life and swiftness, that was before heaven existed and water was, and earth was, and herds were, and trees were and Fire, Ormuzd's son, was . . . tell me this plainly.

Ormuzd answers:

The pure, holy, quick-moving WORD (Honover), I tell thee plainly, Sapetman Zoroaster, was before heaven and before water and before earth.—Creuzer's Symbolik, vol. i. p. 107.

All Hail to Ormuzd's INTELLIGENCE[3] which holds in itself the WORD of excellence.—Ibid. p. 188.

I extol Ormuzd's Working Spirit.—Ibid. p. 188.

The pure, holy, rapidly-powerful WORD was before heaven, and water, earth and herds, &c. I myself the Wrapped in Glory spoke this WORD with Power (mit Grösse) and all pure beings, who are and have been and will be, were (existed) through it and came into Ormuzd's world.—Zendavesta.[4]

The Minokhired says: The Creator Ormuzd made this world and the creatures and the Amshaspands and the Heavenly Reason (Logos) out of his own light, and with the shout of jubilation of the "Time without bounds."[5] Ormuzd is the WORD by which the First Light, the First Fire and the Original Water were created. Ormuzd is the Light as Creator. He spoke the Word (Honover).[6] Ormuzd created through his Word the visible world in six periods of time or thousands of years. First, the Light between heaven and earth together with the heaven and

[1] Creuzer, Symb. p. 224.   [2] Weber, Ind. Stud. i. 373 ; ii. 200.
[3] The Divine Reason, the Logos.   [4] De Wette, Bibl. Dogm. p. 132.
[5] Spiegel in der Zeitschrift der D. M. G. for 1851.   [6] Creuzer, Symb. 210.

the Stars. Second, the Water which covered the earth and
sank into its depths. Third, the earth, fourth, the trees,
fifth, the animals which all spring from the Primal Bull,
sixth, mankind, of whom Kaiomorts was the first. After
Creation was finished Ormuzd celebrated festivals with the
Immortals.[1]

For there are, as it seems, two temples belonging to God; one being
this world, in which the high-priest is the Divine Word, his own First-
born Son.—Philo, On Dreams, ed. Yonge xxxvii.

For it was impossible that any thing mortal should be made in the
likeness of the Most High God the Father of the universe; but it could
only be made in the likeness of the Second God who is the " Word" of
the other. . . . Since the god who stands for the " Word" is superior to
all and every rational nature: and it is not lawful for any created thing
to be made like the God who is above the Word.

Fragment of Philo; from Eusebius.[2]

For the Father of the universe has caused him to spring up as the
Eldest Son whom in another passage he calls the First-born; and he
who is thus born, imitating the ways of his Father, has formed such and
such species, looking to his archetypal patterns.

Philo, de Confus. Ling. xiv.

His First-born Word, the Eldest of his angels, as the great Archangel of many names; for he is called the authority and the name of God,
and the " Word" and Man according to God's image, and He who
sees Israel. . . . For even if we are not yet suitable to be called the
sons of God, still we may deserve to be called the children of his Eternal
Image, of his most sacred Word; for the Image of God is his most ancient Word.—De Confus. Ling. xxviii.

The Word is as it were the Charioteer of the Powers, and He who
utters it is the Rider who directs the Charioteer.—Philo On Fugit. xix.

Having mingled the vital spark from two according substances
Mind and Divine Spirit, as a third to these he added
Holy Love the venerable Charioteer uniting all things.

Lydus de Mensibus, 3.[3]

Aion who first appeared . . . Aion that holds the reins of life.

Nonnus xli. 84; xxiv. 271.

---

[1] Knobel's Genesis, 4 ; Kleuker, Zendav. i. 19 ; iii. 59.
[2] Yonge ; De Wette, Bibl. Dogm. § 156, note.
[3] Taylor ; Cory's Anc. Fragm. 264.

For Aiōn, according to the oracle, is the cause of never-failing life, of unwearied power and unsluggish energy.—Chaldean Oracles.[1]

Plato considered the divine nature under the three-fold modification of the First Cause, the Logos (the Wisdom), and the Soul of the world.[2]   According to Philo, the Spirit of God is one with the Logos.   He designates him as the " Wisdom."[3]

In him (it) was Life ; and the Life was the Light of men.

The Logos is the Mediator between God and man—the Agent of man.[4]   Bel-Mithra (Iao der Anagogeus) is the Mediator between the "Father" and the individual souls, which, like Life-sparks, he sends down and lifts again to the "Father."[5]   He takes the substance of Light (Licht-Materie) the beams of the Sun from the Father, pours them out and makes them return to him again.

πορεύων ἄνω καὶ ἀνατείνων τὰς ψυχὰς ἐπὶ τὸν νοητὸν κόσμον.

Julian, Orat. in Solem, 136.[6]

As Iao is the Mediator, so Christ is the Mediator with the Father.   Christ is the Paraclete (Advocate).[7]   The Paraclete (Comforter) is the Holy Spirit.[8]

And I will pray " the Father" and he will give you another Advocate, THE SPIRIT OF TRUTH.—John, xiv. 17.

Philo speaking of the dress of the High Priest says :

The twelve stones arranged on the breast in four rows of three stones each, namely the logeum, being also an emblem of that REASON (Logos) which holds together and regulates the universe.   For it was indispensable that the man who was consecrated to the Father of the world should have as a Paraclete (One invoked as an Advocate) his Son, the Being most perfect in all virtue, to procure forgiveness of sins and a supply of unlimited blessings.—De Vita Mosis, xiv.

[1] Cory's Anc. Fragm. 240.   [2] Gibbon's Rome, II. chap. xxi. p. 236.
[3] De Wette, Bibl. Dogm. p. 142.   [4] Ibid. p. 128.   [5] Movers, 553, 554.
[6] Movers, 554.   [7] 1 John's Epist. ii. 1.   [8] John's Gospel, xiv. 16, 26.

16

And the Father who created the universe has given to his Arch-angelic and most ancient "Word" (the Logos) a pre-eminent gift, to stand on the confines of both, and separated that which had been created from the Creator. And this same "Word" is continually a suppliant to the immortal God on behalf of the mortal race, which is exposed to af-fliction and misery; and is also the ambassador sent by the Ruler of all to the subject race. And the "Word" rejoices in the gift, and, exulting in it, announces it and boasts of it, saying, "And I stood *in the midst between the Lord and you ;*" neither being uncreate as God, nor yet cre-ated as you, but being in the midst between these two extremities, like a hostage as it were to both parties.—Philo, Who is the Heir, xlii.

And Zoroaster taught that one (Horomazes) resembles Light most of visible things, but the other (Areimanios) on the contrary (is like) Dark-ness and Ignorance : and *between the two* is Mithra. Wherefore the Persians name Mithra the MEDIATOR.—Plutarch, de Iside, c. 46.

According to Mani, " ' Christ the Mediator, like the Mithra of his countrymen, had his dwelling in the sun.' His own system (Mani's religion) was the completion of the imperfect revelation of the Gospel. He was a man invested with a divine mission, the Paraclete (for Mani appears to have distinguished between the Paraclete and the Holy Spirit) who was to consummate the great work auspiciously com-menced, yet unfulfilled, by the mission of Jesus."[1]

According to the prophet Daniel, the kingdom of the Messiah is the fifth of the great world-monarchies.[2]

I will raise up over them one Shepherd (of the people) who shall feed them, my servant David.—Ezekiel, xxxiv. 23.

But in the days of these kings Alah of the heavens shall make a kingdom arise which shall not be destroyed for ages ... It shall break up and con-sume all those kingdoms, but it shall stand for ages.—Daniel, ii. 44.

Ihoh our KING, he shall save us!—Isaiah, xxxiii. 22.

The KING in his beauty thine eyes shall see!—Ibid. 17.

Çaoshyanç (the Helper) is the appellation of the SAVIOR KING whom the Persians looked for at the END of all things.

[1] Milman, p. 278.   [2] De Wette, Bibl. Dogm. i. 159, 160, 170, 187; Daniel, vii. 26, 27.

I will strike the Pari to whom men pray, until that Çaoshyanç is born, the Victorious, from the water Kançaöya.—Vendidad, Fargard 19, § 18.[1]

According to the mythology of Dionysus, as it was related in the neighborhood of Delphi, Dionysus-Zagreus was a Son of Zeus, whom he had begotten in the form of a dragon upon his daughter Cora-Persephone. The young god was supposed to pass through great perils. This was converted by the Orphic poets[2] into the marvellous legend which is preserved by later writers.

According to this legend Zeus destined Dionysus for KING, set him upon the throne of heaven and gave him Apollo and the Curetes to protect him. But the Titans instigated by the jealous Hera attacked him by surprise, having disguised themselves under a coating of plaster (a rite of the Bacchic festivals) while Dionysus, whose attention was engaged with various playthings, particularly a splendid mirror, did not perceive their approach. After a long and fearful conflict the Titans overcame Dionysus and tore him into *seven pieces*, one piece for each of themselves. Pallas (the Divine Wisdom) however succeeded in saving his palpitating heart which Zeus swallowed in a drink. As the ancients considered *the heart as the seat of life* Dionysus was again contained in Zeus and again begotten by him. This Dionysus torn in pieces and *born again* is destined to succeed Zeus in the government of the world and *to restore the golden age*. In the same system Dionysus was also the god from whom the liberation of souls was expected. The Orphic poets looked for a cessation of strife, a holy peace, a state of the highest happiness and beatitude of souls at the *end of all things*.[3] This is IAO the Demiurg called also Sabaoth, the god who is over the seven heavens, and the god of the seven rays, into which he is divided. He is the coming King and Messiah or Mithra.

---

[1] Spiegel, 244. [2] Near the beginning of the sixth century before Christ.
[3] K. O. Müller, Hist. Greek Lit. 237, 238.

I Iahoh am thy Saviour and thy Redeemer, the Mighty One of Iacob.
Isaiah, xlix. 26.

"Zeus the Savior" and Hercules were adored at Xenophon's command by the Ten Thousand Greeks.
Xenophon, Cyri Exp. iv.

Let us make a libation to Jupiter the Deliverer.—Tacitus, xvi. § xxxv.

This is the Zeus-Belus of the Babylonians, Bel the Younger,
the sun-god.

Zeus is THE KING: He is the Author of Universal Life, One Power, One
Daemōn, the Mighty Prince of all things.—Orpheus.[1]

Great KING Osiris.—Plutarch, de Iside, xii.

The Mind of the Father made a jarring noise—understanding by unwearied
Counsel omneiform "ideas" which flying out from One Fountain sprang forth:
. . . . . . for "THE KING" previously placed *before* the multiform world *an
Intellectual Incorruptible Pattern*, the print of whose form is promoted (diffused) through the world, according to which things the world appeared
beautified with all-various ideas of which there is One Fountain, . . . they
are intellectual conceptions from the Paternal Fountain, partaking abundantly
the Flower of Fire in the point of restless time: but the first, self-perfect fountain of the Father poured forth these primogenial[2] "ideas."
Chaldean Oracles.

O KING, dwelling in thy celestial abode the Aether!
Euripides, Troades, 1084, Buckley.

The KING. . . . the SON (Bacchus) of Zeus.—Bacchae, 601.

He praised the KING OF HEAVEN !—1 Esdras, iv. 58, 46.

I speak my works,—to the KING !

Thou art fairer than the children of men : grace is poured into thy
lips ; therefore hath ELOHIM blessed thee forever.

Gird thy sword upon thy thigh O Mighty, with thy glory and thy
majesty.

Thine arrows are sharp in the heart of the KING's enemies ; the
people fall under thee.

Thy throne, O ELOHIM, is forever and ever; therefore ELOHIM THY
GOD (Elohik) has anointed Thee with the oil of gladness above thy fellows.—Psalm, xlv.

Behold the days shall come, saith Iahoh, that I will raise unto David
a righteous BRANCH, and a KING shall reign and prosper. . . .

[1] Cory, 290; Euseb. Praep. Ev. iii.; Procl. in Tim.; Aristot. de Mund.
[2] The first of their race.—Proclus, in Parm.; Cory, 247, 248.

In his days Iudah shall be saved, . . . this is the name by which he shall be called, Iahoh Zedeknu (Jehovah our Zedek.[1])—Jer. xxiii. 5, 6.

In those days will I cause the BRANCH of righteousness to grow up unto David and he shall execute judgment and righteousness in the land.—Jeremiah, xxxiii. 15.

I will bring forth my servant the BRANCH.

He shall be a PRIEST upon his throne.—Zachariah, iii. vi.

FIRST-BORN, . . . radiant BRANCH, . . . bringing brilliant light, holy : on which account I address thee as Phanes.—Orphic Hymn, vi.

Then from the SUN God will send a KING (said of the Messias).

And then God will send from heaven a king (said of Cyrus).

LL. Sibyll. liii. v. 590.[2]

The Children of Chet said to Abram: Thou art a KING sent from God among us![3]

Elohim give thy judgments to the king, and thy justice to the son of the king.

His name shall be to eternity : before the Sun he shall have the name of his son, and we shall be blessed in him, all nations shall call him blessed.

Blessed be Iahoh Alahim Alahi Israel, alone doing wonderful things !

Psalm, lxxii.

According to Mani (in the third century), Christ the glorious Intelligence, called by the Persians Mithra, resided in the sun.[4] This is the Chaldean doctrine of the "Intelligible Sun" considered as the Son of God.

Consider the wondrous works of Al! Dost thou know when Aloh puts his mind on them, and makes the light of his cloud to shine !

Job, xxxvii. 15 ; Schmid.

The heavens declare the glory of El and the firmament showeth his handiwork.

Their voice is gone out throughout all the earth and their words to the end of the world. In them hath he set a tabernacle for the Sun,

Which is as a bridegroom coming out of his chamber; rejoices as a strong man to run a race.—Ps. xix.

---

[1] Sadak, Zadok, Suduk was the name of the Highest God in Phoenicia, "the KING of the Gods." The seven sons of Sydyc were probably the 7 Cabiri, Archangels or Amschaspands. He was the Heptaktis, "the God of the seven beams."

[2] De Wette, Bibl. Dogm. p. 160.   [3] Septuagint, Gen. xxiii. 6; Hebrew Bible, Schmid; Philo, de Somn. xxxvii. ; On Abraham, xliv.

[4] Encyl. Americana, viii. p. 250.

Hymn now Eli Child of Deus, begin Muse. . . . . For Hyperion wedded his own sister Euruphaessa all-renowned, who bore him beauteous children, both rosy-fingered Morn and the fair-haired Moon, and the unwearied Sun (Eeli) like unto the Immortals, who shines unto mortals and to the Immortal Gods, mounting his steeds. And dreadfully with his eyes he glances from his golden casque, and from him the bright rays flash splendidly, and down from his temples the cheek-plates [of his helmet] shining from his head guard his beauteous face, shining afar; and with the gale of the winds his beauteous garments glitter around his form and his male steeds beneath. Here indeed, at even, he, having stopped his golden-yoked chariot and steeds, sends them through heaven towards the ocean. Hail! O King, and willingly grant a pleasant life; and commencing from thee, I will celebrate the race of articulate-voiced men, demi-gods whose deeds the gods have shown forth unto mortals.

Homeric Hymn to the Sun.[1]

The Logos is the Angel of the Lord.

They look upon the Logos, the Image of God, his Angel, as himself.

Philo, on Dreams, 600.[2]

Iahoh said unto Adonai: Sit thou on my right hand until I make thine enemies the footstool of thy feet.—Psalm, cx.; Luke, xx. 42, 43.

The Angel Gabriel is the Son of God begotten upon light; and he undertook to create the world.—Adams, View of Religions, 118.

I am Gabriel that stand in the sight of God.—Luke, i. 19.

The house of David (shall be) as Elohim, as Malak Iahoh (the Angel of the Lord) before them.—Zachariah, xii. 8.

And I saw in the night visions and behold, One like a son of man came with the clouds of heaven and came to the Ancient of days, and they brought him near before him. And there was given him dominion and glory and a kingdom that all people, nations and languages should serve him: his dominion is an everlasting dominion and his kingdom that which shall not be destroyed.

Dan. viii. 13.

Blessed be the King that comes in the name of Lord.—Luke, xix. 38.

And a Shoot shall go forth out of the stem of Ishi (Iasi, Iesse) and a Branch from his roots shall bear fruit.—Isaiah, xi. 1.

I, Iahoh, have called thee in righteousness and will hold thy hand and will keep thee.—Isaiah, xlii. 6.

And then they will see the Son of Man coming in clouds with great power and glory.—Mark, xiii. 26.

---

[1] Buckley's transl.; also Dindorff.

"In the Phoenician polytheism the ideas of El stood originally nearer to those of Jehovah in purity than people seem disposed to believe."—Movers, 296.

[2] De Wette, Bibl. Dogm. 129; Philo, §§ xiii. xxii. Yonge.

Blessed is he that comes in the name of the Lord.
Blessed is the coming kingdom of our father David:
Hosanna in the highest!—Mark, xi. 10.
Then the men, when they saw the sign that Iesus wrought, said: Of a truth this is the PROPHET THAT WAS TO COME INTO THE WORLD.
Then Iesus, perceiving that they would come and seize him to make him KING, departed again to the mountain himself alone.

John vi. 14, 15 ; Sharpe's Griesbach.

The doctrine of a KING who should rise up for the glory and greatness of the nation is found in the Old Persian sacred books. The Persians looked for a prophet Çaŏshyanç and after him two others called Oschedar-bami and Oschedar-mâh: finally (Messias) Sosiosh will appear. The Jewish doctrine of the End of the world has the closest connection with the Persian. The dead rise: after a kingdom which endures a thousand years will come the second resurrection and the Last Judgment. Spiegel considers the Persian expectation of one Messiah following another[1] a borrowed idea from the Buddhistic view that several Buddhas follow in succession. They all agree in expecting the coming of a certain Buddha Maitreya whom Çakya Muni himself foretold.[2]

And, lo, there arose a WIND from the sea!
Thou didst see a MAN coming up from the midst of the sea!
And lo that MAN waxed strong with the thousands of heaven!
The same is HE whom God the Highest has kept a great season, which by his own self shall deliver his creature: and HE shall order them that are left behind!
Behold the days come when the Most High will begin to deliver them that are upon the earth!
And he shall come to the astonishment of them that dwell on the earth.
And one shall undertake to fight against another, one city against another, one place against another, one people against another, and one realm against another.
And THE TIME shall be when these things shall come to pass, and the SIGNS shall happen which I showed thee before, and THEN SHALL MY SON be declared whom thou didst see ASCENDING AS A MAN.

[1] John, xiv. 16.   [2] Spiegel, Vendidad, pp. 16, 35, 37.

Wherefore have I seen the MAN coming up FROM THE MIDST OF THE SEA?

No man upon earth can see MY SON or those that he with him *except in the daytime!*[1]

He gathered another *peaceable* multitude unto him.

Now when he destroys the multitude of the nations . . . he shall defend his people that remain.—2 Esdras, xiii.

Look for your SHEPHERD, . . . for he is near at hand THAT SHALL COME IN THE END OF THE WORLD!

Arise up and stand, behold the number of those that are sealed in the feast of the Lord;[2]

Which are departed from the shadow of the world.

These are they which have put off the mortal clothing and put on the immortal!

In the midst of them there was a YOUNG MAN OF HIGH STATURE, TALLER THAN ALL THE REST. . . .

It is the SON OF GOD whom they have confessed in the world.

2 Esdras, ii.

Both Dionysus and Milichus are the SON OF THE FATHER.[3] "A passage in Martianus Capella designates Ammon Balithon as 'the Father' whom the Son cannot look upon."

Ultra mundanum fas est cui cernere Patrem.[4]

No man hath seen God at any time. The ONLY-BEGOTTEN SON that is in the bosom of the Father, HE hath declared him.

Of that day and hour knoweth no one, neither the angels in heaven, nor the SON—but the Father.

Sol-Mithra is an emanation from the Supreme Light, an image of the Father. The paternal countenance greets him as IAO.[5] In the younger Chaldean oracles the doctrine of a Supreme Being, the Father of all, the Great Father of the Logos, of the Only-begotten Son Iao as Creator, is plainly taught; but the traces of it go back to an earlier period.[6]

---

[1] "While travelling in Egypt and Aethiopia, Dionysius Areopagita was witness of an eclipse of the sun, at the sight of which he exclaimed: 'Now the LORD is suffering something.'"—Seyffarth's Chronology, p. 186.

[2] Compare Rev. vii.; ix. 4; xx. 12.   [3] Movers, 268, 325, 326.

[4] Movers, 266.   [5] Ibid.   [6] Ibid. 263, 264.

And I will bring sackcloth upon all loins and baldness upon every head. I will make it as the MOURNING FOR THE ONLY-BEGOTTEN and its end as the DAY OF BITTERNESS.—Amos, viii. 10.[1]

Over Nebo and over Medaba Moab shall MOURN; on all its heads baldness, and every beard shaven!

In its streets they have girded on sackcloth: upon its roofs, and in its streets every one shall howl, giving way to tears.

And Cheshbon has cried out, and Alalah, even to Iahaz their voice was heard.

The grass is burned up, consumed is the herb, there is no green thing.—Isaiah, xv. 2, 3, 4, 7.

For the fields of Cheshbon languish, the VINE of Sibmah!

Over thy summer fruits and the harvest thy HEDAD has fallen!

And gladness is taken away and exultation from Carmel and in the vineyards there is no singing, no shout of rejoicing: the wine in the wine-presses he does not tread, trampling; HEDAD I have made to cease!
Isaiah, xvi. 9, 10.

Ye shall lament over him as at the lamentation for the ONLY-BE-GOTTEN; on that day the lamentation shall be great as the MOURNING FOR HADAD RIMMON (the Sun).—Zachariah, xii. 10, 11.[2]

Gird thyself with a sack, roll in the dust, set up the WAIL FOR THE ONLY-BEGOTTEN and bitter lamentation!—Jeremiah, vi. 26.[3]

Osiris or Memnon was mourned in Egypt.[4] The Chaldee-Persian Logos is the Only-born of the Father, in the Baby-lonian Cosmogony of Eudemus.[5] Isaac is the Only-begotten, Maneros, Linus (Illinus, Elon) Ieoud (Aud).[6] Maneros (called Palaestinus) is Adonis destroyed by Winter.[7]

And they came to the threshing-floor of ATAD (ADAD the Sun) which is beyond Jordan: there they mourned a great and very heavy Mourn-ing; and he made to his father a lamentation seven days.

And the inhabitants of the land Canaan saw the Mourning on the threshing-floor of ATAD and said: A great Mourning this to the Egyp-tians: therefore he called the name of it Abel Misraim (Mourning of the Egyptians).—Septuagint; Gen. l. 10; 2 Chron. xxxv. 25.[8]

Glorious Eros, renowned son of eternal Night: whom younger mor-tals Phanes call, for he FIRST APPEARED.—Orpheus, Argonautika, 16.

[1] Movers, 249.   [2] Ibid. 249, 196, 308.   [3] Ibid. 248.   [4] Ibid. 250.
[5] Ibid. 268.   [6] Ibid. 252, 302, 303.   [7] Ibid. 245; Plutarch de Is. xvii.
[8] Ibid. 250.

Ulom, Moumis, Phanes, Erikapaius, Aiŏn, are the FIRST-BORN.

> I invoke the FIRST-BORN of a two-fold nature, great, Aether-wandering,
> Egg-born, decorated with golden wings,
> Bull-faced, the Procreator of the blessed gods and mortal men,
> Renowned Seed, many-orgied Ericapaius
> Not named, occult, impetuous all-glittering Branch
> Who scatterest the twilight clouds of darkness from the eyes
> And roamest through the world upon the flight of thy wings
> Bringing brilliant Light sacred, wherefore I call thee Phanes
> And KING Priapos and Light-reflector vivid-eyed.
> But Blessed, very Intelligent, very fruitful, go rejoicing
> To the " Mystic Rites" holy, very-varied, of the orgiophants.
>
> Orphic Hymn, vi. ed. Hermann.[1]

Apollo being asked who he was gave this oracle :

> Elios, Orus, Osiris, Anax, Dionusos, Apollŏn...
> KING of the flaming Stars : and IMMORTAL FIRE !
>
> Eusebius, Praepar. Ev. iii. 15.

> Whether you are Serapis, Egyptian cloudless Zeus,
> Or Kronos, or Phaethon many-named, or thou Mithra,
> Babylon's Eeli, 'in Hellas Delphian Apollo :
> Or Gamos (Chom) . . .
> Or thou Paianeŏn appeasing suffering, or if thou art Aether
> Variegated, and art named Astrochitŏn, for at night
> Thy starry tunics array heaven . . .—Nonnus, xl. 400.

HYMN TO THE SUN.

Sublime POWER of an Unknown Father, or his first Branch (Propago) Ardor who bestowest sensation, *Source of the soul*, Origin of light, great Ornament of Nature, Affirmation of the gods, Eye of the world, Splendor of the bright Olympus : Thou who alone canst see thy Father above the heavens, and contemplate the Supreme Being . . . . Latium names thee Sun, since thou alone, after thy Father, attainest the pinnacle of the light . . . . As thou dost dissipate the darkness and illumine that which is in the azure of the heavens, they call thee Phœbus thou who revealest the secrets of the future and makest clear the crimes

---

[1] Also Cory, Anc. Fragm.

of the night. The Nile venerates thee by the name of the bountiful
Serapis; Memphis sees in thee Osiris; the barbarous races Mithra, Pluto
or the cruel Typhon. Thou art the beautiful Attis, and the divine BOY
of the bent and bountiful plough, Ammon for the sands of Libya, Adonis
for Byblus. Thus the universal world invokes thee by different names.
Hail, veritable Image of the gods and of thy Father's face !

Martianus Capella, l. ii. p. 54.[1]

"Dupuis says, the celestial sign of the VIRGIN AND
CHILD was in existence several (?) thousand years before
Christ. The constellation of the Celestial Virgin by its ascension above the horizon presided at the birth of the god
Sol or Light, and seemed to produce him from her side.
The Magi as well as the priests of Egypt celebrated the
birth of the god Sol or Light or Day, incarnate in the womb
of a virgin which had produced him without ceasing to be
a virgin. . . . This is the same virgin of the constellations
whom Eratosthenes says the learned of Alexandria call
Ceres or Isis, who opened the year and presided at the birth
of the god Day. It was in honor of the same Virgin (from
whom the Sun emanated, and by whom the god Day or
Light was nursed) that, at Sais, the famous feast of lights
was celebrated, and from which our Candlemas, or our feast
of the lights of the purification, was taken. Ceres was always called the Holy Virgin."[2]

"About the eighth month, when the Sun is in his greatest
strength and enters into the eighth sign, the Celestial Virgin
appears to be absorbed in his fires and she disappears in
the midst of the rays and glories of her son.[3] Pelloutier
observes that, more than a hundred years before the Christian Era, in the territory of Chartres among the Gauls, honors
were paid to the VIRGINI PARITURAE who was about to give
birth to the god of Light. It was inscribed on a black
image of Isis.[4] Langevin says this image existed in his

---

[1] Movers, 266; Nonnus, Marcellus, Notes, p. 170.

[2] Higgins, 314, 315; quotes Dupuis, vol. iii. 40, &c. [3] Higgins, i. 314, 315.

[4] Ibid.; Pelloutier, Hist. des Celtes, liv. v. p. 15; Dupuis, iii. 51.

time, about 1792.¹ Albertus Magnus says that the sign of
the Celestial VIRGIN rises above the horizon at the moment
in which we fix the birth of the Lord Jesus Christ.²

" In the first face of the Virgin, the beautiful Virgin ascends, with long
hair and she holds two ears (stars) in her hand, and sits on ' a seat and
feeds a BOY as yet little, and suckles him and gives him food.—Avenar.²

" In the first decan of the Virgin rises a maid called in Arabic Adere-
nosa, that is, pure Virgin, immaculate Virgin, graceful in person, charming in countenance, modest in habit, with loosened hair, holding in her
hand two ears (of corn), sitting upon an embroidered throne, nursing a
BOY and rightly feeding (him), in the place called Hebraea; a BOY, I say,
named Iesus by certain nations, who signify (significantibus) Issa whom
they also call Christ in Greek.—Albumazar.⁴

" Between the houses of Virgo and Libra ascend the GREAT SERPENT
(aspis), which is also called Good Divinity Ophioneus, together with a
CUP of wine, on the testimony of Avenar." ⁵

THREE CONSTELLATIONS CONTIGUOUS IN POSITION, the Raven and SERPENT,
    And in the middle the CUP lies between the two !
On the Ides they are concealed: they rise the following night.
                                        Ovid, Fast. ii. 245.

" In Sanval's history of the antiquities of Paris the Virgin is called Etoile éclatante de la mer." ⁶ Maira means
" the sparkling." ⁷ Maria comes from the name Mar, Amar,
the Sun.

And a great sign was seen in the heaven, a WOMAN INVESTED WITH
THE SUN,⁸ and the moon under her feet, and upon her head a crown of
twelve stars; and, being with child, she cries, travailing and being tortured to bring forth.
    And another sign was seen in the heaven, and lo ! a great FIERY
SERPENT having seven heads and ten horns, and upon the heads of him
seven diadems . . .

¹ Higgins ; Recherches Hist. sur Falaise par Langevin pretre.   ² Ibid.
³ Ibid.; Kircher, Ocdip. Aegypt. iii. chap. v. p. 203.   ⁴ Ibid.
⁵ Ibid. p. 315.   ⁶ Ibid. p. 310.   ⁷ Odyssey, xi. 326.
⁸ The sun in Virgo. The Greek is: " who has come into possession of
the sun."

And the SERPENT stood before the WOMAN about to be delivered, in order that when she should bear her CHILD he might devour it!

And she bore a SON a male, who is about to govern all the nations with an iron staff: and her CHILD was caught up to The God and to his throne!

And the WOMAN fled into the Desert where she has a place prepared there by The God, that there they should feed her a thousand two hundred and sixty days.

And there arose a war in heaven, Michael and his angels fighting against the SERPENT!—Rev. xii. 1-8.

What if you should see the Son of Man ascend up where he was before!—John, vi. 62.

From the bottom of my heart I sing the Great Son of God
To whom the Most High Father gave a throne
When he had not yet been born. Since in the flesh the Double
Existed.—Sibylline Orac. Gallaeus, 649.

The glory which I had with thee before the world was.
John, xvii. 5, 24.

Now THE VIRGIN returns, the Saturnian reigns return:
Now a new OFFSPRING is sent down from high heaven.
O chaste Lucina favor the BOY now being born, with whom the iron race
Shall end and a golden arise in all the world:
Now your Apollo reigns!
This glory of the age will commence, Pollio, in your consulship.
O dear CHILD of the Gods, Great INCREASE of Jove,
Enter upon great honors, the time will now be at hand.
The SERPENT will die!—Virgil's 4th Eclogue.

This people walking in darkness have seen A GREAT LIGHT: those dwelling in the LAND OF THE SHADOW OF DEATH, over them a light has shined!

Thou hast multiplied the nation, thou hast given it great joy: they will rejoice before thee like the JOY AT THE TIME OF HARVEST, as they exult when they divide spoil.

For the yoke of his burden and the staff of his shoulder the rod of his oppressor thou hast broken just like the day of Midian.

For a BOY is born to us, a SON is given to us; on whose shoulder is the sovereignty, but he shall call his name Pela, Ioaz,[1] Al, Agbor, Abi-Ad, Sar-Salom.

To him multiplying the sovereignty and peace, there will not be an

[1] Pelη, Ioηz, El, Gibbor.—Dr. Crusé.

end on the throne of David and over his kingdom, to establish it in
judgment and justice from now and even to (all) time. The zeal of Iahoh
Zabaoth shall do this.—Isaiah, ix.

NEW LIGHT has arisen
Coming from heaven it assumed a mortal form.
First Gabriel showed his sacred mighty person,
Next, bearing his message he addressed in words the maid:
Virgin, receive God in thy pure bosom . . .
And courage returned to her and the WORD flew into her womb.
Becoming incarnate in time and animated by her body
It was formed in a mortal image, and a BOY was created
By a Virgin delivery. This a great wonder to mortals
But nothing is a great wonder to God Father and God Son.
The infant being born, earth at once rejoiced,
The heavenly throne smiled and the universe exulted.
The new God-sent star was adored by the Magi
The infant swathed was shown in a manger to the obedient to God
And Bethleem was called " God-called country" of the Word.

Sibylline Orac. Gallæus, 760–788.

Sending his own SON in the likeness of sinful flesh.—Romans, viii. 3.

And the Word became flesh and dwelt among us and we beheld its
glory, the glory of the ONLY-BEGOTTEN of the Father.—John, i. 14.

God . . . . . hath at the last of these days spoken to us by a Son whom
he hath appointed heir of all things, by whom also he made the Aiōns.
Who being a RAY of his glory and an IMAGE of his substance, and up-
holding all things by the WORD of his POWER (Spirit), when he had by
himself made a cleansing of our sins, sat down on the right hand of the
Majesty on high ; becoming so much better than the angels, as he hath
inherited a more excellent nature than they.

For to which of the angels did He ever say: *Thou art my Son, this
day have I begotten thee ?* . . . . And again, when He bringeth the FIRST-
BEGOTTEN into the world he says: *And let all the angels of God worship
him.* And of the angels he says: *Who makes his angels spirits and his
ministers a flame of fire ;* but of " THE SON :" *Thy throne O God is for
ever and ever; . . . . therefore, O God, THY GOD hath anointed thee with
the oil of gladness above thy fellows. And thou, Lord, in the Beginning
didst found the earth ; and the heavens are the work of thy hands.*[1]

In St. Paul's application of Ps. xlv. and cii. 25, is positive evidence that Iehovah (יחוה Ehoh) was regarded by

---

[1] Ps. xlv. ; cii. 25 ; Epist. to the Hebrews, i.

him as the Son, the Creator, Logos, the "Word of the Power" of God. This settles the question of the identity of the Hebrew, Phœnician, Egyptian and Chaldean philosophy.

"Iao (Iah) was a mysterious name of Bacchus."[1] Iao is the "Light that only the mind can perceive," "the physical and Spiritual Light- and Life-Principle."[2] Iao is the Sun,[3] the Spirit of the sun, the Celestial Sun, Helios Noetos. Zagreus was invoked as the Highest of all the gods.[4]

> Say that the Highest God of all (gods) is Iao!
>> Oracle of Apollo Clarius.
> Appease the Great God Attis, holy Adonis,
> Eubios (Evius) bestowing-riches, fair-haired Dionysus!—Rhodian Oracle.[5]

"The Chaldeans call the god (Dionysus) Iao instead of the 'Intelligible Light' in the Phœnician tongue: and Sabaoth he is often called, as he who is over the seven heavens, that is, the Demiurg."[6] "The Light ($\dot{\eta}$ $\dot{a}\omega$) with the Chaldeans is interpreted 'Intelligible Light' ($\Phi\hat{\omega}\varsigma$ $\nu o\eta\tau\acute{o}\nu$) in the Phœnician tongue: and Sabaōth above the seven heavens, that is, the Demiurgic God."[7] In the Chaldean philosophy this Intelligible Light (Iao) is an emanation out of the Intelligent Life and is the Light-Principle, the Light-Aether, from which the souls emanate and to which they return. The Planets dance their course around the Chaldean sun-god; but "the Father" is the Intelligible World, Bel-Saturn, from whom the seven planetary rays go over to the sun-god.[8]

> And of the seven-wandering (orbs)
> The fourth, the Sun's, is the very centre of the planets.—Nonnus, xli. 347.

Iao, Heptaktis (7 rays) and Sabaoth were names of the Creator (Demiurg) in Phœnicia.[9] Magi from the East bring offerings to the infant Christ "the Creator of the world."

---

[1] Creuzer, Symb. iii. 593.   [2] Movers, 269.   [3] Ibid. 554, 555.
[4] K. O. Müller, 232.   [5] In Socrates, H. E. iii. 23.—Movers, 543.
[6] Lydus, de Mens. iv. 38, 74.   [7] Cedrenus, Tom. i. p. 296; Movers, 550.
[8] Movers, 553.   [9] Lydus, de Mens. iv. 38, 74; Movers, 551, 550.

And SEVEN LAMPS OF FIRE burning before the throne (of God) which are the Seven Spirits of THE GOD!

In the *midst* of the throne . . . stood a LAMB as if slain, having seven horns and seven eyes which are the Seven Spirits of THE GOD sent forth to all the earth!—Rev. iv. 5 ; v. 6.

In the *midst* of the seven golden candlesticks something like to a SON OF MAN GIRT WITH A GOLDEN GIRDLE.

And having in his right hand seven stars . . . AND HIS COUNTENANCE AS THE SUN SHINES! HIS VOICE as the sound of MANY WATERS.

Rev. i. 12, 13, 14, 15, 16.

SABAOTH THE CREATOR: for thus the DEMIURGIC Number (SEVEN) is named by the Phœnicians.—Lydus, de Mensibus, iv. 38, 74, 98, p. 112.[1]

Thou art worthy to take the scroll and to open the seals thereof, because thou wast slain and hast purchased to THE GOD in thy blood (people) of every tribe and tongue and people and nation, and madest them (to be) a kingdom and priests to THE GOD and they shall rule over the earth!—Rev. v. 9, 10.

"Tacitus[2] and Suetonius teach us that the East was full of expectation of this great personage (the Mediator) about the time of Augustus. . . . Socrates, in his dialogue on prayer, speaks of a divine instructor 'WHO WAS TO COME INTO THE WORLD ; AND HAD MAN'S WELFARE AT HEART, AND A WONDERFUL PROPENSITY TOWARDS US.' . . . And this prediction is the most probable ground of Tully's declaration, Neque solum cum Laetitia vivendi Rationem accepimus ; sed et, *cum Spe meliore*, moriendi.—Leges, 2. Thus doctrines obvious to Christians were the *highest arcana* of Paganism ; for instance, Plutarch's Maneros,[3] *a child of Palestine*, his *Mediator* Mithras, the *Saviour* Osiris, is the Messiah."[4]

The Persians held that Meschia was the First Man. The union of the ideas connected with Messias and Logos is said to have been late.[5] Last comes the union of the Messiah, the Logos and Iesus of Nazareth. The idea of the WORD (Logos) or "POWER OF GOD" BECOMING INCARNATE IN A HUMAN BEING was not unknown in the time of the Apostles. Simon Magus claimed to be an incarnation of the Word, the Power of God, the Paraclete.[6]

---

[1] Movers, 551, 550.   [2] Hist. v. 13, Vita Vespasiani.

[3] Plutarch, de Iside, xvii. p. 357 ; Rinck, i. 342 ; Movers, 204.

[4] W. Williams, Prim. Hist. pp. 69, 70.   [5] De Wette, Bibl. Dogm. p. 170.

[6] Milman, Hist. Christ. 205, *a*. Tacitus, a man of the highest rank, chosen

The Supreme Power of the God on high who is above the Creator of the world.—Clem. recogn. i. 72 ; ii. 7.[1]

This man (Simon Magus) is the " Power of God " which is called " Great." Acts, viii. 10.

Hermes (the Divine Wisdom) says to Prometheus :

To such labors look thou for no termination, until some god shall appear as a substitute in thy pangs and shall be willing to go both to gloomy Hades and to the murky depths around Tartarus.

Aeschylus Prometheus, 1027, ff.[2]

" The highest idea of morality to which classic antiquity attained was that just man (δίκαιος) *proving himself by suffering,* whom Plato portrays in the second book of his Republic." Plato predicts to this wise man that he " shall be scourged, tortured, fettered, deprived of his eyes, and, after having endured all possible sufferings, fastened to a post."[3]

He was clothed with a cloak dipped in blood, and his name is called the Word of God (Logos) !

And he has on his vesture and on his thigh a name written, KING OF KINGS AND LORD OF LORDS !—Rev. xix. 13, 16.

The " Reason " of the Creator of all things was before every thing and passed by every thing and was conceived before every thing and appears in every thing.—Philo, On the Cherubim.[4]

But we preach Christ crucified. . . . Christ the Power of God and the Wisdom of God.—1 Corin. i. 23, 24.

But we speak of the Wisdom of God, in a mystery ; the Hidden Wisdom which God ordained before the world.—1 Corinthians, ii. 7.

Who verily was foreordained before the foundation of the world, but was manifested in these last times for you.—Peter, i. 20, 21.

Who is over all God blessed forever.—Rom. ix. 5.

In whom we have redemption through his blood.

Who is " the Image " of the Invisible God, " the First-begotten " of the whole creation.

by Agricola for his son-in-law, a praetor, consul, advocate and man of letters, speaks of Christianity : " And the ruinous superstition, repressed for the time, again broke out not only through Judea, the origin of that evil, but throughout the city also."—Tacitus, Annals, xv. 44.

[1] Movers, 558.   [2] Buckley ; See also Rinck, i. 348.

[3] Plato, Politiae, pp. 104, 105, ed. Stallbaum, 361, E. ; quoted in Schaff, p. 434, note.   [4] Yonge.

17

For by him (Christ) all things were created.
All things were created through him and for him.—Coloss. i. 14–17.

Isis, thrice hapless goddess, thou shalt remain alone on the shores of the Nile, a solitary Maenad by the sands of Acheron. No longer shall thy memory endure upon the earth. . . . And thou, Serapis, that restest upon thy stones, much must thou suffer; thou shalt be the mightiest ruin in thrice hapless Egypt; and those who worshipped thee as a god shall know thee to be nothing. And one of the linen-clothed priests shall say: Come, let us build the beautiful temple of the true God; let us change the awful law of our ancestors, who, in their ignorance, made their pomps and festivals to gods of stone and clay; let us turn our hearts, hymning the Everlasting God, the Eternal Father, the Lord of all, the True, the King, the Creator and Preserver of our souls, the Great, the Eternal God.[1] .

Tertullian says: There is One God no other than the Maker of the World, who produced all things out of nothing by his WORD sent forth first of all: That WORD, called His SON, under the name God seen variously by the Patriarchs, in the Prophets always heard, lastly carried from the Spirit of God the Father and by His power into the Virgin Mary, became flesh in her womb and was born of her a Man and is Jesus Christ.—Adv. Haeret.

THE CREED OF EUSEBIUS OF CAESAREA, A. D. 313.

We believe in One God, the Father Almighty, Maker of all things visible and invisible. And in one Lord Jesus Christ, the LOGOS of God, God of God, Light of Light, Life of Life, SON ONLY-BEGOTTEN, FIRST-BORN of all creation, begotten before all Worlds of God the Father: and by him were all things created: who became flesh for our salvation and lived among men: and suffered and rose the third day from the dead: and ascended to the Father and will come again in glory to judge the living and the dead. And we believe in One Holy Spirit. Believing each of these to be and exist, the Father in truth the Father, the Son truly the Son and the Holy Spirit truly the Holy Spirit: just as our Lord, sending forth his disciples to the announcement, said: Go and teach all nations, baptizing them in the name of the Father and of the Son and of the Holy Ghost. Pearson, On the Creed.

THE CREED CALLED THE APOSTLE'S CREED.[2]

I believe in God the Father Almighty, Maker of Heaven and Earth:
And in Jesus Christ, his only Son, Our Lord; Who was conceived by the Holy Ghost, Born of the Virgin Mary, Suffered under Pontius Pilate, Was crucified, dead and buried; He descended into Hell; The *third day* he rose

[1] Sibylline Books, v. p. 638, Gallaeus; Milman, Hist. Christ. 228.
[2] Traced to the 4th century.

from the dead; He ascended into heaven; And sitteth on the right hand of God the Father Almighty; From thence he shall come to judge the quick and the dead.

I believe in the Holy Ghost; The Holy Catholic Church; The communion of Saints; The forgiveness of sins; The resurrection of the body, And the life everlasting. Amen!

CREED ADOPTED AT THE COUNCIL OF NICE, A. D. 325.[1]

We believe in One God, the Father Almighty, Maker of all things visible and invisible. And in one Lord Jesus Christ the Son of God, begotten of the Father, Only-begotten, that is, of the Substance of the Father: God of God, Light of Light, Very God of Very God: begotten not made: of one substance with the Father: by whom all things were made in heaven and upon the earth: who for us men and for our salvation came down and was made flesh, and was made Man: suffered and rose again the third day and ascended into the heavens and he shall come again with glory to judge the living and dead. And in the Holy Spirit. And the Catholic and Apostolic Church anathematizes those who say "there was a time when he was not," "and before he was born he was not" and those saying "that he was made out of nothing or of another substance or essence, or that the Son of God is created, or altered, or changed."

THE CREED ADOPTED AT THE COUNCIL OF CONSTANTINOPLE,
A. D. 381: PRESENT 150 BISHOPS.

We believe in One God, the Father Almighty, Maker of heaven and earth and of all things visible and invisible: And in One Lord Jesus Christ the Only-begotten Son of God, begotten of his Father before all worlds; God of God, Light of Light, Very God of Very God, begotten not made, of one substance with the Father: by whom all things were made: who for us men, and for our salvation, came down from heaven and was incarnate by the Holy Spirit of the Virgin Mary, and was made man; and was crucified also for us under Pontius Pilate, and suffered and was buried and rose again the third day according to the Scriptures: and ascended into heaven and sitteth on the right hand of the Father: and he shall come again to judge the living and the dead: whose kingdom shall have no end. And [We believe] in the Holy Spirit who is the Lord, the Giver of Life [2] who proceedeth from the Father,[3] who with the Father and the Son together is worshipped and glorified, who spake by the prophets. And [We believe] in one holy Catholic and Apostolic Church. We acknowledge one baptism for the remission of sins. We look for the resurrection of the dead and the life of the world to come. Amen!

---

[1] Attended by 318 bishops.

[2] Iao der Lebendigmacher—τὸ ζωοποιόν.

[3] " AND THE SON " was afterwards inserted by the Spanish Bishops. The insertion of the words " AND THE SON " was finally sanctioned by the Roman Church in 883, but has never been received by the Greek Church.—American Encycl. Art. Creed.

CHAPTER IX.

It shall come to pass that the glory of Iacob shall be made thin!
Isaiah, xvii. 4.

Artapanus says, in his account of the Jews, that, after the death of Abraham and his son as well as Mempsasthenoth the king of the Egyptians, his son Palmanothes assumed the crown and carried himself with great severity towards the Jews. And he compelled them first to build Kessa[1] and to construct the temple that is therein, and also the temple that is in Heliopolis. He had a daughter whose name was Merris who was married to a king named Chenephres then reigning in Memphis; for there were at that time *several kings in Egypt.* And, as she was barren, she brought up a child of the Jews, and named it Moüses: but when he arrived at manhood he was called among the Greeks Musæus.[2]

It was the habit of the ancients to refer important institutions of a preceding period to mythic names.[3] Amos, Amus or Mʊs (Mushi, Mosah) was an ancient Phœnician and Mysian god. Taaut (Hermes, Thoth) is the personified "Wisdom" which, as Sacred Scribe of Saturn, has inscribed the course of Nature and the destinies of the world in the stars. Instead of him, to the seven Cabiri, the planetary Powers, are ascribed these works, and they have written down all as the god Taaut commissioned them to do.[4] The first book of Thoth contained the daily hymns sung

---

[1] Zeus Acas-ios; the HYKS-os; Cush.   [2] Cory, Anc. Fragments.
[3] Movers, 114. The LAWS OF MOSAH!   [4] Movers, 109.

in Egypt in praise of the gods; the second, directions for the life of the kings; the third, fourth and fifth, astrological doctrines: the ten following contained hieroglyphics, cosmogony, geography, the arrangement of the Sun, Moon and five Planets, the description of Egypt, the Nile, rhythm, the holy utensils, &c., theology, medicine, &c., &c. The Babylonian, Phœnician and Egyptian sacred books date back to a fabulous antiquity. The Egyptian sacred books are older than the oldest parts of the Book of Genesis, *which paints the life of the priests just as it was known to be in later times.*[1] A priest-college occupied with expounding of dreams and magic appears at the court of Pharah as early as the history of Joseph.[2] Even the name Hierogrammateus (sacred scribe) occurs in the Hebrew translation, in the Pentateuch.[3] The Chaldeans reckon the age of their sacred books with astronomical numbers.[4]

It is God's law that the human mind is susceptible of increase. The great world-mind progresses continually and adds to its own thought forever. The sacred writings of the Hebrews, Persians and the Egyptian Book of the Dead, have come down to us in the *latest shape* which they assumed.

The Books of Moses *in their present form* were probably completed after the Exile. Many passages of Leviticus (ch. xxvi.) and Deuteronomy (ch. xxviii.) reveal an author who foresees the immediate dissolution of the kingdom and uses the language of the prophets of this period, especially Jeremiah. In the oldest parts of the Pentateuch the language is as completely formed and as perfect as at the time of the Exile.[5] Genesis contains the conception of Homer's Zeus, the frequent introduction of "angels," and the late doctrine of "the Angel of the Lord."

The Hebrews had chiefly Egyptian customs, such as the hierarchy of the Levites, the distinction between clean

---

[1] Movers, 112, 113.   [2] Ibid.; Gen. xli. 8; Exod. vii. 22; viii. 3; Diodor. ii. 70.   [3] Ibid. 112.   [4] Ibid. 113.   [5] Munk, Palestine, 139.

and unclean animals, the circumcision, the division of the
parts of the temple, the ark of the covenant (see Plutarch
de Is. et Osir., c. 35), the resemblance of the cherubim and
the sphynx.[1]

> But ye have borne Sacoth your Malak and your Chion, your ZALAMI (idols).
> Amos, v. 26.

In the worship of Moloch the holy symbols were preserved
in a gold box or chapel. The arcana of the Chaldeans
were preserved in a golden box of Chom. The image of
Mars, called by the Egyptians Chom and Moloch, was kept
at Papremis in a miniature temple of wood covered with
gold. The attendant priests placed it on a four-wheeled
carriage and drew it along.[2] In Egypt the ark was carried
in procession on a boat, the bari of Ammon.[3] The god
himself is either seated in the centre of the bari, or this
place is occupied by a shrine in which he is concealed.
Sometimes the shrine was not carried in a boat; but the image of the god stood upright upon a platform supported by
poles which the priests carried. The ark of the Hebrews
was furnished with rings in which the poles were inserted.[4]
The Ark stood between the cherubim. In the interior of
the Egyptian temples were arks or sacred boxes containing
the symbols and mysteries.[5]

> And they carried the ark of the Alohim in a new cart out of the house of
> Abinadab.
> And David and all Israel played before the Alohim with all might and with
> singing, harps, psalteries, cymbals and trumpets.—I Chron. xiii. 7, 8.
> Behold I will smite with the rod that is in my hand upon the waters which
> are in the River (Nile) and they shall be turned to blood.—Exodus, vii. 17.

In Egypt, the phenomenon of the Green Nile, which is owing to stagnant water carried forward by the new inundation
and once more thrown into the bed of the river, seldom lasts

---

[1] Uhlemann, Thoth, 7, 8.   [2] Herodot. ii. 63 ; Movers, 355. Choum
(Chom) is Satan, Apollo Chomaeus and Baal of the heat.—Movers, 291.
[3] Bryant, Mythol. i. 252.   [4] Kenrick, i. 386, 385 ; Munk's Palestine, 158.
[5] Munk, 158 ; Taylor's Proclus, p. xxviii.

more than three or four days.[1] Osborn saw the phenomenon of the Red Nile. "The river in the sunlight presented
the perfect appearance of a river of blood." During the
entire period of the high Nile the waters never lose the
deep red tinge.[2] The three states of the Nile were the Blue,
Green and Red.[3] The first rise of the waters covered it
with a greenish vegetable matter. In the Amenophion at
Luxor are two figures of the Nile, one which represents its
ordinary state is colored blue, the other red. The red is the
symbol of the inundation and is owing to a mixture of the
red oxide of iron.[4] The plagues of the frogs, lice and flies
are described by Philo with a minuteness not to be found
in the inspired account.[5] The Hebrews crossed the Red
Sea at Hahiroth where it is fordable.[6]

Chæremon says that Isis appeared to Amenophis in his
dreams rebuking him that her temple should have been
overthrown in war. Upon which Phritiphantes the sacred
scribe told him that if he would clear Egypt of all polluted
persons he would be delivered from these terrors. He
therefore collected 25,000 unclean persons and drove them
out. Their leaders were two scribes called Moyses and Josephus, the latter of whom was a sacred scribe; but their
Egyptian names were, that of Moyses, Tisithen, and that
of Josephus, Peteseph. They bent their way towards Pelu-
sium where they met with 380,000 men left there by Amenophis whom he would not suffer to come into Egypt.
With these they made a treaty and invaded Egypt.[7]

According to Lysimachus, Bocchoris assembled the
priests and attendants of the altars and commanded them
to gather together all the unclean persons[8] and deliver them
over to the soldiers *to lead them forth into the desert;* but
to wrap the lepers in sheets of lead and cast them into the

---

[1] Osborn's Egypt, i. 10, 11.   [2] Ibid. 12.   [3] Osborn, ii. 579; i. 3, 8.
[4] Kenrick, i. 73.   [5] Philo, de Vita Mosis.   [6] Champollion, Egypte,
17, Univers pitt.   [7] Josephus, Contra Apion, lib. i. c. 32; Cory.
[8] Compare Exodus, xii. 38.

sea. After they had drowned those afflicted with the leprosy and scurvy, they collected the rest and left them to
perish in the desert. But they took counsel among themselves, and when night came on lighted up fires and torches
to defend themselves, and fasted all the next night to pro-
pitiate the gods to save them. Upon the following day a
certain man called Moüses counselled them to persevere in
following one direct way until they should arrive at habitable places, and enjoined them to hold no friendly communication with men, neither to follow those things which men
esteemed good, but such as were considered evil: and to
overthrow the temples and altars of the gods as often as
they should happen with them. When they had assented
to these proposals they continued their journey through the
desert, acting upon those rules, and after severe hardships
they at length arrived in a habitable country, where having
inflicted every kind of injury upon the inhabitants, plun-
dering and burning the temples, they came at length to the
land which is now called Judaea and founded a city and
settled there. This city was named Hierosyla from their
disposition. But, in after times, when they acquired strength
to obliterate the reproach, they changed its name and called the city Hierosoluma, and themselves Hierosolnmites.[1]

Polemo, in the first book of his Grecian history says:
In the reign of Apis the son of Phoroneus, a part of the
Egyptian army deserted from Egypt and took up their
habitation in that part of Syria which is called Palestine,
not far from Arabia : these indeed were they who went out
with Moses.[2]

Manetho states that the diseased were placed in the
quarries but that they were afterwards established in the
city Avaris which the Hycsos had abandoned. The Shepherds in Jerusalem who had been expelled by the Egyptians were invited to return, and, having united their forces

---

[1] Josephus, Contr. Ap. 34.   [2] Afric. cited, Euseb. Pr. Ev. liber 10.

to the outcasts, took possession of Egypt and treated the inhabitants with great severity until they were again expelled.[1] The Hebrew history really begins with the nomadic period amidst the migrations of tribes. Movers states that Lower Egypt was the resort of Syrian and Arab tribes attracted by its fruitfulness, who conquered the natives.[2]

The Shepherd-kings, according to Manetho, and the Israelites, as Josephus testifies, both came to Egypt 2082 before Christ, and left the country after 215 years (B. C. 1867). Manetho expressly sets the arrival of the Hyksos[3] 2082 B. C., and the Israelites must have come in the same year if they went out in 1867 after having been 215 years in Egypt.[4] Manetho calls the first king of the Hyksos-dynasty Salatis. Joseph, as minister or regent, was called in Hebrew 'Salit.[5] Salatis busied himself with the measuring of corn and made the land tributary. Joseph purchased with the corn collected in the magazines the lands of the Egyptians so that they were compelled to pay rent for the use of them.[6] Josephus expressly asserts that the Hebrews were the Hyksos.[7] It is evident that Exodus and Manetho describe very nearly the same events.[8] The miraculous is largely interwoven with the Hebrew narrative. But it would not have been in accordance with the customs of those times for either side to have given a plain unvarnished historical account. Seyffarth thinks the Hebrews of the Exodus were the Hyksos. His pupil, Uhlemann, inclines to the opinion, that the Hyksos were the Hebrews and that the Jewish account was perverted by Manetho in the Egyptian interest. But it was not so essential for the Egyptians as for the Hebrews to pervert the truth, because

---

[1] Josephus, Contr. Ap. i. c. 26.   [2] Movers, 10.   [3] Acas, Casius, Cush.
[4] Seyffarth, Theolog. Schriften, 106, 151, 152.   [5] Genesis, xlii. 6; Uhlemann Handbuch, iii. 152.   [6] Ibid.   [7] Contra Apion, Book i.
[8] Uhlemann, Handbuch, iii. 154; Die Israeliten und Hyksos, 75, 76.

Josephus defends the Hebrew account; but he (born A. D. 37) lived many (?) centuries after the Books of Moses were written.

the antiquity of the Hebrew nation was made to turn upon
this very question, while the origin of the Egyptians was
not in any way connected with it. The Hebrews came out
of Egypt and settled among the Canaanites. They need
not be traced beyond the Exodus. *That is their historical
beginning.* It was very easy to cover up this remote event
by the recital of mythical traditions, and to prefix to it an
account of their origin in which the gods (Patriarchs) should
figure as their ancestors.

Homer, Hesiod, Pindar, Firdusi, Sanchoniathon's Phœnician antiquities, Eusebius and the Table of nations in
Genesis make the whole thing clear. The mortals mentioned in one are sometimes spoken of as gods in others. The
poets (priests) seem to have seriously set to work to dispose
of the deities as early as the time of the Homeric verses.
In this effort Hesiod and the authors of Genesis have performed their part.

Philo's Sanchoniathon affords a key to the Book of Genesis. Both are composed of "sacred tales" in which the
gods are euhemeristically treated as men and merely human
adventures related of them. "Agrus the Greatest of the
gods" (the Sun Acar, Kur) is called the Husbandman, and
Ali-cus (Ali, Eli, Allah) is called Fisherman from *áls* "the
sea." Kronos, like Noah, has three sons, Kronos, Zeus
Belus and Apollon.[1] Hanoch, Ada, Naama, Zilla, Iubal,
Lamech, appear in the legends of the Phœnicians, Phrygians
and Babylonians.[2] Iodah (Iudah) is the deity-name Adah
(in the masculine). Adah, in the feminine, is a name of
Isis, Juno, Venus, Ceres, Eve, &c. Ephraim is Epurim
(Abarim), Abram, a name of Saturn. Liber, Libanus,
Laban, Lebanon, are names of Bacchus. We find "the As-
surian Libanos" and "the Assurian Adonis."[3] We have
Aroban, or Roben (Re-uben, son of seeing),[4] Saman (Simeon,
hearing), Eloi or Loi (Levi, adhesion), Adas, Odas, Ioudas,

---

[1] Sanchon. Book i. §§ iv. vi. ff.   [2] Movers, 132.

[3] Nonnus, xli.   [4] Compare Arab, Baal-Iarob, Aban.

Dasius, the Tasian Hercules (Iehuda, confession), Adan, Adonis (Dan, judgment), Anaputal (Naphtali, striving), Akad (Gad, a heap, a troop), Asar (Asher, beatitude), and Sabalon, Zebolon (Seb-Elon) " cohabiting," the pun on the name of the Sabellian tribe, the children of the Phœnician deity Asbolos.[1]

And the Children of Sobal were these, Alon and Manahat and Aibal, Sapho and Aonam.—Gen. xxxvi. 23.

The tribe of Asaph is called Ioseph (he shall add). Issachar is Asakar or Zagre-us (Bacchus), and the name is punned upon by assimilating it to the Hebrew word sekari " hire." Abanon becomes Ben-Oni (son of my grief) and Abanaman, Beniamin (son of my right hand).

The ancient religion long before the time of Christ, in Babylon, Egypt, Phœnicia and elsewhere, had become astronomical in character. The gods were placed in the stars. The Phœnician gods were the Sun, Moon, the other Planets and the Elements, which, according to Philo, were men or rather persons under defined human forms.[2] Euhemerism got rid of the gods by turning them into men. Abraham the patriarch and founder of the Hebrews was held to be identical with the original ancestor of the Semitic race, the mythic Bel-Saturn, by the Arabians, the later Persians, Babylonians, Phœnicians and Syrians. Abraham and Israel were names of Saturn.[3]

Conjurantes eos per deum Adonai et deum Israel, qui per legem et prophetas locutus est patribus nostris.—Ev. Nic. pars Altera I.

Deus Israel qui dixit ad Moysen.—Evang. Nic. xii.

For a father, afflicted with untimely mourning, when he has made an image of his child soon taken away, now honored him as a god which was then a dead man; and delivered to those that were under him ceremonies and sacrifices.

Thus in process of time an ungodly custom grown strong was kept as a law.

And so the multitude, allured by the grace of the work, took him now for a god, which a little before was but honored as a man!

Wisdom of Solomon, xiv. 15, 16, 20.

[1] See above, p. 181.   [2] Philo, p. 8; Movers, 110.   [3] Movers, 86.

Sem and Seth (gods) were in great honor among men, and Adam was above every living thing in creation!—Ecclesiasticus, xlix. 16.

Abraham and Israel were mentioned among the mythic kings of Damascus. The first king of Dam-ask-us was Damaskus, then Azel(ns), Ador(es), Abraham and Israel.[1]

Israel spread his tent beyond the tower of ADAR.—Gen. xxxv. 21.

These are all names of the Sun or Saturn. "Kronos (Saturn) therefore whom the Phœnicians call Israel."[2] Adad and Azael, who, according to Josephus, were worshipped as gods in Damascus, are mentioned as kings in the Old Testament.[3]

The lawless fraud of Ischus, SON OF EILAT (Lot).—Pindar, Pyth. iii. 31.

But when her relatives placed the maiden on the mound of wood, and the furious blaze of Haphaistos (Fire) surrounded her, THEN APOLLO SPOKE: I will endure no further in my soul TO DESTROY MY OFFSPRING IN A MOST PITEOUS DEATH! Thus he spoke, and at the first step having reached the boy, he snatched him from the corpse!—Pindar, Pyth. iii.

Abram prepares to offer up to God his Only Son Isaac just as the Phœnicians said Saturn offered up his Only-begotten Son as a sacrifice to his father Ouranos, and circumcised himself and compelled his allies to do the same:[4] This was done on the occasion of a famine and pestilence, like the children offered to Saturn-Moloch at such times.[5] The Mahometan Arabs held Abraham for Saturn in the Caaba, and he was represented as an old man with seven arrows or lots of destiny in his hands.[6]

The Phœnician sacred books of Taaut (Thoth), originally contained, besides the cosmogony (Gen. i. 1), circumstances out of the life of the gods, who, according to the Euhemeristic views of the Orient somewhere from five to eight centuries before Christ, *were men*, ancient benefactors

[1] Kurtz, ii. 177, quotes Justin, Hist. 36, 2; Movers, 87.
[2] Movers, 130; Fragm. Philo, in Eusebius, p. 44.   [3] Ibid. 368.
[4] Sanchoniathon, in Cory, p. 14.   [5] Eusebius, in Movers, 132.   [6] Movers, 86.

and old kings of Phœnicia named after "the Elements" and first deified on account of their services towards mankind.[1] Agenor was a name of Baal,[2] Agenor was an Ancestor of the Phœnicians. Zeus, Apollo and Athena were called by Plato "Ancestors" and "Lords."[3] Perseus was an Assyrian and Grecian god.[4] "The Greeks enumerate these Dorian princes in regular succession to Perseus the son of Danae, *passing over the story of the* DEITY" (Perseus).[5] Among the ancient kings of the Greeks are found the deity-names Azan, Abas (the god Busi), Argus or Arcas, Aegeus, Apis, Danaus, Perseus, Iasus.[6] The Babylonian Euhemerism declared Belus and Annos (Oannes), two names or impersonations of their chief deity Abel or Bel, to be "their oldest sages."[7] The Italians turned some of their gods into men. Thus Janus, whom Scaliger has shown to be the Sun, was set down as an ancient king of Italy. Tages[8] was called the civilizer of the Etruscans. Two kings of ancient Persia appear as gods in the preceding (Indo-Arian) period.[9] Trita, a deity in the Indo-Arian religion, becomes a Hero in the Persian.[10] Abram (Bromius) as a patriarch (?) weighs out four hundred *shekels of silver current money with the merchant,* which, natural enough on the part of a wandering Arabian in the time of Alexander the Great, appears inconsistent with a period of primitive simplicity. Isaac (Asac), the Only-begotten Son, is the name of the god Sichæus (Mercury) and the Carian god Osogo (Suchos). Keb stands for Seb (Saturn).[11] We have "the sons of AKKABA and AKOUPH and ACHIBA and AKBŌS (Acub," Iacobus) in the Book of Esdras.[12]

---

[1] Movers, 90.   [2] Duncker, ii. 489; Movers, Phön. Alt. i. 129–139, 212.

[3] Rinck, i. 309 ; Plato, Euthedem. 302, D.   [4] Movers, 14; Herodot. vi. 53, 54.

[5] Beloe's Herod. iii. 270.   [6] Williams, 565, 567.   [7] Movers, 92.

[8] Tag, Dagur, Dagon, Tagos.   [9] Roth, Sage von Feridun; D. M. G. ii. 228.

[10] D. M. G. 225.   [11] Lepsius, Trans. Berlin Akad. 1851, p. 163 ff. Compare the Turkish and Hebrew deity-names Akb-ar, Cheb-ar, Gibb-or, Gab*A*riel, CAB-ir.

[12] 1 Esdras, v. 30, 31, 38 : also Tischendorf. Vet. Test. Graece, i. p. 587.

The fountain of Ikab (IACAB) shall be upon a land of corn and wine, also his heavens shall distil dew!—Deut. xxxiii. 28.

Akab, Keb (Iakab) is Iacob or Israel (Saturn), "mourned on the threshing floor of ATAD" as the Egyptians, Phœnicians, Syrians and others mourned the Only-begotten Maneros, Ieoud, Linus, &c., Esau (Aso, Oso in Hebrew) is the Phœnician god Ousō (Sanchoniathon's Ousōus). Iacab has his "twelve" sons, the twelve Ancestors of the allied tribes of the Israelites. Hercules, the Sun, has his "twelve" labors and Israel (Hercules) *wrestles* with Elohim.[1] The vowel beginning a name was very commonly omitted as in the names Bel, Baalan, Siris, Chon, Malak, Brahm, Surya, Keb, Seb, Sabos, Sabi in Arabia, Sev, &c., for Abel, Apellōn, Osiris, Akan, Amalak, Abraham, Assur (Asar), Akab, Asab, Asaph, the Arab god Asaf. Iasaf, Ioseph, has adventures in Egypt.[2] Osiris was said to have led a colony into Egypt from Aethiopia.

Primus Assuriorum regnavit Saturnus quem Assurii Deum nominavere Saturnum.

First of the Assyrians reigned Saturn whom the Assyrians named God.

Servius, ad Aeneid, i. 642.[3]

Generally the reducing the gods to the sphere of humanity is any thing but uncommon. They are placed at the head of the genealogies particularly of the kings and princes, from whom in regular succession demi-gods, heroes, ordinary mortals descend. As Wodan forms the last member in the genealogical tree of all ancient German royal families, so Bel does the same among the Semitic races: the Assyrians, Babylonians, Phœnicians, Carthaginians, Lydians. His royal castle defended by walls was shown in Babel, in Phœnicia, and also in the distant West, and the Chaldeans preserved his gravestone which Xerxes destroyed and his body embalmed in oil. Where a divinity was chiefly worshipped there it had reigned in the old time as

---

[1] Movers, 396.   [2] Ioseph's body was put in the sarcophagus (aron) which is in Hebrew the name of the Ark (aron).—Gen. l. 26 ; Ex. xxv. 22.

[3] Movers, 185.

king or queen, Astarte in Byblus or Damascus, and as Dido in Carthage. The guardian deities of a city usually passed for the builders of it. The Phœnician deities had, in the first period of human history, revealed themselves in human shape, taught sciences, &c.[1] The tombs of Tuphoios (Typhon) and "Divine Ilos" (Il, El) "the aged leader of the people," "descendant of ancient Dardanus," are mentioned.[2]

The neighboring lands boast that the hero KOLŌN[3] is their founder and all *bear the name* of him in common, being thus named . . . . bearing the name of *this very god!*—Sophocles, Œdip. Col. 60–65.

For in the division of the nations of the whole earth, he set a ruler over every people; but Israel is the Lord's portion.—Ecclesiasticus, xvii. 17.

Astarte ruled as guardian divinity of the Phœnicians, Demarus of the Arabians, Hadad of the Syrians : the other gods also obtain lands and cities as fiefs of Saturn.[4] So Jehovah has appointed to the Sun, Moon and Heavenly Host, each his land.[5] The land of Israel was the property of Jehovah.[6]

Why does Malcham possess Gad?—Jeremiah xlix. 1.

In the Septuagint, "the division of the nations was made according to the number of the angels of God" and not according to the number of the children of Israel, as the present Hebrew text asserts. This reading was adopted by the most celebrated fathers of the Church, as Origen, Basil, Chrysostom, &c. That this is the genuine reading is proved by Deut. iv. 19 :[7]

And lest by chance thou lift thine eyes to heaven, and look upon the Sun, and Moon and Stars, all the army of the heavens, and art impelled, and bow down to them and serve them, since Iahoh your Elohi hath divided them to all peoples under all heavens.—Version of Schmid.

---

[1] Movers, 153, 155.   [2] Iliad, ii. 785; ᴧ. 415; xi. 168, 370; Compare Pindar, Ol. vi. 70, 71.   [3] Geleon, a name of Zeus. Cullane the mountain with his name. (?)   [4] Compare Sanchoniathon, pp. 34, 38.
[5] Deut. iv. 19; Movers, 287.   [6] Ps. x. 16; Levit. xiv. 34; xxv. 2; Numb. xiii. 13; Judg. xi. 34; Movers, 358.
[7] Preface to Taylor's Proclus; Deut. xxxii. 8.

Individuals having adopted the deity-names, it became in time easier to confound the god with those who anciently bore his name. Hence it was natural for the writers of the myths to say that the gods were their ancestors (especially the sun-god and earth-goddess). Aiakos " the Averter from evil," the son of Jupiter and Ægina, was he a real king of Ægina, or a sun-god euhemerized? In Asia Minor, Asios, the mythic Ancestor of the Asionians, has a name like Sios the Lacedemonian name of Zeus. Asios is the grandfather of Manes (Omanes the Sun). Manes is the Son of Heaven and Earth.[1]

> And Iacob swore by the *fear of his father* Isabak !—Gen. xxxi. 53.
> They joined themselves unto Baal-Peor and ate the sacrifices of the dead.
> > Ps. cvi. 28.

The worship of the manes is connected with the worship of the gods. The spirits of the departed were considered " lights in heaven" by the American Indians, Persians and Hindus.[2]

> But if you will, another tale I will briefly tell you well and skilfully, and do you ponder it in your mind, THAT FROM THE SAME ORIGIN ARE SPRUNG GODS AND MORTAL MEN. First of all, the Immortals holding the mansions of Olympus made a golden race of speaking men. They indeed were under Cronus (Saturn) when he ruled in heaven. And as gods they were wont to live with a life void of care, apart from and without labors and trouble: nor was wretched old age at all impending, but, ever the same in hands and feet, did they delight themselves in festivals out of the reach of all ills: and they died as if overcome by sleep; all blessings were theirs; of its own will the fruitful field would bear them fruit, much and ample: and they gladly used to reap the labors of their hands in quietness along with many good things, being rich in flocks, and dear to the blessed gods. But AFTER THAT EARTH HAD COVERED THIS GENERATION THEY INDEED ARE CALLED DEMONS, kindly, haunting-earth,

---

[1] Duncker, Gesch. des Alt. vol. ii. pp. 506, 507 ; Iliad, ii. 461 ; Dionys. Halic. l. c. Herodot. iv. 45.

[2] See Allen's India, 22, 361; above, p. 3; Zeitschrift, der D. M. G. ix. 238; Spiegel, Vend. Farg. 19; Movers, 90, 152, 155; De Wette, Bibl. Dogm. p. 146; Duncker, ii. 26; Hesiod, Works and Days, 123; Theog. 954–1022.

guardians of mortal men, who, I ween, watch both the decisions of justice and harsh deeds, going to and fro everywhere over the earth *having wrapped themselves in mist*, givers of riches as they are : and this is a kingly function which they have.[1]

The transmigration of men into the circle of the gods belongs in India to the oldest Vedic period. The "Fathers," the souls of the ancestors, are ranked like the gods.[2] The spirits of the departed were considered gods.[3]

I praise the strong souls of the Pure, that aid all created beings.

Vendidad, Farg. xix.

Since they turned their dead men into gods it was just as simple for them to turn their gods into dead men or the ancestors of the nation. This appears to have been done in Genesis to the national satisfaction: but it was also done elsewhere as the genealogical trees of the Greeks show fully.

The Greeks had systems of divine patriarchs (gods) like the Hebrews. In the genealogical table of Aeolus we find first, Zeus or Deucalion, then Hellen, Dorus, Xuthos, Aeolus, Kretheus, Sisyphos, Athamas and Salmoneus. In the genealogical tree of Kretheus, are Kretheus, Aeson, Pheres, Iason-Promachos. In the table of Athamas (Adam) are Aeolus, Athamas who has by Nephele Ino and Themisto. In the genealogical tree of Melampus we find Kretheus Aeson, Pheres, Abas, Oicles, Polupheides (Eos his wife). In the table of Bias are first Bias, who had, by his wife Pero, Talaos, Perialkes, Aretos . . . Adrastos, &c. In the table of the Orchomenian Minyae are Aeolus, Athamas, Sisuphus, Eteocles, Azeus. The table of Phlegyas (Peleg) gives Phlegyas, Ixion and Dia (the Earth). The tree of Elatos gives Elatos (Lot) and Hippia his wife, then Kaineus (Cain) and from him Koronos (Kronos). The table of Thespiae gives first Kanake who by Poseidon has Epopeus;

[1] Hesiod, Works and Days, 108–125; Banks; also ed. Lipsiae.
[2] Wuttke, ii. 391.   [3] Zeitschr. der D. M. G. ix. 238.

18

Aloeus, Amphion, Zethus, Otus, Ephialtes, &c.   In the tree
of Cadmus we find Agenor, Europa, Kadmos, Phoinix, Kilix,
Minos, Autonoe, Ino, Semele, Agave, Polydoros, Oidipus,
Aesanios. The list of the mythic kings of Athens, after
mentioning Kranaos, Kekrops, Deucalion and others, gives
us Itonos, Tithonus, Adonis, Eupalamos, Ion, Achaios, Dorus, Dædal-us (Tidal), Ikaros (Kur, Akar), Talos, Aegeus.
The table of Inachus gives, as the first rulers of Argos, Oke-
anos (Oceanus) and Tethys his wife, Inachus, Phoroneus,
Aegialus, Apis, Niobe, Iasos, Io, Sthenelus.   The table of
Io gives first Io, then Epaphus (the bull-god), Libya, Tele-
gonus, Belus, Agenor, Kadmus, Aiguptos, Danaus. The ta-
ble of Arkas has first Arkas, then Azan, Apheidas, Elatos
(Lot) . . . Auge . . . Epochus (Bacchus). The rulers of
Sicuon were first Helios (the Sun), Aloeus (El, Luaios), Epo-
peus. The Elean-Aetolian table gives Zeus, Aethlios (Atal,
Talos, Tal the Sun), Endymion, Paion (Pan), Epeios (Ap),
Aetolus. The table of Oeneus has Deukalion, Orestheus,
Phutios (Phut, Ptah), Oeneus (Ani), Tudeus (Adad, Thoth,
Tod). We find Tros the Ancestor of Ilos, Assarakos and
Ganymede.[1] The Trojan table has Zeus, Dardanos, Iasion
(Sun), Ilos, Assarak-os, Laomedon. From Laomedon came
Tithonus (the Sun, Titan), Emathion, Memnon. Among the
Heraclidæ is Temen-os.   Temen is an Assyrian deity.

These tables of Grecian genealogies contain the names
of gods, ancestors, patriarchs or heroes, all mixed up together, as seems to be the case with the Phœnician-Hebrew
genealogies of the Old Testament; for these have their
Adam (Athamas, Atamu) Abel (Abelios, Bel, Hobal),[2] Kin
(Akan, Chon, Kaineus), Seth (a god), Anos (Enos), Enoch
(Inachus the Sun), Tubalcain (the gods Tob and Bāl-Chon,

---

[1] Iliad, xx. 236, 239.

[2] The Arabs anciently worshipped Saturn under the name of Hobal. In his
hands he held seven arrows, symbols of the planets that preside over the seven
days of the week.—Pococke Specimen, Hist. Arab. p. 97, sqq. ed. White,
quoted by Movers, 263. The image of Abraham (Saturn) held divining arrows
in its hand.—Movers, 86.

Vulcan),[1] Iabal (Pales), Iubal (Abal, Baal, Apollo), Iavan (Evan=Bacchus), which indicate a mythology which has passed away.[2] It is the same with Sanchoniathon's, in which gods and the names of philosophical dogmas appear as mythic kings, heroes, &c.

The Persian liturgy says:

I invoke and praise the Months, lords of purity.[3]

The Babylonians took twelve names of sun-gods and placed them together as a sacred number. It is probable that the following twelve names are not the oldest but a later system more philosophized. The Invisible God, Apason, Taauthe, Moum, Dacha, Dachus, Kissara, Assoros, Anos, Illinos, Aos, Belus Minor the Demiurg.[4] This number corresponds to the twelve Titans (Suns), to the twelve Great Gods of Homer and the Egyptians. Taauthe is the feminine of Taaut the Phœnician Mercury (Sun). Aoum, or Moum, is Am the Sun or (doubled) Amam (Mom, Moum). Dacha and Dachus are the masculine and feminine of the sun-god Dag (the Day). Assoros is Assur the Sun. Kissara is the feminine of Chusorus a sun-god or Demiurg philosophized. Anos is the Hebrew Enos, the Egyptian god of the inundation Noh (the Hebrew Noah?). Illinos is the Phœnician sun-god Elon the "King of the gods." Aos is As, the God of Asia and a name of the god Assur in Assyria. Bel the Younger is the Demiurgic sun-god, the Creator.

The Hebrew presents a clearer view of the deities than the Babylonian. Thus Adam is the Phœnician Zeus-Demarus of Sanchoniathon, the Demarez (Baal-Tamar) whom the Sea (Typhon) overcame, according to the Phœnician myth,[5] the Hebrew Tamus (Adonis), the Egyptian Re-

---

[1] Vulcan appears in the Iliad quite in the character of Tobalcan the smith.

Il. xviii. 409.

He is the underground Sol, Apollo, Zeus, Tob-alkin or Tuphon, the fire-god Dabal-cain.

[2] De Wette, Bibl. Dogm. i. p. 44.   [3] Creuzer, Symb. i. 321, 327.

[4] Movers, 276.   [5] Seyffarth, Computationssystem, 119, 120, 128.

Athom, King of the gods.[1] Eua or Eva is the feminine of
Euas, Evi, Evius (Bacchus); she is the Mighty Mother
(Rhea), Ceres. Abel is Abelios the Sun. Kin (Cain) is
Iachin, Chon, Akan names of Saturn, in Palestine, Asia
Minor and Egypt. Seth is the god of the Sethites,[2] other-
wise called Asad, Saad, Aseth, the El-Sadai of Genesis; in
Egypt Seth is Moloch. Enos is Anos. Cainan (in Hebrew
Kenan) is the Phœnician god Chanaan, the Syrian god
Kanoon (Canaan) who gave his name to the Syrian month
Kanoon and to the land named after him.[3] Arad, or Iared
gave his name to Erde the E-arth (Arit-imis) who was his
bride like Rhodes (Rhodos) the bride of the Sun. Enoch is
the Phrygian Anakos who foretold the Flood, the Greek Inachus, the Sun. Noah's name is spelled by some Hebrew
scholars Noach, making him agree with this Phrygian Sun-
Noah, Annakos. They say that there was a certain Annakos (Inachus) who lived above three hundred years. And
an oracle was given that at his death all should be destroyed. And the Phrygians hearing mourned exceedingly;
whence the proverb "*the Mourning for Annakos*" applied
to those who grieve exceedingly.[4] This is the Mourning for
Adonis.

And Hanok pleased Elohim three hundred years after he had begotten
Methuselah.

That all the days of Hanok might be three hundred and sixty-five years.

For when Hanok pleased Elohim, he was no more, because Elohim took
him to himself.

---

[1] Osburn, Monument. Hist. Egypt, ii. 271; i. 340.   [2] Movers, 107.

[3] Judges, xi. 24; Amos, i. 14; Jer. 49, 3; 48, 7; Movers, 358; Kenrick,
i. 277; Lepsius Einleit. 144.   Compare Tamuz a Syro-Macedonian month-
name with Thamus, a name of Amon and Thammuz, who is Adonis; Tobi, an
Egyptian month-name, and the land of the god Tob with the compound Hebrew name Tob-Adon-Iaho (three deity-names in one word). The first of
Kanoon and second of Kanoon are two Syro-Macedonian months mentioned
next after Teshreen (November).

[4] Stephanus Byzant. i. 217, 218.   "And he was not; for Elohim took
him," seems to refer to the Mourning for Annakos who suddenly disappeared.
It is the death of Hadad, or Inachus, the Nature-god.

Inac, celebrated citizen of the land Inachia,
Priest ; and the dreadful orgies of the goddess patroness of cities
Which discourse of God after the mystic custom he
Contrived in his meditations.—Nonnus, iii. 261.

Methuselah contains three deity-names. Muth (Pluto),
Maut (Isis), Usel the Etruscan Sol (the Sun) and Ah (Iah)
the Hebrew deity-name : or, differently compounded, we
have Muth (Bacchus Amadios), Uselah (" As," the Babylonian Aos, and Elah (Allah) another name of the Hebrew
God Eloah). Lam-ach or Lamech would correspond with
the Babylonian Ulom, the First-born, whence " lumen" and
illuminate were derived. Ak or Ach is the Arab god
Iauk, the name of Apollo, Agu-ieus, and the German god
Ukko, the name of Adonis, Gauas, and of Bacchus, Gnēs.
If we count these Hebrew patriarchs we find just eleven
names. Nah, the last of the list, makes the *twelfth !* Nah
is the Egyptian Nuh, or Noh, the god of the annual Inundation of the Nile, or, if written Nach, it is Anak, Anakos
the Phrygian Noah (the Sun), Osiris.

Said Iahob Zebaoth Elohi of Israel: Behold I punish Amon of Na and
Pharoh and Misraim.—Jeremiah, xlvi. 25.

The Greeks turned their sun-gods Ion (Ianus), Aeolus
(Ael), Xuthus (Seth), Ach-aeus (Ak), Hellen (Elon), Iber
(Abar), Dorus (Adar, Thor) into chieftains, Ancestors, or
patriarchs of the tribe. The Aeolians were the children of
Aeolus, the Ionians of Ion or Ianus.[1] The Babylonians
turned ten of their gods into kings who reigned before the
Flood. In the reign of Xisuthrus the tenth king of Babylon
the Deluge occurred. In the Bible, Noah is the tenth of
the Patriarchs (leaving out Cain and Abel) and in his time
the Flood occurred. Here is a sufficient coincidence to
show that one idea ruled in both accounts. If with
the philosophical notion of the existence of a River in
heaven, the Great Waters issuing from the sun, we connect

[1] See Gerhard, Berlin Akad. 1853.

the well-known tendency of the Babylonians and Egyptians to carry back their annals far beyond the truth and to claim ages under the reign of the gods themselves, we see a reason why the Flood would be a valuable point of departure for the partisans of a fabulous antiquity among the ancients.

> They tell that the might of waters had overwhelmed black earth, but that by the arts of Zan the sea suddenly received an ebb!
>
> Pindar, Olymp. Ode, ix.

Jehovah in Genesis takes the place of Saturn in the Babylonian Flood story.[1] Zeus is the same as Saturn, for he rules over the empire of Saturn. Kronos being a foreign god, the Greeks connected Zeus with him by calling him the son of Kronos.[2] Homer's Zeus agrees with Genesis ix. 16, 17; xi. 5.

> Rainbows which the son of Saturn has fixed in a cloud, a sign to articulate-speaking men.—Iliad, xi. 27.
>
> Zeus extends a purple rainbow to mortals to be a signal.—Iliad, xvii.
>
> I will set my bow in the cloud to be a·sign of a covenant between me and Earth.—Gen. ix. 13, 14.

The Egyptian accounts differ; but some of them state that the *twelve* Great Gods reigned down to the time of the Flood. The Babylonians said that *ten* kings reigned down to the Flood. The Hebrews counted *ten* Patriarchs from Adam to Noah leaving out Kin and Abel. Thus to correspond with the *ten* Babylonian kings, they gave Adam, Seth, Anos, Kenan, M-ahal-aleel, Iared, Anok, Methuselah, Lam-ech, Noah. If Kin and Abel had been admitted into this list, we should have twelve, agreeing in number with the twelve Great Gods of the Babylonians, Egyptians, Phœnicians, Hebrews, Greeks, Romans, Persians, &c. The names differ of course. Osiris is killed by his brother Typhon while Kin (Iachin) kills Abel (Bel).

---

[1] Movers, 261.　　[2] Rinck, i. 39.

The Italian deity Apell-ōn, the Greek Apoll-ōn, the Cretan sun-god Abeli-os, the Pamphylian sun-god *Babeli*-os was called Bel and Babel (Adonis-El) in Babul-ōn. The terminations *os* and *on* are two different forms of the declension of nouns. The Hebrew author of Genesis has, by punning on the name of the sun-city of ancient learning, derived the idea of babel, "confusion" of tongues. The crowd of strangers that resorted to it from all parts of Asia would suggest such an idea, if the name did not.[1]

> But when the Tower fell and tongues of men
> With various languages were perverted, for all
> The earth was filled with men kings sharing (it),
> Then indeed was the Tenth Generation of speaking men
> After the Flood came upon the Former men.
> And Kronos was KING, and Titan and Iapetus;
> The bravest children of Earth and Heaven men called
> Them, giving the name of Gaia and Ouranos
> Because (these) were the most eminent of speaking men.
>> Sibylline Books, Gallaeus, p. 343–345.

The tenth chapter of Genesis says that the *immediate descendants* of Noah spoke *different tongues*, "every one after his tongue."[2] The eleventh chapter says:

And the whole earth was of *one* language!

Polyhistor remarks: "The Gigantic inhabitants of Babylon were destroyed by the gods for their impiety; except that one of them, Belus, escaped destruction, resided at Babylon and erected and lived in a tower that bore his name."[3] This is the great temple of Belus at Babylon.

The Persians held that, at the END, when Ahriman is overcome, "the earth will be even and regular, and there will be one state and one language and one mode of life

---

[1] The Scythian chief god Papaios (and Paphia), the Egyptian god Apop, the Greek Popoi (gods), the Jewish Abib (Abab), the name of Adonis, Abob-(as), would, compounded with El, Bel, or Bol, give Babul or Babel the Sun; compounded with Elon the deity-name, it would furnish Bab-elon. *There Ihoh confounded the lip of all earth.*   [2] Gen. x. 5.   [3] Eusebius, Praep. Ev. ix. 18.

among happy men who will speak alike." This refers to
the Messiah's kingdom and the resurrection of the dead.[1]
God creates the world in six periods according to the Persians, in six days according to the Hebrews. The Hindus,
Plato, the Hebrews and others agreed that after the work
of creation was over, the Deity changed the time of energy
for the state of repose; he *rested* on the day of Saturn,
Saturday.

In the Beginning also, when the proud GIANTS perished, the hope of the
world (Nah) governed by thy hand escaping on a boat, ...
Wisdom of Solomon, xiv. 6.

Noah is said to have had THREE SONS, Shem (Baal-Semes
the Sun), Ham (Am, Amous, Iamus, Iom the Sun) and Iapet
(Apat, Phut the Egyptian god Ptah the Supreme Deity).
These are Saturn, Jupiter-Sol and Mars-Hercules.[2] Ac-
cording to Sanchoniathon, Kronos (Saturn) had Three
Children, Kronos named like his father, Zeus-Bel and
Apollo.[3] The Sibyl wrote :

Καὶ βασίλευσε Κρόνος καὶ Τιτὰν Ἰαπετόστε.
And Kronos ruled and Titan and Iapetus.
Gallaeus, 344; Williams, 274.

These are Belitan, Zeus-Bel and Baal-Chom or Apollo
Chomaeus.[4] Chom (Χοῦμ) is Satan, Apollo Chomaeus and
" Baal of the heat." Chom was Hercules in Egypt, that
is, the Baal-Chom of the Babylonians.[5] Sanchoniathon,
who gives us Phœnician antiquities, says : "From the race
of AION and FIRSTBORN were born mortal children who had
the names Light, Fire, Flame" (Phōs, Pur, Phlox)[6] the
Sons of Cronos (Saturn), whereas they are the three manifestations of the Sun.[7] Sanchoniathon gave as his authority
the Jewish priest Ierombaal who was priest of the Hebrew

---

[1] Plutarch, de Iside, et Os. xlvii.; Duncker, ii. 387.   [2] Movers, 186, 188.
[3] Sanchoniathon, p. 16.   [4] Movers, 189.
[5] Ibid. 291, 188.   [6] Sanchon. A. iii.   [7] See above, p 191.

god Ieuô.[1] Pherecydes the Syrian also held that Saturn
generated from himself Fire, Spirit and Water, representing
the three-fold nature of the Intelligible.[2] In the Chaldean
Oracles, and on the seal in Dr. Abbot's Egyptian museum,
the trinity is Light, Fire, Flame. Bel-Saturn, Jupiter-Bel
and Baal-Chom are the Chaldean trinity.[3] Saturn, Jupiter-
Sol and Mars (the Devil) are the Babylonian and Phœnician trinity.[4]

The triad, Jove, Pluto and Neptune, are parts or sons of
Saturn. For the Sun is both water-god and god of the two
regions heaven and hell, like Osiris and Hapi who appear
in the three characters. In the same way, Ak (Iacch-os) is
sun-god (Ag-uieus), hell-god (Eacus) and Water (Aqua).
Agni is sun-god, water-god and death-god (Yama) in the
Vedas. The three-fold conception of the male Nature-god
as the Creator, Preserver and Destroyer agrees with the
Triune character of Baal as Year-sun. As Adon-is, he is
the Spring-sun, as Mars or Baal-Chamman, he is the de-
stroying Summer-sun; as Saturn or Baal-Chewan he is
Winter-sun. So he is Morning, Midday and Evening Sun.
The Babylonian Bel was regarded in the Triune aspect of
Belitan, Zeus Belus (the Mediator) and Baal-Chom who is
Apollo Chomaeus. This was the Triune aspect of the
"Highest God" who is according to Berosus either El, Bel,
Belitan, Mithra, or Zervana, and has the name πατηρ "the
Father."

For from this Triad, in the bosoms, are all things governed.

Chaldean Oracles.

For from this Triad the Father has mingled every spirit.

Lydus, l. c. p. 20.[5]

The Chaldean sun-god Mithra is called "TRIPLE." Bel the
Younger contains in himself the already developed ideas of

---

[1] Movers, 128; Sanchoniathon, preface.   [2] Damascius; Cory, 321.
[3] Movers, 263.   [4] Ibid. 186, 189.   [5] Ibid. 189.

Baal-Saturnus (the Good) and Baal-Moloch (the Devil deity), and is Nature-god besides.[1]

The Egyptians arranged their deities in triads containing the Father, the Mother (the Spirit and Matter) and the Son, "the World" which proceeds from the Two Principles; Osiris, Isis and Horus (Light) the Soul of the World, the Son, the Only-begotten. In the same way Plato gives us Thought, "the Father," Primitive Matter the Mother, and Kosmos the Son the issue of the Two Principles. This Kosmos is the ensouled World. The Soul of the World is a third subordinate nature partaking both of Spirit and Matter.

But the Better and "Diviner Nature" is composed of three things, The Intelligible and Matter and That which is composed of both, namely, the World (the god Kosmos).—Plutarch, de Iside, lvi.

Therefore before the heaven was made, there existed Idea and Matter and God the Demiurgus of "the Better." He made the world out of "matter," Perfect, Only-begotten, with a Soul and Intellect, and constituted it a god.—Pythagorean Fragment.[2]

In Egypt we find the Trinity Ammon-Ra the Creator, Osiris-Ra the Giver of fruits, Horus-Ra the Giver of light; —Summer, Autumn and Spring Sun.[3] Uhlemann informs us that the Creator appears as a trinity, the three Kamephi, which, he says, are the three chief divisions of the Zodiac, the three parts of Egypt, &c., &c.[4] He says: On account of the different workings of the Sun in the *three* Egyptian *seasons of the year*, this deity appears in three forms as Ammon-Ra, Osiris-Ra and Horus-Ra.[5] According to one of the Egyptian legends, however, Osiris is born first, next the Elder Horus, then Typhon[6] (the Devil, Apollo Chomaeus, Iapet or Phut, Ptah the fire-god), which agrees with the Babylonian trinity of Baal, Zeus-Bel and Mars (Chom), and with the Edessa triad, Sol, Monimus and Asis (the Devil in

<hr>

[1] Movers, 189, 321.   [2] Cory, 303.   [3] Uhlemann, Thoth, 33.
[4] Thoth, 27. [5] Uhlemann, Handbuch, part 2d, p. 168. [6] Kenrick, i. 343.

Persia). The Egyptian Pimander says : "I deliver the impious to the avenging Demon who loves the guilty and punishes them with fire."[1] In the New Testament we have the Father, Spirit and Son.

The notion of a "triad of gods" is unauthorized by the Rik and Sama Vedas. Vishnu was a god of the Ganges-dwellers who was the impersonation of the beneficent influences of Nature. Çiva was regarded in the valleys of the Himālăya and the southern part of the Deccan as the unrestrained mighty Power of Nature producing new life out of destruction. Soon after Buddha first succeeded in his teachings the Brahmans found themselves unable to contest the three at once. They therefore adopted first Vishnu (the Life in Nature) and ascribed to Brahma only the attribute of creation, to Vishnu the preservation of the world. Later they adopted also Çiva, the Destroyer. Thus the Brahman trinity (Brahma, Vishnu and Çiva) was completed. The fuller development of this Hindu trinity-doctrine belongs to a period later than the Epic poems, that is, later than the second century of our era.[2]

Sanchoniathon gives us a specimen very much resembling the trinity in Genesis x.

"There were born to Saturn (Noah) in Peraea, three sons, Kronos of the same name with his father, Zeus-Belus and Apollōn."—Sanchon. Book I. vi.

Shem (the Sun), Iaphet (Phut, Aphthas, Pthah, Iapetos the Greek Titan, Zeus-Bel) and Cham (Apollo Chomaeus, Baal fervoris, Phut, Puthios, the Hot Deity), in the Bible, are only another version of the Phœnician fable in Sanchoniathon.[3]

Among the immediate offspring of these gods several names of deities are at once recognized. Madai and Iavan (Evan) are names of Bacchus, Tubal is the Egyptian Tob a

---

[1] Champollion, Egypte, Univ. pitt. 142. [2] Duncker, ii. 215.
[3] See Movers, 265, 360, et passim.

name of El, Adoni, Iah, &c.[1]   Among the sons of Cham,
Misraim, Phut (Ptah) and Canaan are gods of the Phœnicians and Egyptians, and the kingdoms Babel, Arach
and Accad are named with names of the Sun.   Elam,
Shem, Lud, Aram, Uz, Hul, Abar or Eber, Assur, Obal,
Ophir and Iobab are all deity-names.   Uzal is Asal or Sol
the Sun.   The principles which lie at the foundation of the
tenth chapter of Genesis are *the naming of countries after
the gods of the nations* and the assumption that the gods
had been men !

[1] Gen. x. 2.

CHAPTER X.

THE GARDEN.

A bower like the garden of youth, a bed of roses bathed in the waters of
life!   A Persian Fable.

> Est ager, indigenae Tamaseum nomine dicunt
> . . . . . medio nitet arbor in arvo.—Ovid, Met. x.

There was God and Matter, Light and Darkness, Good and Evil, in all things
opposed to one another from the Beginning.—Mani, on the Mysteries.

Two females attend the Hindu god Varuna in Hades.[1]
Osiris appears in the under-world attended by two females
Isis and Nephthys. Isis is his goddess corresponding to
Ceres. Nephthys would seem to be the Infernal Isis the
wife of Typhon the ruler in hell. Osiris had his evil side
which is Typhon, the Pluto of the infernal regions.[2] Ceres
and Proserpine would correspond to the two goddesses of
Varuna and Osiris. Osiris is Dionysus and Pluto.[3] To
Ptah also and to Athom the office of presiding in Amenthe
was occasionally attributed.[4] Hel, the Sun, becomes Hell,
Pluto. Ausel the Sun, Sel, Sol, becomes Sheol (Hades).
Iarbas (Apollo), Baal-Iarob, Arab, gives the names Ereb-us
to hell, Orpheus to Pluto (?) and Rephaim to the manes.
Iacchos, Aiakos, Aguieus (Iauk, Ukko) is Eacus in hell.

> Aeacus is his father who laws to " the Silent" (shades) there
> Gives, where a heavy rock urges Sisyphus Aeolides!
> The Supreme acknowledges Aeacus, and Jupiter
> Confesses that the offspring is his own.—Ovid, Met. xiii.

[1] Zeitschr. der D. M. G. ix. 243.   [2] Kenrick, i. 356, 343.
[3] Kenrick, i. 334, 340.   [4] Ibid. 340.

Amanus, the Sun, is Minos (Manu) a judge in Hades.
Mentu is the Sun, Mantus and Rh*ad-am*anthus forms of
Pluto.[1] Xamolxis the sun-god, the Deity of the Getae, was
also god of the dead. At the five-year festivals a man was
offered to him in sacrifice.[2] Herodotus says the only deity
of the Massagetae was the Sun, to whom they offered horses
as did the Persians and Hindus.[3] Varuna the Hindu Saturn is the yellow old man in hell. He sits on a throne on
all four sides of which passages open to the hells. In Egypt
Osiris judges the dead in the under-world. Atus or Attes,
Tius, Deus, Ad, is Dis (Pluto). Adonis is Aidoneus (Hades).
Baladan, Belitan (Baal) is Plutōn. In Hindustan, Yama
the sun-god, "son of the Sun" and brother of Manu, is
Ruler of the dead.[4] The Mexican Sun (Tonatiuh) conducted to heaven the souls of those who died in war.[5] Mercury, the Arcadian sun-god, conducted to the shades the
souls of suitors. Summanus (Esmun the starry Heaven) is
both Jupiter and Pluto.[6] Nebo is Mercury (Sol); Anubis
is the nether Mercury.[7]

According to the Egyptian doctrine, the Sun at the fifth
hour visited the Elysian fields.[8] Horus and Thoth (sun-gods)
weigh the souls in hell. Phre-Atmou is the *Celestial* Sun
(like Tammuz). Atmou (Adam) weighs the souls in the
under-world before their transmigration takes place.[9]

For Iahoh weighs the spirits !—Proverbs, xvi. 2.

Mine is the government, men and women of Egypt! Mine, the Most Holy,
Author of the services before the Most Holy in the temples of both Egypts

---

[1] Arad-Amantus, Erd-Amantus.   [2] Mill, Hist. British India, i. 211;
Herodot. chap. iv. § xciv.; Beloe, vol. ii. p. 393.   [3] Kuhn, Zeitschr. for
1853, p. 183; Beloe's Herodot. i. 183.   [4] Kuhn, Zeitschr. iv. 101, 123.

[5] Lord Kingsborough, vi. 205; Mexique, 25.   [6] Gerhard, Gotth. der
Etrusker, Trans. Berlin Akad.; Eschenburg, Manual, 416.

[7] Anob is the Sun. Anub-is was by some thought to be Saturn.—Plutarch,
de Iside, xliv. He is a god of the souls in Hades. Compare Anob, 1 Chron.
iv. 8, Noph, a land, and "Nob the city of the priests" of Neb, Anubis.—
1 Sam. xxii. 19.

[8] Champollion, Egypte, 131.   [9] Ibid.

(upper and lower), the Measurer and the Weigher of sins; the Most Holy who condemns the sinners, who has made the magnificence of the Sun, the prince of the earth! Mine, the Judge and Weigher of evil deeds, the Most Holy, the Condemner of the wicked, the Creator of the germs that grow on the surface of the earth.—Book of the Dead.[1]

Plato taught that the soul of man is derived by emanation from God through the intervention of the Soul of the World which was itself debased by some material admixture.[2] A philosophical myth in Plato says that the gods formed man and other animals of clay and fire WITHIN THE EARTH and then committed to Prometheus and his brother the task of distributing powers and qualities to them.[3]

The Word of Iahoh who forms the spirit of Adam (man) in the midst of him!—Zachariah, xii. 1.

And Alahim (the gods) said, Let us make Adam (man) in our image.

Gen. i. 26.

All the trees of Adan (Adn, Adonis) in the garden of the Alahim (gods) envied him!—Ezekiel, xxxi. 9.

Burning incense to Bal and departing after other Alahim (gods).

Jeremiah, vii. 9.

Therefore Alohim created HAdam (the man) in his own image in the likeness of Elohim (the gods) he created him, MALE AND FEMALE he created THEM.

Gen. i. 27.

In the second chapter of Genesis a different account is given; for Iahoh Elohim (Alhim) creates Eve from the rib of Adam.

And Iahoh Elohim made HAdam (the man) of the dust of the ground and breathed into his nostrils the Breath of lives: and HAdam was made into a living soul.

Male and female created he THEM and blessed THEM and CALLED THEIR NAME ADAM.—Gen. v. 2.

Adam is the Sun (the Ancestor of men) the Soul of the world, the Life and Breath of all. All souls emanate from their Father the Sun. " The same ' Spirit' which is in the sun rests also in the heart."[4] Bacchus is the Sun (Baga)

---

[1] Seyffarth, Theol. Schr. 5.   [2] Anthon, Class. Dict. Plato.

[3] Anthon, Class. Dict. Prometheus.   [4] Wuttke, ii. 312.

boki is "man," in Egyptian.[1]   Adam is the German words
Odem and Athem meaning "breath;" Adam is the Hindu
Atman, the Sun as the Soul of the universe, the "Charming
Atumnios" (Dominus) of Nonnus.   Adam therefore means
the Breath of Life (Prana) and those in whom is the Breath
of Life, mankind; or, it may be used for Bacchus himself
euhemerized into a man.   Adam means Life, that Life
which is in the *blood* of the sun-born race.

For the Life of the flesh is in the blood.—Levit. xvii. 11.

Adam means blood in Chaldee.[2]   Vitality was supposed
to be in the breath, the Spirit and the blood.[3]   Philo says
Adam is "the mind," and he translates the name of the city
On (Ani the Sun) "the mind."[4]   He quotes Genesis, ix. 4,
"You shall not eat the flesh in the blood of the soul."[5]

But the flesh thereof with the life thereof (which is) the blood thereof,
shall ye not eat.

Your blood of your lives will I require.—Gen. ix. 4, 5.

The VOICE OF THE BLOOD of thy brother calls to me.—Gen. iv. 10.

Philo says: The faculty which is common to us with the
irrational animals has blood for its essence.   And it, having
flowed from the Fountain of the Reason, is Spirit. . . And
the soul of man he (Moses) names the Spirit.[6]   But the
Spirit of God is spoken of in one manner as being Air
(Breath) flowing upon the earth.[7]   In real truth the Breath
is the essence of the soul, but it has not any place of itself
independently of the blood, but it resembles and is combined with blood.[8]

Only be sure that thou eat not the blood: for the blood is the life; and
thou mayest not eat the life with the flesh.—Deut. xii. 23.

---

[1] Seyffarth, Grammar Aegypt. App. p. 75.

[2] Schindler's Penteglott, Art. Adam.   [3] Philo, Quod Deterius, xxii.

[4] Philo, Who is Heir, xi.; De Somniis, xiv.   [5] Philo, Fragm. ed. Yonge,
vol. iv. p. 268.   See Lucretius de Rerum Nat. iii. 43, 35, 36.

[6] Philo, The Worse, &c. xxii.   [7] Philo, On Giants, § v.

[8] Ibid. Fragm. Yonge, iv. 269; Psalm xxx. 9.

Only thou shalt not eat the blood thereof: thou shalt pour it on the ground as water.—Deut. xv. 23.

And the blood of thy sacrifices shall be poured out upon the altar of Iahoh thy Alohi.—Deut. xii. 27.

To the God of Life the Central American races offered the heart of human victims as the symbol of life : the Hebrews and Egyptians offered the blood. The ancients considered the heart the seat of life.[1] Bel orders one of the gods to cut off his own head to make men of the blood.[2]

He called the whole race " Man." And the SOUL of man he names the " spirit," meaning by the term " Man" not the compound being (body and soul), as I said before, but *that godlike creation by which we reason.*—Philo Judaeus.[3]

The Mind which is in us, and let it be called Adam, meeting with the outward sense according to which all living creatures *appear* to exist (and that is called Eve), having conceived a desire for connection is associated with this outward sense.—Philo, Cain and his Birth, xvii.

But Man made according to the image of God was an "idea," or a genus, or a seal *perceptible only by the intellect,* incorporeal, neither male nor female, imperishable by nature.—Philo, On the Creation, xlvi.

The Intelligence, Father of all, who is the Life and the Light, has procreated man like to itself, and received him as his son ; for he was beautiful and the portrait of his Father. God, pleased in his own image, conceded to man the power of using his work. But man, having seen in his Father the Creator of all things, wished also to create : and he precipitated himself from the contemplation of his Father into the sphere of generation. . . . man was then a superior harmony, and for *having wished to penetrate it* he is fallen into slavery.[4]

> The showers perish when Father Aether them
> Precipitated into the bosom of Mother Terra.
> But shining fruits arise. . . . Lucretius, i. 251, ff.

[1] K. O. Müller, Hist. Greek Lit. 237 ; Mexique, plate 12.
[2] Munter, Bab. 41, 42. [3] On the Creation of the World, xxiv. ; The Worse against the Better, xxiii. [4] Pimander Dialogue, Champollion, Egypte, 142.

We all spring from a celestial seed
To all he is the same Father from whom when bountiful
   Mother Terra
Receives the liquid drops of the vapors,
Conceiving, she bears shining fruits and pleasant trees
And the human race and bears all breeds of animals. . .
Wherefore deservedly she has obtained the name MOTHER.
                          Lucretius, ii. 990, ff.

Athamas, Adam, was the husband of Ino (the Moon), the Anna Perenna who is Ceres and Luna.[1]

And Hadam had called the name of his wife Hoh because she was about to be mother of every living (Hi, Hai).—Gen. iii. 20.

AHOH is Bacchus, "HOH" is Eve; or "Huas" (Hoas) is Bacchus and Hoah is Eve or Ceres. The Septuagint calls Eve Eua and Zōē (Life); the Sibylline Books call her Eua. EUAS is the name of Bacchus.[2] Bacchus and Ceres are Heaven and Earth. When united into one Being, Kosmos, they form the hermaphrodite Adam of the Kabbalists.[3] In Egypt, Athom, Atumn, Atmn, Tmo, Tmu, is the sun-deity. Adamus is Thamus (Amon) and Thammuz, the Hebrew name of Adonis in the Mysteries.[4] Damia is Isis. As, the Sun, and HES (Isis), Aos, Euas (Bacchus) and Eua (Ceres), Evius (Dionysus) and Eva (Demeter), Gauas (Adonis)[5] and Gaia (Earth), are the Adam and Eve euhemerized into mortals who dwelt in Edem or Eden; they are the Adonis-Osiris-Kronos and Venus of the sacred Mysteries. The Homeric Hymn calls Earth "Mother of all" and Aeschylus calls Venus "Original Mother of our race." "Armaiti, the spirit of the earth, the Earth-goddess, is the daughter of Ahura-mazda, called Çpenta (holy), *Dâmis* (*creative*)."[6]

Four Oannes (or Suns) appeared in four different periods according to the Babylonian belief.[7] The Mexicans believ-

---

[1] Ovid, Fasti, iii. 656, ff.   [2] Movers, 548, ff.   [3] Ibid. 544.
[4] Ezekiel, viii. 14.   [5] Movers, 199.   [6] Haug, in der Zeitschr. der D. M. G. viii. 770.   [7] J. Müller, 515; Creuzer, Symb. ii. 68, ff.

ed that there had been four ages, those of Earth, Fire, Wind and Water, and that they lived in the age of the fifth Sun.[1] The Hindus and Persians have four ages, the Tibetans and Hesiod five. The Orphic theologists hesitate between four and six world-ages. The Greeks, Romans and others believed that the world had passed through three periods, the Golden, Silver, Brazen, and was then in the Iron age. It was a continual fall of man from Paradise to a state of human suffering. The Hindus at first held three periods, the first that of Perfection, the second the Waning, the third Darkness. The first period is usually divided into two, the first of which is an ideal state; so that there are four Yuga. The last, the Kaliyuga, began 3102 before Christ.[2] Among the Egyptians the ages vanish alternately, by floods and fire; among the Hindus, by floods alone. According to the Orphic philosophers, Heraclitus and the Stoics, this present age or world will be destroyed by fire.[3] In the Golden age Saturn ruled.

Primus Assuriorum regnavit Saturnus quem Assurii Deum nominavere Saturnum.—Servius ad Aeneid, i. 642; Movers, 185.

The Garden of Eden was a most ancient idea common to the Persians and Arabs. The Arab tribe Ad deduced their origin from Ad[4] the son of Aus, or Uz,[5] the son of Aram, the son of Shem, the son of Noah. Ad had two sons Sheddad and Sheddid. Sheddid dying first, his brother became sole monarch, and having built a sumptuous palace made a delightful garden in the deserts of Aden[6] in imitation of the Celestial Paradise.[7] This Aden is Eden; the Hebrew A standing for both a and e.[8] The Eden story in the Bible is probably another form of the Arabian legend and the Persian story of Jima's Paradise in the golden age of man-

---

[1] J. Müller, 512.   [2] Wuttke, ii. 416.   [3] J. Müller, 511.
[4] The Sun, At, Attys.   [5] "As." All these are names of the Sun or Saturn.
[6] Adan is the Assyrian sun-god.   [7] Universal Hist. xviii. 370.
[8] Rödiger's Gesenius, Gram. 31, 37, 38.

kind. Philo asks, "What is the river which proceeded out of Adin" and " Why in Adin or Eden is God said to have planted the paradise towards the East." [1]

And God planted a paradise in Edem.—Septuagint.

And a River issues from Edem to irrigate the garden.—Gen. ii.

In Egypt we find the Celestial City of God, Tantatho [2] a City of the Skies. It is not unlikely that the idea of Saturn's palace in heaven was connected with some notions of the Celestial Paradise which served the Hebrew priest and poet as a basis for the conception of an aboriginal earthly Garden of God. In Persia we find Garon-mâna the dwelling of Ahura-mazda, the seven archangels and the other pure ones. [3]

We find among the Persians the story of Jima's Paradise. Jima is an old name of the sun-god and Saturn. Saturn's was the Golden Age of mankind. So was the Persian Jima's. There was during his reign neither cold nor extreme heat nor old age nor death nor envy produced through the evil spirits. Food was abundant and the streams did not dry up ... And Jima the famed in Airiana Vaedja held a meeting of the best men ; to this the Creator Ahura-mazda came attended by the Celestials most worthy of devotion and said to Jima : Thou shalt protect creatures with life from the evils of winter, &c. Therefore make a garden with four corners for a dwelling to men and women the greatest, best and most beautiful on earth, for cows provided with milk ; there bring the seeds of all kinds of cattle the greatest, best and finest on earth, let the birds dwell there, collect there the waters to the greatness of a hathra (10,000 paces), there bring the seeds of all sorts of trees the most beautiful and fragrant upon earth, there bring the seeds of all viands which are the sweetest and most fragrant on this earth. Do all this *by pairs* and so that they will not come to an end.

[1] Philo, Quaest. et Solut. 7, 12.   [2] Seyffarth, Theolog. Schr. p. 4.
[3] Vendidad, xix. 121.

And Jima made the garden and erected dwellings therein, stories, halls, courts and enclosures, and brought there
the germs of the finest, largest and best men and women,
and the seeds of all kinds of cattle and the seeds of all trees
and viands: there was neither altercation nor displeasure,
hostility or enmity, no beggar and no complaint, no poverty
and no sickness, no form great beyond measure, no mon-
strous teeth and no other evil of the fiend (Ahriman) in the
body of man in the gold-colored everlasting spot where
food is inexhaustible. These men led the finest life in the
garden that Jima had made, they held a year but as a day,
and every forty years from every pair was a pair produced
a male and a female child; the same happened of every
kind of animals. After Vivanghvat, Athwja was the
second of mortals who pressed out the sap of the Soma
plant and brought it an offering to the gods. Therefore a
son Thraetona was born to him, the offspring of a noble
race in the district Varena. The Evil one had created the
Serpent Dahak the destroyer with three heads, three mouths,
six eyes and a thousand powers, a horrible Demon to annihilate the purity in the existing world, a sinful being to
lay waste the world.[1]

Indra's heaven contains his palaces of gold ornamented
with precious stones; it is embellished with fresh fountains,
grottoes, gardens always in flowers, perfumed by the ex-
halations of a CELESTIAL TREE that grows in the centre and
fills the whole with its aromatic odors.[2]

Men gathered acorns fallen from the wide-spreading TREE OF JOVE.
Ovid, Bohn i. p. 10 ; See Rinck, i. 326.

The TREE OF THE LIVES (HaHiim, or HaChiim), in the midst of the garden.
Gen. ii. 9.

And he went to the harmonious nymphs and the Hesperian retreat, in
order to pluck with his hand the golden fruit from the apple-bearing boughs,
having slain the swarthy-backed Dragon, who, wreathing his vast orbs around
[the tree] kept guard.—Euripides, Hercules Furens, 395.

---

[1] Duncker, ii. 302; see Weber, Ind. Stud. iii. 438.   [2] Iude, 196.

Jupiter disguised as a dragon obtains the favors of Proserpine.[1]

The garden of the Hesperides was the garden of the gods. Hercules killed the DRAGON which guarded it and plucked the fruit; but Minerva carries it back again.[2]

And Ceto, mingling in love with Phorcys, brought forth as youngest-born a terrible Serpent, which in hiding-places of dark earth *guards all golden apples.*
Hesiod, Theog. 333.

The DRAGON whom CHTHONIOS ECHĪŌN (Iachin, Kin, Iekun, Chiōn, Chiun) begat . . . as a bloody GIANT hostile to the gods!—Euripides, Bacchae, 540.

He who lies in dread Tartarus, the foe of the gods, Typhōs the hundred-headed.—Pindar, Pyth. i.

And before the throne was as it were a SEA of glass like crystal.
Rev. iv. 6.

And he showed me a RIVER OF WATER OF LIFE brilliant as crystal, proceeding out from the throne of THE GOD and the LAMB!

In the midst of its expanse and on either side of the river, the TREE OF LIFE making twelve fruits, in each month giving out its fruit, and the leaves of the tree for the healing of the nations!

And night shall not be, and no need of a candle and light of the sun, for God, the KURIOS, gives light upon them.—Rev. xxii. 1, 2, 5.

The Assyrians and Persians had their sacred tree Gaokerena which grew in the sea Var-kash the gathering of the waters.[3] Ahura-mazda drove forth the purified water with wind and clouds, in order to let it descend in rain a second time.[4]

Purified flow the Waters out from the Sea Puitka to the Sea Vouru-kasha; off to the tree Huapa. There grow my trees, all, of all kinds.[5]

Then I brought forth, I who am Ahura-mazda, the healing trees—
Many hundreds, many thousands, many ten thousands,
Round about the one Gaokerena.[6]

This tree was considered by the Persians to have the power to render those immortal who ate its fruits.[7]

When I created this abode, the beautiful, shining, worthy to be looked

[1] Nonnus, v. 566, 569.　　[2] Movers, 443, quotes Apollodorus, ii. 5, 11.　　[3] Spiegel, Vend. p. 256.　　[4] Duncker, ii. 372.　　[5] Zendavesta, Spiegel's Vendidad, p. 107, 108.　　[6] Vend. Farg. xx. 15, 16, 17.　　[7] Knobel's Gen. 25.

upon (saying) I will go out, I will depart; then the Serpent Agra-mainyus who is full of death created diseases.[1]

Now the Serpent was more subtil than any beast of the field which Ihoh Elohim had made: and he said unto the woman, Yea? Hath Elohim said ye shall not eat of every tree of the garden?

And the Serpent said unto the woman, Ye shall not surely die.

For Elohim knows that in the day ye eat thereof your eyes shall be opened and ye shall be as gods knowing good and evil.[2]

And Ihoh Elohim said: Behold the Man is become as one of us, to know good and evil.

Philo asks: Whence was it that the Serpent found the plural word " gods"?[3]

In that hour Samael (the Devil, Typhon) descended from heaven riding on this Serpent.—Targum to Genesis, iii. 6.[4]

The Egyptians said that, in the contest between Horus the Good Divinity and Typhon, a serpent pursued Thueris (Terra?) when she goes over to the side of Horus.[5] Mars has his Serpent. Mars is here Typhon, or an evil Demon.[6] Ovid says Dione (Terra, Venus) fled from Typhon to the Euphrates.[7]

> Terribilem quondam fugiens Typhona Dione,
>   Tunc quum pro coelo Jupiter arma tulit,
> Venit ad Euphratem comitata Cupidine parvo,
>   Inque Palaestinae margine sedit aquae.
>   . . . Succurrite, Nymphae,
> Et Dis auxilium ferte duobus, ait.—Ovid. Fast. ii.

And to the Woman were given the two wings of The Eagle The Great (Eagle) that she might fly into the Desert to the place of her, where she is nourished there for a Kairon and Kairons and half a Kairon from the face of the Serpent!

And the Serpent cast out of his mouth water like a river after the Woman, that he might cause her to be carried away by the stream.

And the earth helped the Woman!—Rev. xii. 14, 15, 16.

---

[1] Vend. Farg. xxii. 24.   [2] Cahen's Hebrew Bible; Septuagint, ed. Tischendorff. This is the reading of the Septuagint Version of the Scriptures over two hundred years before Philo existed.   [3] Philo, Quaest. et Solut. 36.

[4] Ascensio Isaiae, ed. Ric. Laurence; Movers, 371.   [5] Plutarch, de Is. xix.

[6] Nonnus, ed. Marcellus, pp. 41, 42; Movers, 370, 393, 232, 365, 367.

[7] Fast. ii. 451; Williams, 264.

The story of the tree of the knowledge of good and evil is of the same nature as the story of the apple of discord which Paris assigned to Venus, thus bringing upon himself the unrelenting hatred of Juno and Minerva. The account of the Fall of Man is an attempt to account for the origin of evil. Homer says Two Jars lie at the threshold of Zeus, one containing good the other evil gifts.[1] He also represents Zeus weighing the fates of the Trojans and Greeks in his balance.

For Zeus himself appoints the happiness and the unhappiness of all below.

Homer had also the philosophy of Light and Darkness in his mind, because he makes Zeus reluctant to invade the realm of Dread Night. In the Hindu myth of Indra slaying the Dragon, the clouds are conceived of as a covering in which a hostile demon, Vritra "the Enveloper," extends himself over the face of the sky, hiding the sun, threatening to blot out the light, and withholding from the earth the heavenly waters. Indra engages in fierce combat with him, and pierces him with his thunderbolt, the waters are released and fall in abundant showers upon the earth, and the sun and the clear sky are again restored to view. Or, again, the demons have stolen the reservoirs of water represented under the figure of herds of kine and hidden them away in the hollows of the mountains. Indra finds them, splits the caverns with his bolt and they are set again at liberty.[2]

Dualism of the Deity dates back to a time when the Old Bel was not yet changed into a Bel the Younger (Belus Minor).[3] The Phœnician gods Belus and Canaan[4] are Cain and Abel. We have here the conflict of the Good and Evil Deities or Principles. These are the Two Sides of Hercules. The Deity is conceived of as two separate Beings always in contention like Ormuzd and Ahriman. The Hostile Brothers Adrastus and Agathon were Lydian,

[1] Iliad, xxiv. 527–532.   [2] Prof. Whitney, Journal Am. Oriental Soc. iii. 320.
[3] Movers, 414.   [4] See above, p. 181.

Phrygian and Phœnician gods.[1] Chiun and Moloch, Hyp-suranius and Usō are the two Hostile Brothers. Mars kills Adonis, Pygmalion kills Elion and Sichaeus (Asac).[2] Adras-tus kills Atys in hunting. Osiris and Typhon, like Sol and Apopis in Egypt, are Brothers in continual hostility, and the Devil kills the Good Divinity. Typhon boxes up Osi-ris and sets him adrift on the Nile. Typhon is represented by a hippopotamus on the top of which a Hawk (Horus) contended with a Serpent. On the monuments Horus is represented piercing the Serpent Apop who is connected with the Giant Apophis, said to have made war on Jupiter.[3] The swine was an emblem of Typhon in Egypt.[4] The Apa-latchis in Florida had an Evil Spirit Cupai who rules in the world below.[5] The Peruvian Cupay was the child of cold death and the gloomy under-world.[6] The Dacotah Indians sacrificed more frequently to the Bad Spirit than to the Great Spirit. The Floridians did the same because the last did not trouble himself about them, while they were very much afraid of the Bad Spirit who troubled them greatly, re-quired to be appéased with festivals and human sacrifices and made cuts in their flesh. In Virginia the Bad Spirit was exclusively worshipped for the same reasons.[7]

The Phœnicians and Hebrews had Two Pillars the em-bodiment of these two hostile gods.[8] The Hebrews called them Iachin and Boz (Cain and the sun-god Abas, Busi). Cain is *in Hebrew* KIN. The Highest Demon in the Book of Henoch is named Iekun (Chon).[9] "Iachin the pillar that stood in the temple at Jerusalem is in name, Phœni-cian origin and symbolic meaning, the same as Chijun" (Saturn).[10] It was the usual opinion of the ancients, which came chiefly from Egypt, that the God of the Jews was Saturn ; and, since this last was from his bad point of view regarded as Typhon in Egypt, the idea became general

[1] Movers, 16.   [2] Ibid. 398, 393.   [3] Kenrick, i. 353.
[4] Movers, 204, 376, et passim.   [5] J. Müller, 140.   [6] Ibid. 320.   [7] Ibid. 151.
[8] Movers, 394.   [9] Ibid. 293.   [10] Ibid. 295.

among the Egyptians that the Jews worshipped the evil-demon Saturnus-Typhon.[1] The Egyptians considered the God of the Israelites to be Typhon-Saturnus, the Bad Principle that continually governs the Sun.[2] Typhon was represented with the head of an ass in Egypt. The golden head of an ass worshipped in the holy of holies was borrowed from an Egyptian Typhoeum.[3] The Egyptians held that Apopis, Brother of the Sun, made war against Jupiter.[4] Saturn as president over all hurtful and destructive powers of Nature was especially represented under the form of Typhon, who, as the Hostile Principle (the Enemy or Fiend) opposed the beneficial and wholesome workings of the Sun and Moon. His name is found in Homer (Tuphōeus) as that of a powerful giant.[5] The Egyptians worshipped Saturn under the symbol of a pillar.[6] Josephus says Moses erected pillars under which was the image of a boat on which the shadow of the top of the columns fell, to indicate that he who is in the Aether always accompanies the Sun on his course.[7] The Egyptians adored Typhon with the usages of the Moloch-worship.[8] The Israelites in Egypt worshipped El-Saturnus as Moloch, who in his Bad Side is Typhon.[9] Pimander says: I am myself the INTELLIGENCE for good men, pure, pious, holy; my presence aids them, and immediately they know all, and the Father is propitious and full of pity for them. On the contrary I remove myself from the ignorant, the wicked, the envious, the homicides and the impious; I deliver them to the Devil, the Avenger who loves the culpable and punishes them with fire.[10]

Twelve goats for the sin of all Israel!—1 Esdras, vii. 8.

Bel Minor is Baal-Saturnus the Good and Baal-Moloch

---

[1] Movers, 297, quotes Seyffarth, System astronom. Aegypt. 124.
[2] Movers, 298, 294.   [3] Ibid. 297.   [4] Plutarch, de Iside, xxxvi.
[5] Uhlemann, Thoth, 50.   [6] Movers, 298.   [7] Ibid. 296.
[8] Movers, 365, 367, 368–371.   [9] Ibid. 369; 368–370.
[10] Champ. Egypte, p. 142.

the Evil Principle. The Egyptians made Nephthys (the Infernal Isis) the wife of both Osiris and Typhon in hell.[1] Zeus-Bel is Aiōn, Demiurg; the Good and Bad Principle, and the Mediator.[2] Azazel and Typhon are Mars-Moloch. The fiend Emathion corresponds to the Arabian Lycurgus or Mars-Dionysus, the Antaeus-Typhon who dwells at one time in the Arabian desert, at another, in the Libyan.[3] Babys-Typhon, the brother of Osiris-Adonis, is Typhon the Devil.[4] Azazel is the head of all the bad demons of the Hebrews and dwells in the desert like the Egyptian Typhon.[5] Azazel is Moloch and Samael.[6]

The Two Sides of Hercules.

Saturn against Moloch
Tabal-IAH against Tobal-KIN.
Iaho versus Iachin (Ihoikin, Jehoiachin).
Iah versus Con, Acan, Agni (Coniah).[7]

EL versus ASAS-EL.

He shall put on the holy linen coat and he shall have the linen breeches upon his flesh, and shall be girded with a linen girdle, and with a linen mitre shall he be attired: these are the garments of holiness. He shall also wash his flesh with water when he puts them on.

Then from the congregation of the Children of Israel he shall take two kids of goats for a sin-offering, and one ram for a burnt-offering: . . .

And Aharon shall cast lots upon the *two goats*, one lot for IHOH and one lot for AZAZEL.[8]

And Aharon shall bring the goat on which ascends the lot for Ihoh and shall make him a sacrifice for sin.

But the goat on which the lot ascends for Azazel shall stand alive before Ihoh for an expiation upon him: to send him to Azazel into the desert (where Typhon, Satan, was supposed generally to be found). . . .

He shall go out to the altar which is before Ihoh and make an atonement for it; so as to take of the blood of the bullock and of the blood of the goat and put it upon the horns of the altar round about.

And let him sprinkle upon it with blood with his finger seven times; and let him purify it and sanctify it from the impurities of the sons of Israel. . . .

---

[1] Champ. Egypte, p. 129, *a*; Kenrick, i. 343, 356; De Iside, xliv. xii.
[2] Movers, 391. [3] Ibid. 232. [4] Compare 233. [5] Friedlander, p. 122.
[6] Movers, 397. [7] IekunIAH, Jeconiah. [8] Aziz in the Zendavesta is a devil.

And Aharon shall lay both his hands upon the head of the live goat and shall confess upon it all the iniquities of the sons of Israel and all their prevarications in respect to all their sins: yea he shall *put them upon the head of the goat* and shall send him into the desert by the hand of a man appointed (for the purpose).—Leviticus, xvi. 4, 5, 7, 8, 9, 10, 18, 19, 21.

Plutarch says that the Egyptians, in a drought accompanied by pestilence and other misfortunes, drove some of the holy animals quietly and secretly forth and sought to frighten them away by threatenings. This purification offering was made to the Demon in the Arabian desert by the Phœnicians, in the Libyan (desert) by the Aegyptians.[1]

The notion of a hostile pair is continued in the Bible. Israel (Saturn) contends with Elohim and conquers. Israel and Uso (Aso, Esau) are opposed. Esau is Samael which is the name of Azazel and Satan; he not unfrequently obtains the epithet Mars, "wild boar," Old Serpent Satan.[2] Samael is Satan and probably the Angel of Death.[3] Abel (Bel) is killed by Kin (Iachin, Agni, Chon, Moloch). So Siva strikes off the head of Brahma.[4] Baal is both sun-god and Malachbel (Baal-Moloch).[5] So the Hebrews have their Malak Ihoh, the Angel of the Lord, who wrestles with Jacob.[6] Both Sides (of Hercules) were regarded as Two Beings united into one personality and adored together as Moloch and Chiun. In Tyre they were Usō and Hypsuranius or Baal-Moloch and Baal-Chiun who constitute the dualistic conception of the Tyrian Hercules.[7] Movers says that the Two Pillars in the temples were the emblems of these two hostile sides or Brothers, and that they were regarded as the Greatest Gods of the Phœnicians.[8]

He formed Two PILLARS of brass: eighteen cubits the altitude of each pillar; and a web of twelve cubits surrounded either of the two columns...

And he set up the PILLARS before the portico of the temple: he erected the RIGHT PILLAR and called its name IACHIN; and he erected the LEFT PILLAR and called its name BUZ (Abas, Iehus, Bus).—1 Kings, vii. 15, 21.

And the Pillars of brass that were in the house of Ihoh, and the bases and

---

[1] Movers, 369.   [2] Ibid. 397.   [3] Munk, Palestine, 522.   [4] Movers, 398.
[5] Ibid. 400, 180.   [6] Ibid. 390; 2 Sam. xxiv. 16.   [7] Movers, 393.   [8] Ibid. 394.

brazen sea that was in the house of Ihoh the Chaldees broke in pieces; and carried the brass of them to Babylon (Babel).

Two Pillars, one sea and bases which Salamah made for the house of Ihoh.

Eighteen cubits was the height of one Pillar and the capital upon it of brass, and the height of the capital three cubits, moreover the brass net-work and pomegranates round about upon the capital, all brass. And just like these were on the other Pillar over the net-work.—2 Kings, xxv. 13–17.

The sun-pillars at On are mentioned. The Phœnicians called the Hercules Pillars Usō and Hypsuranius and celebrated great festivals in honor of these pillar-gods. They were also called Haman and Amon,[1] the Fire (Destroying) and the Spirit.[2] They were the Darkness and the Light. The shadow that fell from the top of the sun-pillar upon the Sun's boat and always accompanies the Sun upon its annual course is Typhon.[3] Sol becomes Typhon.[4] Hercules, the manifestation of the Highest God, is regarded as a dualism consisting of the destroying Moloch, Hhamman or Mars, and the beneficent Chon, Chiun, Saturn.[5]

The Hebrews adored the Good and Evil Principles. Paul opposes Christ to Belial,[6] just as Horus is opposed to Typhon in Egypt. The Babylonian Bel was Mithra in the Assyrian period. The two elements Good and Evil constitute the essence of the Chaldean Mithra. Ahriman was adored in the shape of reptiles by the Seventy Elders.[7]

When I entered and saw, lo every form of reptile and beast, abomination; and all the idols of the house of Israel; depicted on the wall round about!

And seventy men of the Elders of the house of Israel (and Iazan-Iaho son of Saphan standing in the middle of them) standing before them; and to (each) man his censer in his hand and an abundance of a cloud of perfume ascending.

Ezekiel, viii. 10, 11.

Afterwards he showed me Iahosha the GREAT PRIEST standing before the ANGEL of Ihoh and the SATAN standing at his right hand to oppose him!

Zachariah, iii.[8]

Michael, the Archangel, when contending with the Devil disputed about the body of Moses.—Jude, 9.

---

[1] Movers, 294, 295.   [2] Sanchoniathon; in Movers, 344.   [3] Ibid. 298.

[4] Ibid. 300.   [5] Ibid. 395.   [6] 2 Cor. vi. 15.   [7] Movers, 390, et passim.

[8] Undecaying Nasatyas, you bore away by night in your foe-overwhelming car Jāhusha.—Wilson, Rig Veda Sanh. i. 312.

Job makes Satan one of the sons of Elohim. Chom is Satan, Apollo Chomaeus and "Baal of the heat."[1] He is Camus or Chemosh (Ariel) the idol of the Moabites.

Zarathustra gave leaders to the good and bad spirits.[2] His system is an irreconcilable dualism like that of the ancient Hebrews. Sam at the bidding of the Highest God goes forth against Dahak (the Enemy).[3] The Persians call the Good Principle of God Yezad (Asad) or Yezdan (Iasdan, a name of Ormuzd); the Evil Demon they call Ahariman or Ahriman.[4] Rimmon (Ar-Amon) was a Syrian god.[5] Hadad-Rimmon is Adonis, the late Autumnal-Sun,[6] and was probably the same god whom the Persians turned into Ahriman the Prince of devils. Winter was the work of Typhon, as much as the hot destructive summer-rays of the sun.[7] Iahi the Persian devil, the Hindu Ahi, is perhaps the Hebrew Iah (as Moloch). Bel "the Prince of devils" was the Phœnician and Hebrew sun-god and the Babylonian chief divinity. Iasdan the Good God Ormuzd is the name Satan, Shitan (Asatan), a name of Ahriman. Asas (Iasus, Asios, Zeus, Iesous, Iesus) is the name of the Sun; Asis is Mars (the hot fiend) in Edessa and Aziz a devil in Persia.[8] Ramas is the Phœnician chief god; Baal-Ram is the terrible Deity appeased with the offerings of children by way of atonement.[9]

Yea they sacrificed their sons and their daughters to demons (SDIM, Sadim).

And poured out innocent blood, blood of their sons and their daughters whom they sacrificed to the idols of Canaan.—Psalm, cvi. 38, 39.

They sacrifice to shedim (demons), not Alah (God): to Alahim (gods) they did not know; to new, they came from the neighborhood, your fathers did not fear them.—Deut. xxxii. 17.

We have Bharata, Berith, the Deity, and Vritra the Devil;

[1] Movers, 291. [2] Duncker, ii. 323. [3] Spiegel, Zeitschr. der D. M. G. iii. 247.
[4] Universal Hist. vol. xviii. 388; Duncker, ii. 310. [5] 2 Kings, v. 18.
[6] Movers, 206, 197. [7] Ibid. passim. [8] Spiegel, Vendidad, 231, note.
[9] Movers, 132, 396.

Bedan, PADAN (Aram, Put) the Sun, and Puthōn the Serpent (Abadon). Baal-Berith is the Good God; Baal-Zebob is the Evil One.[1] Apollo slaying the Serpent Pytho is only a mythical statement that Good overcomes Evil. Apollo destroys Put or Phut (Ptah) anciently the Sun and Fire-god, afterwards the Destroying Sun; the sun-serpent then becomes the emblem of Evil. Originally the serpent was the emblem of the sun-deity Saturn; now like Saturn himself, he is the Author of Evil.

I saw the Satan as LIGHTNING from heaven falling.—Luke, x. 18.

And the GREAT DRAGON was cast out, THE SERPENT OF OLD, called DIABOL and the Satanas.—Rev. xii. 9.

And he (the angel) seized the DRAGON the SERPENT OF OLD who is Devil (Dabal, Tabalcan) and Satanas,[2] and bound him for a thousand years . . . and after that, he must be loosed a little while.—Revelations, xx. 2, 3.

Samiel is Satan and the name of the Sirocco;[3] the Sirocco is also called ATABUL-us (Diabol-os).

The mountains which ATABULUS PARCHES!—Horace, Sat. i. 5, 78.

Atabal, Tobal, Dabal-cain, Diable-Cain, is the god Vulcan the father of Cacus (the Devil, Typhon).[4] Vulcan (Thubalcain) is Moloc-Abar (?) or MulciBER,[5] the Fire-god Moloch.

Proxima Vulcani lux est; Tubilustria dicunt:
Lustrantur purae, quas facit ille, tubae.—Ovid, Fasti, v.

As the sun rose from the waves of the sea in the morning, it was natural to give him the appendage of a fish's tail. The deities of Asia Minor were represented with fish-tails[4] like Odacon, Dagon, Oannes, Vishnu; those of Phœnicia

[1] Bebōn, Smu, Abaddon, Apolluōn.—Revelations, ix. 11; Plutarch de Iside, lxii. Semo (Smu) is Hercules. Asmo-deus (Sem-odeus) is an Evil Spirit.—Tobit, iii. 8.

[2] Compare the name SATNIOS.—Iliad, xiv. 443.   [3] Movers, 224, 397.

[4] Ovid, Fasti, i. 454, 473. Compare Atabal, king of the Sidonians:—1 Kings, xvi. 31; King Tab-Rimmon.—Ibid. xv. 18; Tubal the name of a land. —Ezekiel, xxxii. 26; Ithobal-us (compare Tobal, Devil, Bel-zebub), priest of Astarte.—Whiston's Josephus, iv. 377.   [5] Pur "fire."

Yucatan and Mexico with the tails of serpents. The serpent was the symbol of the sun-gods. Ra, Ar, or Erra, Iar, Horus was in Egypt represented with the serpent (Uraeus) and the sun's disk.[1] Eros (Ar) was represented as the beginning of life, with a serpent on his head.[2] The asp was likened to the Sun because it does not grow old and moves rapidly without the aid of limbs."[3] "Taaut first attributed something of the divine nature to the serpent and the serpent tribe; in which he was followed by the Phœnicians and Egyptians. For this animal was esteemed by him to be the most inspirited of all the reptiles, and of a fiery nature (καὶ πυρῶδες ὑπ' αὐτοῦ); inasmuch as it exhibits an incredible celerity, moving by its spirit without either hands or feet or any of those external members by which other animals effect their motion."[4] Moses made a Brazen Serpent for the Hebrews which was worshipped until the days of Hezekiah.[5]

And Moses made a Serpent of Brass and put it upon a pole, and it came to pass that if a serpent had bitten any man, when he beheld the Serpent of Brass he lived.—Numb. xxi. 9.

This is the Good Divinity the sun-god, not the Devil. To the Serpent the beauty and harmony of the universe is ascribed. Ophion is the Daimōn (Dominus) that by his Wisdom assisted the Creator Saturn.[6]

Iahoh by Wisdom has founded the heavens.

The Hawk-headed Serpent was the Egyptian emblem of the Divine Mind.[7] The Devil is called Kadmon, which is the name of the Beneficent Deity, Ophion-Kadmus the Wisdom of God.[8] Hermes (Aram, Remus, Haram, Harameias) is Kadmus the Divine Wisdom. Baal-Ram is the Devil. Asasiel, Asasyal, the Angel, and Asasel the Devil, Atus

---

[1] Kenrick, i. 328.   [2] Rinck, i. 62.   [3] Kenrick, ii. 17.
[4] Sanchoniathon, in Euseb. Praep. Evang. Lib. i.; Cory, p. 19.
[6] 2 Kings, xviii. 4.   [8] Movers, 109.   [7] Deane, Serpent-worship, 145.
[5] Movers, 517, 213.

(Adas, Deus) and Dis (Pluto), Iacchos and Eacus, Adonis and Aidoneus (Hades), Iabe and Ob (the Serpent-god), Indra and Andra (the Dev), afford instances of the same principle.

Bel contains in himself the full idea of the Deity in the Nature-religions of antiquity. He is not merely the Creative but the Preserving or Sustaining, and the Destroying Principle. As Saturn, he is the Principle of order and harmony in the universe, and as Mars, he is the wild destroying Fire, the Cause of all disorder and confusion and contention in the world.[1] The elements of this dualism are seen in the Jewish idolatry. The Evil or Darkness is adored, as personified in Ahriman, by the Seventy Elders who pray in the gloomy chambers of the temple before all sorts of reptiles : while the Light, the Good Principle Ormuzd, is worshipped by the twenty-four priests with the High Priest at their head, with their faces turned towards the Sun, and holding the HOLY BRANCH to the nose.[2] This Bel of the Chaldean Magi, so often interchanged with the Persian Mithra, usually called Jupiter-Bel (Zeus-Belus) and previously shown to be Mithra, is the representative of the Chaldean Triad consisting of the Old Bel (Zervana akerana), Ormuzd and Ahriman. As Manifestation of Zervana or the Old Bel, he is called, like him, "Father"; in the grottoes of Mithra he appears as Aion, and, like the ancient Bel, is the Creator. Then he represents the Good and Hostile Principles, Ormuzd the Being of Light (Gabriel ?) and Ahriman the god of Darkness, and Plutarch describes him as the Mediator between the Good and Evil sides of the Dualism, drawing a parallel between him and those Planets which the Chaldeans believe are between the good and the hostile, and partake the nature sometimes of the former, sometimes of the latter.[3]

---

[1] Movers, 184, 185.   [2] Ibid. 390 ; Ezekiel, viii. 8–12, 16, 17.
[3] Movers, 391.

Zoroaster taught that from the Beginning the Principles of things were Two ; one the Father, the other the Mother: the former is Light the latter Darkness.[1]   The Chaldean Zaratas taught Pythagoras that there were Two Original Causes of all things, called the Father and the Mother. The Father is Light, the Mother Darkness.[2]

I form the Light and create Darkness . . . I Ihoh do all these things !
                                                           Isaiah, xlv. 7.
The Light shone in Darkness and the Darkness comprehended it not !
                                                           John, i. 5.

Nearly four centuries before Christ Plato taught that there was in Matter a blind refractory force which resists the will of the Supreme Artificer.[3]

For the Flesh lusts against the Spirit !
It is the Spirit that quickens, the Flesh profits nothing !
                                                           John, vi. 63.

Hermogenes in the second century considered Matter co-eternal with God and the First Cause of all evil.[4]

There is one event to the righteous and to the wicked—all things come alike to all !—Ecclesiastes, ix. 2.

Munter, Bab. p. 46.   [2] Movers, 265 ; Origenis, Philosophumena, p. 38.
[3] Anthon.   [4] Jean Yanoski, Afrique Chretienne, p. 4.

CHAPTER XI.

POLYTHEISM.

Never, O Destinies, never may ye behold me approaching as a partner the couch of Jupiter: nor may I be brought to the arms of any bridegroom from among the Sons of Heaven.   Aeschylus, Prometheus, 896, 897.

Neither did the Sons of the Titans smite him nor high GIANTS set upon him!   Ioudith, xvi. 6, 7.

PHILO's Sanchoniathon says: "The mortals becoming proud and insolent married the daughters of Kronos and Taut."[1] Homer says the Titans are the "Sons of Heaven."[2] They are the deities under the earth whom Zeus cast with their leader Saturn (Lucifer) into hell.[3]

The furthest limits of land and ocean where Iapetos and Kronos sitting are delighted not with the splendor of Huperion Eeli nor with the winds, but profound Tartarus is around!—Iliad, viii. 479–481.

Titan gods . . . the earth-born Titans . . . sent beneath the broad-wayed earth . . . in a dark, drear place, the extremities of vast Earth . . . And there are the sources and boundaries of dusky Earth, of murky Tartarus, of barren Pontos and starry Heaven, all in their order: . . . and the dread abodes of gloomy Night stand shrouded in dark clouds. In front of these the son of Iapetus stands and holds broad heaven with his head and unwearied hands unmovedly, where NIGHT and DAY also drawing nigh are wont to salute each other as they cross the vast brazen threshold. The one is about to go down within whilst the other comes forth abroad, nor ever does the abode constrain both within; but constantly one at any rate being outside the dwelling wanders over the earth, while the other again being within the abode awaits the season of her journey until it come!—Hesiod, Theog. 735–758 ; Banks.

[1] Book 2, § viii.   [2] Iliad, v. 898.   [3] Ibid. xiv. 203, 274, 279. Christ preached to the SPIRITS IN CUSTODY, DISOBEDIENT IN THE DAYS OF NŌE!— 1 Peter, iii. 18–20.

The ANGELS who kept not their first estate, but left their own habitation, he hath kept in everlasting chains under darkness.—Jude, 6.

I keep for Neptune the bonds of Iapetus (Phut).—Nonnus, ii. 295.

The Old Kronos found an excellent auxiliary O Tuphoe (Typhon, Tophet, Devil)!—Nonnus, ii. 565.

Homer calls the Giants Otus and Ephialtēs who contended against Jupiter " Sons of El (Aloe)." [1]

There were the GIANTS famous from the Beginning, that were of great stature and expert in war!—Baruch, iii. 26.

And they were destroyed by not having wisdom.—Baruch, iii. 28.

On what principle it was that " Giants" were born of Angels and women. Sometimes Moses styles the Angels " Sons of God."

Philo, Quaest. et Solut. 92.

And the fourth is like a son of the gods.—Daniel, iii. 25.

You will see one according law and assertion in all the earth, that there is One God, the king and father of all things, and many gods, Sons of God, ruling together with him.—Maximus Tyrius (A. D. 150).[2]

And it came to pass when mankind (HAdam) began to multiply on the face of the earth and daughters were born to them,

That the Sons of the gods (HAlahim) saw the daughters of men, that they were beautiful ; and took to themselves wives of all which they chose.

The Nephilim (Giants) were on earth in those days ; and also after that the sons of *H*Alhim (the gods) came in to the daughters of *H*Adam (men), these (women) bore (children) to them.

These are those Valiant (the Gibborim) who once were men of renown !

Gen. vi. 1, 2, 4.

It is evident from the following quotation from the Book of Enoch that the SONS OF HELOHIM were the Angels of the stars, the SONS OF EL.

It happened after the sons of men had multiplied in those days, that daughters were born to them, elegant and beautiful.

And when the angels, the Sons of heaven, beheld them, they became enamored of them, saying to each other : Come let us select for ourselves wives from the progeny of men, and let us beget children . . .

Then they swore all together, and all bound themselves by mutual execrations. Their whole number was two hundred, who descended on

---

[1] Iliad, v. 386.   [2] Preface to Taylor's Proclus.

Ardis, which is the top of Mount Armon ... These are the names of their chiefs: Samyaza, who was their leader, Urakabarameel, Akibeel, Tamiel, Ramuel, Danel, Azkeel, Sarakuyal, Asael, Armers, Batraal, Anane, Zavebe, Samsaveel, Ertael, Turel, Yomyael, Arazyal. These were the prefects of the two hundred angels, and the remainder were all with them. Then they took wives, each choosing for himself; whom they began to approach, and with whom they cohabited; teaching them sorcery, incantations, and the dividing of roots and trees.

And the women conceiving brought forth Giants;

Whose stature was each three hundred cubits..... Moreover Azazyel taught men to make swords, knives, shields, breastplates, the fabrication of mirrors, and the workmanship of bracelets and ornaments, the use of paint, the beautifying of the eyebrows, the use of stones of every valuable and select kind, and of all sorts of dyes, so that the world became altered.

Impiety increased; fornication multiplied; and they transgressed and corrupted all their ways.

Amazarak taught all the sorcerers and dividers of roots;

Armers taught the solution of sorcery;

Barkayal taught the observers of the stars;

Akibeel taught signs;

Tamiel taught astronomy;

And Asaradel taught the motion of the moon.

And men being destroyed, cried out; and their voice reached to heaven.

Then Michael and Gabriel, Raphael, Suryal and Uriel looked down from heaven, and saw the quantity of blood which was shed on earth, and all the iniquity which was done upon it and said one to another; It is the voice of their cries;

The Earth deprived of her children has cried even to the gate of heaven.

And now to you, O ye Holy Ones of heaven, the souls of men complain saying; Obtain justice for us with the Most High. Then they said to their Lord, the King; Lord of Lords, God of gods, King of kings,

... Thou hast seen what Azazyel has done, how he has taught every species of iniquity upon earth and has disclosed to the world all the secret things which are done in the heavens.

Samyaza also has taught sorcery, to whom thou hast given authority over those who are associated with him. They have gone together to the daughters of men; have lain with them; have become polluted;

And have discovered crimes to them.

The women likewise have brought forth Giants....

Then the Most High, the Great and Holy One, spoke;

And sent Arsayalyur to the son of Lamech,

Saying; Say to him in my name; Conceal thyself.

Then explain to him the consummation which is about to take place; for all the earth shall perish; the waters of a Deluge shall come over the whole earth and all things which are in it shall be destroyed.

Again the Lord said to Raphael: Bind Azazyel hand and foot; cast him into darkness; and opening the desert which is in Dudael, cast him in there.—Book of Henoch, by Archbishop Lawrence, p. 208.[1]

When therefore Ihoh saw that the wickedness of HAdam (the ADAM) was multiplied on earth and moreover that every imagination of the cogitations of his heart was only evil every day, ...

Ihoh said: I will destroy HAdam (the "man," mankind), whom I have created, from the face of the earth.—Gen. vi. 5, 7.

God spared not the ANGELS THAT SINNED, but in bonds of darkness casting them down to hell ... spared not the old world but saved Noah, bringing the Flood upon the world of the ungodly.—2 Peter, ii. 45.

Then the Lord said to me: Enoch, scribe of righteousness, go tell the Watchers of heaven[2] who have deserted the lofty sky and their holy everlasting station, who have been polluted with women

And have done as the sons of men do, by taking to themselves wives, and have been greatly corrupted on the earth ....

But you from the beginning were made spiritual possessing a life which is eternal, and not subject to death forever.

Therefore I made not wives for you, because being spiritual, your dwelling is in heaven.

Now the Giants, who have been born of Spirit and of Flesh, shall be called upon earth Evil Spirits .... and the Spirits of the Wicked shall they be called!—Book of Henoch, pp. 5–24.

The Persians adored Ormuzd, the six Amshaspands and angels, the Hindus Brahma and the gods considered as angels[3] emanating from the One Essence, the Hebrews Iah, the archangels and the angels, the Babylonians Bel and the gods, the Chinese Shangti, the six Chief Spirits and other spirits, the Greeks Zeus and the gods.

[1] About 110 B. C. Kurtz, Die Ehen, 13; Dillmann.

[2] These are the names of the angels who watch: Uriel, Raphael, Raguel, Michael, Sarakiel and Gabriel; seven in number. A Watcher and a Holy one descending from heaven.—Dan. iv. 13 (10). Compare the seven Amshaspands and archangels.—Munter, Bab. 13. The Chaldeans believed in the gods of the planets.—Plut. de Iside, xlviii.; Movers, 162.   [3] Wuttke, ii. 292.

I perceive the throne of Zeus and all the holy glory of the gods!

Euripides, Kuklōps, 579, 580.

At last the gods or angels were held to be merely Powers of God. Minerva, Apollo, Vulkan, Mars, Mercury, Prometheus, Bacchus, Thoth, Taaut, Adam, are but Powers of God.[1]

And the Lord hastened from Mount Pharan with myriads of Holy Ones (Kadesh), on his right his angels were with him!—Deut. xxxiii. 2, Septuagint.

The Stars shined in their watches and rejoiced: when he calls them, they say, Here we are; and so with cheerfulness they showed light unto him that made them!—Baruch, iii. 34.

They deemed either fire or wind or the swift air, or the circle of the stars, or the violent water, or the LIGHTS OF HEAVEN to be the gods which govern the world!—Wisdom of Solomon, xiii. 2.

Among the EL-im (gods) there is none like unto thee, O Adoni!

Psalm, lxxxvi. 8.

Alahim (God) stands in the ASSEMBLY OF AL, in the midst of the gods (Alahim, Elohim) he shall judge!—Psalm, lxxxii.

For Ihoh is GREAT AL and a great king over all Alahim.—Psalm, xcv. 3.

Though there be that are called gods whether in heaven or in earth (as there are gods many and lords many): but to us there is One God, the Father; of whom are all things and we in him.—1 Corinth. viii. 5.

Paul, like Plato, considered the gods deiform processions from the One; distinct from and yet abiding in him.

God has exalted Christ far above every Beginning (soul, god) and Power, and Authority and Lordship.—Ephesians, i. 21.

In Ephesians vi. 12, Paul conjoins with Principalities and Powers "the World-rulers."[3]

Look ye upon Me, all men in the house of praise, and also on the multitude of POWERS, on the brilliant woof of heaven, on the carpet of honor, the abodes of the HOST OF POWERS.—Book of the Dead, chap. i. Seyffarth.

For the gods ought we to call Lords.—Euripides, Hyppolyt. 88.

The God of Angels, Powers and of every creature.

Polycarp's Prayer; Milman's Hist. Chr. 284.

According to the Chaldeans, the Aeons are gods . . . they are analogous to the "Ideas" of Plato which also are gods.[4]

[1] Compare Nonnus, x. 300, ff.; Proverbs, viii. [2] Preface to Taylor's Proclus, p. xxv. [3] Ibid. xxiii. [4] Preface to Taylor's Proclus.

Thee, Father of the Worlds, Father of the Aeons, Artificer of the gods it is holy to praise. Thee, O KING, the intellectual sing, Thee O Blessed God, the Cosmagi (Rulers of the World), those Fulgent Eyes, Starry Minds round which the illustrious body dances in chorus. All the race of the blessed sing thy praise, those that are about and those that are in the world, the Zonic gods, and the Azonic also, who govern parts of the world, wise Itinerants stationed about THE ILLUSTRIOUS PILOTS [of the universe.]—The Platonic Bishop Synesius.[1]

" Of all beings and of the *gods that produce beings* One exempt and imparticipable Cause pre-exists—a Cause ineffable . . . . and unknown by all knowledge and incomprehensible, unfolding all things into light from itself."[2] The Hindus said Mahan Atma (the Great Soul, Breath or Adam) had drawn the first man out of the waters.[3] The old story was that the Germans grew on trees, the Greeks sprung from the stones which Deucalion and Pyrrha threw behind them after the Deluge.[4]

For you are not born of the old-fabled oak nor of a stone !
Odyssey, xix. 163.

According to a myth of the Sioux, the first man stood many ages growing with his feet in the soil like a tree. Another tree grew near him. A snake gnawed them off at the root so that they could walk away as men.[5] The Indians considered men as formed out of the earth.[6] The Bible declares that man was made of the dust of the ground. The Peruvians called the body " animated earth."[7]

The American aborigines believed that the sun-god was assisted in the work of creation by other spirits or gods.[8] The Mingoes believed that animals (spirits) aided the Great Spirit, Michabu, in the creation of the earth.[9] Many Indian myths represent the Great Spirit as Creator, and at the head of the other gods. The Virginia tribes thought the Great Spirit first created other gods who assisted him

---

[1] The wisest and best of the ancient Christians.—Preface to Taylor's Proclus.
[2] Proclus; by Taylor.   [3] Weber, Ind. Stud. i. 321.
[4] Grimm, Deutsche Mythol. 538.   [5] J. Müller, 109.   [6] Ibid. 110.
[7] Perou, 868, b; Univers pitt.   [8] J. Müller, 107, 108.   [9] Ibid. 110.

in the Creation. These were especially animal gods who were of more assistance than the Manitus who looked on.[1] Compare Plato, Timaeus, 41, where the other gods are called upon to aid in creating animals.[2] In one of the Babylonian cosmogonies the other gods assist Bel in creating.[3] Among the Lenni-Lennape Indians, the idea existed that the Great Spirit swam on the surface of the waters, then he created the earth out of a grain of sand.[4]

And Alahim said: Let us make man in our image.—Gen. i. 26.

In the account of the building of Bel's tower in Babel (Babylon) Ihoh says: Come let us go down.[5] Philo the Alexandrian Jew states that God is surrounded by a number of "Powers" and that they made man.[6] In the ancient Persian Cosmogony, "the pure and holy spirits" have created the world.[7]

Most of the Egyptian gods are identified with the Sun.[8]

I am Alahi the Creator, God .... Therefore I will cut in pieces the garment of the crowd of the wicked, I whom no one is like not even the princes of the people; (of those) who vex me the Horus, who torment me the Phatha (Ptah), who hew asunder me the Thoth, who cut in pieces me the Tamo (Creator), who twine bonds for my feet, beat with their fists me who call: Fear ye! Fear ye! No one is like to me, not even the princes of the people.[9]

"Egypt believed in and worshipped but One God; and the great number of the divinities were but Manifestations of his unity."[10] In India, Agni is Sun, Indra, Varuna, Soma, &c.[11]

The Eternal Only God is Narayana. Narayana is Brahma, Çiva, Çakra, the twelve Aditya, the Vasu and the two Açvin .... Time ... Narayana is above and beneath, within and without, all that has been and will be!

Narayana-Upanishad.[12]

---

[1] J. Müller, 107, 108; Picard, 115.   [2] See above, p. 159, note.
[3] Munter, Bab. 41.   [4] J. Müller, 107.   [5] Gen. xi. 7.
[6] Philo, De Confus. Ling. xxxiii. xxxiv. Bohn.   [7] Duncker, ii. 390.
[8] Kenrick, i. 336.   [9] Seyffarth, in der Zeitschr. der D. M. G. for 1845, p. 93; Grammat. Aegypt. App. pp. 61, 62.   [10] Champollion Figeac, Egypte.
[11] Benfey, Samaveda, p. 266.   [12] Weber, Ind. Stud. i. 381.

Thou, Agni, art Indra, the Showerer on the good; thou art the adorable
Vishnu, the hymned of many:

Thou, Agni, art the royal Varuna, observant of holy vows: Mitra, the
Destroyer: thou art Aryaman the protector of the virtuous, whose (liberality)
is enjoyed by all .... thou art the divine Savitri the possessor of precious
things: protector of men, thou art Bhaga, and rulest over wealth .... leader
of a radiant host, thou art lord over all offerings: thou art the distributor of
tens, hundreds and thousands of good things.

Wilson, Rig Veda Sanh. ii. 210, 211.

The Assyrian priest bore the name of his god.[1] Nergal
Sarezer is the Assyrian God; Nergal Sarezer is the Assyrian chief of the Magi (Rab Mag). Perseus (the Sun) was
the name of the priest of Mithra and the Persian god. Sadak, Zadak, Suduk is the Highest Phœnician god; Zadok
was the name of a Hebrew priest.

From the extremity of the earth we have heard songs:
GLORY TO ZADIK!   Isaiah, xxiv. 16.

Malak, Moloch, has his prophet (priest) Malachi. Malchi-
Zedek was priest of Elion, the Most High God of the Phœ-
nicians and Hebrews. The Hebrew priest Eli bears the
name of his God Eli, El. El-Iaho or Elijah, the man of
God, has two names of the Hebrew God Eli and Iah. David's seer (priest) was called Gad from Achad the Sun.
Oded the name of a Hebrew priest is Adad the Sun. Eden
the Hebrew priest has the name of his god Adan the Sun.
Ezra the priest has the name of the Sun Asar, Azar. We
find Haman a name of Baal and Heman a Hebrew priest;
Merodach (Baal) and Mordecai; Amos the priest and
Amus the god, Amar the Sun and Immer the Hebrew
priest; Sebad-ios, a name of Bacchus, and Iozabad the
Hebrew priest (Zebedee). In the "Ascension of Isaiah,"
we find Amada the name of a Hebrew priest; Bacchus is
called Omadios and Muth (Amat, Hamath).[2] We find
Abar the Sun, Abaris a Greek priest; Koios the Titan,
Koias the Greek priest; Ag the Sun (Agù-ieus, Ukko, Iauk,
Apollo) and Aggeus the Hebrew priest; Ad the god (Ado-

---

[1] Movers, 70.   [2] Ibid. 372; The Ammidioi, 1 Esdras, v. 20.

nis), and Addo the priest, 1 Esdras, vi. 1; Mus, the god, and Moosi-as the priest, 1 Esdras, ix. 31; Adan the God, Dani-el his priest;

I will confess to thee Adani Alahi! Adani Al!—Ps. lxxxvi. 12, 15.

Mentu the Egyptian sun-god, Mantus a name of Pluto, Manetho, the Egyptian priest and historian; Chnuphis, the god Kneph, Chonuphis an Egyptian priest; Iaho, Iah, the Hebrew God; Ihoa, Iahoa, the Hebrew priest, "the prophet:"[1] the Egyptian god Seb (Saturn), the Phœnician god Sabos, the Arabian Sabi, names of Bacchus[2] and Eusebius the priest.

But you who desert IHOH, who forget Har-Kadesh, who lay out a table to GAD and who fill a libation to MANI.—Isaiah, lxv. 11.

Jehovah is the One God by many names, Salam,[3] Adoni, Alah, Alahah, Eloah, Elohi, Elohim, El, Eli, Eloi, Elon, Elion, Iah, Sabaôth, Aisi, Iabe (Eubios, Evius) Sadai, Baal, Ahoh, Ihoh, Ahiah, Aô, Iaô, Israel, Rabboni, &c.[4] Iao is the Hebrew God proclaimed by Moses![5]

My strength my song is IAH; he has been my safety.
This is my ELI . . . my father's ALAHI.
Extol him that rides upon the heavens by his name IAH.

Exod. xv. 2; Ps. lxviii. 4.

[1] 1 Kings, xvi. 12.   [2] Movers, 23.   [3] The Solumi, between Lukia and Kilikia (Cilicia), spoke Phœnician.—Movers, 15; Duncker, ii. 489.

And in his army went up a race wonderful to behold,
Uttering Phœnician words from their mouths.
It dwelt in the SOLUMian Mountains by a wide lake.
Wild as to their heads: shorn all round, but on top
They wore the smoke-dried skinned heads of horses.   Choerilus.

Josephus quotes this passage, and claims these mountaineers for his nation in the time of Xerxes, which is hardly probable, because these Solumi lived on the Taurus range in Asia Minor, and the Jews dwelt in Palestine. Their name was that of their God Salom, which is found also on the Hebrew altar inscribed IHOH-SALOM, Judges, vi. 24, and in the name of their city Salem, the island SALAM-is, and the city Salamis in Cyprus opposite the Phœnician coast.—Odyssey, v. 283; Iliad, vi. 184; Herodot. i. 173.

[4] Gesen. Thes.; Hosea, ii. 16; Samaritan Pentateuch, Gen. i. 1.

[5] Movers, 552.

He that sends forth LIGHT and it goes ; calls it again and it obeys with fear !—Baruch, iii. 33.

I am Iahoh the Alahim, beside me is no Alahim !—Isaiah, xlv. 5.

He is the One Existence, simple abstract existence as in India.

I AM that I AM.   Ahiah asur ahiah !

Aнɪᴀн (Aнᴀн, Iᴀнoн) has sent me !—Exod. iii. 14.

From the time of Homer down, we find Zeus constantly mentioned apart from the other gods : so also with his epithet " Father." [1]

The Great Leader in heaven, Zeus driving a winged chariot, arranging in order and caring for all things. And the army of the gods and daemons marshalled in twelve parts follows him, but Hestia alone remains in the house of the gods.—Plato, Phaedr. ii. p. 344.[2]

O Zeus, what daring pride of mortals can hold back thy power, which neither sleep making all weak ever seizes, nor the unwearied Months of the gods.—Sophocles, Antig. ed. Boeckh, 585.

Woe, Woe, 'tis by the Will of Zeus, Cause of all, Doer of all: for what is accomplished among mortals without Zeus ! What of these things is not Divinely accomplished !—Aeschylus. Agam. 1456–'9.

When Homer wrote :

The Will of Zeus was being accomplished,

He acknowledged the One God as much as the Hebrew who said,

Hear, O Israel; Iahoh, our God Iahoh, Oɴᴇ.—Deut. iv. 6.

But perhaps there is some man by the banks of the Nile possessing the name of Zeus: for in heaven there is but One !

Euripides, Helen. 491.

There is a mighty Zeus in heaven who overlooks and sways all things.

Sophocles, Elektra, 174, 175.

O Zeus, Zeus, that crownest all, bring my prayers to pass.

Aeschylus, Agamemnon, 973.

And may Zeus render the earth fruitful at all seasons : and may the herds that feed before [the city] . . . bear young abundantly !

Aeschylus, Suppliants, 685, 689.

[1] Buckley, Aeschylus, p. 4, note ; Euripides, ii. p. 44.

[2] Bohn ; see Macrob. Sat. p. 319.

King of Kings, most blest of the Blessed, and most perfect might of the perfect, Blessed Zeus, be persuaded and may it come to pass.

Aeschylus, Suppl. 528.

Whatever is fated that will take place! the great, immense MIND of Zeus is not to be transgressed.

How can I behold the Divine MIND, a fathomless view!

Aeschylus, Suppl. 1046, 1054.

To be free from evil thoughts is God's (Theou) best gift.

Aeschylus, Agam. 928.

But I call upon the KING of heaven Hallowed Zeus.

Euripides, Iphig. in Tauris, 749.

And I invoke Zeus the Lord of oaths.[1]—Sophocles, Philoctetes, 1324.

O Thou that dost inhabit the shining clouds of heaven, O Zeus, preserve us!—Euripides, Phoenissae, 84, 85.

Osiris is the Weaver of threads, who moves the shuttle from morning unto evening to prepare a covering for your body.[2]

I slaughter the holy offering of the lamb for thee at Tan-tatho, who burn it in my flames.

I am the Weaver of the garments, also the Inventor of the loom, the Contriver of the woof.

There is One who has kindled the stars, who has woven the path of the chaff of the stars (the Milky Way) for the Servants the statues in the house of the Most High: who has lighted the stars for you; who has woven for you the path of the chaff of the stars, the Most Holy One your Governor: He, praised by my voice in the house of the Most Holy, exalted by the song of praise, celebrated by the song of the choir, Most Sacred, Just . . .[3]

Glory upon thy face, Weaver of the plenitude of the lands of earth, O Most Holy! Lord of all that breathes! Beautifier of the world! Let me praise the Architect, the Author of the fulness of the Worlds; who, at his time, let all things upon the earth and beyond this world exist, constructed them for me.

Hymns and songs of praise to the Architect, who made them for me, for the home of man the image of the Former of men; to Him who once created the girdle of delight, the course of the two stars for all years (sun and moon).[4]

Consideration of the Tamo (Creator) of the grain-kernels for man, of the stalks for clothes, the God who has spread out the circle of the earth.

---

[1] Movers, 171; Exodus, xvii. 16; Hosea, ii. 16.   [2] Uhlemann, Thoth: quotes Turin. Hymnol. vi. 3.   [3] Seyffarth, Theol. Schr. der alten Aegypter, pp. 10, 9, 8, 7.   [4] Ibid. Book of the Dead, chap. 1.

Thus says Os-har-ham N. N. the Just:

It is I who let the corn grow for the servant, splendid wheat flour for the laborer of the vale at the hour of his life, also garments for the naked, raiment for the uncovered, mantles for the denuded.

Book of the Dead, Seyffarth, Theolog. Schr. p. 34.

O Good Divinity, Lord of Abydos,
Thou givest fruit-bearing trees of all kinds,
The splendor of the clouds of heaven
And the light of sight
To those who pray to
Thee and the leaders of the star-house.
Devote to me, my God, a place of rest.

Uhlemann, Todtengericht, 13.

Let me enter into thy people to all times !

Seyffarth, Theolog. Schr. p. 30.

Osiris, the Good Divinity, the Lord of life, the Great Mighty God, King to eternity, Creator of the plenitude of the lands and of heaven, Weaver of the rich girdle of the lands, the Great God, Lord of the lovely city Abydos, Ruler of his slaves to all times !

Uhlemann, Todtengericht, 15.

I sing the works of Neb (the Lord) delighting my heart as long as I walk in the house of Neb (the Lord).[1]

His is the End as his is the Beginning !!![2]

In one of the oldest Persian hymns that have come down to us is the following :

Who made the course of the Sun and the Stars ?
Who gives increase to the Moon and lets her vanish?
Who holds the earth and the clouds above it ?
Who the waters on the fields and the trees ?
Who lent swiftness to the winds and streams ?
Who made good lights and the darkness ?
Who made the good warmth and the frost?
Who made the morning-red, the evening and the night?
Who made Armaiti (Earth) the wide, the rich in fields ?
Who holds up the son to the father when he departs
If not Thou Ahura-mazda ! Thou thyself the
Purity ! Praised high above all Thou All-Spirit,
Thou original fountain of all that live !

Jaçna, 44.[3]

---

[1] Nebo, "lord."
See Rev. xxii. 13.

[2] Book of the Dead, Seyffarth, Theolog. Schr. p. 15.

[3] Haug, Zeitschr. der D. M. G. vii. 328 ; Duncker, ii. 359.

In later invocations is found:

I praise Ahura-mazda the shining, the very good and very great, very perfect and very strong, very discerning and very beautiful, Who clothes himself in a star-embroidered robe in which no end is visible; Conspicuous in purity, Who has the good gnosis, Who is the fountain of well-being, Who has created us, Who has formed us, Who has nourished us, the most Perfect of intelligent beings! For the sake of the Holy Word we will to honor the Wisdom of Ahuramazda, for the Revelation of the Holy Word we honor the tongue of Ahuramazda.—Jesht Fravashi.[1]

I pray to Ahuramazda the abounding in light, to the Holy Immortals (the Amesha Çpenta), to the body of the Steer (Heaven, the Divine Male), to the Soul of the Steer.

I praise thee O Fire, son of Ahuramazda, the quickest of the sacred Immortals, I invoke the Fire of Ahuramazda with all fires!

I celebrate Mithra the elevated, immortal, pure, the Sun, the KING, the Potentate of the lands, the quick Steed, the Eye of Ahuramazda, who increasest the pairs of beeves ; and Ramakhathra.

I praise the holy Çraosha endowed with holiness, the victorious, who gives the world abundance, and Raçnu (the Spirit of Righteousness) the very just, and ARSTAT (the SPIRIT OF TRUTH)[2] who gives the world all blessings . . .

I praise the Fravashi, the heavenly Mount which preserves the WISDOM, the Navel of the waters: and all heights, effulgent with purity, which Ahuramazda has made, and the pure water and the trees which Ahuramazda has given . . .

I praise the Moon which preserves the Steer's keim . . . I praise the Months . . . I celebrate the Years and the Stars, the holy and heavenly creations, and the Uncreated Lights that have no beginning; and the resplendent, brilliant Tistar (Sirius).

I praise the holy word, the pure, the active, which is given against the Evil Spirits (Devs), given through Zarathustra's mediation; I praise all the Lords of Purity that Ahuramazda has revealed and Zarathustra published . . .—Zendavesta.[3]

---

[1] Duncker, ii. 359. [2] But when he comes, the SPIRIT OF TRUTH, he will guide you in all truth.—John, xvi. 13. [3] Duncker, ii. 357–359.

CHAPTER XII.

In living beings slumbers the Primal God under the name Purusha and
under the form of the living soul.

Bhagavat-Purana, vii. 14, 37, 38; 13, 4.

Est Deus in nobis: agitante calescimus illo;
IMPETUS HIC sacrae semina mentis habet.

Ovid, Fasti vi. 5, 6.

The heart is the seat of the Atman.

Chândogya-Upanishad.

THE further we go back in the history of mankind
whether in Italy, Greece, Africa, Barbarian Europe, Palestine, Asia Minor, the Caucasus, Margiana, Baktria, Scythia,
across Iran through Cashmere to the Indus, the tribal organization is the earliest found. Mankind were divided
anciently into tribes speaking different dialects or languages.[1] Niebuhr says : " The further we look back into
antiquity, the richer, *the more distinct and the more broadly marked* do we find the dialects of great languages. They
subsist one beside the other with the same character of
originality, and just as if they were different tongues. The
notion that there was a universal German, or a universal
Greek language in the beginning is purely ideal. It is only
when the dialects, after having been gradually impoverished
and enfeebled, become extinct, and when reading grows to
be general, that a common language arises."[2] These differences of language have been gradually lessened by the
fusion of tribes through conquest and the gradual accumu-

---

[1] Ranke, Hist. Popes, p. 11. Am. ed.　　[2] Niebuhr's Rome, Am. ed. i. p. 49.

lation of many tribes into a single nation. Such nations after becoming consolidated were in time perhaps combined into an empire or that fusion of states which Rome govern- ed in Italy. "This name was in the earliest times a national one *in the south;* and it was not extended to the more northerly regions until the Roman sway had united the peninsula into one state, and by colonization and the dif- fusion of the Latin language had moulded its inhabitants into a single nation." "No country that was divided amongst a variety of nations ... bore any general name in the early ages of antiquity until some one people became master of it. Had Asia Minor for instance continued a united state after Croesus subdued all the country to the west of the Halys (Alus),[1] the name of Ludia would pro- bably have come into use for the whole, as that of Asia did subsequently for the countries which made up the kingdom of Pergamus, and that of Asians for their inhabitants."[2] We read of petty kingdoms throughout Syria, Palestine, Arabia, Egypt, Persia, Cashmere and on the Indus. In Edom, when Iob-ab was dead, Husham of the land of the Temanites (Ataman) reigned ... and after him Hadad.[3] We find also the Nat-ophath-i, the Sucath-i, Ken-i, the children of Gad, the Robani, the Hagari, the Hadadites or Hittites, the Iabusi, the Amori, the Amalekites, the Ban- iami, the Akroni, the Asadothi, the Avi, the Asak-Aloni, the Gashuri, the Machati, the Anaki, and many kings;[4] the kings of Madon, Shimron, Achasaph, Gazar, Makadah, Iaracho, Dabar (Debir), Habron (Hebron) Iarmuth, Lachish, kings of the Amorites on the west side of the Jordan, kings of the Canaanites, the king of Iaroshalam, of Tappuah, Hor- amah, Arad, Libnah, Adullam, Bethel, Aphak, Dor, Tanach, Kadash, Iokaneam and very many other small principalities. Compare also the number of tribes and nations assembled to besiege Troy, according to Homer.

---

[1] Ilus, Aloh, Allah.   [2] Niebuhr's Rome, Am. ed. p. 30.
[3] 1 Chron. i. 45, 46.   [4] Joshua, xi. xii. xiii.; 1 Chron. ii. iii.

21

Larger states were formed out of the smaller ones and finally the Babylonian, Persian and Greek world-monarchies
arose causing a more general prevalence of one language
within the empire.

A fusion of peoples to some extent must have taken
place in the countries about the Caucasus and north of it
from the Black Sea to the Caspian. The Median, Assyrian,
Sclavonian, Goth and the Pelasgic-Greek dwelt near together, based as to language upon a primitive element, the
earliest grammatical forms, having the same general philosophy of the structure of language. Similar ideas and
mutual intercourse must have taken place from Austria to
Baktria. We know that recruits for the Persian armies
were drawn from their northern neighbors, and intercourse
must have existed long previously. As semi-civilized
nations they grew up together with many resemblances between them. Then came the gradual descent from Iran
and Baktria upon Cashmere, later upon the Indus, at last
into the valley of the Ganges. Finally, many centuries
later, from the same hive north of the Euxine and the Caspian we find an emigration west, south-west and north-
west into France, Italy, Scandinavia and the British Islands.
From these causes and especially from mutual intercourse
between the nations the verbal resemblances have arisen
which are now traced from Ireland and England across
Europe, Sclavonia, Media and Persia to India. " In fact,
long before the time when our history happens to commence, the face of Europe had been changed by migrations
no way inferior in power, or as to the swarms that took part
in them, to those which gave rise to the later revolutions in
the destinies of mankind. Such a movement of countless
hosts, of which no recollection would have remained but
for an incidental mention of it by Herodotus, without any
indication of its date, was the expedition of the Illyrian
Enchéleans who seem to have penetrated into the heart of
Greece and even to have sacked Delphi. I conceive

that this must refer to a migration of the whole Illyrian people from remote northern regions : and I incline to think that the earlier Pelasgian population in Dalmatia which was overpowered by them, was not quite exterminated." " I have ascertained the existence of Pelasgian tribes, firmly settled as powerful respectable nations in a period for the most part prior to our historical knowledge of Greece. It is not a mere hypothesis, but with a full historical conviction, that I assert there was a time when the Pelasgians, then more widely spread than any other people in Europe, extended from the Po and the Arno almost to the Bosporus."[1]

Two languages may in some points be nearly akin, in others altogether alien. Such is the relation between the Sclavonic and the Lithuanian. In this manner the Persian is connected with the Sclavonic in many of its forms and roots. In Latin there are two elements mixed up together ; one of them connected with the Greek, the other entirely foreign to it.[2] The whole country between Media and the Danube was occupied by a series of cognate tribes. These Scuthians (Scythians) and the Medes were in continual contact and collision. The Pelasgians may be traced step by step to a primitive settlement in Media.[3] The Thracians, Getae, Scuthae and Sauromatae were so many links in a long chain connecting the Pelasgians with Media. The Sauromatae were at least in part allied to the Sclavonians ; and the Pelasgian was unquestionably most nearly allied to the Sclavonian.[4] Sclavonian is the point of transition from the Semitic to the Indo-germanic languages.[5] There are resemblances between Sclavonian, Semitic and Old Italian.[6] The Sclavic peoples have notoriously remained in connection with the Persa-Arians up to a tolerably late period.[7] "Indi, Persians, Greeks, Romans, Germans,

[1] Niebuhr's Rome, i. pp. 47, 48.   [2] Ibid. p. 49.
[3] Donaldson's Varronianus, p. 40.   [4] Ibid. p. 59. The Sclavonians originally dwelt in the north of Media, in the countries joining Assyria.—Ibid. 72, 74.
[5] Ibid. 72.   [6] Ibid. 75.   [7] Weber, Ind. Stud. i. 291, note.

Sclaves, all probably dwelt together in an earlier time."[1]
The Sclavonians came from the banks of the Borysthenes
into Dalmatia and later into Italy.[2]　They were the ancient
Sarmatians, a nation living on the Don and near the Caspian
Sea.[3]　Sanskrit is nearest to the Greek after the Old-Persian.
"Homeric-Greek, Old-Persian and the language of the
Hindu Vedas are alike in some points."[4]　In respect to language the Assyrians belonged to the Zend peoples, to the
Indogermanic family.[5]　The Sclavonians dwelt in the
northern part of Media joining Assyria.[6]　Strabo confines
the name Ariana to the races which inhabit the region extending from the Indus to the Medes and Persians, up to a
line which he draws from the Kaspian Gate to Kerman.[7]
The language of the Caucasian Hindus is only a dialect of
the language in which the Zendavesta and the inscriptions
of Cyrus, Darius and Xerxes are composed.[8]　As early
perhaps as four thousand years ago, a race uttering words
related to our own gradually descended from Ariana as the
conquerors of India.　They were a pastoral people bearing
the name which Herodotus gives to the Medes (Areioi),
Arya.　Their country was Airiana, Iran, Aria, called also
Aryavarta, Airyana Vaedjo, Eran Vej.

Some of the oldest deities of the Vedic peoples were
those of the Medo-Baktrians and Persians.　The color of
these tribes, who are first found on the Indus, was white.
They speak of the Arian color which distinguished them
from the aborigines who were black races.[9]　The Varani,
the Aparnoi in Baktria, the Parni in Margiana, the Pasianoi
and the Tambuzi in Baktria, are names of peoples which
connect India with the countries south and west of the Cau-

---

[1] Spiegel, Vendidad, p. 4.　　[2] Universal Hist. xix. 638.
[3] Bunsen, Phil. of Univ. Hist. ii. 8.　　[4] Haug, Zendstudien; D. M. G. vol. vii.
[5] Movers, 69; Munk, Palestine, 434.　[6] Donaldson's Varronianus, pp. 72, 74.
[7] Duncker, ii. 308.　　[8] Ibid. ii. 14, 308.　　[9] Ibid. ii. 245, 11, 12, 13, 14;
Roth Zur Lit. und Gesch. des Veda; Weber, Ind. Stud. i. 161, ff.; Allen's
India, 23, 24.

casus. Parthia is the country of the god Bharata, the
Abrat or Euphrates is his river.[1] The Varani must have
adored the burning god Varan or Varuna; the Aparnoi the
same god under the name ABARAN, Pharan or Baran, for
ancient nations and tribes usually bore deity-names. The
Pasianoi seem to have the name of the god Pushan in India,
Apasson in Babylon. The Arii adored the sun-god Ar;
the Asii worshipped As, the Sun; the Getae Achad, Choda,
God; the Gēlai served Agal the Sun; the Mēdoi, Amad;
the Zugoi Asak or Osogo; the Bati served Abot, Phut, or
Buddha the sun-god, the Soanes adored Sonne, Asan or San
the Sun; the Artaei Arad.[2] The Nisaei adored the Babylonian god Anos, Nuseus or Dionysus.

Like the Babylonian and Persian peoples the tribes on
the Indus had originally but three castes: the priests, warriors, and the third caste composed of agriculturists, traders,
artisans, &c. But from the conquered people of India a
fourth class was subsequently created called the Sudras,
who were the servile caste. "A Sudra is born to serve."
"The language of the Vedas is an older dialect, varying
very considerably, both in its grammatical and lexical character, from the classical Sanskrit. In many of the points
in which Vedic and Sanskrit disagree, the former strikingly
approaches its next neighbors to the westward, the language
of the Avesta, commonly called the Zend, and that of the
Persian inscriptions."[3] "It has long been looked upon as
settled beyond dispute that the present possessors of India
were not the earliest owners of the soil, but, at a time not
far beyond the reach of history, had made their way into
the peninsula from its north-western side, over the passes of
the Hindu-Koh, through the valley of the Kabul, across the
wastes of the Penjab. And the Vedas show them as still
only upon the threshold of their promised land, on the In-

[1] Aprathah, Gen. xxxv. 19.
and Median names, passim.
Am. Oriental Soc. iii. 296, 297.

[2] See Strabo, xi.; Universal Hist. Persian
[3] Prof. Wm. D. Whitney, in the Journ. of the

dus, namely, and the region on either side of it, covering the whole Penjab, extending across the little neck of territory, which, watered by the holy Sarasvati, connects the latter with the great basin of Central Hindustan, and touching the borders of this basin on the courses of the Yamuna and Ganges.''[1] The ring of the Magi is found in India; also the deities and the basis of the philosophy of the countries surrounding Babylon.

We find the following resemblances in name between Hindu gods and deities further west: Bhaga (Bog, Baga, Bacch-us), Aditya (Adad, Adat, Tat, Taaut, Tot, Thoth), Damunas (Dominus, Daimon), Atman (Temen, Atumn-ios, Autumn-us, Adam), Iama (Ioma, Iom, Am, Euim-os, Yima); Varun, Varuna (Avaran, 1 Maccabees, ii. 5, Paran, Perenn-a, Huperion, Hebron, Brenn-en " to burn"),[2] Bharata (the Shachamite god Berith,[3] the Macedonian god Perit-ius the name of a month-deity, Huper-BERET-aeus a Macedonian month-god, Ephrath, Gen. xxxv. 16, the River Euphrates or Frat), Pramati (Pharmuthi an Egyptian month-god; Prometheus),[4] Agni (Ignis in Latin, Akan, Kan, Chon, Kin, Iakin, Guni in Hebrew), Mithra (the Babylonian Bel-Mithra, the Persian Mithra), Pushan (Apasson), Ahû (Ehoh, Ehou, Ahoh, Iahoh), Ansa the Aditya (Anos, Nuseus), Brahma (Abram, Bromius),[5] Hari the Sun (Har, Horus in Egypt, ArIEl, Ar-es, Ar=Fire), Aryaman (Rimmon, Areimanios).

"Without thee Varuna I am not the lord of a moment." To Varuna men pray that their sins may be forgiven. He watches over what is morally right and repels and punishes the wrong. He knows all men's thoughts and deeds. Therefore the poets surround him with spies

---

[1] Prof. Wm. D. Whitney, in Journ. of the Am. Oriental Soc. iii. 311.

[2] Compare the sun-name of Brenn-us, the king ; Bariônâ.—Matthew, xvi. 17

[3] Judges, ix. 4, 46 ; EL-Berith and Baal-Berith.

[4] The months bore deity-names.—Kenrick, i. 277 ; Lepsius, Einleit, p. 144.

[5] Sanskrit scholars derive Brahma from Brih, the verb " to strain " in prayer.

like the Persian Mithra.[1] Varuna is the Sun.[2] Varuna in glittering glory sits throned afar in his hundred-gated palace. When the dawn appears he mounts with Mitra a golden chariot; at evening one of iron.

One of you is Lord and sacred ruler; and he who is called Mithra summons men to exertion.—Vasishtha.[3]

The sun is the eye of Varuna, the wind is his breath. The God of the highest heaven (Varuna) has shown to the sun, the sea and the stars their path and has ordered the seasons.[4]

The regal Varuna verily made wide the path of the Sun to travel on his daily course.—Wilson, Rigv. Sanhita, i. 62.

Thou Indra, art KING: they who are gods (are subject) to thee: therefore Scatterer (of foes), do thou protect and cherish us men: thou art the protector of the good, the possessor of wealth, the extricator of us (from sin): thou art true, the investor (of all with thy lustre), the giver of strength.—Wilson, ii. 166.

"The oldest system of philosophy confines itself closely to the explanation and commentating of the Veda, to the traditional side of the religion. Also the name Vedanta, End of the Veda, indicates that it is the conclusion and the sum of the commenting theology. After the explanations of Veda-passages follows the doctrine of the means of salvation, which are either outward, as the observance of the ceremonial, the laws of purification, the offering; or inward, as soothing and taming of the senses, listening to and understanding the revelation, recognition of Brahma."

"It is different with Speculative Inquiry which issued not from the traditional side of religion, but directly from the idea of God. It let alone all these endless torturings to deduce the God-conception from the Vedas and to place it in harmony with them, and attempted to deduce the existence and nature (Wesen) of Brahma from its own conception. Out of this *Conception* then must also the Creation of the world be explained and the existing reality be brought into agreement with it. For a sharper piercing reflection,

[1] Wuttke, ii. 263; Roth, Die Höchsten Götter der Arischen Völker.
[2] Wilson, Rigv. Sanh. ii. p. 8, § 8, *note.*
[3] Roth, Die Höchsten Götter der Arischen Völker.   [4] Duncker, ii. 62.

the difficulty in bringing together the Brahma-conception
and the material world lay in this, that Brahma, as World-
soul, was considered absolutely immaterial, not perceptible
by the senses, and Non-Matter; and yet the Matter, the
world of the senses, must stream out of him so that he must
be not only the intellectual but also the material Basis of the
world. To remove this dualism and contradiction, the
Hindu philosophy grasped a simple but confessedly very
bold means: it denied the entire sensible world; it sunk
the whole world in Brahma. This is the doctrine of the
system of the Mimansa (Inquiry). There is but One Existence; this is the Highest Soul (Paratma, the highest Breath)
as Manu's Laws already name Brahma. There is nothing
outside of this Highest Soul; what seems to exist outside of
it is only delusion. The Energy (çakti) of the Highest Soul
and its unfolding (prakriti) is the seed out of which the visible world proceeds. NATURE is nothing but a play of the
World-soul with appearance, it begins to shine and vanishes
again. Only the deception of the senses mirrors manifold
forms before man where but One inseparable Actuality exists. Like sparks out of the sputtering Fire, living beings
come forth from the World-soul and return to it again. The
conduct and action of the living beings is not caused by the
spark of Brahma indwelling in them (which is considered
altogether logically as simple and at rest), but through the
body and through the senses, which, themselves appearance and deceptive, take up into themselves and mirror
forth the deception of the Maja (the world of external
things). Through this appearance (Schein) is the soul of man
in darkness, that is, held in the belief that the external
world exists and that man is subjected to the passions of
grief and joy, and man acts determined through the appearance and the emotion which has proceeded from this. In
truth the human soul is an unsevered part of Brahma the
Highest Soul; only the deception of the senses lets the soul
believe that it exists by itself (für sich), that the perceptible

world exists, that there is a manifold world independently existing by itself. This deception must be removed by inquiry which lets us know that all that is, is the Highest Being, the World-soul himself: thereby vanishes the illusion of a many-formed world. The freedom of men from the senses, from the sensible world and the passion caused by it, is the perception that the sensible world has no existence, that the human soul is not severed from the Highest! Thus man finds the right way back from the sensible world and its independent existence to Brahma by earnest thought, which convinces him that his soul is of divine nature, an unsevered part of the Highest Soul, that all is the Highest Soul and that he is himself Brahma!" [1] The doctrine of the "two Mimansa" seems to have been brought into its present systematic form *later* than the Sankhya doctrine. This system seeks to show that the doctrine that Creation is a deception and the transcendent Brahman the only actual existence is the fundamental doctrine of the Vedas, since all the passages are brought into harmony with this monotheistic pantheism. [2]

I have beheld the Lord of Men with seven sons (the seven solar rays); of which delightful and benevolent (deity) who is the object of our invocations there is an all-pervading middle brother, [3] and a third brother, [4] well-fed with (oblations of) ghee.

They yoke the seven to the one-wheeled car: one horse NAMED SEVEN bears it along: the three-axled wheel [5] is undecaying, never loosened, and in it all these regions of the universe abide.

The Seven who preside over this seven-wheeled chariot (are) the seven horses; seven sisters ride in it together, and in it are deposited the seven forms of utterance.

Who has seen the Primeval (Being) at the time of his being born: what is *that endowed with substance* which the Unsubstantial sustains: from earth are the breath and blood, *but where is the soul*: who may repair to the sage to ask this?

. . . What is that One alone, who has upheld these six spheres in the form of the unborn?

Let him who knows this (truth) quickly declare it; the mysterious condi-

[1] Duncker, ii. 162, quotes Colebrooke, &c.   [2] Weber, Vorles. p. 217.
[3] Vayu, Air.   [4] Agni, Fire.   [5] Present, Past and Future.

tion of the beautiful ever-moving (Sun): the rays shed milk from his head, investing his form with radiance; they have drunk up the water by the paths (by which they were poured forth).[1]

The Mother (Earth) worships the Father (Sun) with holy rites, for the sake of water; but he has anticipated (her wants) in his mind: whereupon, desirous of progeny, she is penetrated by the dews of impregnation, and (all) expectant of abundance, exchange words (of congratulation) . . . .

The twelve-spoked wheel of the true (Sun) revolves round the heavens, and never (tends) to decay: seven hundred and twenty children in pairs (360 days and nights) Agni, abide in it . . . .

The even-felled undecaying wheel repeatedly revolves: ten united on the upper surface bear (the world): the orb of the Sun proceeds, *invested with water, and in it all beings are deposited.* . . . .

He who knows the Protector of this (world) as the inferior associated with the Superior and the Superior associated with the inferior, he is, as it were, a sage; but who in this world can expound: whence is the Divine Mind in its supremacy engendered? . . .

Two birds associated together[2] and mutual friends take refuge in the same tree: one of them eats the sweet fig; *the other*, abstaining from food, merely looks on.

Where the smooth gliding (rays) cognizant, distil the perpetual portion of ambrosial (water); there has the Lord and steadfast Protector of all beings consigned me, (though) immature (in wisdom).

In the tree[3] into which the smooth-gliding, feeders on the sweet, enter and again bring forth *light* over all, they have called the fruit sweet, but he partakes not of it who knows not the Protector (of the universe).

I ask thee (Institutor of the rite) what is the uttermost end of the earth: I ask thee where is the navel of the world: I ask thee what is the fecundating power of the rain-shedding steed: I ask thee what is the supreme heaven of (holy) speech.

This altar is the uttermost end of the earth: this sacrifice is the navel of the world: this Soma-juice is the fecundating power of the rain-shedding steed:[4] this Brahma is the supreme heaven of (holy) speech. . . .

---

[1] The sun drawing water. The rays give out and absorb water.

[2] The human soul and the Great Soul of the world.   [3] The sun.

[4] The swift horse (of the Sun) approaches the place of immolation, meditating with mind intent upon the gods; the goat bound to him is led before him; after him follow the priests and the singers.

They have seen thy doings, O God! the goings of my God my King in the sanctuary.

The singers went before, the players on the instruments after, among them were the damsels playing on the timbrels.—Ps. lxviii. 24, 25.

The Persians called the Sun "the Swift Horse," "the Eye of Ahura-Mazda." —Duncker, ii. 357; Spiegel's Vendidad, iii. 5.

I distinguish not if I am this All; for I go perplexed and bound in mind; when the first-born (ideas) of the truth reach me, then immediately shall I obtain a portion (of the meaning) of that (sacred) word.

The immortal (part) cognate with the mortal, affected by (desire of) enjoyment, goes to the lower or the upper (sphere): but (men beholding them) associated, going everywhere (in this world, together), going everywhere (in other worlds, together) have comprehended the one, but not comprehended the other . . .

They have styled him (the Sun), Indra, Mitra, Varuna, Agni, and he is the celestial, well-winged Garutmat; for learned priests call One by many names, as they speak of Agni, Yama, Matariswan . . .

The fellies are twelve; the wheel is One; three are the axles; but who knows it? Within it are collected 360 (spokes, days), which are, as it were, movable and immovable . . .

The uniform water passes upwards and downwards in the course of days; clouds give joy to the earth; fires rejoice the heaven.

I invoke for our protection the celestial, well-winged, swift-moving, majestic (Sun), who is the germ of the waters; the displayer of herbs; the cherisher of lakes; satisfying with rain the reservoirs.[1]

Agni, the embryo of the waters, the friend accomplishing (all desires) with truth, has been placed (by the gods) amongst men, the descendants of Manu.

Agni when kindled is Mitra; and, as Mitra, is the invoker (of the gods); Varuna is Jatavedas: Mitra is the ministering priest: Damunas is the agitator (Vayu): Mitra (is the associate) of rivers and mountains.[2]

The seven rivers display his glory; heaven and earth and sky display his visible form: the sun and moon, Indra, perform their revolutions that we may see AND HAVE FAITH IN WHAT WE SEE.

We invoke to become our friend, Indra, who is attended by the Maruts; whose great power (pervades) heaven and earth, in whose service Varuna and Surya are steadfast, and whose command the rivers obey.

May we continue in the favor of Vaiswanara, for verily he is the august sovereign of all beings: as soon as generated from this (wood) he surveys the universe; he accompanies the rising Sun.

Who Agni amongst men is thy kinsman? Who is worthy to offer thee sacrifice? Who indeed art thou, and where dost thou abide?[3]

Above all spirits reaches Agni upon earth, in the air, in the sun: and this is because he is the purifying Offering of fire by which human, inhuman and superhuman demons on earth, in the air and in heaven are driven out. This

---

[1] Wilson, Transl. Rigv. Sanhita, ii. pp. 125-144. [2] Mitra, Agni, Varuna, are all one.—Wilson, Rigv. ii. 332. [3] Wilson, i. 263, 261, 254, 198.

feeling of offering (Opfergefühl) is most closely connected
with the material-spiritual Light-feeling (Lichtgefühl) with
the human feeling of repentance, with the physical-moral
sentiment of purification. This Vedic Pramati, the thinking, time-measuring Fire-light upon the altar, is, like the
Greek Fire-spirit Prometheus, the civilizationsprinciple
among the oldest shepherds and cultivators of the earth ; ...
from this civilizationsprinciple proceeds later Brahma, the
Power of the meditating and creative Light-Word (Licht-
wort) and prayer. Through the ceremony of offering upon
the altar, the Fire-ghost becomes the Offer-ghost; "the
offerer" who is a priest is, symbolically, "the offered up"
(Geopferter). Agni, who is father and mother, son and
daughter; who enters into all human relations and is the
Fire in the Airy Sea, in the Lightning considered as a
purifying, atoning fire-offering, is, in the later performance
of the ceremony, the priestly Agni become World-Spirit:
the purifying gloom-expelling primal Offering in which the
Spirit of the World is at once the offerer and the offering;
so that from his mouth issue the words and the rhythm, from
his body break forth the objects of Nature and are distributed to the universe as parts of the offering. In this system
all the individual Element-gods appear proceeding out of
the heart (Manas, Mens) of " the offered up," together with
the Senses that connected with the Manas find their oneness in it. When these ideas are united with the Atomic
theory, the living atoms are considered as seeds which externally expand themselves into life but in the heart (Manas)
are the archetypes, images or undeveloped "ideas" of the
senses. Their origin is the Manas, the inner Sense (as Soul
of the world). The Heart (Manas) wakened by Love becomes creative ; from it the Senses emanate, make the Inner
Space within the Heart external, render it the World-Space,
and become the causes of all things. Brahma issuing in
the Senses fills all Space and is every thing.[1]

[1] Baron v. Eckstein, Weber, Ind. Studien, ii. 376–379.

Agni immortal sustainer of the universe, bearer of oblations, deserving of adoration, I will praise thee, who art exempt from death, the preserver, the sacrificer!—Wilson, Rigv. i. 119.

The Sun is the Soul of all that is fixed or movable.[1] There is only one single Deity, the Great Spirit (Mahan Atma the Great Soul); this is also named Sun, for he is the "Spirit" of all beings.[2] "The Vedas say in many passages : There is in truth but One Only God, the Supreme Spirit, the Lord of the universe, and the universe is his work."[3]

In shoreless ocean, in the midst of worlds, greater than the great (das Grosse), streaming through all light with his radiance, stays Pradshapati (Brahma, Lord of creatures) in the interior within : into him this All enters, again streams forth, in him the gods stay all together. This is what was and will be; it dwells in the highest unchangeable Aether... This alone is the Right, this is the True, this is the highest Brahman of the godwise.—Mahânârâyana-Upanishad.[4]

The Spirit is One and Everlasting![5]

Brahma through whom all things are illumined, who with his light lets the sun and the stars shine, but who is not revealed by their light.
Sankhara, Atma-Bodha, 61.[6]

God is concealed in all things; whoever recognizes Him as the only Lord and as Him who compasses All, he becomes immortal. He is the mouth of all beings, their head and throat, He dwells in the heart of all beings; He fills the All; He is omnipresent; He, the Spirit (Purusha), He the Cause (Beweger) of Being, He is Light, and imperishable; the Spirit, as large as the thumb, dwells always in the heart of men, and makes itself known through the heart, the will and thought.
Kaivalya-Upanishad, 7–9.[7]

"There are, here and there, prayers especially to Çiva which in religious fervor and childlike trust can be confidently placed by the side of the best hymns of the Christian Church : but their number is in truth very small."[8]

[1] Wuttke, ii. 262. [2] Ibid. ii. 254. [3] Jancigny, Inde, 172; Allen's India, 368. [4] Weber, Ind. Stud. ii. 80, 81. [5] Sankhara, Atma-Bodha, 36, 38, 39, 60, 64; in Wuttke, ii. 259. [6] Wuttke, ii. 324. [7] Wuttke, ii. 328. [8] Weber, Akad. Vorlesungen.

"The beginnings of philosophical speculation go back to a very high antiquity. As early as the Samhita of the Rik Veda, at any rate in the latest parts of it we found hymns which indicate a high degree of reflection : in particular, here as among all other peoples it is the question respecting the origin of the world which gave the strongest impulse to philosophical reflections. The mystery of existence, being and life, forced itself immediately on the mind and at the same time with it the question how is this riddle to be solved, what is the cause of it. The most natural suggestion and obviously the most primitive is the idea of an eternal Matter, a chaotic mass, into which gradually comes order and clearness, whether owing to its own native capacity of development or through an impulse from without. This implies then an object, a being external to that chaotic mass. When we have got so far we are near the thought that this Being that gives the impulse is higher and more exalted than that chaotic primitive-Matter, and with the advance of speculation this primal Matter sinks ever into a less prominent position until at last its existence even appears as caused by the will of that Being, and consequently the idea of creation arises. We can follow this gradual gradation in the Vedic texts with tolerable certainty. In the older passages it is everywhere said that the worlds were established with the help of metra."[1]

From Spirit and Matter, the Two Principles of all things, we find, besides many others, three main schools derived. These three philosophies are the Brahman which retained the Spirit (the One Being) and denied Matter; the Sankhya which retained Matter and denied the One Existence; last, the Buddhist school which denied both Spirit and Matter and assumed the existence of unintelligent souls[2] (or living atoms[3]) and adopted abstract Existence in place of Matter. The Chi-

---

[1] Weber, Vorlesungen, 210, 211.   [2] Duncker, ii. 178, 183; St. Hilaire, Bouddhisme, 194; Cousin, Hist. Mod. Phil. i. 374.   [3] Ind. Stud. ii. 376.

nese Tao is Non-existence considered in reference to Creation, but is simply abstract Existence, if compared with total nullity.

While Pythagoras derived his numerical harmony (Kosmos), the orderly arrangement of the world, from the Monad, the Brahmans affirmed that ONE EXISTENCE alone exists. While Plato taught that the EIDE, the spiritual bases of the true and the beautiful, came out from the Father and were clothed with material forms by the Efficient Cause; the Sankhya philosophers held that "the souls" assumed their bodies of their own accord. Kapila taught that the "self" is a SELF-CREATING POWER.[1]

In the dualism of the Greek Philosopher Anaxagoras, the Spirit ("Nous"), in the Beginning, gave to the material Atoms which lay in a state of disorder the impulse by which they took the forms of individual things. Anaxagoras seems to have had as little reference as possible to the "Nous" after the Atoms were once set agoing by it.[2] The Sankhya school asserted that "the individual souls" clothed themselves with material forms out of Matter. Kapila takes his stand on the idea of the "I" (individuality) and the idea of "Matter."[3]

We have seen how the earliest Greek systems of philosophy, as well as those of Egypt, Phœnicia, Judaea, Babylon, China and Persia were based on the assumption of the Two PRINCIPLES as the causes of all life within this material universe. While the Hindu schools passed through this stage of thought (Purusha and Prakriti) and believed that ALL THINGS WERE THE PROGENY OF ONE FIRE, there is little left of the Two Principles in the Hindu religious and philosophical writings; but the point of closest resemblance between the Hindu and the Babylonian or Hebrew conceptions is the emanation of all souls (in the Bible philosophy) out of the Spirit of God (the Purusha, as the Hindus would say). All souls emanate from and are a part of the Great

---

[1] Duncker, ii. 165.   [2] K. O. Müller, 247, 248.   [3] Duncker, ii. 164, 165.

Soul Brahma, in the Hindu Philosophy.[1] In the Baby-lonian Philosophy the life-influence comes from the Most High to Iao who pours it out (as Creator) over the world.[2] Starting then from the Two Principles, instead of placing a First Cause (God) above them, the Brahman philosophy preferred to deny one of the Two Principles, namely Mat-ter—and to assert that the Spirit was the ONE EXISTENCE, the Cause of all things, the Only Existence, and that what we call " Matter" or "Body " is an error of the senses. It does not exist. All things are an emanation from the One Essence alone; from Brahma; and returned to him. All things are forms of Brahma.

Their idea was that the Creation is only a deception and the transcendent Brahman alone the Reality; but without personal existence. "The Brahman[3] has two forms, the formed and the formless" (the world and God).[4] The human soul is not separated from the Highest Soul. Man's thought is Brahma's thought. There is no other being than Brahma—he is all alone. The Primal Existence does not create the individual beings of this world, but changes him-self into them. The world has flowed from Brahma, it is the unfolded Brahma.[5] The Spirit is Purusha ; the Unreal, Illu-sive Material of the world is called Prakriti. This is descend-ed from the old philosophy of the Sun and Earth, the Father and Mother, the two causes of all things, with the Earth struck out entirely and all existence declared to be the Sun and the influences or emanations from him. Only One Being! One Existence ! the Life in Nature. Thus the Spirit and Matter philosophy of the Chaldean Magi is entirely ignored by the Hindu philosophical schools. It is retained by the Old Chinese and Old Persian philosophies.

The philosophy of Xenophanes and Parmenides leans decidedly towards pantheism ; and the Grecian philosophi-

---

[1] The Greeks considered the soul to be breath or air.—K. O. Müller, 249. See above, pp. 152-155.   [2] Movers, 553-556.   [3] In the neuter gender.
[4] Wuttke, ii. 264.   [5] Wuttke, ii. 265, 287, 299, 303.

cal writings are said to have been favorably received by the Brahmans. The philosophy of Strato of Lampsacns, B. C. 286, resembles Buddhistic notions. According to him, what is called God, Intelligence and Divine Power is nothing else than the power of NATURE DEPRIVED OF ALL CONSCIOUSNESS OF ITSELF. The school of Leucippus and Democritus, in the fifth century before Christ, regarded the soul as a collection of round and igneous atoms whence result movement and thought. It is materialist. Anaximander in the first half of the fifth century before Christ taught that the world arose out of the ETERNAL or rather INDETERMINABLE SUBSTANCE which he called THE INFINITE (τὸ ἄπειρον). The Buddhists held that Swâbhâva (self-immanent substance) preceded every thing else.[1] The Buddhists assert that Swâbhâva (literally " its own existence" from Bhâva, existence, and Swa or Sva the pronoun), the Basis underlying the merely *apparent* existence which is revealed by our senses, is the First Cause. This is the Chinese idea of Tao which is Non-existence, because we do not perceive it in existing things; but is really existence when compared with absolute nullity.[2]

The Buddhists believed neither in God nor in Matter; only in Nature or Existence (Swâbhâva). The Chinese school of Lao-Tseu regarded their Tao "the Reason Supreme" not as " a person" or a god ; but as ·"the intelligent working· power in Nature." The Sankhya school of India held that " Intellect is produced from Nature : Self-consciousness is derived from Intellect."[3] " The Babylonians like the rest of the barbarians pass over in silence the One Principle of the universe." The First Cause among the Egyptians was " unknown darkness."

We have thus reached the point of union between all the old philosophies and religions from four to six centuries

---

[1] Bhava means existence, Abhava non-existence. Swa-bhab means particular constitution, disposition, quality or nature.—Wilkins, note to Bhagavatgita.

[2] La Chine, ii. 354.   [3] Cousin's lectures, i. 376, 377.

before Christ—the culminationspoint of a prior civilization.
It is "simple abstract Existence" as the "First Cause" of
all things.

Philo, a contemporary of Christ, held that "the existence"
of God was all that could be predicated of him, the only
appreciable thing about him; he is invisible, not recogniz-
able by the soul, like no created thing; he lives not in
Time but in Time's IMAGE or archetype.[1] We may say with
Hesiod (?) that Chaos was the first Existence, or with
Anaximander that "the boundless" (τὸ ἄπειρον) was the
original substance from which all things arose and to which
they return; or with Heraclitus that Fire is the First
Cause, the Igneous Principle of Life; or with Pythagoras,
that there is One Universal Mind diffused through all things,
the Source of all animal life, in substance similar to Light.

Instead of stating, as the Bible does, that, in the Beginning, the SPIRIT of God moved on the face of the waters
while the earth was yet unformed and void, the Brahman
story of the Creation is, that the SOUL OF THE WORLD existed
alone in the Beginning. He having willed to produce
various beings from his own divine substance, first, with a
thought, created the waters and placed in them a productive
seed. In common with the Greek cosmogonies (except the
Orphic) which make the gods a part of the world, the
Brahman philosophy has for its First Cause something not
separated from Nature or the world. Brahma does not
stand above Nature as its Master, but is mixed up with it.
Brahma and the world form one being, one existence,
together. He did not create it, it proceeded out of him.

Then neither the One Existence, nor the unreal, was. There was neither
world nor heaven, nor any thing above it: nothing anywhere concealing or
enveloped, nor water deep and dangerous : Death was not, nor Immortality,
nor separation between day and night. But IT (the First Cause) breathed
without exhalation. . . . Darkness was there ; this universe was enwrapped in

[1] De Wette, Bibl. Dogm. i. p. 122.

darkness and undistinguishable water; but the Covered Mass[1] was brought forth by the power of meditation. Desire (Love, Eros, Kama, Apason, Cupid) was first formed in His SPIRIT, and this was the original *creative seed* which the wise recognize by their acuteness as unreality, which is the fetter of Being (des Seins).[2]

This universe existed only in darkness, imperceptible, undefinable, undiscoverable by reason, undiscovered, as if it were wholly immersed in sleep.

Then the self-existing Power, himself undiscerned, but making this world discernible, with five elements and other principles, resplendent with brilliance the most pure appeared dispelling the darkness.

He whom the mind alone can perceive, whose essence eludes the external organs, who has no visible parts, who exists from eternity, even He, the Soul of all beings, whom no being can comprehend, shone forth in person.

He having willed to produce various beings from his own divine substance, first with a *thought* created the waters and placed in them a productive seed.

The seed became an egg bright as gold—and in that egg He was born himself, Brahma, the great forefather of all spirits. By that which is, by the imperceptible Cause, eternal, who really exists and to our perceptions does not exist, has been produced the Divine Male (Purusha) celebrated in the world under the name Brahma.

In that egg the great Power sat inactive a whole year, at the close of which, by his *thought* alone, he caused the egg to divide itself;

And from its two divisions he framed the heaven and the earth: in the midst the subtil Aether, the eight regions and the permanent receptacle of waters.[3]

He whose powers are incomprehensible having created this universe was again absorbed in the Spirit, changing the time of energy for the time of repose.

In the Beginning this ALL was non-existing. "THAT"[4] was existing; it changed itself, it became an egg. This lay a year, it split; the two shells were gold and silver. The silver is the Earth, the gold the Heaven. The mountains are the womb, the cloud the covering . . . what is there born is the Sun. When he was born, then arose after him rejoicings, all beings, all wishes.[5]

Divine, without form is the "Spirit" (Purusha), pervading the internal and external of beings, unborn, without breath, without heart (Manas), shining elevated above the highest and unalterable. Out of him comes the Breath of Life, the mind and all senses.—Mundaka-Upanishad.[6]

According to a very ancient Hindu legend, Varuna,

---

[1] "The Earth. . . . Thou coveredst it with the Deep as with a garment."— Ps. 104.   [2] Wuttke, Geschichte des Heidenth. ii. 282.
[3] Laws of Menu, by Jones, Pauthier, Haughton.   [4] The One Existence, "It."
[5] Weber, Ind. Stud. i. 261; Wuttke, ii. 293.   [6] Wuttke, ii. 294.

Lord of all, is throned in the midst of heaven, and on all four sides about him lie the places of punishment for the unrighteous, the hells.[1] The fancy of the priests metamorphosed the realm of Jama from heaven into hell, in which the impure and unholy must be punished for the trespasses which they have committed during their life and have left unatoned for. In time the different tortures of hell were painted in detail. As in Egypt and other hot countries, so in India glowing heat is a means of punishment.[2]

From the head of Brahma came the Brahman caste, from his arms the warriors, from his thighs the Vaicja caste, and from his feet the Sudras, the caste ordained to serve. The gods issue from Brahma and are sparks of the Soul of the world, although stronger than the souls of men. The Brahmans had made their doctrine succeed mainly through the fear of hell and the rebirths of the soul.[3] In connection with the Brahman philosophy the priests taught that men must pass through all the inferior stages of existence until they became absorbed in the One Essence; and for their sins they might, between each stage of existence from the fly up to the elephant or the Sudra caste up to the Brahman caste, pass ages in some one or other of the numerous hells which had been conjured up to terrify the imaginations of the people. The Brahmans conceived the idea that, as the successive emanations were more and more remote from Brahma's One Essence, the different orders of being were so many gradations of existence to be passed through before the Soul finally became absorbed in the Supreme Essence. As all beings have proceeded from Brahma so must all return to him. The idea of the transmigration of souls into various states of existence was retained, together with the innumerable hells that the Hindus appended to their worship of Varuna and later of Indra. If then a sinning soul must go through all orders of being,

---

[1] Weber, D. M. G. ix. 242.   [2] Duncker, ii. 69.   [3] Ibid. ii. 118.

from that of an insect through many other existences until it at last entered the body of a pious Brahman and thence obtained absorption in the bosom of the Deity; and if, after each stage, it must undergo tortures for thousands of years in the various hells, what a terrible prospect was offered to the soul after death ! For a punishment of wrongs done in one existence the soul is condemned to begin again at the foot of the scale of emanations from Brahma and retrace each stage until the final absorption is attained. In every worm, in every ant or other creature, was perhaps the soul of a man, of a friend, a relative or ancestor. Such a philosophy must necessarily seek relief in its very opposite. The Sankhya sect declared the reality of Matter and the existence not of One Spirit, but of innumerable souls who clothed themselves with matter. Kapila places himself upon the idea of the " I," and the idea of Matter. There is no eternal Substance, no Creator and Lord of the world. Brahma is like the other gods, self-created and not free from grief, age and death, although he may have power over the elementary Creation. Only the MANIFOLD MATERIAL " NATURE" exists which produces and perpetuates itself by its own inherent power. The souls did not issue from Brahma nor do they return to him. With the variety of Nature, with her variableness of manifestation, there exists also the multitude of human souls of themselves from eternity !

These souls, the only intelligent principle in Kapila's doctrine, wander through the world and clothe themselves with the material of the body which they take from the material world. When this is laid aside they do not die but survive the body and adopt a new material. The existence of the soul is owing to its very nature. The true aim of life is to be freed from the bonds of Nature. This is attained by recognizing that the body is not the soul. The Spirit is freed by acknowledging that it is not Nature. This conception of its own independence is the redemption according to Kapila. Thus instead of the philosophy of

Brahma and the deceptive world of appearances, the Sankhya
system gives us the "self" and Matter. Instead of the One
Intelligent Principle without Matter, we have the multitude
of individual souls and the existence of Matter.

The Buddhists met the Brahman philosophy with a new
and before unheard of system. Not only was the One
Spirit, the One and only Existence of the Brahman philosophy denied, but they set up its direct opposite, Non-existence. Nothing exists, only variable mutable Nature in
its innumerable apparent forms. Nothing is! The Brahmans had shown that Matter is Unreality. The Buddhist
accepted the Unreality of Matter as the Only Existence.
The souls of the Sankhya system are admitted. Nothing
exists but individual spirits and Matter pervaded with unrealness. While the Brahmans had denied the existence
of Matter and the Sankhya had affirmed it, but denied "the
Spirit," the Buddhists, on the contrary, denied both together. The Brahman said, There is nothing but Brahma.
The Buddhist said, There is nothing at all. The Brahman
declared all things delusion and vanity. "True," says the
Buddhist, "and Brahma is as much a delusion as the rest."
Nothing is!

The Buddhists consider Sensibility the only source of
knowledge. Thought appears only with Sensation and does
not survive it. They call the soul "the existing know-
nothing;"[1] the visible material world they consider non-
existence, the illusion of the senses. It is the intellectual
substratum of men which clothes itself out of the five Elements (Fire, Water, Earth, Air, Aether) with Matter and
Body.[2]

"The things—says an old orthodox Buddhist-writing—
are not created by a God (Isvara, Lord), nor by the Spirit
(Purusha) nor by "the Matter" [as the Sankhya teaches].
If God, or Spirit, or the Matter were really the only Cause,

---

[1] Duncker, ii. 182; Burnouf, 488–509.   [2] Duncker, ii. 178.

then the world must have been created in its entireness at
once through the single fact of the existence of this Cause,
because the Cause cannot be without its working exists.
We see however the things come after one another into the
world, some out of the mother, others out of a seed. We
must therefore conclude that there is a succession of causes
and not that a God is the only cause. But, one answers,
this multitude of causes is the working of God's will who
has said: Let such a being arise now and another afterwards; thus the succession of beings is explained and God
is still the Cause. To this it may be replied that as soon as
many " acts of will" in God are assumed many causes are
confessed, and thus the first proposition is overturned that
there is only One Cause. Moreover this plurality of causes
can be brought forth only at a single time, because God,
the Source of defined acts of will, is one and indivisible;
we must also confess that the world is created at one time.
But the sons of the Çakja (Buddha) hold fast to the principle
that the course of the world has had no Beginning." [1]

The oldest and purest philosophical school of the
Buddhists, the Suabhavikas, which is related to the Sutras
as the Vedanta is to the Vedas, denies with the clearest
distinctness the existence of a Spiritual world-basis. There
is, it teaches, nothing else but Nature. This Nature exists
in two modes, in a positive and in a negative. In the first
state, in Pravritti, the Existence, she is active, moves living : in the second, in Nirvritti, the Rest, the Non-living,
Nature rests, its life ceases. Between waking and sleep,
between life and death, between movement and rest, the
existence of Nature goes on in constant interchange, not by
the will of a being different from it, but by its own force.
A Buddhist high-priest in Ava in writing to a Catholic
bishop enumerated among the six most exceptionable here-
sies the doctrine that there is a Being which has created

---

[1] Wuttke, ii. 527, 528 ; Burnouf, 117, 119, Note 2.

the world and should be prayed to. The emanation of the world out of Brahma passed already in the old time for one of the greatest errors.[1] All becomes at last as it was in the Beginning, "the great rest of Nothing."[2] "The highest symbol of the All are the prayer-wheels put in motion by wind or water."[3] The use of these prayer-wheels is general in the northern lands, but in India and the South they are not found.

The Buddhists waive all questions about the origin of the world as unanswerable. The old Buddhist writings are silent respecting the origin of the soul.[4] "The inner nature of that which exists is transitoriness." The world is a clouding of the pure nothing and turns back into non-existence. The world ought not to be, and yet it is! This then is from evil: all Being is wrong, all is pervaded with sorrow, and the deepest feeling of the discerning wise man is a great general world-sorrow.[5] Birth, age, sickness, death, is the character of the misery of the world.

When one sees heaven and earth, let him think that they are not eternal: when he sees mountain and vale, then shall man think that they do not last forever. . . . When one also adds the original component parts of the body's being, yet are they still unsubstantial since their being ceases in a short time and they are then as phantoms. "How long does human life last?" asked Buddha of a Çramana; the latter answered: It lasts some ten days. "Thou art not yet on the path purified!" He asked a second, and this one says: About as long as a meal continues. "Go, thou also art not yet purified!" But the third spoke: So long as is needed to be able to exhale and inhale! Buddha allowed that the last possessed the right knowledge.[6]

The Buddha-doctrine is called the doctrine "of the nothingness of the ALL," "the inspiring doctrine of the void."[7] Only one feeling befits the pious WISE, the feeling of un-

---

[1] Wuttke, ii. 528.   [2] Ibid. ii. 570.   [3] Ibid. 525.   [4] Ibid. ii. 530, 532.
[5] Wuttke, 535.   [6] Ibid. 536.   [7] Ibid. ii. 535.

speakable grief.[1] Nothing exists but individual spirits and Matter pervaded with unrealness. Every thing is deceptive. Nothing *is ;* except that of which we have but the visible changeable form. The True is the endless Void. Penetrated with pity for the sufferings of men afflicted by the evils of life and cursed with the fear of an almost eternal transmigration of their souls after death, Buddha taught "the consoling doctrine of nothingness." To those who feared to be reborn he offered the way of escape—Extinction, Annihilation of the thinking self. The soul is compelled by its own nature always to assume new forms. How can the soul, the intellectual substratum, be prevented from doing this? By annihilating itself extinction is attained, nirvana (freedom from THOUGHT) is arrived at.[2]

His doctrine was that the events of this life are controlled by the acts committed during a former existence: that no wrong action remains unpunished, no good deed unrewarded. From this fatality which attaches to man within the circle of his transmigration he can only free himself by directing his will upon the one thought of freedom from this destiny, and by doing good works, whereby, after throwing off the bonds of the passions, and recognizing that the world and its appearances are illusions, he obtains entire freedom from rebirth. By destruction of the intellectual basis, the soul, this freedom is attained. Thought stops, the individual existence ceases. Nirvana, Extinction, is reached.[3]

The origin (Entstehung) of every existence is caused through passion (Leidenschaft) in an earlier existence.[4] The essential properties of existence are enumerated in order to convince us that there is no self or soul. We are to contemplate the unreality of our being that we may learn to despise it, and place ourselves in such a position that we

---

[1] Wuttke, ii. 542.   [2] Duncker, ii. 183.   [3] Ibid. 183, 184.

The impermanence of Matter, the existence of suffering in all things, the annihilation of the thinking spirit.—Neve, 24 ; Lotus, p. 372.

[4] Weber, über den Buddhismus, p. 48.

may live above its agitations and secure its cessation. There
will be a future state of existence but not of the individuality that now exists; there is a potentiality inherent in existence (Karma). Every being, until nirvana or extinction,
necessarily produces another being unto whom are transferred all the merit and demerit (Karma) that have been
accumulated during an unknown period by an almost endless succession of similar beings, all bound by this singular
law of production to every individual in the preceding links
of the chain so as to be liable to suffer for their crimes or
be rewarded for their virtues. The soul *in its own nature*
is pure and composed of happiness and wisdom. The properties of pain, ignorance and impurity are those of Nature,
not of soul. The chief end should be to escape from the
unreal state in which our souls are placed. By destroying
within ourselves the cleaving to existing objects (upadana)
this can be attained. Nirwana, or freedom from evil desire, is the end of successive existence, is freedom from sorrow and the evils of existence. It is the annihilation of all
the elements of successive existence.[1]

The universe is created by the works of its inhabitants;
it is their effect; and if, by an impossibility, there had not
been any guilty, there would not have been hells and places
of punishment.[2]

Buddha said to one, " Friend, this way does not lead to
indifference respecting the things of this world, does not
lead to freedom from passion, does not lead to prevention of
the vicissitudes of existence, does not lead to calm, does not
lead to perfect intelligence . . . to the state of Çramana . . .
to nirvana."

Nirvana is complete annihilation.[3] Some Buddhists
(400 years after Christ) rendered a worship to the " Perfection of Wisdom."[4] Swâbhâvikas or " naturalists" are veritable atheists, who say that all things, the gods as well as

---

[1] Eastern Monachism, 291, 292.   [2] St. Hilaire, 187 ; quotes Lotus de la
bonne loi, 835, Burnouf.   [3] Burnouf, Introduction, 110.   [4] Ibid. 113.

men, are born from Swabhâva or their own nature.[1] Nowhere is Çâkyamuni (Buddha) named God, nowhere does he receive the title of Adibuddha. The notion of a Supreme God represented by Adibuddha was foreign to primitive Buddhism.[2]

The doctrine of a theistic sect in Nepal which sets an endless, existing through itself, all-knowing, world-creating Ur-Buddha, Adibuddha, at the head of existence, is a later perversion of the true doctrine, which first arose probably after the tenth century after Christ.[3] There is no trace of it in the Chinese Buddhistic writings—and its philosophical sister, the school of the Aiçvarikas, who assume an abstract, spiritual God Adibuddha, but deny him the government and control of the world, ascribe to Nature a life and development independent of him.[4]

It has been remarked that, about the fourth and fifth centuries before Christ, instead of the calm enjoyment of outward Nature which characterized the early epic poetry of the Greeks, there existed a profound sense of the misery of human life and an ardent longing for a condition of greater happiness. This feeling was not so extended as to become common to the whole Greek nation but it took deep root in individual minds. The Orphic poets believed that human souls are punished by being confined in the body as a prison. In India, in the fifth century before Christ, Buddha starts from the conviction that the earth is a vale of sorrow and the world nothing but a mass of griefs. The worst is that misery is not ended with this life, that man is constantly reborn to new sufferings, that he is driven restless through the eternal interchange of birth and death, never to find rest. While other nations feared death, the Hindu feared immortality of suffering. The good tidings of a life of peace and the hope of a death without resurrection opened the hearts of the people to Buddha's teachings.

---

[1] Burnouf, Introduction, 118.   [2] Ibid. 119.   [3] Wuttke, ii. 529; Burnouf, 117, 119, *note* 2.   [4] Ibid.; Burnouf, 442.

He was a king's son penetrated with the conviction of
the vanity of earthly things. "The dark side of life had
cast a deep shade of sombreness over Buddha's susceptible
mind." The legends relate that one day he saw a decrepid
old man with broken teeth, gray locks and a form bending
towards the ground, his trembling steps supported by a
staff as he slowly proceeded along the road. The prince in-
quired "Shall I become thus old and decrepid?" and he was
told that it was a state at which all beings must arrive. The
prince now saw that life is not to be desired if all must thus
decay. After four months he sees a leper, full of sores, and
afterwards a dead body in a putrid condition. He reflected
deeply on the evils which filled the world and resolved to
renounce crown and throne, and search out the causes of
human misery in the hope of alleviating it. He preached
to the people directly, disregarding all the distinctions of
castes, and his gentleness and humility, contrasted with the
pride and pretension of the Brahmans, made a deep im-
pression. All without distinction might become his followers, and to all he opened the hope by the adoption of his
doctrine to be freed from the bonds of their birth.

He taught self-denial, chastity, temperance, the control
of the passions, to bear injustice from others, to suffer death
quietly and without hate of your persecutor, to grieve not
for one's own misfortunes but for those of others. As every
one seeks to lessen his own griefs, so shall he also lessen
those of his fellow-men. Hence the exhortation to love, forbearance, patience, sympathy, pity and brotherly feeling.
One great secret of Buddha's success was that he preached
morality to the people instead of metaphysics; but his morality is founded less on *love* than on *human misery*. He
admitted slaves and malefactors among his disciples and opposed the system of castes on the ground that body, birth
and the whole external world possess but an inferior worth.
Whoever more closely considers the body will find no difference between that of a slave and that of a prince. The

body is to be regarded only according to the spirit that is in it. In the midst of oppressed peoples he showed how evils could be patiently borne or avoided by the aid of his doctrine. Salvation and redemption have come for all; even the lowest and most abject classes can be freed from the necessity of rebirth.[1] The soul, the intellectual basis, can be annihilated.[2]

The Buddhist worship is the worship of an idea. Buddha has not been raised to the rank of a deity. He is and continues to be considered a man! The devotion is offered to the idea of NOTHINGNESS. As the distinctive peculiarities of Buddhism are philosophical and moral it could enter into any religion and extend its principles everywhere. It entered China as the religion of Fo, it conquered Cashmere, Thibet, Nepal, Birma, Siam, and entered Japan. At this day it numbers at least one-fourth of mankind among its converts. His followers regard him as the Ideal of knowledge and goodness (the incarnation of the Supreme wisdom). He was to them in the place of a god and relics of him were venerated. A great part of the respect paid to Gotama Budha arises from the supposition that he voluntarily endured throughout myriads of ages and in numberless births the most severe deprivations and afflictions that he might thereby gain the power to free sentient beings from the misery to which they are exposed under every possible form of existence. It is thought that myriads of ages previous to his reception of the Budhaship he might have become a rahat and therefore ceased to exist; but that of his own free will he forewent the privilege and threw himself into the stream of successive existence, for the benefit of the three worlds.[3]

The fearful night of error is taken from the soul, the sun of knowledge has arisen, the gates of the false ways which lead to the existences filled with misery are closed: I am

---

[1] Duncker, ii. 191.   [2] Ibid. 183.
[3] Spence Hardy, Manual of Buddhism, p. 98.

ON THE OTHER SHORE, the pure way of heaven is opened, I have entered the road to Nirvana. On this road the oceans of blood and of tears are dried, the mountains of human bones are broken through and the army of death annihilated as the elephant overturns the reed hut. He who without distraction follows this way escapes from the circle of transmigration and the revolutions of the world. He can boast: I have performed what was incumbent on me, I have annihilated the existence for myself, I will not again be born, I am freed, I shall see no more existence after this! [1]

[1] Burnouf, Intr. pp. 462, 510; in Duncker, ii. 184.

CHAPTER XIII.

Omnia paullatim tabescere, et ire
Ad scopulum spatio aetatis defessa vetusto.
                                        Lucretius, ii. 1170.

He made of one blood every race of men to dwell on all the face of the earth . . . that they should seek God if haply they might trace and find him, since he is not far from each one of us!   Paulus.

THE "One Existence" of the Hindus and other orientals appears as the "First Cause" in the Jewish Philosophy. It is the EN-SOPH ("without end") of the Cabbala. This is all things, and out of it there is nothing. No substance has proceeded out of absolute nothing; all which is has drawn its origin from a source of eternal light, from God. God is only comprehensible in his manifestation: the not-manifested God is an *abstraction* for us. Under this point of view he is called the "NOTHING." This "NOTHING" (AYIN) is the indivisible and infinite unity; hence it is called EN-SOPH. This is "boundless," and not limited by any thing. Here we have Anaximander's TO APEIRON, the Buddhist's non-existence and the Chinese TAO, as analogous ideas. The Buddhist Swabhava is not a person; neither was the TAO, nor the Babylonian ONE PRINCIPLE OF THE UNIVERSE, nor the Egyptian UNKNOWN DARKNESS.

The Primitive Light of the God-NOTHING filled all space; it is space itself. All creation has gradually emanated from the Divine Light. According as it removes itself from its

source it approaches Darkness; and Matter, which is the
most remote, is the seat of Evil.[1] Here is also a variation
of the Brahman idea that all creatures issued from this
Highest Being in such a manner that the most spiritual
were nearest to him, the most material, sensual and coars-
est forms the furthest removed from him.[2] The EN-SOPH
manifests itself freely by its WISDOM and thus becomes the
First Cause, the Cause of causes. The INFINITE EN-SOPH
manifested himself, in the Beginning, in One First Principle or Cause, the "PROTOTYPE OF CREATION" or "Macro-
cosm," called the SON OF GOD, the Primitive Man. This is
the "figure of a man" which hovers above the symbolic
animals of Ezekiel. It is the Adam-Kadmôn, from whom
the Creation emanates.[3]

The New Testament shows the abundant superstitions
of the times, especially among the common people. There
we find dumb devils, demoniacs, spirits of weakness, &c.,
&c. Sins, mistakes, diseases, must be atoned for as in
Egypt by offerings. Pigeons, meat, grain, wine and salt
must all be offered to the Lord by way of ATONEMENT for
their sins. Paul preached an ancient doctrine when he
taught that Christ died an atonement to the eternal justice
of God for the sins of men. The ideas which prevail in the
New Testament were many of them old before the time of
Christ. We find the doctrine of purification in Leviticus,
in the laws of Manu and the Zendavesta. Innumerable
sects existed, and all sorts of doctrines came from Greece,
Babylon, Persia, India and Egypt to influence the Hebrew
mind. The End of the world was expected in Persia and
Judaea; and this event was connected with the appearance
of the expected Messiah and the Resurrection.

" Philo imagined an eternal atonement already made

---

[1] Munk's Palestine, p. 523.   [2] Duncker, ii. 68.   [3] Munk, 523. The
Epistle to the Hebrews, i. 10, 11, applies Psalm cii. 24 (25), 25 (26), and its
expression ELI (Ali, O God) to Christ. See above, pp. 245, 246.

and eternally being made by the Logos.[1] This Jewish-
Heathen philosophy of religion was carried into *practice* by
the Therapentae, *the servants of God*, who considered themselves the genuine spiritual contemplative worshippers.
They are to be viewed as Jewish monks like the Essenes,
whom they strongly resemble, though no outward connection can be shown. They dwelt in a quiet, pleasant conn-
try on Lake Moeris, not far from Alexandria, shut up in
cloister-like cells (σεμνεῖα, μοναστήρια) and devoted to the
contemplation of divine things and the practice of asceticism.
They generally lived on nothing but bread and water, and
ate only in the evening, being ashamed to take material
nourishment in daylight. Every seventh Sabbath was with
them specially sacred. They then united in a common love-
feast of bread and water seasoned with salt and hyssop,
sang ancient hymns and performed mystic dances emble-
matic of the passage of their fathers through the Red Sea, or,
according to their allegorical exegesis, of the release of the
Spirit from the bonds of sense. These Jewish ascetics regarded ' *the sensible*' as intrinsically *evil*, and *the body as a
prison of the soul*. Consequently the aim of the wise man
was outward mortification. The ascetic death was the birth
to true life." [2]

The Essenes were an association of practical philosophers
who joined to the doctrines of the Pharisees the principles
of an exalted morality, and applied themselves to the practical virtues, to temperance and labor. They divided the
day between prayer, ablutions, labor and repasts in common.
No profane word was uttered before the Sun rose, which
they saluted every morning with prayers after the ancient
usage.   Then the superiors sent each to his occupation;
after laboring until eleven o'clock they bathed themselves
in cold water and joined in the repast. They entered the
dining room solemnly as if it were a temple, and sat down
in the most profound silence. Each received a piece of

---

[1] Schaff, Hist. Apost. Church, 180.   [2] Ibid. 181.

bread and a dish with one mess. Before and after the meal a priest pronounced a prayer. Before returning to their work they put off the garment which they had assumed for the meal and which they looked upon as sacred. At evening they united for a second repast.[1] Yea and nay were with them a sufficient guaranty of veracity.[2]

Let your word be yea yea, nay nay; for what is more than these comes of evil!—Matthew, v. 37.

The Essenes like the Buddhists lived in associations or monasteries and generally disinclined to marry. They believed in equality among men (like Buddha and Christ), in giving to those who are in want, they avoided splendid garments and generally all cleaving to existing things, rejecting pleasures as an evil and esteeming the conquest over the passions as a virtue. They studied morality, and held that the soul, having descended from Aether the most pure, being drawn to the body by a certain natural attraction, remains in it as in prison.[3] For the rest, they resembled the Pythagoreans and differed from the Buddhists by believing in a God. The Essenes kept up relations with the world beyond their community and sought to serve society by giving it the example of a laborious life, a sincere piety, and a constant virtue which controlled all the human passions. Those who entered their society must bring to it all that they possessed; the property of the society confided to administrators was held in common and belonged to all: and there were no rich and no poor. John the Baptist was apparently a stricter sort of Essene.[4]

[1] Munk's Palestine, 515, 516.   [2] Schaff, 175.

[3] According to an Orphic notion more than once alluded to by Plato, human souls are punished by being confined in the body.—K. O. Müller, Hist. Greek Lit. 238. This was the idea of Philo, who considered that the soul existed before the body was created.—Preface to Philo, by Yonge; De Wette, Bibl. Dogm. 149.

[4] Milman, Hist. Christ. p. 77; Munk's Palestine, 515–519; Josephus, Wars of the Jews, ii. ch. 8.

"The Phœnicians, who were Canaanites, worshipped the Sun, Moon and Stars two thousand years before Christ, and practised Magianism." The Magi worshipped the heavenly bodies. The Assyrian religion, which was almost exclusively the worship of the heavenly bodies and stars, had its origin in the ancient belief that the heavenly bodies, especially those which move in their orbits, like the Sun, Moon and the Five Planets, were gods and rulers of the fate of men.[1]

They fought from heaven, the Stars from their courses contended with Sisara!—Judges, v. 20.

"Even the Jehova-religion did not entirely throw off this aspect, but only made it subordinate to its scheme; and the One God appears as the Ruler of the heavenly host." The Stars were always considered living divine natures and Powers of heaven.[2]

And a fourth is like a son of the gods (Alahin).—Daniel, iii. 25, 28.

For who in the heavens shall compare himself with Ihoh? (who) shall be equal to Ihoh among the sons of Alim (Elim "the gods")?—Psalm, lxxxix. 6.

And all the HOST OF HEAVEN shall be dissolved and the heavens shall be rolled together as a scroll: and all their HOST shall fall down as the leaf falls off from the vine.—Isaiah, xxxiv. 4.

I am the God of the gods, the sublime Creator of the Wandering Stars (Planets) and of the army celebrating me above thy head; I am the Former of the august race of the gods, princes and directors.—Book of the Dead.

The gods are called the children of Heaven because they presided over certain constellations of heaven.[3]

When Christ appeared there existed a belief in astrology. The Chaldeans, Phœnicians, Jews, Egyptians and others believed in it. Hence the Magi *saw the star of Jesus.*

For the MAGI FROM THE EAST had seen his star in the east!

Matthew, ii. 1, 2, 7, 9.

Christ says that they who rose from the dead were as angels

[1] Gesenius Jesaia, ii. 529.   [2] Ibid; Daniel, iv. 32 (35), 13, 17; Job, xv.; iv.; xxxviii.; xxv.; Matthew, xxiv. 29; Coloss. i. 16.   [3] Seyffarth, Theolog. Schriften, p. 3, ff.

in heaven. The idea of the Resurrection from the dead had long been held among both Persians and Jews; in many cases however it was connected with the doctrine of trans-migration. "Çaoshyançç, a KING, will come and annihilate Agra-mainyus and his bands—a doctrine peculiar to the earlier Parsees which seems first to have had its commence-ment in the Avesta." The Parsee idea of the Resurrection is set down by Spiegel about the time of Artaxerxes Ochus B. C. 337. This idea already existed in Persia in the time of Alexander the Great, for Theopompus says that "men will return to life again."[1]

Then will the KING say to those on his right hand : Come ye blessed of my Father, inherit the kingdom prepared for you from the foundation of the world.—Matthew, xxv. 34.

For the world hastes fast to pass away.—2 Esdras, iv. 26.

For the EVIL is sown, but the destruction thereof is not yet come!

For the grain of evil seed has been sown in the heart of Adam from the Beginning!—2 Esdras, iv. 30.

What shall be the parting asunder of the TIMES : or when shall be the END OF THE FIRST and the BEGINNING OF THE ONE THAT FOLLOWS?

Esau is the END of the world and Iacob is the BEGINNING OF THE ONE THAT FOLLOWS.—2 Esdras, vi. 7, 9.

And when the world that shall begin to vanish away shall be finished, then I will show these tokens : . . .

And the trumpet shall give a sound which when every man hears they shall be suddenly afraid ! . . .

Whosoever remaineth from all these that I have told thee, shall escape and see my salvation and the END of the world.—2 Esdras, vi.

The kingdom of God is preached and every one presseth into it.

Luke, xvi. 16.

Buddha preached extinction, the unrealness of the world; Christ taught that the END of the world was at hand.

The kingdom of heaven is like a net cast into the sea, and gathering up of every kind; which when it was full, they drew to the shore, and sitting down gathered the good into vessels and *cast away the bad.* So will it be at the END OF THE AIŌN (age, world). The angels will come forth and sever the wicked from among the just and will cast them into the furnace of fire.

Matthew, xiii.

[1] Spiegel, Vend. pp. 16, 32 ; quotes Journal Asiatique, 1840, T. X.; Zeitschr. der D. M. G. p. 360, ff; Theopompus; Diog. Laert. prooem. sec. 9.

John the Baptist and Christ both taught that the END OF THE WORLD was approaching.[1]

Verily I say to you, Ye will not have gone over the cities of Israel till the Son of man be come.

Hereafter ye will see the Son of man sitting on the right hand of power and coming on the clouds of heaven.—Matthew, xxvi. 64.

They will see the Son of man coming in clouds with great power and glory. And then he will send his angels and will gather together his chosen from the four winds, from the uttermost part of earth to the uttermost part of heaven.
Mark, xiii. 26.

Verily I say unto you, There are some of those standing here, who will not taste of death till they see the Son of man coming in his kingdom.
Matthew, xvii. 28.

Because they thought the kingdom of God was to appear immediately.
Luke, xix. 12.

We have heard out of "the Law" that Christ abides till the End of the world.—John, xii. 31.

Then cometh the End (of the world) when he shall have delivered up the kingdom to God the Father.—1 Cor. xv. 24.

Why say the scribes that 'Elias must first come?
'Elias indeed comes first and restores all things!—Mark, ix. 11, 12.

The origin of the expectation of the End of the world may be sought for among the conceptions of the Chaldeans and ancient Egyptians, from whom in all probability it passed to the Etruscans and other nations. There is every reason to suppose that the Old Italian learning was to some extent imported from the East. The Etruscans believed in a Creation of six thousand years, and in the successive production of different beings the last of which was man.[2] This was the doctrine of the Old Persians and the Hebrews. "It has been ascertained according to the chronology of the ancient Egyptians that the first age of the world began 5871 years before Christ on the 10th day of May, according to the Julian reckoning, on a Saturday, being at the same time the vernal equinox. The day on which Christ rose from the dead was the same on which the creation of the world was completed."[3] The Egyptians had a chronology based

---

[1] Matthew, iii.; x.; John, vi. 40, 51.   [2] Italie Ancienne, ii. 347.
[3] Seyffarth's Lectures, Evang. Review, p. 43.

on the idea of a general Flood which was set down as having occurred at a certain date. The world had existed 2423 years up to the time of the Flood, which took place 3447 before Christ. As in their computation[1] the Flood came 3447 B. C., the six thousand years of the world's duration would expire not long after the Baptist's announcement of the approach of the End of the world. Preachers and prophets naturally referred to it in their addresses to the multitude.

> In those days came John the Baptist preaching in the wilds of Judaea, saying: Repent, for the KINGDOM OF HEAVEN is at hand!

And immediately after *his baptism by John,*

> From that time Jesus began to preach and to say: Repent, for the KINGDOM OF HEAVEN is at hand![2]

He commences his walk as a preacher of the advent of the End of the world, and he ends with the same doctrine:

> For many will come in my name, saying: I AM HE, AND THE TIME IS AT HAND!
> And when ye shall hear of wars and commotions be not afraid; for these things must first be: BUT THE END IS NOT YET AT HAND!
> > Luke, xxi. 8, 9 ; Mark, xiii. 6.
> When ye see these things come to pass, know ye that the KINGDOM OF GOD is nigh.—Luke xxi. 31 ; Matthew, xxiv. 33.
> This generation will not pass away till all these things come to pass.
> > Mark, xiii. 30.
> What will be the sign of thy coming and of the END OF THE WORLD ?
> > Matthew, xxiv. 3.

The Egyptian theory of a Creation lasting six thousand years agrees with the Hebrew computation.[3] Theopompus of Chios relates that Ormuzd's reign was three thousand years and Ahriman's would last as long. After these six thousand years the two Gods would contend until at last Ahriman would yield and mankind be made happy. They

---

[1] According to Seyffarth, Theol. Schriften der alten Aegypter, p. 108.
[2] Matthew, iv. 17.　　[3] Seyffarth's Lectures, p. 43.

would no longer require nourishment, and would cast no shadows; the dead would rise, men would become immortal . . . . But, at the END, the appointed time comes at which Areimanios is overcome by sickness and hunger which he has himself caused, and vanishes. Then the earth becomes level and uniform, and there will be one kingdom, one language and one manner of life for happy and unilingual mankind. The fragments of the Zendavesta contain nothing of the periods of three thousand years of the reigns of Ormuzd and Ahriman, nothing of the happy future. The Vendidad casually mentions that hereafter a new Prophet will come from the East, and yet shorter mention is made of the time of the Resurrection. The views of Theopompus and Plutarch conform so entirely to the Persian style of thought and agree so well with the Zendavesta, that we can hardly doubt that such views of the future existed in Iran in the fourth century before Christ.[1] The Babylonian and Persian doctrine of the End of the world is proclaimed by the prophet Daniel.[2] "It was universally believed that the End of the world and the kingdom of heaven were at hand. The near approach of this wonderful event had been predicted by the apostles."[3]

I know that he will rise again in the Resurrection at the LAST DAY.

John, xi. 24.

Clangor tubae per quaternas
Terrae plagas concinens
Vivos una mortuosque
Christo ciet obviam.

Dies irae, dies illa
Solvet seclum in favilla
Teste David cum Sibylla.

Tuba, mirum spargens sonum
Per sepulcra regionum,
Coget omnes ante thronum.

[1] Duncker, ii. 387, 388; Plutarch, de Is. c. xlvi. xlvii.; Vend. xviii. 110.
[2] Daniel, ix. 25, 26, 27.   [3] Gibbon, i. 411.

Iudex ergo quum sedebit,
Quidquid latet apparebit,
Nil inultum remanebit !

I udicii fuerit cum signum, terra madebit.
E coelo veniet Princeps per saecla futurus.
S cilicet, ut carnem praesens, et judicet orbem.
O minis homo hunc fidusque Deum, infidusque videbit,
U na cum sanctis Excelsum fine sub aevi,
Σ αρκοφόρον. Ψυχὰς ἀνϑρώπων βήματι κρινεῖ.

Eruthraea Sibylla.[1]

When we consider the many systems and schools of philosophy more than two thousand years since in which "Love" was a prominent feature, when we call to mind the throng of cultivated writers and distinguished men of those times, can we for a moment think that the idea of love for others was unknown until Christ appeared? It may not have been prominently associated with morals, but the bare idea could have been no stranger to the human mind when the Love (Apasson) of the Unrevealed Being was named by the Babylonian and Sidonian philosophers and even Plato spoke of love. The noblest sentiments had already been uttered for ages. Confucius in China had inculcated "the perfecting one's-self," "the cultivation of the moral faculty," "the enlightenment of the people."[2] Near five hundred before Christ, Lao-Tseu·said : Embracing all beings in one common affection, one is just, equitable towards all beings.[3] In the Book of Proverbs we find :

He that despiseth his neighbor is void of sense !

Towards the year three hundred before Christ, Simeon the Just held that "the world is founded on three things : the Law, Worship and Works of charity."[4] Christ taught : Thou shalt love thy neighbor as thyself. Love your enemies, and do good, and lend hoping for nothing back.

---

[1] Boissard, De Divinatione, &c., p. 206.   [2] La Chine, 184, 185.
[3] Tao-te-king, § 16 ; La Chine, i. 116.   [4] Munk, 486.

Judge not. Forgive. Do good to them that hate you, bless them that curse you, pray for them that insult you. To him that smites thee on the cheek offer also the other; and from him that takes away thy cloak forbid not thy coat also. Give to every one that asks of thee, and of him that takes away thy goods ask not again. Blessed are ye that weep now, for ye will laugh. Blessed are ye when men shall hate you and when they shall avoid you and shall reproach you and cast out your name as evil, for the Son of man's sake.

"It was above all among the Essenes that the more elevated ideas of the Messiah's reign had their birth; but there were also a great number of Pharisees who shared them, and among the most illustrious are cited those who made the whole of the Law to consist in the practice of morality and the love of one's neighbor"... "That which you do not like done to you," said Hillel, "do not do it to your neighbor; this is all the Law, the rest is only commentary." Hillel was one of the most illustrious chiefs of schools in the time of Herod. Many other passages of the same nature are found in the Talmud and the other collections of the old Rabbis. "Joseph de Voisin, in his notes to the Pugio fidei of Raymond Martin has collected numerous sentences of the ancient doctors of the synagogue which offer parallels to the discourses of Jesus."[1]

The New Testament and Buddha's teachings both proclaim the vanity of worldly things.

Verily I say unto you that there is no one that has left house or parents or brethren or wife or children for the sake of the kingdom of God, who will not receive much more at this time, and in the age to come life everlasting.

Luke, xviii. 30.

Lay up for yourselves treasures in heaven.

What is valued among men is an abomination in the sight of God!

Luke, xvi. 16.

Blest are the poor; for yours is the kingdom of God!

Blest are you that now hunger, for you shall be filled!

Munk's Palestine, p. 565, note. Thalmud of Babylon, traité Schabbath, fol. 31, a. quoted by Munk.

But alas for you that are rich, because you have had your consolation!

Alas for you that laugh now, for you will mourn and weep!—Luke, vi.

And it came to pass that the poor man died and was carried by the angels into Abraham's bosom: the rich man also died and was buried.

And in hell he lifted up his eyes, being in torments . . .

Abraham said: Child, remember that thou *in thy life-time* didst receive thy good things and in like wise Lazarus evil things; but *now* he is comforted and thou art tormented.—Luke, xvi.

The New Testament here teaches that the rich and the poor shall change places in the world to come.

Blessed are the poor in spirit, the meek, the merciful, the pure in heart, the peace-makers: Ye have heard that it was said to them of old; Thou shalt not kill; and whosoever shall kill, will be deserving of the judgment. But I say unto you, that every one that is angry with his brother without a cause, will be deserving of the judgment.

What is born of the Flesh is Flesh; and what is born of the "Spirit" is "Spirit."—John, iii. 6.

And the KURIOS is the "SPIRIT"!—2 Cor. iii. 17.

Now is Christ risen from THE DEAD, the "First-fruits" of those AT REST!

1 Cor. xv. 20.

For if the "first-fruits" are holy, so is the kneaded!—Rom. xi. 16.

O death, where is thy sting: O death, where is thy victory!

1 Cor. xv. 55.

I heard a voice from heaven saying, Write, Blessed are the dead who die in KURIOS, from henceforth: YEA, says the SPIRIT, that they may rest from their labors!—Rev. xiv. 13.

Out of Siōn the Deliverer shall come!—Rom. xi. 26.

A Savior who is Christus KURIOS!—Luke, ii. 11.

Veni Redemptor gentium,
Ostende partum Virginis.
Miretur omne seculum,
Talis decet partus Deum.

Non ex virili semine,
Sed mystico spiramine
Verbum Dei factum est caro
Fructusque ventris floruit.

Alvus tumescit Virginis,
Claustra pudoris permanent,
Vexilla virtutum micant, .
Versatur in templo Deus:

Procedens de thalamo suo,
Pudoris aula regia,
Geminae GIGAS substantiae
Alacris ut currat viam.

Egressus ejus a Patre,
Regressus ejus ad Patrem;
Excursus usque ad Inferos,
Recursus ad sedem Dei.

Corde natus ex Parentis
Ante mundi exordium.

Esaias quae cecinit
Completa sunt in Virgine

Enixa est puerpera,
Quem Gabriel praedixerat.

Adam vetus quod polluit,
Adam Novus hoc abluit:

Jam nata lux et salus,
Fugata nox et victa mors:
Venite gentes, credite,
Deum Maria protulit.

Gloria tibi Domine
Qui natus es de Virgine![1]

One of the legends represents Buddha as saying: "I direct my scholars not to do wonders; I rather say to them: So live that you conceal your good actions and confess your faults."[2] "In the midst of oppressed peoples he showed how the unavoidable evils could be patiently borne, how they could be mitigated by mutual help."[3] It was the evangelium of a peaceful life and the hope of a death without resurrection which opened the hearts of the people to Buddha's teachings.[4] He declared that there was no distinction between the body of a slave and that of a prince. The body is to be esteemed or not, according to the spirit that is in it. "The virtues do not ask about the castes."

---

[1] Rambach, Anthol. i.   [2] Bournouf, p. 170; Duncker, ii. 202;
St. Hilaire, p. 144.   [3] Duncker, ii. 192.   [4] Ibid. 193.

Salvation and redemption are come for all. "My law is a law of grace for all."[1] The people were deeply impressed by the gentleness and humility which Buddha opposed to the haughtiness and pride of the Brahmans and by the compassionate commiseration which he exhibited for the distress of the people, for all the wretched and laden.[2] So Christ said, "Come unto me all ye who are weary and heavy-laden, and I will give you rest." Buddha taught the people his moral rather than his metaphysik which denied all but the thinking "self." Men must bear wrong from others with patience; mishandling, even maiming and death, must calmly be endured without hating the persecutor. "The maiming frees man from members which are but transitory; and execution from this foul body which yet dies."[3] Not one's own misfortune but that of our fellow-men is a ground of sadness. Control the passions, "bring rest into the senses," avoid as much as possible contact with the world. "As every one seeks to lessen for himself life's sufferings, so shall he also lessen the sorrows of his fellow-men. All men without regard to rank, birth and nation, form, according to Buddha's view, one great suffering association in this earthly vale of tears. Therefore the commandments of love, forbearance, patience, compassion, pity, brotherliness of all men.[4]

If one has committed a sin in word, thought or deed, let him repent and confess before his companions in the faith, and before those who have attained a higher grade of holiness.[5] The power which controls the universe is Karma (action), consisting of Merit and Demerit. At the death of any being the aggregate of his merit and demerit is transferred to some other being, which new being is caused by the Karma of the previous being, and receives from that Karma all the circumstances of its existence. The manner in which being first commenced cannot now be ascertained. The cause of

[1] Duncker, ii. 191; Wuttke, ii. 533.   [2] Duncker, ii. 190.   [3] Ibid. 187.
[4] Ibid.   [5] Duncker, ii. 188.

the continuance of existence is ignorance, from which merit and demerit are produced, whence comes consciousness, then body and mind, and afterwards the six organs of sense. Again, from the organs of sense comes contact; from contact, desire; from desire, sensation; from sensation, the cleaving to existing objects; from this cleaving, reproduction; and from reproduction, disease, decay and death. Thus like the revolutions of a wheel there is a regular succession of death and birth, the moral cause of which is the cleaving to existing objects, while the instrumental cause is Karma. It is therefore the great desire of all beings who would be released from the sorrows of successive birth to seek the destruction of the moral cause, the cleaving to existing objects, or evil desire. They in whom evil desire is entirely destroyed are called Arhats. The freedom from evil desire ensures the possession of a miraculous energy. At his death the Arhat invariably attains Nirvana, or ceases to exist.[1]

In the sixth century before Christ, at the age of 36, Buddha attained the triple science which is the negation of existence in three degrees—the supernatural perception of the three great facts: "the impermanence of Matter, the existence of grief in all things, the annihilation of the thinking spirit." At his birth he had said: I will put an end to birth, to old age, to sickness, to death! Now, considering the evils of created beings he cried: I will put an end to this sorrow of the world![2]

At the hour of Buddha's birth precursory signs were perceived in the gardens and parks of Kapilavastu; Nature became immovable; the rivers stopped; the flowers ceased to blow, the birds were silent. At school, he revealed a superior knowledge by giving the definition of sixty-four kinds of writing whose names were unknown to the master himself. By his mere presence thirty-two thousand infants were by degrees entirely grounded in perfect and complete

[1] Eastern Monachism, p. 5.   [2] Neve, p. 24.

intelligence. On the Nepalese pictures of Buddha a vast luminous circle surrounds his head! [1]

The womb that bears a Budha is like a casket in which a relic is placed; no other being can be conceived in the same receptacle; from the time of conception, Mahamáya was free from passion and lived in the strictest continence.

Whilst reposing on her divine couch, Bódhisat appeared to her, like a cloud in the moonlight, coming from the north and in his hand holding a lotus. After ascending the rock, he thrice circumambulated the queen's conch. At this moment San-tusita (Bódhisat) who saw the progress of the dream, passed away from the déwa-loka and was conceived *in the world of men;* and Mahamáya discovered, after the circumambulatious were concluded, that Bódhisat (Buddha as claimant for the Budhaship before birth) was lying in her body as the infant lies in the womb of its mother.[2]

At the time of the conception thirty-two great wonders were presented. The 10,000 sakwalas (systems of worlds) trembled at once; there was in each a preternatural light so that they were all equally illuminated at the same moment; the blind from their birth received the power to see; the deaf heard the joyful noise; the dumb burst forth into songs; the lame danced; the crooked became straight; those in confinement were released from their bonds; the fires of all the hells were extinguished so that they became cool as water, and the bodies of all therein were as pillars of ice...

The father of Gótama Budha, Sudhódana, reigned at Kapilavastu, on the borders of Nepaul; and in a garden near that city the future sage was born, B. C. 624. At the moment of his birth he stepped upon the ground, and after looking around towards the four quarters, the four half-quarters, above and below, without seeing any one in any of these ten directions who was equal to himself, he ex-

[1] Neve, 29, note 2.　[2] Manual of Buddhism, 142, 143; see Sale's Koran, ii. 125.

claimed, Aggo hamasmi lókassa ; jettho hamasmi lókassa; settho hamasmi lókassa ; ayamantimájáti ; natthidáni punabbhawo: "I am the most exalted in the world ; I am the chief in the world ; I am the most excellent in the world ; this is my last birth ; hereafter there is to me no other existence." When five months old, he sat in the air without any support at a ploughing festival.[1] "The wonders that he performed were of the most marvellous description : but in those days the possession of supernatural power was a common occurrence, and there were thousands of his disciples who could with the utmost ease have overturned the earth or arrested the course of the sun." He died at the age of eighty years and his relics were preserved and became objects of worship.[2]

When Buddha was told that a woman was suffering in severe labor, unable to bring forth, he said, Go and say: "I have never knowingly put any creature to death since I was born ; by the virtue of this observance may you be free from pain !" When these words were repeated in the presence of the mother the child was instantly born with ease.[3] He also tamed an infuriated elephant. The sage charged him not to take life in future, to hate no one and to be kind to all ; and the elephant in the presence of all the people repeated the five precepts.[4]

Buddha was tempted by the Demon Wasawartti Mára, who said, as Buddha was leaving the palace of his father: "Be entreated to stay that you may possess the honors that are within your reach ; go not ; go not!" The prince declared, "A thousand or a hundred thousand honors such as those to which you refer would have no power to charm me to-day ; I seek the Budhaship ; I want not the seven treasures of the Chakrawartti ; therefore begone, hinder me not." Then Mara ascended into the air and said to Sidhártta (Buddha), gnashing his teeth with rage, "We shall

---

[1] Eastern Monachism, p. 2.   [2] Ibid. 4.
[3] Manual of Buddhism, 252.   [4] Ibid. 321. See Wuttke, ii. 566.

see whether thou wilt become Budha; from this time forth
I shall tempt thee with all the devices I can imagine; until
the reception of the Budhaship I will follow thee incessantly
like thy very shadow, and on the day of its attainment I
will bring a mighty army to oppose thee.[1] The Devil (Diabol) tempts Christ by the offer of all the kingdoms of the
world.

The great problem which Buddha sought to solve was
the origin of human suffering and its remedy.[2] In the sixth
century before Christ he said, "I will put an end to the
grief of the world. In perfecting this doctrine, which consists in poverty and the restriction of the senses, I will attain to the true deliverance! Indifference to the objects
of the world, freedom from passion, hindrance of the vicissitudes of being, calm, perfect intelligence, the state of a
Çramana (a Buddhist elect), Nirvana (Extinction)!" "In
Nirvana, say the older legends, nothing exists but the
void."[3]

All phenomenon is void; no phenomenon has substance proper.
Lalitavistara.
Within is the void; without is the void. The personality is itself without
substance. Every thing put together is perishable, and like the lightning in
heaven it does not last long. THAT is temporary, THAT is misery, THAT is void.
Buddhist Sutras, St. Hilaire, 194.

In his miracles, Jesus is said to have used the formula
THY SINS ARE FORGIVEN THEE! His disciples asked Jesus:
"What sin has this man or his parents committed that he
was born blind?" Buddha taught that the misfortunes and
sufferings of this life are the result of evil actions performed
in a former life. The Jews said to the blind man: Thou
wast *altogether born in sins*, and dost thou teach us![4] The
doctrine of the disciples is analogous to the "MERIT AND
DEMERIT" of the Buddhists; for the sick recovered *if their
sins were forgiven*. The Pharisees believed in transmigra-

---

[1] Hardy, Manual of Buddhism, 160.   [2] Duncker, ii. 176.
[3] Ibid. 183.   [4] John, ix. 34.

tion.[1] Pythagoras taught it in the fifth century before Christ. The Egyptians also believed in transmigration, and the disciples of Jesus were persuaded that a man might have sinned before he was born.[2]

The Egyptians and the Pharisees believed in superior beings or angels between the Divinity and men.[3] The Pharisees also believed in bad angels or demons who were the causes of all kinds of evils. Josephus sees in the demons the souls of wicked men who after their death come sometimes to torment the living. In the New Testament and in the Talmud the angels and demons play a very great part, and it is evident that the popular belief of the Jews had adopted to a certain point the dualism of the Parsees, which was subordinate however to the Mosaic monotheism. Satan was surrounded with bad angels or demons like the devs of Ahriman. At the head of the good angels they placed seven princes or archangels; these are the seven Amshaspandas of the Persians of which the First is Ormuzd. Allusion is made to them in the Book of Daniel written at the epoch of the Maccabees, and they are represented as the protectors of different peoples and empires. The doctrine of angels took the greatest development in the Christian doctrine and in that of the Cabbalists.[4] Demons were considered certain divine powers, of a middle nature, situated in the interval of the Air, between the highest Aether and the earth below, through whom our aspirations and our deserts are conveyed to the gods.[5] Plato attributes to the deities of Olympus and heaven all which is fortunate, and all that is sinister to the demons.[6] The New Testament holds that insanity, epilepsy, &c. were "being possessed of a devil." This is the Hindu doctrine.[7] Luke mentions dumb demons.[8]

[1] Gibbon's Rome, iv. 385.   [2] John, ix. 2; Munk, 512, 521, 522.
[3] Munk's Palestine, p. 513; Seyffarth, Theolog. Schr. p. 2.   [4] Munk, 513.
[5] Apuleius, Rel. of Socrates.   [6] Plut. de Iside, xxvi.   [7] Allen's India, 382.
[8] Luke, xi. 14; Matthew, ix.

24

Some mighty demon came so that he had not his right senses.

Aeschylus, Persians, 725.

A woman that had *a Spirit of weakness* eighteen years . . . whom Satan has bound!—Luke, xiii. 11, 16.

Inasmuch as they are possessed by demons!—Euripides, Phœnissae, 888.

A legion of devils are in one man, and depart from him into a herd of swine.[1]

Buddha renounced his wife and family, not even allowing himself a last embrace of his infant son, in order to release the various orders of being from the sorrows of existence.[2]

If any one come to me and hate not his father and mother and wife and children and brethren and sisters, yea, and his own life, he cannot be my disciple.

Luke, xiv. 26.

Christ sent out the seventy on their mission: Buddha made it the duty of his followers to go forth as missionaries and spread his doctrine everywhere. A rich merchant name Pûrna, who had left all his goods and become an enthusiastic disciple of Buddha, determined to win over a wild tribe to the new faith. Buddha put his firmness to the proof, saying the people are wild, fierce, cruel, and that he would have to endure from them the greatest insults and injuries. Pûrna answered: Then I will hold them still for good, dear people, because they neither beat nor cast stones at me. "When however they do even this?" Then I say still the same, for they could indeed wound me with weapons. "But this also will happen!" Now then they are dear good people because they do not rob me of my life. "But when they kill thee?" Then I thank their love and goodness that they free me with so little pain from this miserable body. "Go Pûrna," said Buddha, "thyself redeemed, redeem them. Thyself saved and consoled, save and console them. Lead thou, thyself perfected, them to perfection." As Pûrna really succeeded by his invincible

---

[1] The swine was Typhon's emblem. [2] Hardy, Manual, pp. 158, 177, 120, 121.

mildness in converting the savages, this instance explains also the fruits which the Buddhist missions generally have had afterwards.[1]

After Buddha's death, there were three famous councils of the Buddhist Church. The first was summoned by his disciple Kaçjapa under the protection of Agataçatru, king of Magadha, in the chief city Radshagriha, to collect and write down from memory Buddha's teachings. One hundred and ten years after Buddha's death Revata summoned a second council at the new capital of Magadha, Pataliputra, which, the legend says, was attended by a million bhikshu (monks). Revata chose seven hundred prominent men to lay down a new "confirmation of the Good Law" (about 430 before Christ). At a third synod attended by a thousand bhikshu one hundred and eighty years later, which was held in the time of king Açoka of Magadha, about 250 before Christ, the Buddhist canon was a third time purified and settled.[2] Fa Hian states that, at the time of his visit to Ceylon, in the beginning of the fourth century after Christ, there were 5000 ecclesiastics in one of the monasteries at Anurádhapura, and that upon a mountain not far distant 2,000 priests resided.[3] Another Chinese traveller, who visited Magadha not far from the year 630, presided at a meeting of a great number of the Buddhists in which two thousand Brahmans sat.

Buddhism and Christianity both have their miracles; but the Buddhist miracles far outnumber the Christian.[4] Buddhist worship,which was, originally, mere worship of his image and relics, regard to his memory, later a worship of the relics of his chief followers and pious kings, has now become a pompous and splendid ceremonial. This worship of relics, the monasteries, the use of bells to summon the followers of Buddha to worship, rosaries, and many other

---

[1] Weber, über den Buddhismus, p. 54.   [2] Duncker, ii. 197, 198, 199.
[3] Spence Hardy, Eastern Monachism, 310.   [4] Manual of Buddhism, passim; Neve, 17.

peculiarities, have so much resemblance to Christian rites that it may be questioned whether the last has not been the borrower.   It is notorious that the Buddhist missionaries very early, perhaps even in the first two centuries before Christ, had penetrated into the west as far as Asia Minor. This is however still an open question.[1] The course of trade between India and Mesopotamia would bring a knowledge of eastern ideas to the western world.   It is not probable that Judaea, with its knowledge of Babylon and Persia, could have been even a century without hearing of Buddhistic doctrines taught five hundred years before Christ.

It was but a journey of some months' duration for caravans to pass by land from the Indus to Persia and Babylon. Alexander's army penetrated to the Indus and returned. " In the second and third centuries before the Christian era Buddhist missionaries must have come into the Persian lands.   In the following period these missions became constantly more frequent, and Manicheanism in the third century after Christ appeared as an express mingling and union of Christian, Persian and Buddhist religious views." Gnosticism borrowed both from Brahman and Buddhist doctrines. This is certain respecting Bardisanes, Ammonius and Scythianus.[2] The Buddhists practised " confession," they had monks, nuns, celibacy, tonsure, the use of bells and rosaries, the worship of relics, the building of church towers, the " glory," &c.   Buddhism entered China one or two centuries before Christ, and in the year 61 after Christ was openly recognized.[3] " The Buddhists appeared for the first time in China in the reign of Schi-hoang-ti, 217 before Christ, but were repulsed. A hundred years later scattered traces of Buddhism are here and there found."[4] It was not introduced into Japan at all before the first century of our era, and was not established there until the fifth or *sixth* century. The pa-

[1] Weber, Akad. Vorles. p. 267.   [2] Weber, Ueber den Buddhismus, pp. 64, 63, ff.   [3] Ibid.   [4] Wuttke, ii. 590, quotes Foue-Koue-Ki, v. Abel Remusat, pp. 41, 44.

triarch of the Indian Buddhists in the year 495 of our era transferred his seat to China, and the succession was no longer continued in India.[1] It is without exception the most wide-spread religion on the globe. The most moderate estimate carries the number of Buddhists to 350 millions.[2] But notwithstanding their numbers they have far less liberality than the Christians, for these have established numerous missions for their conversion, while neither Buddhists nor Brahmans have reciprocated the attention.

The Buddhist literature is very considerable. The sacred religious writings comprise one hundred and eight thick volumes. They were confirmed at the three councils. Since the middle ages the Christian influence is perceptible in many traces: for instance the parable of the lost son is distinctly found in the Buddha-writings. Manicheanism was an attempt to found a new religion with reference to Parsism (Zoroastrianism), Buddhism and Christianity.[4] In the middle of the fifth century Buddhism began to be overpowered in India and in the Indus country, and its profession was not tolerated in Hindustan after the seventh century. Kumarila Bhatta in the seventh century was a chief expositor of the Mimansa philosophy, and by his influence overthrew Buddhism.[5] "Let those WHO SLAY NOT be slain; the old man among the Bâuddhas and the babe: from the bridge of Rama[6] to the Snowy Mountains" (the Himâlâya). Buddhism with its monastic usages was carried to Japan in 418 and in China it flourished in the sixth century. The Panjab and the eastern borders of Afghanistan were Buddhistic about the year 400 of our era.[7]

While Christ was regarded in the West as the Creator of the world, the Hindus in the third century of our era regarded Crishna (in accordance with their idea that all

---

[1] Journ. Am. Orient. Soc. i. 129.   [2] Jancigny, Japon, 148.

[3] Wuttke, ii. 522; quotes Burnouf, pp. 136, 43, 45, 578; Spiegel, in d. Allg. Monatssch. Halle, 1852, p. 552, &c.   [4] Spiegel, Vend. 30; Milman, Hist. Chr. 278.   [5] Journ. Am. Orient. Soc. i. 129.   [6] The strait between the continent and Ceylon.—Am. Orient. Soc. i. 129.   [7] Fa Hian, Ibid. p. 130.

things emanate out of the One Being) as the Soul of the
world.   Crishna is the Buddha of the Brahman schools,[1]
and like Buddha corresponds in position to Christ in the
Christian theogony.   Crishna says: Behold in this my
body the whole world animate and inanimate, and all things
else thou hast a mind to see.[2]   He is an incarnation of the
Supreme Deity, and was declared to have originally appeared on earth in the form of one of the ancient heroes of
the nation.   Christian missionaries penetrated into India in
the first century of our era ; and there would be nothing
surprising in their doctrines having some influence upon the
Brahman religion while they failed to establish Christianity
among the people.   God was manifest in Christ.   The Brahmans would find it very well suited to their views to teach
that Vishnu became manifest in Crishna ; while it might
be useful in getting up a revival of the Brahman religion
in opposition to the growing importance of Buddhism in
the second century.   The Crishna sect predominates among
those who profess Brahmanism.   It extended itself widely
in the fifth century after Christ.   The preaching of Christian
doctrines in India probably developed the LATER Krishna-
worship ; at any rate, after the appearance of Christianity
we find important traces of a Christian influence.   Then
thoughts come forth which stretch far beyond the ancient
doctrine without throwing off the pantheistic character and
without the idea of an absolute personal Spirit, the Creator
of heaven and earth.[3]   Krishna's name has not yet been
found in the oldest sutra.[4]

Mahomet based his religion on Judaism and Christianity.   He drew from both, regarding Moses and Christ as
divinely inspired teachers of former times.   He enjoined
charity, abstinence, temperance and bravery.   The injunc-
tion of self-denial is common to Buddhism, Mahometanism,
and Christianity.   When asked by the young man, "What

---

[1] Wuttke, ii. 339.   [2] Bhagavatgita.   [3] Wuttke, ii. 264, 329.
[4] Lassen, Ind. Alt. p. 736.

shall I do to inherit eternal life?" Christ answered "Sell all that thou hast and give to the poor." It is probable that from the Essenes or Eastern Monachism or Buddhism this idea of absolute poverty and entire self-denial was obtained. Some of the Christian sects took vows of dirt, ignorance and poverty. The ancients totally failed to conceive that the circumstances in which they found themselves were ordained of God: but they felt it incumbent on them *to alter Nature* and set up a theory. Nature, according to them, was not the servant of God. In respect to the civil laws Mahomet followed step for step the laws of Moses and the decisions of the Rabbis, only adapting them to the customs and prejudices of his countrymen. He even borrows expressions from the Jewish and Christian scriptures. He taught the Last Judgment, the Resurrection and Predestination. To the Jews he said that he came to restore the faith of their fathers in its purity; to the Christians, that Jesus is the best of prophets.[1] Mahomet's unitarianism stretches from the Atlantic to the Ganges. "There is no god but God!" Mahometanism, after conquering India from the tenth to the fifteenth centuries and seeing the ruin of the successors of the Prophet under the English rule, is still ready to argue its claims with the Buddhists and Vishnu-worshippers. It writes books and makes converts in Northern India still. While Brahmanism is nearly effete and Buddhism has attained the highest point of its progress in making converts, while many Hindus of the upper classes have reached that state of indifference that they are infidels, it stands forth between the opposing sects as, in some sort, a mediator between the Hindu and the Christian, the Oriental and European doctrines.

"There is a large and important class of natives in the large cities of India at the present day who are deists. The editor of one of the oldest papers in Bombay, after inserting two or three articles in his paper to prepare the minds of

---

[1] American Encycl. Art. Koran.

his readers, said 'it was obvious to all that the state of religion was very sad and becoming worse, that all classes of
people appeared to have lost all confidence in their sacred
books ; that Christians do not believe in their Bible, for
they do not keep the Sabbath, many of them are intemper-
ate, &c. ; that the Jews, the Mohammedans, the Hindus
and the Zoroastrians do not believe in their respective sacred
books, because if they did they would not do so many things
which are forbidden, and neglect to do so many that
are commanded.' He then proceeded to say that the sacred
books of all these different classes of people may have been
of divine origin, and when first given they may have been
adapted to the then state and circumstances of the people,
and have been very useful ; but that they had become un-
suitable to the present advanced state of knowledge and
improved state of society ; and that none of these sacred
books could ever again have the confidence of their people,
and become the rule of their faith and practice : and that
if people should continue as they are, without any
system of religion or standard of moral conduct, they
would become worse and worse, and at length become
depraved beyond recovery or endurance.   He then
suggested that a religious convention be held in Bombay, and that each class of people send a delegation
of their learned and devout men with copies of their sacred
books, and that the men of this convention should prepare
from all these sacred books a Shastra suited to the present
state of the world, and adapted to all classes of people : and
he expressed his belief that a Shastra thus prepared and re-
commended would soon be generally adopted.   In his next
paper he proceeded to mention some of the doctrines which
such a Shastra should contain, and among these he said it
should inculcate the existence of *Only One God*, and the
worship of him without any kind of idol or material symbol ; and then he would have no distinctions of caste, which
he thought one of the great evils and absurd things in the

Hindu religion. Now these opinions and suggestions are chiefly remarkable as exhibiting the state of the native mind.... The writer of these articles was a respectable and well-educated Hindu, who had not renounced the principles or practices of his hereditary faith, nor the rules of caste. He knew the state of religious opinion among the Hindus, and he was well assured that such opinions and suggestions would not be to the prejudice of his character nor to the injury of his paper. This man, the readers of his paper, and the circle of his acquaintance, show the state of hundreds and thousands in India, who are dissatisfied with the Hindu religion, and having no confidence in it would gladly embrace something more reasonable, more easily practised, and which they hope would exert a better influence upon society and the state and character of their nation." [1]

[1] Allen's India, 584.

NOTES.

---•●•---

P. 12.

THE Mazzarōth, mentioned in Job xxxviii. 32, are, *according to Ewald*, to be distinguished from Mazzalōth (2 Kings, xxiii. 5), and mean a single constellation.—Weber, Ind. Skizzen, Die Verbindungen Indiens, 76.
Munk says the Mazzalōth are the constellations of the Zodiac.

Munk, Palestine, p. 91.

The Septuagint identifies Mazourōth with the Hebrew Mazzalōth, " the houses " or constellations in the Zodiac.

2 Kings, xxiii. 5. B. C. 285.

Wilt thou bind together the delights of KIMAH,
Or the trailing bonds of CHESIL wilt thou loose,
Wilt thou lead forth MASSARŌTH in his time,
And AISH WITH HIS SONS wilt thou bring?

Hebrew Bible, Sebastian Schmid.

Pp. 14, 15.

The Sun was regarded as a gold-feathered bird.

Weber, Zusammenhang Ind. Fab. 9.

P. 33.

The names of the months are derived from the names of the gods.—Lepsius Einleitung, 144. Each month and day had its tutelary god.—Kenrick, i. 277; Herod. ii. 82.

P. 37.

The author has made use of the language of Lepsius at the beginning of Chapter Third of this work, to introduce the subject, and merely to indicate that Mentu and Atmu are sun-gods, without adopting the distinction into day-Sun and night-Sun. Since, however, Atmu (Athom) is sometimes represented as presiding in Hades, there is no more objection to regarding him sometimes as the Descending Sun, than for the poet to describe Bacchus as going to Hades. We have Aidoneus or Hades, the Descending Sun ; Nebo, Anubis, Mercury of the Dead ; Adad, (Thoth,) the Sun; Thoth, Tod, Death. See above, pp. 285, 286, 200; Uhlemann, Handbuch, i. 187.

Pp. 272, 267, 270, 276, 280.

After passing over the obsequies of Osiris, "because many of the Mysteries are mixed up with them," Plutarch says: "The priests not only of THESE (Apis and Osiris, &c.), but also of the OTHER GODS SUCH AS ARE NOT UNCREATED NOR INCORRUPTIBLE, say that their bodies lie dead and are taken care of, but the souls shine in heaven (being) Stars, and are called, that of Isis, the DOG by the Greeks, but by the Egyptians Sōthis, and that of Hōrus, Ōriŏn, that of Tuphŏn, ARKTOS (THE GREAT BEAR) . . . ; but that the inhabitants of Thebais (in Egypt) REGARD NO GOD AS MORTAL, but think Him whom they call Knĕph to be uncreated (unborn) and immortal.

But because many such things are said and pointed out, some, thinking that these great and terrible works and sufferings were commemorated, being those of kings and rulers who through superior virtue or power inscribed upon their glory the dignity of DIVINITY or who had good fortune, use a very easy circumlocution, and not badly transfer WHAT IS BAD TO RELATE from the gods TO MEN, and have *these* helps from the things historically narrated. For the Egyptians narrate that Hermes was in body short-armed, but Tuphŏn red-skinned, but Horus white and Osiris black-skinned, as if in nature they had been born men. Moreover they name Osiris general, and Kanŏbos governor, and they say the star named after him is his : . . .

But I fear lest this is moving the immovable, and that *these* wage war not only with a long time, according to Simonides, but with many nations and families of men seized with the reverence FOR THE GODS; *who* have left nothing undone to bring down from heaven to earth so GREAT NAMES, and unsettle and dissipate reverence and belief ingenerated in nearly all from the very Beginning; not only opening great doors to the godless crowd that brings divine things down to human, but affording a brilliant license to the impositions of Euēmerus the Messenian, who putting together copies of incredible and unreal legends scatters every sort of impiety in the habitable world, those who are esteemed GODS all equally expunging, (changing them) into the names of generals and admirals and kings who once existed, having been registered in Pagchōn in a golden writing which neither Barbarian nor Greek, but Euëmerus alone, as it seems, having sailed to the neither born nor being anywhere on earth Pagchöoi and Trifulloi, chanced upon !

Truly great exploits of Semiramis are hymned among Assyrians ; but the great (deeds) of Sesöstris in Egypt: but Phrygians to this day call the brilliant and wonderful works MAN-ica, because a certain MANis, one of the former kings, was a good and powerful man among them, whom some call MAss-ēs: but Kûros led Persians, and Alexander Macedonians, conquering, to almost the end of the earth ; but they have the name and memory of good kings. . . .

They do better, therefore, who think that the things related of Tuphön and Osiris and Isis are neither sufferings of gods nor of men, but of great DAEMONS whom both Plato and Pythagoras and Xenocrates and Chrysippus, following the old theologians, say are more robust than men, and far surpass in power our nature, but not having "the divine" unmixed or pure. . . . As in men, there are also in DAEMONS differences of virtue and of evil. For the Giant-stories and Titan-myths sung by the Greeks, and certain lawless actions of Saturn, the contests of Puthön against Apollön, and the FLIGHTS of Bacchus and the WANDERINGS of Dēmētēr are not different from the Osiriac and Typhoniac ceremonies and others which all can freely hear covered up with myths: but whatever things veiled by sacred Mysteries and rites are kept undivulged and unseen by the masses, *have the same story.*—Plutarch, de Iside, xxi.—xxvi.

Plutarch is very orthodox ; and this is a proof of the great antiquity of the belief that the gods were not mortals, for the orthodox never favor any thing that is new. Plutarch, though an orthodox Greek, would have been considered a heretic by the Hebrews, because *they* related the adventures of these deities *when they were men or patriarchs.* The Old Hebrews would not have blamed Euhemerus.

Pp. 277, 278.

According to the Babylonian myth ten Zodiac gods, preceded by Bel and Beltis (Adam and Eve), ruled before the Flood. They are the old kings: Alorus, Alaparus, Almelon, Ammenon, Amegalarus, Daon, Aedorachus, Amempsinus, Otiartes, Xisuthrus (Noah, Deucalion). Xisuthrus, with his wife, his daughter and steersman, was taken up among the gods. In Egypt also every one of the Twelve Gods of the Zodiac going about in boats had his steersman.—Movers, 165. The humanizing of the gods existed in Phœnicia, especially in later times.—Movers, 166. The gods were gradually looked upon as "merely human-personal beings" and were separated from the original ideas of them. Philo's Sanchoniathon may have had many predecessors ; and it appears as if this mode of treating the subject of the divinities first sprung up in Phœnicia.   The travesty of the Cadmus-myth which Euhemerus learned in Sidon seems to indicate that the philosopher of the school of Aristippus here had, *already earlier*, kindred spirits.—Movers, 156.

Pp. 137, 219, 221.

But Enuŏ (Luna) was equally balanced; common to both Deus and Typhon.—Nonnus, ii. 475.   One might perhaps say that Noah (Enuŏ) was the Man *in the moon.*   Compare p. 219 above; Nahaliel, Numb. xxi. 19; Nahsŏn, Naassŏn, 1 Chr. ii. 11; nass " wet." Nuseus (Bacchus).

Pp. 206—216, 356.

To the dead
No future resurrection ever hereafter!
Aeschylus, Agam. 568, 569.

Pp. 216, 217, 218, 159, 160.

But only if the Son (Aisaculapius, Asklepius, Esmun, Attis) of Phoibos-were viewing with his eyes this light could she come, having left the dark habitations and the gates of Pluto : for he *raised up the dead* before the God-sent (Diobolon) spear-point of thunderous fire destroyed him.—Euripides, Alcestis, 124 ff. See Movers, 160, 527, 532–534, 504.

Thus said Adni (Adoni) Ihoh to these bones : Lo, I bring my Spirit upon you *that you live!*

For I will give nerves upon you, and will make flesh ascend upon you, and will draw skin over you, and will put Spirit in you *that you live:* . . .

While I prophesied a sound was made and lo, a shake of the earth; and the bones came together, bone to his bone: . . .

Prophesy over Spirit ; O son of man, prophesy and say to the Wind: Thus said Adni Ihoh : From the four winds come, O Spirit, and breathe into these slain, *that they live!*

I will open your sepulchres and will make you ascend from your sepulchres, O my People!—Ezekiel, xxxvii. (B. C. 500—600?)

My soul drew near unto death, my life was near to Hades below!
Ecclesiasticus, li. 6.

Pp. 356, 359, 247, 248, 210–217, 159, 160.

We all shall not be put to sleep, but we all shall be changed, in a moment, in the twinkling of an eye, at the last trump : it shall sound and the dead shall be raised incorruptible, and we shall be changed!
1 Cor. xv. 51, 52.

Pp. 216, 218, 200, 206—209.

HERCULES (the Sun) who has *gone out from the chambers of earth*
Leaving the nether house of Ploutōn!

Euripides, Herc. Fur. 807, 808.

DATES.

Aeschylus, born B. C. 525. Sophocles, B. C. 495. Euripides, B. C.
480. Plato, born about 429, B. C. Philo of Alexandria, contemporaneous with Christ, lived before and after Christ. Philo of Biblus, in the
first and in the second century, A. D. in the time of Nero—Adrian.
Plutarch, born about the middle of the first century, A. D. Nonnus, at
the end of the fourth century, A. D.

P. 218.

Rambach, i. 106, instead of Deu*s* has Deu*m*, which is better:
Laudant rite Deum lux, polus, arva, fretum.
Light, heaven, fields, sea, duly praise GOD *going above the stars.*

Mundi renovatio
Nova parit gaudia,
Resurgenti DOMINO
Conresurgunt omnia.
Elementa serviunt
Et auctoris sentiunt
Quanta sint sollemnia.

Coelum fit serenius
Et mare tranquillius,
Spirat aura lenius.
Vallis nostra floruit,
Revirescunt arida,
Recalescunt frigida,
Post quae VER intepuit.

Vita mortem superat,
Homo jam recuperat
Quod prius amiserat,
Paradisi gaudium.
Viam praebet facilem,
Cherubim versatilem,
Ut deus promiserat,
Amovendo gladium.

Rambach, i. 289.

Pp. 317, 352.

And bring LAMBS—one white, the other black—to the EARTH and to the SUN: and we will bring another to ZEUS.

Iliad, iii. 103, 104; Rev. xiv. 4.

P. 252.

ANTIPHONA DE MARIA VIRGINE.

ALMA Redemptoris MATER, quae pervia coeli
Porta manes et STELLA MARIS . . . .

11th century.   Rambach, i. 230.

AVE MARIS STELLA,
Dei MATER ALMA
Atque semper VIRGO,
Felix coeli porta.

10th century.   Rambach, i. 219.

Save those who hope in thee, Mother of the never-setting SUN, Mother of God!

Rambach, i. 148.

Hymn we the BOY of a MAID
The pure, unespoused
In the couches shared by men,
By the ineffable will of the FATHER!

Synesius; died about 430.   Rambach, i. 70.

A STAR showed the LOGOS before the SUN,
Coming to cause sin to cease, to the Magi . . .

John of Damaskus, died 754.   Rambach, i. 141.

Patris SAPIENTIA,
VERITAS divina
DEUS HOMO captus est
Hora matutina,
Nocte a discipulis
Cito derelictus.

Rambach, i. 356.

P. 93.

El, called Aldos, Aldemios, names of Zeus.

Movers, 262; quotes Etym. M.

P. 160.

I will ask the NYMPH BENEATH, the Daughter of the fruitful goddess Ceres, to send up his soul.　　　　　　　Euripides, Rhaesus, 963, 964.

Kroniŏn quickly took away the Breath of the breasts, and the burning thunderbolt inflicted death!　　　　　Pindar, Pyth. iii. 57, 58.

Pp. 186, 187, 188.

These (Chaldaeans) were of opinion that this KOSMOS, among the things that exist, is single, either being itself GOD (Theos), or that in it is God (Theos) comprehending the soul of all the things.

Philo, Migration of Abraham, § 32.

P. 202, line 3; p. 209.

That they may know that thou by thy name art Ihoh alone, ALION over all the earth!　　　　　　　　　　　Ps. lxxxiii. 18.

P. 222.

And when the Feast of Bacchus was kept, the Jews were compelled (by Antiochus) to go in procession to Bacchus carrying ivy.—2 Maccabees, vi. 7. If Antiochus had called it the Festival of Adonis, perhaps no compulsion would have been required.—Movers, 25.

Pp. 219, 221, 222, 200.

Compare, page 39 *note*, Ihoh-Nasi: also, MI NH, "the waters of NOAH."

Isaiah, 54, 9. See above, p. 48.

Pp. 295, 223, 225, 315.

The Egyptian-Dodonean Dione was originally the same as the Phœnician goddess Ashtoret (Astarte, Aphrodite), just as Ammon (the Spouse of Dione) was identical with ADONIS (the SPOUSE OF ASTARTE).

Rinck, Relig. der Hellenen, i. 223.

P. 271.

The district of the Ammonites was considered the property of the god Chamosh-Ariel. The Israelites regarded their land as the property of Jehovah, which he had given them for a possession.

Movers, 358; Judges, xi. 24; Amos, i. 14; Jer. xlix. 3; xlviii. 7.

Pp. 276, 286, 321.

And at that time came Iahosha and cut off the ANAKI from the mountains, from Habaron, from Dabar, from Anab.—Josh. xi. 21.

The ANAKI (were) there, and the cities great and fenced.

Joshua, xiv. 12.

Pp. 314, 315.

Zagreus (Zagareus) the god ; Zachariah (Zacharias) the priest.

P. 326.

With Pushan, Apasson, deity-names, compare BASHAN (ABASAN):
Har-Alahim (is) Har-Bashan.

Adoni said : From BASAN I will bring.

Ps. lxviii. 16, 23.

P. 372.

There is no reason to doubt that Buddhism had extended itself into Cashmere in the third century before Christ.

Prof. Salisbury, Journ. Am. Oriental Soc. i. pp. 101, 119.

P. 367.

Mara, " sensual attachment."—Ibid. i. 282. Mar "the Lord " in Syriac.
—1 Cor. xvi. 22, Dr. Crusé ; Movers, 28, 663.

P. 284; p. 291.

Amon, Anan, Iohanan, *H*asad-IAH, Anani, Assir, SAN-azar, *P*arez, *H*alah, *I*abaz, Aharhel, *H*athath, Alah, Ar, Saraph, *I*amin, Iarib, Azam, ASAN, Ahi, Guni, Baal, Baki, Ahitob, Zadok, Ethan, Kadash (Kedesh), Rimmon, *H*ilen, *H*ukok, Bari, Arad, Adar, Elam, Eliel, Sh-ASHAK, N-OHAH, Nah-ash, Rapha, Uzal, Ebal, Salma, Abida, Bela, Baor, *H*usham, *H*adad and Bedad, Aliah, Teman, Baal-hanan, Carami, Uri, Aram, Ram, Boaz, Attai, Iaho, Zaza, *I*ada, Ah-aban, Akar, *H*alaz, *H*-USI the ARCHITE[1] are single or compounded Sun-names. The land of Aos (AUS), Job, i.

Thy BALI thy ASI (OSI, USI): Ihoh Zabaoth is his name !

"Thy Husband (is) thy Creator."—Isaiah, liv. 5.

Thou shalt call me AISI and no more BALI.—Hosea, ii. 16.

The names of the " suns " or " kings " Asa, Shalom (Shallum), Alah, Iaho, Basha, Adon-Iaho, Sol-Am*ah*, Saul, DOD (Dvd), Abas-Alom, king Tai, Agag, Abadon, Elon, Aphthah (Ptah) or *I*ephthah, Arab or Oreb

---

[1] 1 Chron. the first six chapters; 1 Esdras, v. 30; 2 Sam. xvii. 5.

(Iarib, Rab), Zeb, Zebul, Agalon (Eglon), Og, ATABAL king of the Sidonians, 1 Kings, xvi. 31 ; and kings TAB-RIMMON, H-azion, 1 Kings, xv. 18 ; Aluattes or Haluattes, king of LUD-ia, ADOD, a Phœnician king-name and deity-name mentioned in Sanchoniathon, are Sun-names.

And BALA son of Azaz son of Shemu (Samo) son of Ioal : he dwelling in Arar (city of Aroer=Horus) even unto Nabo (Nebo) and Bal-Maon.

1 Chron. v. 8.

Pp. 37, 77, 78, 310.

> But when Immortal God's imperishable ANGELS,
> ÊKAR, 'EromiEL, OuriEL, SaniEL and AzaEL.
>
> Sibylline Oracles; Gallaeus, 274.

P. iv OF THE PREFACE.

To the believer, who holds that God has regulated all progress by general laws, it would be natural to look for some similar principles of development in the Sanskrit and Hebrew, and primarily in the mode of writing.[1]

Lepsius says[2] that the Indian (Hindu) Alphabet has a common origin with the Semitic : that all Semitic and Indogermanic alphabets carry us back to one and the same primal alphabet : this was a syllabic alphabet; that is, every letter contained a consonant and vowelic element united into an indivisible unity. The Dêvanâgari, the holy writing of the Hindus, was a pure syllable-writing before the vowel-marks were added above and below the line : it can, however, always be read without them, because every letter includes in itself, besides the consonant-element, also the vowel a, and is spoken with it.[3] T is Ta, B Ba, K Ka. The Hebrew likewise was anciently written without the vowel-points, which date from about the seventh century after Christ. If, therefore, any one would read the language of the Old Testament as it existed prior to our era, he must fill up the blanks between the consonants with vowels; and if no particular vowel is indicated, which should he take of the five vowels ? The *first*, of course, since it was included in the consonant. Prof. Heinrick Wuttke, speaking of the Semitic-Phœnician Alphabet, says : Neither consonants nor vowels were pure, separated in their peculiarity, because *to the former a short vowel was added*, to the latter a slight breathing.[4]

---

[1] Compare Weber, On the Semitic Origin of the Indian Alphabet, 1, 139, 149, et passim.   [2] Lepsius, Ueber die Anordnung und Verwandschaft des Semitischen, Indischen, Aethiopischen, Alt-Persischen und Alt-Aegyptischen Alphabets, pp. 40, 44, 46, 47, 19.   [3] Ibid. 23, 24, 26.

[4] Zeitschrift der D. M. G. xi. p. 96.

Seyffarth, speaking of the Egyptian Hieroglyphics, says: As in Hebrew and other Semitic languages, the vowels were commonly left out of the account.[1] Take for instance the Hebrew name *Abimlk bn Irbal*. It may be read Abimalak ben Irabal, or Abemelek ben Irebel, or Abimelek ben Ierobal, &c.; but as we must select one of the vowels, Aleph (Alpha), which stands for the sounds A and E, has the preference. Take the name *iroslm* (Ierusalem), and putting in the vowel *a*, we have Iarosalam. Take *alhi* and *alhim*, and inserting *a*, we have Alahi and Alahim, names of Jehovah. Take *ahitpl*, and this rule gives us the word Ahitapal (Ahitophel). There are cases where the Hebrew with its *old* vowels can dispense with all additions: as *arim* "fires," from AR "fire." In almost all cases where Hebrew names are introduced in this work, they are to be read without the vowel-points.

In the subordinate position which vowels occupied in reference to consonants, and more especially from accidents and the usages of colloquial utterance, the vowel sound *a* has been exchanged for all the other vowels in turn even in the same word—first in conversation, later in writing. Thus we have Asak, Isaak, Osogo, Such-os, Sichae-us, all sounds representing the same name originally. It is best to lay little stress on vowels as being a variable and mutable element, and to adhere to the CONSONANTS as the ancients did.

The broad *a* becomes *o* and *au;* the short *a* becomes a short *i*, and frequently is dropped entirely at the beginning of a word: as, Pidaura, anciently Epidaurus, Sar for Asar, Kur for Akar, Keb for Akab, Seb for Asab, Sarak for Asarac, Mardi for Amardi, a people of Asia, Media for Amadia. Very often *a* is misread *e* in the Bible; for Aleph, the first character of the Hebrew alphabet, is both *a* and *e*. The consonants were continually transmuted into their middle and aspirated forms. P is B and Ph. T becomes D and Th, as in Methone and Modon, two names of the same city. K passes over into G and Ch. The letters i, j and y have all the same sound, and are written indiscriminately one for the other in this work. In the Hebrew, *i* was constantly prefixed to words beginning with a vowel. The same occurs in Egyptian words. It is also added at the end of names, as a suffix and otherwise. S softens to *sh* and *h*. Sometimes a word beginning with a vowel was written both with and without an aspirate. The ancient *u* in Greek and Latin words has been turned into a *y* (Ludia, Musia, Dionusos). S is z.

Pp. 266, 380, 381.

Philo says the Taaut-writing contained only a history of the gods *during their life* in Phœnicia, and not the *later added* allegories of the

[1] Seyffarth, Chronology, 40.

priests. Philo adduces this document as proof that the gods of the Phœnician religion were only men. This is the doctrine of Genesis which corresponds to Philo's description of the Taaut-document of the Phœnicians. Compare Movers 91 (Orelli's Sanchoniathon, pp. 6, 8), 102, 107, 125.

P. 381. *Masses.*

Compare Masa, or Massa, one of the CHILDREN of IsamaEl.—Gen. xxv., 14. KADMAH.—Ibid. 15.

P. 381.

The FLIGHTS of ADONIS.—Movers, 200. Adonis died Sept. 23.—Movers, 211. The WANDERER Kadmus.—Nonnus, Dionys. xiii. 350.

P. 200, 286.

"The kings (of the Thracians) say that they are born from Hermes" (Kadmus). — Herodot. v. 7. Hermes-Kadmus (as Hades, Vulcan, Thoth).—Movers, 520, 521, 21, 23, 43, 83, 142, 155. Kadmah, Gen. xxv. 15.

Pp. 216; 383, *Hercules.*

The soft-footed Hours in the twelfth month brought the ADONi*s* from ever-flowing Acheron!—Theocritus, Id. xv. 103 ; Movers, 233.

P. 251.

A Festival of Fires (PURA).—Movers, 14. Diana, Virgo. Movers 31.

P. 284.

The names Danaus, Aegyptus, Dorus, Tarah (Terah), Cilix, Phoinix, Mus, Oar, Misor, Misraim, Assor, Tur, Sidon, are used in the same way as the names in the Table of Nations, Gen. ix. 8–13, 15, 22.

P. 362.

KUR is the Sun.—Movers, 228 ; Anthon, Art. Cyrus. Kyr=Adonis and Memnon.—Movers, 199. Agr-*adat*es (Cyrus) from Akar the Sun and Adad, Aditya, Tat, the Sun ; like MITHRA-dates. Kōras ; Achor. Ichōr " SPIRIT."

P. 269, *Note* 11. P. 145, *Note* 2.

Achab.—Movers, 179. K-ōKEB BAÁL=the Planet JUPITER.—Movers, 174. IKAB-od, haCAB-od, CUP-ido, COBad, AIGUPtah, COPtos.

P. 301.

The hurtful elements in Nature are emanations from the sun and are personified in the idea of Typhon.—Movers, 160.

P. 268.

With IscHU*s* compare the name Isaca*h*, Gen. xi. 29.

Pp. 297, 299.

With Iacab and Asau compare Asak and SamaEL (Ishmael), Nit
(Anat) and Antaeus-Typhon.—Movers, 397, 419, 232, 435, 371.

Pp. 362. 389.

ADONI is the KURIOS (KUR).—Psalm ii. 4, Septuagint; 2 Cor. iii. 17;
Luke ii. 11.   Mar KURI, Mar the SUN (Mer-KUR).—Movers, 522.

Pp. 389, 216, 225.

Thammuz and Adonis die in June.—Movers, 210.   Compare the
Horus-festival in Epiphi (June 25th to July 25th).   The DEATH of
Adonis was celebrated *both* in Summer and in the Autumn.

Huēs Attēs, CHI Ata, or CHI Aba, Attēs LIVES!   The εὐάζειν of
the Attes-worshippers in the Bacchanalia and CHI AZŎN were in Phœni-
cia the CRY OF JOY which succeeded to the sad DEATH-LAMENT HOI
ADŎN.—Movers, 205.   Semele was also called Huē (Hua).   In the
Mysteries they "go shouting aloud that EUA" (Eve).—Euseb. Praep.
Ev. p. 62.   Eusebius also mentions the WANDERINGS of Ceres and Pro-
serpine.—p. 62.   Bacchus was called Euas and Huas, and Guās.—
Movers, 547, Hesychius; Scholia ad Aristoph. Aves, 583.

P. 382.

Aisculapius, Asklepius (Esmun).   Osiris (Adonis, Bacchus), Ammun,
Smun, Thoth, identical.   Movers, 150, 528, 233, 125, 435, et passim.   Tat-
Aesculapius, Ibid, 500, 501, is Sarapis and Thoth.

Pp. 160, 210 ff, 383, 389.

The prevailing doctrine maintains that Sarapis is Pluto.   Some consider him Osiris, Jove, Aesculapius.—Tacitus, Hist. iv. 84.

Kad(a)mus who sowed the earth-born crop.—Euripides, Bacchae, 264.

Kadmus is Thoth (Death), Taaut, Hermes.—Movers, 62, 89, 205,
519, 501, 537.   Compare the names Sarp-EDON in Homer (Sarap-*is*),
Zaccur (Zagreus), Nehemiah, iii. 2; Mar-amuth (Muth, Pluto).—Ezra,
viii. 33.

Pp. 199 *Note* 2, 205, 206.

And often too she struck very-nourishing earth with her hands,
Invoking Aidēs (AD) and awful Persephoneia
To give death to her son.—Iliad ix. 568 ff.

Pp. 381, 290.

The MOURNING FOR HUAS!—Crusius, Iliad, Heft, v. p. 71.   HUAh
חוה would be Ceres (Eve) Demeter.

Whom a little before they had buried they say has RISEN.—Julius Firmicus, de Errore Profani Religionis.

Reviviscens canitur et laudatur!—Hieronymus ad Ezechiel, viii.; Movers, 205.

Pp. 216 ff; 257, 383, 399 ff.

According to Menander, Hiram first celebrated the RESURRECTION OF HERCULES in the month Peritius (Berith).—Movers, 385; Josephus, Antiq. viii. 5, 3. On the 2d of Peritius, the twenty-fifth of December in the Roman Kalender, the Festival Natalis Solis Invicti corresponding to the Hercules Tyrius Invictus was celebrated. Hiram of Tyre first performed this ceremony.—Ibid. 386.

Not even the POWER of Hercules escaped Death;
Who was the DEAREST to King Deus (Zeus).—Iliad, xviii. 117, 118.

Pp. 290. 225.

For AHOH (Adam) and HOH (Eve), read HUAS and HUAH, or GUAS and CHOAH, Iacchos (ACHOS) and CHOH (Eve, Ceres): or Gauas (Adonis) and Chauah (Agauā, Agavē, Eve); or Akab (Iacob), KAB, KEB (Saturn), and Chavah (Eve). חוה or חוה (Eve) can be read in *either* way without the *modern* vowel points. יהוה (Iachoh, according to Movers, p. 548) is Iacchos (Bacchus). חוה (Choh) is Eve (Ceres).

P. 92.

Adani or Adoni (Adni, Adonai, Atten) and Athena (Adana) would be Adonai (Jah) and Wisdom the Goddess of Pindar and Proverbs vii. Compare Brahma and Sarasvati the Goddess of Science; Apollo and Minerva in Athens; Agag, Ukok, Gog and Ogka (Athena); Adonis (who is Bacchus.—Movers, 25, 545; Eusebius, H. E. iii. 23; Plutarch, Quaest. Conv. iv. 6) and Autonoe, Danae. See p. 209 *above.*

P. 206.

For Succoth (tents?) read perhaps Saga, Siga, Sicca (Venus).—Movers, 642, 587, 597 *note*, 596, 14, Cotys a goddess, Cuth a place, KUTHereia, TarKAT, AdarGATis, MeleCHET. Two cities named Succoth, from the Sun-god perhaps. Compare M-ASSAGET-ae.

Pp. 48, 72, 90, 191.

Compare Aiiar (Jair) the Hebrew month (April-May), Ear, Eiar, "Spring" in Greek, IAR the Egyptian god, the "god IARibolos" named in Palmyrene inscriptions.—Movers, 434; Gesenius, 229; Iar-BAS (Iarob), Movers, 427; Ier-obal: YEAR in English, IAR meaning month in Egyptian.

—Seyffarth, Theol. Schr. p. 23. Ar (Arēs) the fire-god Mars.—Movers,
335 ff. Aʀ of Moab ; Aur, the city of the fire-priests : Aʀ the Sun-god.

P. 94.

Aʀɪᴇʟ (Adoni)———Aʀɪᴀᴅɴᴇ (Venus-Proserpine). Aʙᴀʙ (Adonis)
———Pᴀᴘʜia (Venus), Phoebe (Moon), Bhava (Existence).   Pharo
(Mithra)———Freia (Venus). Neb, Nabo———Niobe. Amas, Mus
———Amaz*ah* (Artemis). Sᴛʀᴀᴛɪ*os* and *A*storet.   Akabar, Cᴀʙᴀʀ
(Cabir),———Cupris (Venus). Kᴇᴅᴀʀ———Kᴜᴛʜᴇʀeia (Venus).

Let the Desert and its cities cry, the villages Kᴀᴅᴀʀ inhabits.—Isaiah,
xlii. 11.

Zeus (Sɪos-Atham*as*) encircled his wife (Iuno, Ino) in his arms
And under them the divine earth produced fresh herbage,
Dewy lōtus and crocus and hyacinthus.—Iliad, xiv. 346 ff.

P. 208.

Aᴅᴀᴍ*as* the son of Asɪ, and Asɪos son of Hurtac*us*.—Iliad, xiii. 759.

Atumn*ios*, a Trojan, son of Amis-odar-*us*.   Atumn*ios*.—Iliad, v. 581.
Idomen-eus.—Il. xvi. 317.

I saw Aᴅᴏɴɪ standing on the altar, Who said :
If they dig into Sᴀol (Hell) there shall my hand take them !—Amos
ix. 1, 2.

Pp. 35, 86.

Adonis was called Iᴛaios (Eᴅ).   Ada, the Babylonian Heʀa (Era)
or Juno, was called by the Turians Iᴛea.—Movers, 199, quotes Hesychius.

From the Psalms.

Iʜᴏʜ Aʟᴀʜi, vii. 2.   Iʜᴏʜ Aᴅᴏɴino, viii. 10.   Aʟɪōɴ, ix.   Aʟ, x. 11.
Iʜᴏʜ Aʟ, x. 12.   Iʜᴏʜ Malak Aolam o Aᴅ═Iahoh is Kɪɴɢ, to ᴛɪᴍᴇ
(Oulom) and ᴇᴛᴇʀɴɪᴛʏ, x. 16.   Thou saidst to Iʜᴏʜ Aᴅᴏɴɪ, xv. 2.   I
invoked Ihoh and to Aʟᴀʜɪ I cried ! xviii. 7.   Aʟɪōɴ═God, xlvi. 5.

And he rode on a Kʜᴇʀoʙ and flew and was borne on the wings of
the Wind, xviii. 11.   Who is Aʟoʜ except Iʜᴏʜ? Aʟᴀʜino, xviii. 32.

Who is this Kɪɴɢ Hᴀᴋᴀʙoᴅ ? Iʜᴏʜ Azoz and Gᴀʙoʀ, Iʜᴏʜ Gᴀʙoʀ !
—xxiv. 8.   Iᴀʜ, cii. 19.

Give to Iʜᴏʜ, O Sons of Aʟ-im (the gods), glory and strength, xxix. 1.
Malak Iʜᴏʜ═Angel of Iahoh, xxxv. 6.   Aᴅᴏɴɪ, xxxv. 17, 22.   Aʟᴀʜɪ
and Aᴅᴀɴɪ, xxxv. 23, Iʜᴏʜ Aʟᴀʜɪ, 24.   Aᴅᴀɴɪ shall deride him, xxxvii. 13.
Aᴅᴀɴɪ Aʟᴀʜɪ, xxxviii. 16.   Iʜᴏʜ Aʟᴀʜɪ. Ibid. 22.   Adani Ihoh, lxxi. 5.
Iʜᴏʜ Zᴀʙᴀoᴛʜ, . . . Aʟᴀʜɪ Iᴀᴋᴀʙ, xlvi. 12.   Aʟ, Aʟᴀʜɪᴍ, Iʜᴏʜ, shall
speak, Psalm ʟ.   Iʜ (Iᴀʜ) Aᴅᴏɴɪ, cxxx. 3.   The name Aᴅɴɪ═Adani,

or ADONI is used thirty-two times besides, in the Psalms, as a name of
IAHOH.

P. 244.

Therefore, O Alahim, thy ALAH has anointed thee with the oil of
joy before thy companions!—Ps. xlv. 8; Schmid & Septuagint.

Pp. 242, 243, 245, 247, 362, 390.

Wherefore are the nations agitated and the peoples meditating
vanity ?

The kings of the earth have united and the rulers have consulted
together against Ihoh and his Massiah (anointed king):

Shall we tear off their fetters and cast off their cords from us ?

Dwelling in the heavens he shall laugh, ADONI shall deride them !

Then he shall speak to them in his anger, and in his ire shall terrify
them :

But I have anointed my malak (King) upon Siōn the mount of
KADASHI ! [1]

I will announce concerning the decree ; Ihoh said to me : MY SON art
Thou ! I this day have begotten thee !

Ask of me and I will give nations (for) thine inheritance and (for)
thy possession the ends of the earth.

Thou shalt subdue them with an iron sceptre !

Kiss the SON, lest he be angry (O kings) !—Psalm ii. Schmid.

Pluribus persuasio inerat, antiquis sacerdotum libris contineri, fore
ut valesceret Oriens et e Judaea profecti rerum potirentur.—Tacitus,
Hist. v. 13.

Pp. 252, 280 ff.

From TROS (TURus, Thor, Thore) were descended THREE illustrious
SONS,

ILus, ASSARAcus and divine GAN-UMEDE !—Il. xx. 231, 232.

Ovid Met. x. 160 calls the CUP-bearer Ganymede ILiádes (Son of IL
or Son of Ilium). Attis, Adonis and Bacchus are all occasionally
represented holding the CUP.

P. 278.

Numbers, xxxi. 37-50 ff, contains appropriations out of the spoil like
those given to Apollo at Delphi after victories.

---

[1] Kadash-BARANA (Baruna ?), a place —Joshua, xv. 3; Kadash, a city.—
Numbers, xx 14. Compare AKDEStis (AKADAS Atys)=Mars. Compare Movers,
382, 383, 306. Kadasho means "his Sanctity."

Pp. 80 ff, 275, 284.

With Amon compare Iamin and the Iamini; with Iachin the Pillar-god compare Iachin and the Iachini (Agni). With SUN (SAN) compare Suni and the S*h*uni; with Ariel (Moloch); Areli and the Arelians. With Pars, Perseus, compare Pharez, the Apharsi, the Pharezians and the Aphar*asaki*; with Azrael (Israël), Asriel and the Asrieli; with Abar (Eber) *H*eber, compare the Heberi (Hebraioi); with Arad, Arod and the Arodi; with Aran (Ouranos), Eran; with Agni (Chon, Akan) compare Guni, the Kan-ites (Kin) and the Gunites; with Azar, Iezer and the Iezeri :—Numbers, xxvi.; xxiv. 21, 22, 24; Ezra, vi. 6; iv. 9.

And the children of Azar are these : Bel-ahan and ZAUN and Akan. —Gen. xxxvi. 27. Zauan*as* was a god in Sidon, Movers, 216; Siôn (Sivan) a Hebrew Month-god. Compare Azôn, p. 390 above : Zān (Zeus), and "the princes of Zoan (ZAN)."—Isa. xix. 11. Comp. Z͟ON.—Movers, 216.

Pp. 181, 267.

Asabel, family of the Asabeli (Asbolos).—Numb. xxvi. 38. Baal-Chanan, son of Ak*a*bor (Akbor, Chebar.)—Gen. xxxvi. 38. Phoenix is son both of Agen*or* and Can*aan*. They must be the same.

P. 270.

Jupiter was euhemeristically called a mortal king of Crete.—Jupiter Minos or Jupiter Ammon !

Pp. 152, 55, 146, 290, 138, 186, 195.

Ouranos and Gē as Man-woman.—Movers, 147. Uranos formerly named ᾽Επίγειος (Adam) separated from his spouse Gē (Adama); which is a Euhemeristic account of a primitive union of heaven with earth, which the Demiurg divided into two halves.—Movers, 271. Epigeios (earthy), in Sanchoniathon, is the name Abachus (Ibycus) or Bacchus slightly changed. The First Man was of the earth, earthy.—1 Cor. xv. 47. It is probable that Sanchoniathon's stories were intended to depreciate the ancient polytheism in favor of something like Mosaicism.

Pp. 251, 252, 389.

Isis is Proserpine. Ariadne is Proserpine. Theseus is the Tasian Hercules who goes through the TWELVE CHAMBERS of the Labyrinth devoted to the 12 deities of the Babylonian Zodiac. Compare Movers, 81. She is the Bride of Bacchus in the Mysteries. Mino*taur* would be the Equinoctial Bull or the SIGN of the Bull, the Creator-Sun. Labrand-EUS was the Ludian god (Liber-Anid, Anait) also called Zeus Stratios.— See Movers, 476, 17, 19; Plutarch, Quaest. Gr. 45. Zeus was the husband of Ceres! Sab-Azios = ZEUS-Dionysus.

P. 171.

DIVINE WISDOM (Thoth, Kadmus) as a CLOUD. Compare Jupiter as GOLDEN SHOWER wedding Danae (AriAdne) the daughter of Acri*sius*, who is Saturn, great grandson of Danaus—Movers, 398; Iliad, xiv. 321 —and grandfather of PERSEUS most illustrious of all *men*. Acrisius is son of ABAS.

P. 326, *Note* 3.

Compare PEIRITH-O-*us* euhemerized into a COUNSELLOR equal to the gods, the son of Zeus.—Iliad, xiv. 318. Compare the name PROIT-OS; Pryd = a British Sun-god.—Bunsen, Phil. of Univ. Hist. I. 149, 150.

Pp. 245, 359, 360.

E coelo REX adveniet per secla futurus
Scilicet in carne praesens ut judicet orbem,
Unde Deum cernct incredulus atque fidelis.—Sibylla Erythraea.

Pp. 266, 389, 381, 284, 273.

Compare Sanchoniathon's AGREUS and Homer's AGRIUS, Iliad, xiv.; Homer's Adrastus, xv. 120, and the ADRASTUS who kills ATUS (Adonis): the names ALT-es (Alates, Aluattēs), Iliad, xxii. and LOT, Laothoē and LEIT-as

Pp. 389, 390, 268, 297, 206.

PugmALIŌN murders ZAKI, SAKI (Sichaeus), the *pure* BROTHER.— Movers, 398, quotes Cedrenus I. 246; Malala, p. 163.

P. 220.

Plutarch precedes the dissertation on the Jews by the assertion that Bacchus and Adonis are the same.—Plutarch, Morals, 816. He also declares that Neptune presides over the *humid and generative* Principle. —p. 821., Quaest. Conv. III. i. The pine was consecrated both to Neptune and Bacchus, and all the Greeks adored Neptune Phutalmios and Bacchus Dendrites.

Neptune and Ceres were worshipped in the same fane.—Ibid. 812.

Ceres is SENDING FORTH GIFTS for you and Bacchus is
  Much-cheering, increasing the germ of trees,
    Holy Light of Autumn!—Pindar. Plutarch, pp. 910, 926.

Empedocles names Venus LIFEGIVER, but Sophocles named her the FRUITFUL.—Ibid. 924.

Osiris is the *Nile* according to the Egyptians.—Plut. de Is. xxxii. They call Bacchus Huēs.—de Iside xxxiv.

Pp. 152, 153, 160.

" The SPIRIT in the mouth."—Plutarch, Moralia, p. 900.

Pp. 197 *line* 3, 158, 362.

For as that which is filled with Holy Ghost (Pneuma) is called EMPNOUN (*breathed into*), and that which is filled with understanding is called *sensible*, just so this DANCE OF SOUL has been named ENTHOUSIASMOS on account of the communion and communication of DIVINER FACULTY: and THE PROPHETIC of enthousiasmos is from Apollo's inbreathing and *possession*; but THE BACCHIC is from Dionysus:

And with Corybantes ye will dance!

says Sophocles; for the rites of the Mother and the rites of Pan agree with the orgies of Bacchus.—Plutarch, Erōtik, xvi.

P. 213.

To those who LOVE there is a return (Anodos) from Hades to light! Ibid. xvii. 22.

Pp. 206, 209, 381.

However there are some slender and obscure emanations of truth scattered through the mythologies of the Egyptians. . . . Xenophanes ordered the Egyptians if they think Osiris a mortal not to honor him as God, but if they think him God not to MOURN him!—Plutarch, Erōt. xvii. xviii. For Osiris and Isis have passed from GOOD DAEMONS into gods; but there are sacrifices by which they appease and soothe the obscured and crushed power of Typhōn, which is yet half dead and struggling! . . . . In the Sun's sacrifice they exhort those worshipping the God not to carry gold ornaments upon their body and not to give food to an ass (Typhon's emblem). Some say that from the fight (between Horus and Typhon) Typhon fled *seven* days on an ass, and, escaping, begat the boys 'Ierosolumos and Ioudaios (Jerusalem and Judaeus). Plut. de Iside, xxx. xxxi.

MYSTERIES AND SACRED STORIES.

Osiris having been put in the box or ark by Typhon and thrown (as the Fruitful Principle) into the Nile on the *seventeenth* day of the month when Sol passes through Scorpio, the myth proceeds to state that the Pans and Satyrs revealed the facts and produced *panics* (panikas) which gave rise to the name. Isis WANDERING everywhere and perturbed met no one without CALLING TO HIM, but meeting with little children she asked about the ARK (or box): these happened to have seen, and told the mouth of the Nile by which the friends of Typhon had sent the vessel to sea. But Isis, perceiving that Osiris had united himself in love to her sister as to herself by mistake, and seeing as evidence the melilōtine crown which he left with Nephthys, seeks her little Boy (for she had exposed him as soon as he was born for fear of Typhon). He is found after tracking him with dogs, he is grown up, and her guardian and companion is called Anubis (Mercury), said to guard the gods as the dogs do men.

From him she learns that the ark has been washed by the sea to Byblus and the wave had mingled it with some heath. But the heath, giving out in a little time a very great and very beautiful shoot, embraced and grew round and concealed it (the ark) within itself. . . . Isis comes to Byblus. . . . . She nurses the Boy of Astarte by giving him her finger in his mouth instead of her breast. At night she burns the mortal (parts) of his body. . . . The Mother makes a noise and the child's IMMORTALITY is lost.

As soon as Isis finds herself alone she opens the ark and putting her face upon his (Osiris's) kisses him and sheds tears. She frightens to death a Boy who observes her. This is MANEROS PALAESTINUS.

When Isis has gone home to Horus in Boutos and has put the ARK out of sight of men, Typhon hunting by night near the Moon falls in with it (the ARK), and knowing the BODY, divides it into fourteen pieces and throws them away separately. . . . But Isis made IMAGES and gave them to each city, as if she was giving them the body : so that he might be honored by *more*, and, if Typhon should conquer Horus, seeking the genuine body he would despair after hearing so many stories. Then Osiris *from Hades* being present with Horus prepared and trained him for the fight.

This is a small part of Plutarch's story, while many other things, such as the dismemberment of Horus, etc., etc., are left out by him. The Egyptians fable that on the seventeenth day of the month Osiris died, on which day the full-moon is evidently most full. On the nineteenth day of the month by night they go to the sea. And the stolists and the priests bring out the HOLY ARK of gold, having inside a box into which taking drinking water they pour, and there is a shouting of those present that OSIRIS IS FOUND ! Then they mix fruitful earth and water, and, commingling aromatics and incense of the costly kinds, they form a LUNIFORM LITTLE IMAGE; and this they robe and adorn, signifying that they consider these gods the essence of earth and water.—Plut. de Is. xxxix.

A certain Pamulas heard a voice proclaim in the temple that

OSIRIS the Great Beneficent King IS BORN !

He therefore brought him up receiving him from Saturn. In his reign the Egyptians were freed from a hard life and the chase, he giving them fruits and laws, and teaching them to honor the gods.—Plutarch de Iside. All this is the covering up of the old religion by Sacred Stories in principle not unlike those of the Hebrews.

The celebration of the ADONIA began with the disappearance of Adonis, after which follows the SEARCH FOR HIM by the women. The Myth represents this by the SEARCH of the goddess after her BELOVED; which is analogous to the SEARCH of Persephone in the Eleusinia, of Harmonia at Samothrake, of Io in Antioch. In Autumn when the rains washed the red earth on its banks the river Adonis was of a blood-red color, which was the signal for the Byblians to begin the LAMENT. Then they said that Adonis in hunting was KILLED by MARS, or the BOAR, and his blood running into the river colored the water. Hence the name of the river ADON; for ADM (interchanged with ADN) means "blood."—Taken from Movers, 200. "Adonis is mourned in most states of the Orient as the HUSBAND of Venus, albeit this evil has passed over even to us."—Firmicus, p. 15, ed. Wovver; Movers, 193, 154.

Bethleem nunc nostrum et augustissimum orbis locum, de quo Psalmista canit

VERITAS DE TERRA ORTA EST!

lucus inumbrabat Thammus, id est, Adonidis: et in specu ubi quondam Christus parvulus vagiit, Veneris AMASIUS plangebatur.—Hieronymus Ep. 49. ad Paulin. Tom. iv. part II. pag. 564. ed. Martianay. Movers, 193.

Pp. 219, 220, 256 5 .

And immediately issued BLOOD and WATER (SPIRIT)—John, xix. 34.

P. 185.

The Egyptians like the Greeks make two Cupids, the common and the CELESTIAL; and the third Eros they think the Sun. Aphrodite they greatly venerate. And we see that there is a great resemblance of Eros to the Sun and of Aphrodite to the Moon; for FIRE is neuter as some think; but brightness and heat is sweet and generative, that borne by the Sun gives nourishment, light and increase to the *body ;* but that which comes from Eros, to the *minds.*—Plutarch, Mor. p. 934.

Pp. 244, 285.

The altar of Deus the Savior in the Peiræus.—Ibid. p. 1031. The temple of AIAK-os in Aegina.

Pp. 213.

Proserpine is in the moon and what are connected with the moon.—Ibid. 1152. She bounds upon Pluto in Hades.—See p. 1154. The Athenians anciently called THE DEAD Dēmētreos, that is Cereales. Proserpine was called Only-begotten. Luna is Diana.—p. 1157.

P. 145.

" God indeed, just as the ancient saying says, holding the Beginning and Middle and End of the ALL!"—Plutarch, p. 1375. This is the Alpha and Omega!

P. 102.

In support of the opinion that the *longer* ancient names are compounded of *shorter names*, it is only necessary to glance at the Babylonian names which Movers (Phönizier, pp. 479, 478, 166, 341, 645) divides *on this principle*.

Movers divides *by names of gods* the names Nabo-chodon (Achad, Adon)-osar, Nergal-sar-azar Bel-sh-azar, Bal-adam, Belitan (Baal-Ethan,) Chun-El-Adan (Chyneladan), Chin-zer-us, Adar-melech, Adr-ammelech, An-ammelech, Nabo-col-assar, Sar-dan-apal, Nab-opal-asar, Asar-dan-apal, Asar-adon, Bal-adan, Nab-uzar-adan, into the *dissyllabic* deity-names Asar, Adan, Neb, etc. If we seek to go *further* and divide these dissyllables into *names of one syllable each*, Grimm's article on the Origin of Language, p. 47, line 3d, and pp. 102, 103 *above*, where eight monosyllabic Sun-names are shown to exist, would certainly suggest the attempt. Moreover, the habit of reading for a special purpose hundreds, perhaps thousands, of Bible-names and other ancient names in the countries around the Mediterranean, renders familiar the smaller names contained in the larger, so that one knows them at last intimately and sees at once the principles of their composition. The *fact* is the main thing; it matters very little what speculations or theory the *fact* overthrows. In the Bible-names Adoni-bezek, Adoni-jah, Tobi-jah, Abi-jah, Ammin-adab and Tob-adoni-jah, it is obvious that these longer names contain the shorter ones, Jah, Adoni, Tob, or Adab, etc. A familiarity with the names Abas and Asak or Ezek, would at once suggest a name compounded of both, namely, Bezek, Buzac-*ium*. Abas, Buz (Bushi, Iebus) and Anata, Anait-is, Nit, would suggest Buz-anati-um, Byzantium. Sarch-edon-us and the Edonians suggest Asarac and Adan, two names of the Sun-god. Sath-rab-uzan-es would come from As, Athur, Abus, Azan, or, differently, Seth, Arab, Azan. Liber (ELAbar), Asar (Osar) and Achad (Choda) would give the ancient Persian name Labor-osoar-chod. Asis the Edessa deity-name and Ani or Ina (the Sun) would make Sis-inn-es, or, differently, As-isinn

(Asan, the Sun).   Iethro (Jethro) would suggest Athur, Hator, Ietur,
Thuro, Atar (in Atar-gatis).   Iethro is *later* translated by the *common
language* into "his excellence," or "posterity." Iethro (if he was a god
euhemerized) and Thuro (Athuri, Hathor) would be god and goddess,
Hatur and Hathor.   The names Ar, Ur, and El, would suggest Ariel and
Uriel.   El and Jar or Jaho would suggest Elijah or Eliaho.   The god-
names Bar, and Tom, Tmu, would suggest Bar-tim-aios.   The names Malaki
and Zadok would suggest Melchizedek.   The names *Am* (Iom) the Sun
and *Ani, On,* the Sun, would suggest Aman, Hamman, Amanus, Amon,
Omanes.   To all of which somebody replies, this violates the artificial
system of language which I and my teachers have laid down and the
idea that proper names are translatable.   Of course, if an author *dis-
believes* some of their dicta he will not follow them, but stand upon
facts understood rationally and naturally.   Ariel, Arasal (the god
Arsalus), Salmon, Salman-assar, Azar-iel, El-izur, El-Azar, Ellasar,
Shash-abaz-zar (Asas-Abas-Azar) ; Anata, N-athan, El-n-athan, Ionathan,
Nathan-Ael, Nethan-Iah, Neb-ushas-ban, Pani-el (Pniel), Pen-uel, Adad,
El-idad, Adad-ezer, Abar-ban-el (Abar-aban-el), Abr-avan-el, Aban-azar
(Eben-ezer) Bani-amin, Artem-is, Artem-idor-us, Ari-obar-zan-es, the
Obar-es, Nab-onid, Abas, Bushi, Pos-*eidon, Edon*-ians, K-*udon*-ians,
M-ak-*Edonians,* Th-eocrit-us, Et-eocret-ans, Cret-ans, Kuret-es, Ahaz,
Ahaz-Iah, Iaho-ahaz, Nahum, Nehem-iah, Zedek, Zadok, Zedek-Iah,
Echen-eus, Chon, Can-an, Chenan-iah, Chen-an-ah (Chan-Anah).   Iah-
azak-El, *H*ezek-Iah, Azak, Adad, Iedid-iah, Iahi-el and Eli-Iah, Aram,
Ierem-Iah, Baal-Ram, Ram-as, *H*arameias, Herm-es ; Ah-imaaz and
Amaz-iah, Kedar, Chedor-*E*laomar (Omar, Mar).

     It is a generally received opinion that Hebrew proper names are
translatable by common Hebrew words.   The author is compelled
to dissent from this view,—except as a *subsequent,* not a *primitive* interpretation of them.   The Hebrew names are very frequently two-syllable
names of sun-gods.   Even among us, proper names cannot always be
translated by ordinary words, and it is not unreasonable to suppose the
same to be true of ancient names, especially when facts and common
sense reasoning are both in favor of this view.   If kings and priests
were called by names of the Sun why should not others in time have
borne similar appellations.   If long names were considered as *more
dignified,* would not the agglutination of short names be as rational a
way of accounting for the longer names as to insist that they were made
up of ordinary words which sounded a little like them, and that the
Hebrews were called by such significant names as Tempest, Abomination, Strength of the Lord, Resurrection of the Lord, Knowledge of the
Lord, "Son of my right hand," or, "The Lord says" (Amariah, com-

pounded of Amar the Sun, Mar "Lord," Marna "Zeus," and Iah "Jehovah"). It is not denied that even the Hebrews punned upon the ancient names by *thus* translating them, but the author has no hesitation in asserting his belief that this was not the earliest manner of deriving them. Imagine a whole nation called by the names of abstract ideas! The names were generally and mainly formed by the *agglutination* of monosyllable and dissyllable names. This mode of formation is *old* in the history of thought and *primitive* in the history of language. It is prior to *all* the German-Sanskrit grammatical systems.

POSTSCRIPTA.

P. 4, read Tlavizcalpantecutli. P. 26 *note* 3, insert after Amous, Rinck, I. 223. P. 27 *note* 3, read Aegyptens. P. 34 *note* 1, add Movers, 14. P. 35 *note* 3, add Eusebius, Praep. Ev. 36. P. 37 *note* 10, read v. 31. Pp. 37, 38, Ziōn is Siōn in the Septuagint. Castor and Pollux are called "the Siō." P. 45, after Delawares, add J. Müller, 116. P. 49, insert *Compare* the rivers Oanis, etc. P. 56, line 9, after "Serpent" insert *in Egypt.*—Deane, 165. P. 56, after *note* 15, add Amas, Massēs, Amus, Mus the Sun; Meisi, Serpent. P. 61 *note* 6, add Bunsen, Phil. of Univ. Hist. i. 102. P. 62 *note* 1, after 687 add 689. P. 66 erase Aoum. P. 69, *note* 2 belongs to Bore and Pharo; to line 27 add Adan, Dan, or Odin. P. 71 *note* 2, Mattan-ah, Numh. xxi. 19. P. 75 *note* 6, add Baal-Perazim.—1 Chron. xiv. 11 ; Pharez.—Ibid. iv. 1. P. 79, Pharah, or PARseus. P. 80, erase Ar. It may have stood originally Areshamesh (?). Air means "city." P. 81, line 13, add Obad-Iah, Obad-Adom, Iochabad, Bethuel; Baitulos in Sanchoniathon. P. 82, line 11, add PAPEL-agonia (Paphlagonia). P. 86, Adonis is Mars.—Movers, 234. *Note* 5, add 263, 414. P. 88 *note* 6, Phil. of Univ. Hist. i. 79. P. 90, read PHC. P. 91, add ARATHis, the Dea Syria; Arad*us*, the city. P. 91, Hilaira.—Pausanias, iii. cap. 16. After Athro and Thuro add :—Movers, 629, 507 ff; also Iethro (Jethro). P. 92, add Dione after Diana; Pentheus after Banoth. P. 97 *note* 2, Wagenfeld is quoted to this word. Wagenfeld's *names* appear to be genuine enough, although all *except the first chapter* has been pronounced spurious by scholars. P. 104, The LIFE-BEARING FIRE is the "SPIRIT." P. 124 *note* 5, add Movers, 195. P. 128, Nature. P. 160, for Demeter read perhaps Persephone. P. 161, Sanskrit Vira (Viras) "man," Umbrian veir, Teut. ver, Zend vira, Latin vir, Sanskrit Nara. Erase *vir in Zend.* Add Umbrian viros; Gothic vair; Ir. fear. P. 161, derive aham from Asam (Shem, Samos), Aham. P. 164, for (of heaven) read (of the rains). Pp. 115, 178, read Soul of the world. P. 190, for winding read spiral ; round (?). P. 191, *line* 3, read MI ŌS MI ŌS IAR MISI MI EPHEPH NOU EILE ŌS. P. 203, for Idean read Idaean. P. 205 *note* 7, Sōcus in Homer. P. 206, As(a)c-Ani-us. P. 208, Abel ECHEN "Mourning for the ONLY-BEGOTTEN ;" — IEUD.— Amos, viii. 10. P. 208, with pp. 207, 210, 213, 214, compare Movers, 201. P. 244, insert O before Elohim Thy God. P. 254, Exaneteile Neon Phōs ! Exorta est Nova Lux !—Gallaeus, 760. P. 254, *line* 35, confirmed by the Septuagint, Psalm xxii. 1, 2, 3. See *above*, p. 191, lines 4, 5. P. 260 *note* 1, Compare KUZAH (AKASas?) the Arab Cloud-god. P. 266, p. 271 *note* 4, Eusebius, Praep. Ev. pp. 37, 38. P. 271 *note* 6, add O people of Chamos /—Numh. xxi. 29 : *Note* 6, read Judges, xi. 24 for 34. P. 280, add Eusebius, Pr. Ev. 37, 38. P 282, Azis in Homer.—Iliad, ii. 514. See p. 392, *line* 28. P. 295, *line* 9, The Man (ha Adam). P. 308, SATNIO the name of the (Sun's) river in Homer.—Il. xiv. 445. The king-name TABEAL.—

Isaiah, vii. 6.   P. 305, Gabriel or Adonai.   P. 315, for *their* city read the Hebrew city.   P. 326 *note* 2, compare the *name* Par(a)nass-*us* (Bar-Anas, Nuseus). P. 360, for sense read Wisdom.   P. 363, line 3d, compare Ps. xix. 4, 5.   P. 382, Isa. xxvii. 13.   P. 383, see Movers, 445.   P. 383, read Byblos for Biblus.   P. 386, read Salam-ah for Sol-Ama*h* (Salomo).   With the name Apasson compare the king-uame Apisaon.—Iliad, xi.   P. 389, after Danaus insert Perseus.   Diana is Virgo. —Plutarch, p. 1057.   Pp. 251, 389, Astarte was Virgin.—Duncker; I. 166.   Dido was Virgin.   Anna was worshipped by the Giblites.—I. 169 ; See p. 222, *above.* P. 393, the sons of El (Il) were the angels.   P. 394, Isis.   See Plutarch, de Facie in Orbe Lunae, xxvii.   P. 397, *line* 41, the Festival of the Pamulia which is like the Phallephoria was celebrated by him.—De Iside, xii.   P. 392, Iacob and Cupris; Chabar (Venus).—Univ. Hist. viii. 353.   P. 38, Sana, a city near mount Athos. Saon of *Samothrace*, Son of Jupiter.   Pp. 271, 274.   Dardanus, Iasion and Har-monia the children of Jupiter.   Pp. 85, 86, Corubas, son of Cubele and Iasion, taught the Mysteries of Cubele.—Ibid. 356.   P. 394, for Kin read Ken.   Pp. 271, 296, Ceneus an ancient hero ; Abas an ancient bero.—Ibid. 371, 368.   Pp. 82, 97, 208, 392, Temenus son of Hercules, ancestor of Caranus (Kronos).—Ibid. 398.   Pp. 249, 270, 389, compare Iacob (Keb, Kabus) Mourned in the sacred rites of Palaestinus and Cubele.—Gen. l. 10 ; Plutarch, de Iside.   The Angel Akibeel and Cubele. Compare *H*ecura.   P. 72, King Anius.—Virgil, Æn. iii. 80.   P. 66, the angel-name Iomiael, and the Scandiuavian god Iumala.   P. 94, add Babia, the Syrian God-dess.—Univ. Hist. ii. 282.   P. 206, compare the king-name I*a*donsac, the successor of *H*arsal.—Univ. Hist. ii. 110.   Pp. 209, 290, "Tomas, a name of the Sun."— Book of Enoch, 98, ed. Lawrence.   P. 278 read Mal-albel (in Enoch).   P. 175, light-aether.   P. 116, *line* 20, for *ring* read Frost.

Its walls too as well as pavement were *formed* with stones of crystal, and crystal likewise was the ground.   Its roof had the appearance of agitated (the course of the) stars and flashes of lightning; and among them were cherubim of fire in a stormy sky. . . .   No trace of delight or of life was there. . . .

Attentively I surveyed it and saw that it contained an exalted throne, the appearance of which was like that of frost, while its circumference resembled the orb of the brilliant sun ; and there was the voice of the cherubim !   From under-neath this mighty throne rivers of flaming fire issued.—Book of Enoch.   I beheld the receptacles of light and thunder.—Enoch.   P. 310 *note* 2, for seven read *six.*

I beheld seven Stars of heaven bound in it (Hades) together, like great mountains, and like a blazing fire. . . .   These are those of the Stars which have transgressed. . . .   This is the prison of the angels.—p. 26.   The name of the first (chief of the bad angels) is Yekun ; he it was who seduced all the sons of the holy angels, and causing them to descend on earth led astray the offspring of men. —p. 77.   Pp. 316, 248, 253.   No man has seen God at any time; the Only-begot-ten Son who is in the bosom of the Father, he has declared him.—John i. 18.

There I beheld the Ancient of days, and with Him Another. . . .   This is the Son of man.   In that hour was this Son of man invoked before the Lord of all spirits, and his name in the presence of the Ancient of days.   Before the sun and sions were created, before the stars of heaven were formed his name was invoked in the presence of the Lord of spirits !   Therefore the Elect and Concealed One existed in His presence before the world was created and forever.   From the Be-ginning the Son of man *existed in secret !*   He shall judge Azazeel and all his asso-ciates.   The earth shall be immerged and all things which are in it perish, while judgment shall come upon all, even upon all the righteous.—Book of Enoch, *passim.*

Lightning Source UK Ltd.
Milton Keynes UK
UKHW010729040521
383104UK00006B/845